B

London

Hints for using the Guide

Following the tradition established by Karl Baedeker in 1844, sights of particular interest, outstanding buildings, works of art, etc., as well as good hotels and restaurants are distinguished by stars as follows: especially worth attention ★, outstanding ★★.

To make it easier to locate the various places listed in the "A to Z" section of the Guide, their co-ordinates on the large map of London are shown in red at the head of each entry: e.g., Buckingham Palace F 4.

Coloured lines down the right-hand side of the page are an aid to finding the main heading in the Guide: blue stands for the Introduction (Nature, Culture, History, etc.), red for the "A to Z" section, and yellow indicates Practical Information.

Only a selection of hotels and restaurants can be given; no reflection is implied therefore on establishments not included.

In a time of rapid change it is difficult to ensure that all the information given is entirely accurate and up-to-date, and the possibility of error can never be entirely eliminated.

Although the publishers can accept no responsibility for inaccuracies and omissions, they are constantly endeavouring to improve the quality of their Guides and are therefore always grateful for criticisms, corrections and suggestions for improvement.

Preface

This guide to London is one of the new generation of Baedeker Guides.

These guides, illustrated throughout in colour, are designed to meet the needs of the modern traveller. They are quick and easy to consult, with the principal places of interest described in alphabetical order. and the information is presented in a format that is both attractive and easy to follow.

This guide covers London, the capital of the United Kingdom of Great Britain and Northern Ireland. The guide is in three parts. The first part gives a general account of the city, its population and administration, economy, transport, art and culture, famous people and the history of London. A small selection of quotations and a number of suggested tours leads into the second part in which the principal places of tourist interest are described. The third part contains a variety of practical information. Both the sights and the practical information are listed in alphabetical order.

The new Baedeker guides are noted for their concentration on essentials and their convenience of use, and contain numerous specially drawn plans and colour illustrations. At the end of the book is a large map making it easy to locate the various places described in the "A–Z" section of the guide with the help of the co-ordinates given at the head of each entry.

Contents

Baedeker Specials

London is

Those coming to London for the first time are certain to feel that they already know at least a little about the city they have chosen to visit – wherever they go they will come across names which are known worldwide. Is there anyone who has not heard of Buckingham Palace, Piccadilly Circus, Trafalgar Square, Carnaby Street and Hyde Park? Even less well-known streets and squares like Oxford Circus, Charing Cross or Regent Street have a certain familiar ring to them, and everybody knows Eaton Place. So there is no reason not to feel at ease in London.

You must
have at least one ride on a London double-decker bus

Having said that, what does one have to do to get to know the city? First there are the places that everyone wants to see – those that call to mind the days of the British Empire, such as the Government Buildings in Whitehall, monuments of British history like the Tower and Westminster Abbey, architectural masterpieces such as St Paul's Cathedral and the magnificent, world-famous museums, especially the British Museum, the National Gallery and the Victoria and Albert Museum – enough to make even a longish stay in the capital quite an exhausting experience.

Having duly seen these "obligatory" sights, however, visitors can then enjoy the rest of London at their leisure, depending on how much time they have at their disposal. Those who are content

Chinatown
a piece of China in the middle of London

still swinging!

just to learn a little about it need simply do a few things which are not included in the official programme. The parks are a "must". Enjoy a peaceful stroll through Hyde Park – either in the morning, when it is still a bit misty and the first joggers and horse-riders are about, or else in the early evening, when boys are playing football and families are picnicking on the grass. Visit a pub when workers in the City have left off work and experience the noisy scene as bankers and stockbrokers relax over a pint, or else on a quiet sunny afternoon in Greenwich or, if you can manage it, in the early morning to join the butchers at Smithfield Market. Discover London from the top of a double-decker bus, amble through Chinatown and afterwards enjoy high tea at the Ritz; a day in London will provide a fascinating and contrasting picture of the different faces of this city and its cosmopolitan population. And do not be afraid of British food! It is by no means as bad as it is made out to be, in fact quite the opposite; however, anyone who does not fancy steak and kidney pie or Yorkshire pudding will probably enjoy Chinese *dum sum*, spicy Indian lentil soup and a *tandoori* dish, or a shark steak from a Caribbean cooking-pot – the choice is endless. It is these varied attractions and its free and easy atmosphere which make London a truly cosmopolitan city, and thanks to this same diversity – and regardless of any imperial pomp and the stiff dignity of the English "gentleman" – London is still a swinging city thirty years after the invention of the mini-skirt!

Treasures
of the Orient in the British Museum

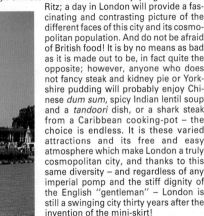

uckingham Palace
is one of the most popular attractions – even if you do not see the Queen!

Londons Pubs –
they alone make the journey worthwhile!

**Nature, Culture
History**

Facts and Figures

General

Capital and world metropolis

London is the capital of the United Kingdom of Great Britain and Northern Ireland, seat of the royal residence, the two Houses of Parliament and the Government, as well as the capital of the Commonwealth. Not only is it the economic and cultural hub of Great Britain and one of the world's major financial centres, it is also a truly cosmopolitan city in which people from all countries contribute to a wide cultural background.

Geographical situation

London is situated in south-east England, on latitude 50°31' north. Surrounded by hills averaging 150m/500ft above sea-level, it lies in a gently undulating basin on both banks of the River Thames some 47 miles/75km upstream from where it enters the North Sea. The Greenwich meridian (0° longitude) runs through the borough of Greenwich.

Climate

The climate of London is temperate. The average temperature in January is 40°F/4·3°C and in July 63°F/17·5°C, the yearly average being about 49°F/9·5°C. Rain falls annually on some 170 days. However, the once notorious London fog is now almost a thing of the past.

What does one understand by "London"?

Depending on how one thinks of it, the name "London" can mean different things. First of all, the name can denote the original heart of the city, the "City of London", which covers an area of only 1 sq.mile/ 2·6 sq.km, which is why it is often known as "The Square Mile". It has a resident population of only some 5000, although more than 400,000 people work there. In the evenings it is relatively deserted. The actual municipal area of London, known as the County of London, was established in 1888 and had an area of 117 sq.miles/303 sq.km and a population of 3·2 million. In 1965 it gave way to an even larger unit by the amalgamation of the County of London with the county of Middlesex and parts of the adjoining counties of Surrey, Essex, Kent and Hertfordshire to form Greater London with an area of

◀ *Piccadilly at night*

609 sq.miles/1579 sq.km and a population of about 6·8 million. The districts in which they live are so varied that many of the inhabitants will say that they come from, say, Richmond rather than London. In 1986 Greater London was again dissolved. In a still wider sense the name of London is now applied to the conurbation known as the Capital Region, measuring some 125 miles/200km across with a population of over 12 million and which, broadly speaking, is encircled by the M25 London Orbital Motorway and dominates the south-east region of Britain.

Population and Administration

By the middle of the 17th c. London already had a population of over half a million and was thus by far the largest city in England. Thereafter the population continued to increase until it reached the million mark in the early 19th c. From the middle of the 19th c. the City of London

Population growth

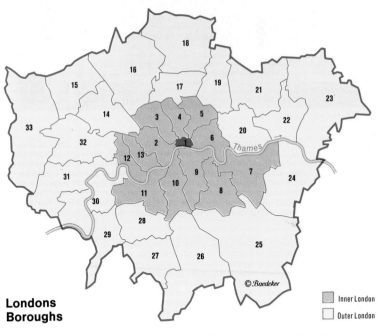

Londons Boroughs

| | Inner London |
| | Outer London |

1 City of London
2 City of Westminster
3 Camden
4 Islington
5 Hackney
6 Tower Hamlets
7 Greenwich
8 Lewisham
9 Southwark
10 Lambeth
11 Wandsworth

12 Hammersmith and Fulham
13 Kensington and Chelsea
14 Brent
15 Harrow
16 Barnet
17 Harringey
18 Enfield
19 Waltham Forest
20 Newham
21 Redbridge
22 Barking and Dagenham

23 Havering
24 Bexley
25 Bromley
26 Croydon
27 Sutton
28 Merton
29 Kingston upon Thames
30 Richmond upon Thames
31 Hounslow
32 Ealing
33 Hillingdon

Lunch break in the legal district

showed a steady decline in population (1851: 130,000; 1881: 50,500; 1921: 13,700; 1931: 11,000 and now only 5000), while the population of Greater London grew from 2·2 million in 1841 to its present figure of over 6.8 million (3·2 million of whom live in Inner London). This great increase in population not only involved steady outward extension of the built-up area but also led to the creation of nine "New Towns" around the capital: Basildon, Bracknell, Crawley, Harlow, Hatfield, Hemel Hempstead, Stevenage, Welwyn Garden City and Milton Keynes.

Incomers

London's increasing importance as an industrial and commercial centre attracted numerous immigrants and other incomers. In the 17th c. many Huguenot refugees came from France; in the 18th and 19th c. there were many Irish immigrants; in the early 19th c. Africans and Chinese settled in London's dockland; after 1880 there was an influx of Jewish families to the East End; after the Second World War a flood of immigrants came from the West Indies, Africa, Cyprus, India and Pakistan; and in more recent years Arabs have established themselves in London, making their presence felt in the business world.

London and its environs continue to see the greatest concentration of immigrants in the whole of the United Kingdom. Many of these ethnic groups tend to be concentrated in particular parts of London – Jamaicans in Brixton, Trinidadians in Notting Hill, Indians in the East End and Southall, Chinese in Soho, while rich Arabs show a preference for Kensington. All this has resulted in a rich ethnic mix, leading in turn to a diversity of culture which is almost unique in Europe and which is reflected in the wide variety of restaurants, shops, festivals and customs. On the other hand, however, this mélange of cultural differences has indisputably caused problems and conflicts in the spheres of self-administration, educational and cultural establishments, equality of opportunity at work and in religion. There are also social problems which affect others beside coloured Londoners.

As a result of the decline of London industries and the Port of London large numbers of unskilled workers have lost their jobs in recent years, and cut-backs in public expenditure have also put many Londoners out of work. For the unskilled there are often only poorly paid jobs available which provide a low standard of living, while housing, whether to rent or buy, is very expensive. Many factors have meant that, according to conservative estimates, 25% of Londoners live below the poverty level – ethnic minorities, the sick, the old, those living alone and the homeless, the numbers of which are growing, are particularly vunerable.

Problems of a large city

The religions practised in London are as varied as the ethnic composition of its population. The established church is the Church of England, and London is the seat of an Anglican bishop and also of a Roman Catholic archbishop. In addition there are Methodist, Baptist and United Reform churches (a union of Congregationalists and Presbyterian). Non-Christian faiths are practised mainly by Commonwealth immigrants, including Hindus and Buddhists. The Jewish community forms another minority.

Religion

The area of Greater London is divided between the City of London and 32 boroughs. Twelve of these boroughs, which are situated closely around the City, form "Inner London", while the remainder are known as "Outer London".

Administration

The administrative structure of the metropolis is not simple to explain. When the Greater London Council (G.L.C.) was abolished in 1986 the various areas of responsibility of the former council devolved upon the boroughs and government departments. Thus, for example,

Tourists in Trafalgar Square

the head of the London Metropolitan Police is responsible to the Home Office, while the City of London has its own police force (see *Baedeker Special*, pages 196–97). In certain fields the boroughs have formed commercial organisations while remaining largely autonomous as regards town planning. Nevertheless, London is unique as a metropolis as it is without a unified administrative body.

The administration of the City of London is based on medieval attested rights; this subject is dealt with at greater length in the *Baedeker Special* on page 15.

Economy

World financial centre

London's position as the capital of a world empire gave it international importance as one of the world's leading financial centres. The most decisive date in the recent history of the city was October 27th 1986, the day of the "Big Bang". On this day the London Stock Exchange relaxed many rules which had hitherto been strictly applied, in particular those concerning membership and the limitations placed on the way in which the members conducted their business, and it became an open market for stocks and shares. At the same time trading in shares by computer was introduced which enabled transactions to be finalised much more quickly. This move led to an influx of broking firms from abroad, the most important from New York, and an immense increase in capital turnover. Today 22% of all bank transactions in the world are conducted in London (New York 18%; Tokyo 10%). With a daily turnover of 300 billion dollars the London Stock Exchange is the largest foreign exchange centre in the world and over 520 banks have offices in the city. In addition it is one of the major centres of trade in raw materials and precious metals, and has 20% of the valuable worldwide insurance business, with more than 500 international insurances companies having offices in London. The Baltic Exchange handles bids for cargo space in ships and aircraft; over half the international business in this field is handled here. London is also one of the leading markets for trade in derivatives. Finally, since 1945 Sotheby's and Christie's have made London the leading world centre for trade in art.

Centre of British economy

As the capital of Great Britain and Northern Ireland, London is the centre of government, trade and industry. Almost all the major British shipping lines and industrial undertakings have their headquarters here, and in the exhibition halls of the capital more than 80 important international and national trade fairs and exhibitions are held each year. Although the importance of the city as a centre of administration, trade and other major services continues to increase (some 80% of London's gross domestic product comes from these sources) industrial production in and around London has declined since the 1960s, with many new firms preferring to be located outside London or in the provinces.

Industry

London's traditional industries are the manufacture of clothing and furniture, and the printing trade; the city has a virtual monopoly of the British press. Another old-established trade is diamond-cutting, especially in Hatton Garden. Precision engineering (developed out of the older trade of clockmaking) and the electrical industries have largely migrated to new industrial sites. The existence of the Port of London led to the development in the 19th c. of an industrial zone, with woodworking and furniture manufacture, sugar refineries and other food and semi-luxury production (e.g. brewing) and the chemical industries.

Between the two world wars cement-making, paper-making and vehicle manufacture (e.g. Fords of Dagenham) were established along the lower reaches of the Thames. A major post-war development has

The Corporation of London – a city within a city

The administration of the City of London is based on medieval attested rights, and the Corporation is still elected and carries out its functions according to traditional custom. The *Corporation of London* has the same powers as other boroughs and in addition it is responsible for the City Police Force and for the health and safety of the port. Furthermore, it administers the Central Criminal Court ("Old Bailey") and the markets of Billingsgate, Smithfield and Spitalfields.

The Court of Common Council, which meets in the Guildhall, is headed by the Lord Mayor and consists of 24 Aldermen and 131 Common Councillors. The latter are elected annually in December to represent the 25 wards into which the City is divided; the Aldermen, who are elected for life, together with the Lord Mayor, also represent the wards. The Common Council was established in the 12th c. following informal talks between the Lord Mayor and the Aldermen; the first official election took place in 1384.

The Lord Mayor, the senior representative of the City, is always a businessman. He is elected annually on Michaelmas Day. For this purpose the Liverymen, the representatives of the City Livery Companies, meet to consider a list of candidates, all of whom must previously have held the office of Sheriff. By a show of hands they chose two names which are communicated to the Aldermen who make the final decision. On the Friday before the second Saturday in November the Lord Mayor is inducted by his predecessor in the "Silent Ceremony", in which scarcely a word is spoken. On the following day the "Lord Mayor's Show" takes place, when there is a colourful procession through the streets of the City and the new Lord Mayor takes the oath of office. On the Monday of the following week the "Lord Mayor's Banquet" is held in honour of the outgoing Lord Mayor, and this glittering function is usually attended by members of the Royal Household and by the Prime Minister.

Among the traditional officers of the City are the Sheriffs, whose origins go back to the 7th c. The Liverymen chose the Aldermanic Sheriff from among the Aldermen, and also the Lay Sheriff, who is not an Alderman. The Sheriffs have to carry out all instructions of the High Court of Justice and they accompany and support the Lord Mayor. Other important officers include the Town Clerk, the Chamberlain of London (a financial officer), the Comptroller and Solicitor, the Remembrancer (responsible for ceremonies), and the Secondary Sheriff and High Bailiff of Southwark whose duties include the business of the Central Criminal Court.

Named after their traditional forms of dress, the *Livery Companies* were trade guilds which laid down standards of quality and training regulations for apprentices. Today they are mainly concerned with various charitable and educational aims but they still play an important role in the government of the City. There are still 97 guilds in London. The first dozen are known as the "Great Twelve"; these are the Grocers, the Spicers, the Clothmakers, the Furriers, the Haberdashers, the Ironmongers, the Vintners, the Salters, the Clothiers, the Tailors and Cutters, the Goldsmiths and the Fishmongers. Only the Goldsmiths, the Fishmongers and the Vintners still supervise their guilds; the Guild of Apothecaries still functions as an examining body.

been the establishment of a large refinery and petro-chemical complex at Tilbury.

Tourism

Tourism continues to grow in importance. London attracts almost 10 million visitors each year, as many as any city in the world.

Building boom

The increasing attraction of London as a financial centre drew a large number of firms to the City, but they found it difficult to acquire adequate accommodation. So the townscape of London has completely changed in recent years following the construction of more and more office tower blocks. At the same time the confines of the City are extending as even the adjoining districts become increasingly attractive. Other gigantic projects are under construction or in the planning stage. Thus Spitalfields Market, together with Broad Street Station, where the Broadgate Centre is already opened, Liverpool Street and Bishopsgate Street Stations, will be Europe's largest office and commercial complex under one roof. The same thing is happening at Charing Cross Station, with the office complex London Bridge City in Southwark, and with the rebuilding of the King's Cross/St Pancras area where the new British Library has been constructed. The most ambitious project, however, was the redevelopment of the old docks; here, at Canary Wharf, a residential and office complex with Europe's highest office tower as its central feature has been developed.

Transport

Commuter traffic

More than 1½ million people work in London. Every day over one million commute to the capital from the suburbs, the vast majority by public transport. Most travel by British Rail trains to one of the capital's thirteen main stations, as well as by Underground, the quickest and cheapest form of transport in London. The latter serves 273 stations and carries 5½ million passengers daily on a network of 260 miles/420km. The line with the highest succession of trains – 33 each hour – is the Bakerloo-Northern line, while the busiest Underground station – 73 million passengers a year - is King's Cross (see Baedeker Special, pages 252–54). London also has a well-developed network of bus services with a total length of some 4040 miles/6500km. Its 5500 double-deckers and single-deckers carry about 5,100,000 passengers a week. The Docklands Light Railway (DLR) was opened in 1987 to serve the redeveloped Docklands area. It is now also linked up to the City (Bank Station) and east London (Stratford Station). The Jubilee Line is at present being extended to the Docklands area.

Road traffic

London is the most important motorway junction in the country. Motorways from all parts of Britain enter the 115 mile/185km-long M25 orbital motorway. In central London, however, traffic tends to come to a standstill, and the Underground is a far quicker way to travel.

The Port of London

London lies on both banks of the Thames, some 47 miles/75km above its mouth, and has a port open to sea-going vessels which ranks among the principal ports of the world (freight turnover in 1991 amounted to 52·8 million tonnes). The development of the port, however, suffered a decline in recent decades and part of the freight traffic was lost to other places, including Dover and Felixstowe. The building of terminals in the north of Great Britain to handle North Sea shipments also contributed to the decline of the Port of London. Port installations built in the 19th c. – St Katharine's Dock, Millwall, East and West India Docks, Royal Victoria and Royal Albert Docks – in the east part of the capital are in danger of falling into decay but have been redeveloped as a financial, high technology and dormitory complex; the main port installations are now to be found on the stretch of river 15–20 miles/25–30km downstream from

Tower Bridge. These include Tilbury, with a huge container terminal and London's passenger terminal for voyages to Australia, South Africa and the Far East. Still further downstream lie the oil terminals of Shellhaven, Thameshaven, Canvey Island and Coryton, which can handle tankers of up to 90,000 tonnes.

In the Port of London mainly vehicles, machinery, chemical products and electrical goods are loaded for export, the main imports being crude oil, timber and corn.

There are five airports close to London. The largest is Heathrow, 15 miles/24km west of the city; handling about 54,500,000 passengers annually (1997), it is the third largest international airport.

Gatwick, 27 miles/45km south of London. handles mainly charter and tourist traffic, although it is being increasingly used by scheduled services, because Heathrow is becoming increasingly congested.

At the end of 1987 London's newest airport, London City Airport in Docklands (10 miles/16km east of the city centre), was opened for use by light aircraft. It is used mainly for business flights.

The two airports of Stansted (37 miles/59km north-east of London) and Luton (32 miles/51km north-west) are being used more and more for flights to and from London.

Airports

Art and Culture

Architecture and the History of Art

Roman Londinium

Before the Romans, the Celts inhabited the London region, and small sculptures, ceramics, jewellery, everyday objects and weapons from that period have been dug up – a selection of these can be seen in the London Museum. From A.D. 43 onwards, when the Romans established their rule under the Emperor Claudius, Londinium grew up on the site of a pre-Roman settlement; initially it consisted of a fortified enclosure surrounded by a *vicus* or village, but quickly developed into an important commercial centre. The erection of a wooden bridge near the present-day London Bridge (confirmed by the discovery of coins on the site) aided its rapid growth.

Basilica and forum

By about A.D. 80 Londinium was already the largest town in the British province and boasted among other things a massive basilica where Leadenhall Market now lies, with a large adjoining forum, a well-constructed sewerage system and many baths. A harbour, goods warehouses and the governor's palace were built close to the Thames.

Temple of Mithras

In 1954 a Temple of Mithras, designed with a main nave, side-aisles, apse and columns, was excavated. Statues displayed in the Guildhall and in the London Museum are further evidence of this Mithras cult; many other items on display provide background to life in Londinium at the time.

City wall

The building of the city wall commenced in the 2nd c. A.D.; 6m/20ft high and 2·5m/8ft thick, it curved round from the present Tower Hill to Ludgate Hill. There are no signs in London of the grid street system so characteristic of the Romans in other towns.

Norman London

Apart from a few wall remains and some coin finds little remains of the Anglo-Saxons who, in A.D. 410, superseded the Romans. The first important remains date from the 11th c., after the Normans had arrived. The latter engaged on an immense building programme: round arches, doorways with archivolts, rectangular, later clustered or rounded columns, arcades, simple wooden ceilings which developed later into barrel or groin vaulting, are all characteristic of this architecture which employed simple geometric patterns and capitals in the form of human figures or animals as decoration.

White Tower

Between 1078 and 1097 William the Conqueror built the massive Tower, his first example of Norman architecture. The stone blocks used in its construction were imported from Caen and the walls were coated with chalk, which explains why it was described as the "White Tower". The impression of power and stability conveyed by this massive square building, four storeys in height, with its rounded windows is emphasised further by the enormously thick walls (3m/10ft at the base, becoming thinner towards the top). At the south-eastern corner, instead of a tower, can be seen the apse of St John's Chapel, one of the most important examples of early Norman art in London. Its side aisles

St John's Chapel in the Tower of London: finest example of Norman architecture

continue round the choir, in the upper storey a walkway leads round the whole building; near the chapel this walkway takes the form of a gallery, a feature which is typical of similar buildings in the south of France. The plain, uncarved, arcaded arches of the lower storey rest on massive round pillars with simple cubic or folded capitals. The nave is barrel vaulted, the side aisles have groin vaulting.

The choir of St Bartholomew the Great also presents an impressive picture of Norman architecture: the sheer size of the walls, the round-arched arcades, the sturdy columns and distinctively profiled screen arches of the upper storey dating from the Romanesque period contrast sharply with the Late Gothic Perpendicular-style windows.

St Bartholomew the Great

London Bridge, with its twenty arches the first stone bridge over the Thames and built about 1200 by Peter Cole of Church, is a technical masterpiece. Immediately after it was completed houses, shops and a chapel were built on either side of the road.

London Bridge

High Middle Ages: Gothic

Gothic forms were appearing in English architcture before the middle of the 12th c.: pointed arches, ribbed vaulting, limb structure and triforia or arcaded galleries. In Early Gothic many Norman elements can still be detected, but the walls display more and more tracery, the columns become more slender and the windows lancet in form. This first phase is known as Early English, of which Westminster Abbey is an outstanding example. This triple-aisled edifice with choir, sanctuary and radial chapels has more the proportions of a French cathedral. The varied wall structures display the characteristic ogival and wide arcade arches below, surmounted by trefoil and deep lancet arches, together with rose

Architecture

Early English style

Gothic perfection: choir and nave in Westminster Abbey

and lancet windows. The wide, tall windows of the polygonal chapterhouse are very impressive. The simple, clear tracery shows the influence of Amiens and Rheims, while the trefoil arches above the sedilia are rounded and date from the very early Gothic period. The rosette patterns on the unique floor tiles (*c.* 1250) are very similar to the rose window in the transept and exemplify the great interest shown at the time in pierced tracery.

Decorated style

The Decorated style which followed portrays Gothic architecture in its richest and most complex forms. Walls are more pierced, windows and door openings decorated with rich tracery and arch designs. Stonemasons bring emphasis on detail to a fine art: heavily pierced decoration is placed above doorways, the capitals of columns are less severe and receive ornamentation, and roof vaulting, including ribbed vaulting, becomes more complex. The spacious appearance of buildings remains unaffected by these changes. One outstanding example of this style is St Ethelred's Chapel (late 13th c.) near Smithfield Market.

Perpendicular style

The Perpendicular style dominated English architecture until the beginning of the 16th c. In this insular form of English Late Gothic detail on walls and vaulting becomes more elaborate while shapes are more rigid and methodical and ornamentation less exuberant. In arches and windows the emphasis is more on the horizontal and windows become larger so that the wall surface is less obtrusive. A further feature is the use of vertical members in lattice-work. In addition to net and star vaulting, fan vaulting is introduced, in which the ribs radiate outwards from a central point. The Henry VII Chapel, formerly Lady Chapel, in Westminster Abbey (1503–19), with its extraordinary fan vaulting and truncated vertical patterns is a superb example of the Perpendicular style.

Of the few remaining examples of Gothic secular architecture, Westminster Hall, today part of the Houses of Parliament, stands supreme.
A further important example is the Guildhall, the crypt, assembly hall
and main doorway of which are so typical of the period in which it was
built, 1411–39.

Secular
architecture

The development of medieval sculpture can be studied in some detail
through the medium of monuments and tombstones. In the 13th c. the
types of tombstone figure found, for example, in Temple Church were
common. New guidelines were employed in Westminster: the tomb of
Edmund Crouchback (d. 1296) has a canopy attached with niches
containing figures of women in mourning; above the sculpted likeness
of the deceased are three gabled arches in the middle of which is an
equestrian statue of the Count. This expensive architectural structure
has its origins in holy shrines. A further example is the tomb of John of
Eltham, where the petitioning figure shows the body curved in the
manner employed by English sculptors before 1250 to portray emotion
and grief. In Westminster Abbey full-length sculptures have been preserved on the doorway of the chapterhouse and the internal end walls
of the transept; some of the angels still retain their original colouring.

Sculpture

Monuments and
tombstones

Book illumination in England reached its peak in the 12th c. Traditional
outline drawing was combined with Continental influences, promoting
a lively interchange of patterns with the ruling house of Anjou. Matthew Page, the renowned English painter of miniatures, decorated the
"Historia Anglorum" manuscript, the miniatures in which on the one
hand owe much to ancient Classical styles while on the other hand
reflecting contemporary thinking by adhering to nature and emphasis-
ing emotional values. The panels of the Westminster Reredos (Westminster Abbey) date from about 1280; the tall, elegant figures of Christ
and the Apostles, standing closely one behind the other, have a most
pleasing softness of form with their robes sweeping gently to the floor.
Their faces and curly hair are also softly portayed. Examples of secular
painting are the frescoes – mainly battle scenes from the Old Testa-
ment – which Henry II had painted in his palace at Westmninster from
about 1235 onwards. Unfortunately, these works by the court painter
Walter of Durham were completely destroyed in 1834 and so those
now seen in the Painted Chamber are only 19th c. copies.

Painting

London in the Renaissance

The Perpendicular style remained important during the whole of the
Renaissance. Renaissance features – a striving for harmony, symmetrical façades, a revival of the ancient Classical column orders – are
initially to be seen only in a few details here and there. The Tudor style
(c. 1485–1558) marks a period of transition and radical change.
Although not in the Tudor style, the above-mentioned Henry VII Chapel
falls in this epoch. Tudor buildings in London include the gatehouse,
audience chamber and chapel of St James' Palace, as well as the
former Staple Inn in Chancery Lane. Hampton Court Palace (1514–40)
is a Gothic edifice with Italian interior decoration in the form of terracotta medallions with the busts of Roman emperors. Its brick and tile
construction and above all the slender chimneys with geometric decorations are typical of the Tudor period.

Architecture

During the Elizabethan era (1558–1603) the economic prosperity
enjoyed was reflected in a glittering culture at court, but few new
building projects were undertaken. However, some major theatres
were built at the time, in particular the now restored Shakespearean
Globe Theatre. In the Jacobean period (c. 1603–25) Gothic forms fall
out of favour, Classical columns and entablature and symmetry again
come to the fore and decoration becomes considerably more lavish.

Elizabethan
style

Architecture and the History of Art

The Stuart period (from 1625) was dominated by the Palladian style, the chief exponent of which was Inigo Jones (1573–1652), whose exclusive and aristocratic edifices pointed the way ahead for English architecture in the centuries that followed. The distinguishing features of his style are modesty and simplicity of décor together with solidity of construction; a superb example of his work is the Queen's House in Greenwich (1616–35), a two-storey rectangular building in strict Classical and Palladian style with a balustrade and Corinthian columns. Jones' *chef d'œuvre*, however, was Whitehall Palace, of which only the Banqueting House (1619–22) still remains.

**Painting and
sculpture**
The interest in miniature painting was initiated by the Dutch Hornebotte family, who were invited to England from the Netherlands by Henry VII in about 1530. Nicholas Hilliard (1537/38?–1618) favoured portraits showing only the head and shoulders, with particular emphasis on the ruff and jewellery. Under Elizabeth I, whose major portraits they painted, Hilliard and his followers were among the most important painters of miniatures.

Hans Holbein
New ground in painting was also broken by Hans Holbein (1497–1543), who spent several long periods of residence in England, initially engaged in painting portraits for German merchants of the Hanseatic League and was then appointed as court painter to Henry VIII. His portraits are noted for their rational observation of detail, the countenances precisely drawn, differences in materials clearly shown. The first Renaissance sculptures in London were created by the Florentine Pietro Torrigiano (1472–1528) on the tombstone of Henry VII and his Queen Elizabeth of York (1512–18) in Westminster Abbey. It shows the pair in the traditional manner as isolated recumbent figures, richly attired and with hands folded in supplication, their heads resting on pillows. This manner of portraying individual countenances and body forms, the shape of which can be detected under the clothing, can be seen in many other examples in London.

The century of Sir Christopher Wren

17th century:
the Architectural
Age
The 17th c. was the great age of architecture in England. First of all Inigo Jones' methods set the tone, but in the second half of the century Sir Christopher Wren (1632–1723) came to the fore, especially in connection with the rebuilding of London following the Great Fire of 1666. His St Paul's Cathedral and 52 other city churches display a great variety of building styles, some of them quite surprising. In many cases, however, he respected local traditions. Initially, in co-operation with Inigo Jones, he extended the Royal Naval Hospital in Greenwich with the Queen's House and the Greenwich Observatory. Wren's masterpiece is St Paul's Cathedral (1675–1711): the façade with two towers and the dome are novel developments. The two rows of colonnades are attributable to the Parisian architect Perraults, while the upper floors of the towers are reminiscent of the Baroque designs of Francesco Borromini in Rome and are similar to a number of other towers built by Wren. The interior represents a compromise between the Anglican preference for a basilica with a nave and spacious choir, and the architect's concept of a central edifice crowned with a dome. St Stephen's Walbrook was built almost as a prototype for St Paul's; it is a cruciform pillared basilica with an architrave and two flat-roofed side aisles; in the choir a large, square area is left empty and roofed with a dome, thus trying out Wren's ideas for St Paul's. Although Wren did design some secular buildings for the royal court, these are rare; mention should be made, however, of the massive, somewhat over-plain square building of the east wing of Hampton Court Palace (1689–92). Towards 1700, in conjunction with Sir John Vanburgh and Nicho-

19th century London architecture: Princes Gardens

las Hawksmoor, Wren developed a uniquely heterogeneous form of English Late Baroque. Otherwise he perpetuated the English tradition, a semi-mixture of styles in which Gothic is enriched with Renaissance and Early Baroque details.

In London, sculptural works concentrate on decorative sculpture, especially in churches and prestigious buildings. Occasionally some captivating pieces appear, such as the marble bust of Wren by Edward Pierce (1673; now on display in the Ashmolean Museum in Oxford). Inspired by French sculpture and by Bernini, this is London's first Baroque bust.

Sculpture

18th century

The stark dissociation of English architecture from the international Baroque began in 1715. Richard Boyle, Earl of Burlington, the chief exponent of Classico-Palladian ideology, regarded Baroque as a form of hostile propaganda on the part of the Catholic church and gathered around him a circle of architects – Adam, Chambers, Stuart, Revett – who favoured the architectural styles of southern Europe, especially those of Italy. Thus, William Chambers (1723–96) introduced French and Roman influences into his classical Somerset House, as the north front clearly portrays. Robert Adam (1728–92) employed a number of styles in building Kenwood House and emphasised the façade by means of an *ædicula* and a porticus; however, he laid more emphasis on the Neo-Roman, elegantly-refined decoration of the interior rooms.

Architecture

In 1630, when designing the Covent Garden Plaza, Inigo Jones produced London's first example of standardised rows of houses modelled on the the Place des Vosges in Paris. Great Queen's Street and Lincoln's Inn are on similar lines. However, following the Great Fire of

Residential buildings

William Hogarth: "Beer Street" . . .

London in 1666 re-building was done in a disjointed fashion, without taking advantage of the situation to introduce a form of overall planning or to re-design the city in a spacious and completely new form. It was not until the east side of Grosvenor Square was built that the idea of a standardised façade design was adopted, which can now be seen governing the design of the many-storied Georgian houses in numerous squares, crescents or circuses. Grey and yellow brick, bright stucco decoration, a certain rhythmic effect resulting from the use of such architectural features as columns, gables and entrance porches, are characteristic of this simple style.

John Nash

One of the prime exponents of this trend was John Nash (1752–1835), whose most important legacy to the nation was Regent Street and Regent's Park, built from 1811 onwards and at the time Europe's largest municipal building project.

Painting

Until the early 18th c. artists from mainland Europe were setting the tone in England: the German Godfrey Kneller (1646–1723) painted elegant portraits, Italians painted historical scenes. Among the English painters, only Sir James Thornhill (1675–1734) stood out with his decorative work – for example, the dome of St Paul's or the ceiling-paintings in Hampton Court Palace.

William Hogarth

However, the following generation again brought English painting to the forefront of international ranking. William Hogarth (1697–1764)

... and "Gin Lane"

first had success with his "conversation pieces", before he introduced moral themes into his popular pictures which presented their characters as they really were without any false gloss. Hogarth's reputation resulted from his large output of copper engravings, which satirised society life, of which he was a careful observer, and which also served to denounce abuses and corruption.

Sir Joshua Reynolds (1723–92), whose work was inspired by a study trip through Italy and the Van Dyck tradition as well as by the *chiaroscuro* treatment of light and shade employed by Rembrandt, had a considerable influence on the development of portrait painting. He portrayed his distinguished models posing as famous antique statues or followed the lines of major Renaissance compositions, thereby achieving accuracy of character, depth and liveliness in his paintings. Reynolds enjoyed great respect among his aristocratic patrons and his ranking in London art circles was further enhanced when he was elected the first president of the Royal Academy in 1768. Together with Reynolds, Allan Ramsay (1713–84) and Thomas Gainsborough (1727–88) numbered among the most important portrait painters of the time. Landscape painting also gave Gainsborough a fresh impetus when he founded an Anglo-Arcadian tradition and produced extremely carefully executed landscapes in skilfully balanced and soft colours.

Sir Joshua Reynolds

Architecture and the History of Art

19th century

Architecture

The major 19th c. building project centred around the Houses of Parliament, which were to be built in Gothic or Elizabethan style, showing on the one hand that Gothic was still highly prized as a "rational style", while on the other hand the proximity to Westminster Abbey may also have played a part. In 1836 the draft plans of Sir Charles Barry (1795–1860) were accepted; these proposed a finely structured but strictly symmetrical façade. However, it was 1860 before the use of the Neo-Gothic style in secular buildings finally became fully accepted, an example being the Royal Courts of Justice. It is clear from his designs for the Traveller's and Reform Clubs in the Italian quattrocento style that Barry was an architect with a wide range of ideas. Sir John Soane (1753–1837) was the architect of the Bank of England back in 1788 and was responsible for an extraordinary number of new buildings and extensions to old in the city. His buildings were varied and elegantly classical in form.

Industrialisation necessitates buildings of a new kind

The type of buildings needed in a city such as London changed considerably in the course of the 19th c. Large residential buildings, docks, markets and railway stations became important projects. For example, between 1835 and 1839 Robert Stephenson and Philip Hardwick designed Euston Station, with an impressive entrance in the form of a Doric porticus in wrought iron which – in spite of fierce opposition – was pulled down in 1963; King's Cross Station, built by Lewis Cubitt in 1851–52, had barrel-vaulting 24m/80ft wide over the track and platforms and a glazed entrance façade. The *pièce de résistance* of glass and iron constructions was the hall built for the Great Exhibition of 1851. In 1860 the city made a start on building the first underground, the stations of which were simple flat barrel-vaulted affairs with deep window niches to admit daylight, while at night illumination was provided by gas-lamps. Shortly after the first stretch of underground rail was opened advertising rights in the stations were leased out, and the resultant bright and cheerful hoardings added to the charm of the various stops. Market halls and galleries such as Burlington Arcade, Covent Garden and Leadenhall Market serve as a reminder of London as an economically prosperous metropolis. Tower bridge, erected in 1886–94, was a new London landmark and a fine example of Victorian Gothic.

Painting

Landscape painting remained an important genre. John Constable (1776–1837) initially followed in the footsteps of his 18th c. predecessors and practised copying older landscapes. Soon, however, he forsook conventional forms of composition and evolved his own ways of portraying light and colour. In his studies of nature he tried to convey delicate nuances of light and atmospheric conditions, interested himself in cloud forms and movements, while employing relaxed and economical brush strokes and thus giving his pictures more the character of oil sketches than of finished paintings.

William Turner

Joseph Mallord William Turner (1775–1851), initially self-taught, then a student in Reynold's art classes, was inspired by studying the works of Poussin and Lorrain. He became famous for his delicate rendering of the shifting gradations of light. Landscape impressions flooded with light, misty atmospheres, iridescent reflections were all conveyed without any discernible outline, conveying a generalised visionary mood sometimes accentuated with an arbitrary choice of colour of a semi-symbolic character.

Pre-Raphaelites

The imaginative force and visionary power of William Blake (1757–1827) made him the forerunner of the Pre-Raphaelites. In their romantic and retrospective approach the latter concentrated their attention on the period before Raphael, namely, the Pre- and Early Renaissance

John Constable: "Chain Pier, Brighton"

periods, which were particularly attractive to artists because of the way they expressed emotional situations and moods. Their subjects were religious, literary and historical as well as contemporary.

20th century

From the end of the 19th c. until immediately after the Second World War architecture fell back into its traditional 18th c. mould, as exemplified by Reginald Bloomfield's Piccadilly Hotel or Regent Street, and Lutyen's Britannic House and the Midland Bank. Academic pomp tended to govern the architecture of the generations which followed. New urban developments came to the fore; the "Tecton" group planned the Highpoint One and Highpoint Two apartment blocks, without equal in their elegance and skill. Post-war residential and school architecture was aimed almost solely at meeting the urgent need for such accommodation. The Royal Festival Hall and the Royal National Theatre set a new trend; this cultural complex by Denys Lasdun on the south bank of the Thames displays the use of concrete, an emphasis on the horizontal and a "landscape" impression created by means of platforms and bridges. Finally, in the 1980s, interesting high-tech and futuristic buildings appeared. In 1980 James Stirling was commissioned to extend the Tate Gallery, and in 1988 Richard Rogers completed the spectacular new Lloyd's building; Charing Cross Station, rebuilt in the early 1990s, possesses many post-modern features. The most ambitious project, however, is Docklands, an example of modern architecture containing such interesting architectural solutions as the One Canada Square office-block by Cesar Pelli or The Cascades apartment block by Piers Gough, the varying shades of colour and shape of which range from an eclectic mix of styles to a Neo-Classical coldness.

Architecture

At the end of the 20th century, the "Millenium", the face of London will change once again. Although the ambitious plans of the architect Sir Richard Rogers to construct a glass canopy along the South Bank had to

Architecture at the end of the 20th c.

27

New building in Docklands: "The Cascades" by Piers Gough

be aborted, the world's largest giant wheel, 495ft/151m high, is to be erected in the nearby Jubilee Gardens, Sir Richard Rogers will, however, build in Greenwich where the year 2000 will be ushered in with huge celebrations in a new amusement park. The park's main attraction will be the gigantic Millenium dome embracing everything the high-tech leisure industry can offer. Britain's other top architect, Sir Norman Foster, is constructing a fine lattice-work pedestrian bridge over the Thames between Southwark and Blackfriars Bridge, and plans to refurbish the Great Court of the British Museum by the year 2003. In the centre of the Great Court stands the famous round Reading Room of the British Library which, following the removal of the library to new premises the Reading Room, will be used for other purposes. Sir Norman intends to cover the Great Court with a glass dome.

Painting and sculpture

Three main trends govern modern art prior to the Second World War: a number of European artists who took up residence here, including Hans Arp, Naum Gabo, Laszio Moholy-Nagy and Piet Mondrian, favoured the move to Constructivism, the harmonies of pure geometric form and the rejection of concrete subjects. In the avant-garde sphere Surrealism developed, a form which theoretically was founded in England as a result, for example, of Roland Penrose's manifesto which was published shortly before the war. The two forms came together in "Unit One". The third stream reflected the Impressionist origins of Modernism. In their work the exponents of Modernism covered such subjects as the First World War and human sexuality; Jacob Epstein produced sculptures in bronze and stone. After the Second World War the fine arts relished an unprecedented wave of popular enthusiasm. Figurative work enjoyed a revival and fresh mediums were employed: Richard Hamilton and Eduard Paolozzi took advantage of the demand for art emanating from the new consumer society and encouraged by the media and the use of computers. Pop-art become the art form of the sixties. In the 1950s

Henry Moore produced sculptures with a spatial, three-dimensional quality which was further developed in the abstract work of Anthony Caro. In the 1960s the principles of Constructivism expanded into expressive and emotional forms, as exemplified in the sculptural work of the "New Generation" (King, Caro, etc.). Francis Bacon went his own way, using cruelty, force and suffering as the major themes for his large works, as did Frank Auerbach, who produces wild and spontaneous-looking paintings with thickly-applied oil paints which are then scraped away to allow an image to appear through the impasto, and Lucien Freud who paints the human form from peculiar angles. The Performance artists Gilbert and George and Bruce McLean have since turned to Photorealism.

London – a city of culture

London is the cultural and scientific centre of Great Britain. Radio and television companies, including the British Broadcasting Corporation (BBC), have their headquarters here, and almost all the national and Sunday newspapers are published in London. The city has five major orchestras (Royal Philharmonic, London Philharmonic, BBC Symphony Orchestra, the Philharmonia and the London Symphony Orchestra), more than 100 theatres, including the Royal Shakespeare Company housed in the Barbican Centre, the largest opera house in Britain (the Royal Opera House, Covent Garden), and two well-known ballet companies, the Royal Ballet and the English National Ballet.

A scientific and cultural centre

London boasts the country's leading museums and art galleries, at least six of which – the British Museum, the Victoria and Albert, the National Gallery, the Tate Gallery, the Natural History Museum and the Science Museum – are world-renowned.

Museums and libraries

The British Library is one of the great libraries of the world. In the Guildhall is the renowned Guildhall Library which includes the Greater London Record Office and the History Library containing the most important collection of documents concerning the development of London and its charters.

The University of London, which was originally founded in 1836 as an examining body for the various colleges in the city, became a teaching university in 1900. The university, with nine faculties, comprises a number of largely autonomous colleges and schools in various parts of London and the surrounding counties. In 1878 London University was the first university to grant degrees to women.

Universities and colleges

The main university buildings are in Russell Square. The colleges forming part of or associated with the university include University College, the largest, founded in 1826, King's College, housed in one wing of Somerset House, Bedford College near Regent's Park, the Imperial College of Science and Technology in South Kensington, the London School of Economics (LSE, near Kingsway) in New Cross south-east London, and Birkbeck College.

Two other universities were established in London in the 1960s, the City University and Brunel University.

Other colleges of note include the London Business School (with university status), art colleges such as the Chelsea School of Arts, the Royal College of Art, the Royal Naval College in Greenwich and numerous research institutes. The Guildhall School of Music and Drama enjoys a world-wide reputation.

Famous People

The following alphabetical list of famous people includes personalities who, by reason of birth, death, residence, occupation or death, are connected with London and are well-known not only in Britain but throughout the world.

Francis Bacon (1561–1626)

Francis Bacon was born in Highgate. He studied at Trinity College, Cambridge, and returned to London via Paris to join Gray's Inn. In 1584 he entered Parliament and became the protegé of Lord Essex, a favourite of Queen Elizabeth I. However, Bacon did not flinch from prosecuting his erstwhile patron in a case of high treason in 1601. In 1603 he was raised to the peerage, and in 1618 was finally made Lord High Chancellor. Yet three years later he himself was accused of high treason and temporarily thrown into the Tower. Subsequently he withdrew to the country and devoted himself to philosophical writing in which he founded the empirical method. His motto was "knowledge is power", and this knowledge could be won only by experiment, exact investigation and the results emanating therefrom. His most famous work, "Novum Organum", appeared in 1605; in his total of 85 essays he revealed himself as a master of English prose.

William Booth (1829–1912)

Nobody can fail to respect the soldiers of the Salvation Army who preach indefatigably the word of God in "red-light" districts, in shelters for the homeless and on the streets. The founder and first General was William Booth from Nottingham. After an apprenticeship to a pawnbroker and years as a preacher, he came to London in 1864 and founded the Christian Mission in Whitechapel in 1878. From this beginning emerged the Salvation Army which Booth modelled on the British Army. Although faced with hostility and ridicule, by the end of the 19th c. General Booth and his supporters had succeeded in extending the organisation throughout the world and gaining general acceptance.

Charles Spencer Chaplin (1889–1977)

Oversized shoes, a baggy coat, a jacket too tight for him, a moustache, a bowler hat and a walking-stick: with "The Tramp", who sympathises with his fellow men and who, in spite of every injustice, stands up for doing what is right, "Charlie" Chaplin created an immortal figure in the history of the cinema. He was born in London, the son of a poor variety artiste, and trod the boards when still a child; during a tour in the USA he was engaged by the Keystone Film Company. His first appearance in "The Tramp" in 1915 was to bring him fame in the 1920s and he remained true to this character in subsequent films such as "The Kid" and "The Gold Rush", made by United Artists, the production company which he founded in 1919 together with Mary Pickford, Douglas Fairbanks and D. W. Griffith. Chaplin continued his successful career when the "talkies" arrived, notably in "Modern Times" and especially in the controversial film "The Great Dictator" which, in spite of all its comic elements and satire directed at Nazi Germany, nevertheless lodged a deeply moving appeal against inhumanity and barbarism. After the Second World War his political involvement during the McCarthy era was the cause of his being brought before the Committee for Un-American Activities; the Department of Justice used a visit by him to Great Britain as an excuse for barring his return to the USA. Chaplin then settled in Switzerland. In his later films he revealed another side to his nature, notably in "Monsieur Verdoux" in which he played a false suitor for marriage and a murderer. Charles Chaplin died in Vevey on Lake Geneva, and although his fame was won in the USA he remained a British citizen.

Charles Chaplin

Charles Dickens

George Frederick Handel

Winston Spencer Churchill is without doubt the dominant figure of British politics in the first half of the 20th century. A member of Parliament from 1900 he was, as First Lord of the Admiralty, until 1915 largely responsible for the armament of the Royal Navy to counter the expansionist aims of the German Reich. From 1917 until 1929 he held a number of cabinet posts, including being Minister of War from 1918 until 1921 and finally Chancellor of the Exchequer. In the 1930s his star began to fade, but at the outbreak of the Second World War he was brought back into the government, again as First Lord of the Admiralty. Finally, in 1940 Churchill became Prime Minister at No. 10 Downing Street, at the head of an all-party administration. With President Roosevelt he concluded the Atlantic Charter and at the "Big Three" conference (United States, Soviet Union and Great Britain) was instrumental in laying down decisive guidelines for post-war order in Europe. Although he had led his country to victory in the war his government lost the 1945 parliamentary election largely because of a weak economic and financial policy. However, from 1951 to 1955 he was again Prime Minister. Churchill was also admired as a painter and as a writer; in 1953 he was awarded the Nobel Prize for literature. His saying "An iron curtain runs through Europe from north to south" epitomises the time of the "Cold War". Winston Churchill died in London.

Winston Churchill
(1874–1965)

The writings of Charles Dickens portray in an outstanding and sensitive manner the life of the poor of London. He had known poverty himself in his youth in the port area when his father was in a debtor's prison, and later he could only attend a mediocre school. Dickens worked his way up from being a lawyer's assistant, a parliamentary stenographer and journalist to become the most sucessful author of his time, as well as the proprietor of the "Daily News". He became known in 1837 for his "Pickwick Papers"; in the novels which followed, including "Oliver Twist", "Nicholas Nickleby" and "David Copperfield" he created heroes of world-wide literature. Again and again London is the scene of the action, turning on the plight of the poor and the injustice shown to them, and showing Dickens as a champion of the under-privileged. With all his social concern, however, Dickens never neglects humour, and his books still provide pleasure to countless readers. He is buried in Westminster Abbey.

Charles Dickens
(1812–1870)

The son of a respectable Yorkshire family, Guy Fawkes was a committed Catholic, and so left Protestant England in 1593 and enlisted as a soldier in the Spanish Netherlands. Increasing oppression of the Catholics in England led to the emergence of a number of conspirators who made plans for an attack on Parliament – the "Gunpowder Plot".

Guy Fawkes
(1570–1606)

To put their plans into action they needed a man with military experience, and they found him in Guy Fawkes, who had made a name for himself in the Netherlands as a man of courage, and so they brought him back to England in 1604. Fawkes deposited 20 barrels of gunpowder in a cellar beneath the Parliament buildings, but before he could ignite them he was arrested on November 5th 1605, tortured and condemned to death. He was executed outside Parliament on January 31st 1606. "Guy Fawkes Day" is still celebrated in England on November 5th with fireworks, masquerades and burning of effigies of the plotter.

Alexander Fleming
(1881–1955)

In 1928 the Scottish bacteriologist Alexander Fleming of St Mary's Medical School, London University, made a rmarkable discovery. Around a culture of certain fungal spores appeared an area which was free of bacteria. Fleming had discovered penicillin and had made the most important advance in the fight against infectious diseases. For this he was awarded the Nobel Prize for medicine.

George Frederick
Handel
(1685–1759)

The composer and organist George Frederick (Georg Friedrich) Handel, born in Halle in Saxony, is regarded as the first German musician to achieve world-wide fame. In 1711 he came to London for the first time to supervise the production of his opera "Rinaldo" at the Haymarket Theatre; a year later he finally settled in London where he resided in Brook Street near Hyde Park. In 1719 he was commanded by the king to found an opera house, but this was obliged to close down in 1728 as public taste preferred such middle-class operas as John Gray's "Beggar's Opera" to the aristocratic Italian forms favoured by Handel. However, Handel's outstanding works were composed during his stays in London, including his "Messiah" (1742), "Water Music" (1715–17), "Judas Maccabaeus" (1747) and "Music for the Royal Fireworks" (1748). He is buried in Westminster Abbey.

Henry VIII
(1491–1547)

Henry VIII of the House of Tudor ruled England from 1509 to 1547. He has gone down in history as the founder of the Anglican church, and because of his dissipated life-style and his six wives. Henry, born in Greenwich on June 28th 1491, was prepared as the future king from the age of eleven. He was educated along humanist and theological lines, was extremely well-mannered, an accomplished dancer and hunter and an imposing figure of a man. The first years of his rule seemed to confirm what had been expected of him, thanks largely to his Chancellor Wolsey. In recognition of a polemic he published castigating Luther (although in fact most of it was the work of Wolsey) Pope Leo X granted him the title of "Defender of the Faith". When his marriage to Catherine of Aragon failed to produce the male heir he desired, he tried to divorce her, but the Pope refused to give his permission. The resultant dispute ended in 1533 with the secession of the English church from Rome and the founding of the Anglican Church with the king at its head. Henry then married Anne Boleyn (mother of Elizabeth I), who was beheaded in 1536. His next wives were Jane Seymour, who died in 1537, Anne of Cleves (the "Flanders mare"), whom he soon divorced, then Catherine Howard, who was executed in 1542, and finally Catherine Parr, who survived him. In the last years of his life – he died on January 28th 1547 – after executing his chancellors Thomas More and Thomas Cromwell, Henry VIII became a solitary figure, mistrusting all around him and treating in the harshest fashion all those to whom he took a dislike.

Alfred Hitchcock
(1889–1980)

The central theme in the films directed by Alfred Hitchcock, who was born in London, was "suspense". Not the normal suspense of a "who dunnit?" but the tenseness created in the viewer by his treatment of threatening situations in such films as "The Invisible Man" or "Rear Window", or else the opposite approach, whereby he lets the viewer know more than the actors (in "Psycho", for example), aided by excellent production techniques and camera work.

Hitchcock, who was educated at a Jesuit seminary and studied aesthetics and engineering, is considered one of the greatest exponents of his craft. He made his first two films in Munich in 1926; in the 1930s he worked in England ("The 39 Steps"; "The Lady Vanishes") and from the 1940s in the United States. The leading Hollywood stars appeared in his films – "Rebecca", "Dial M for Murder", "Strangers on a Train", "The Birds", and others – all of which were undoubted masterpieces.

In London Hogarth learned the craft of a silversmith, yet he pursued his education in a parallel field by being apprenticed to an engraver, and was later a pupil of Sir James Thornhill, whose daughter he secretly married. His creed as a painter, and more especially as an engraver, was to observe and portray life as it was. His works are full of an intense irony, portraying the vices and foibles of the age (e.g. "Moral Pictures"), making him one of the keenest critics of his time. He can be said to have established the genre of caricature in England. As the founder of the St Martin's Lane Academy he presided over the leading educational institution of drawing and engraving and he became court painter in 1757. Among his best-known engravings are "A Rake's Progress", "Marriage à la Mode" and "The Four Stages of Cruelty".

William Hogarth (1697–1764)

Born at Augsburg in Germany, Holbein the Younger was the son of a talented painter. In 1515 he went to Basle where he became known for his murals, altarpieces and especially for the woodcuts of "The Dance of Death". Eventually, after several journeys, he came to England where he won acclaim for his lifelike portraits. In 1536 Holbein was appointed court painter to Henry VIII. He died of the plague in 1543.

Hans Holbein the Younger (1497–1543)

Born in Lichfield, Samuel Johnson lived in London from 1737, where he made his name as an essayist, journalist, satirist, novelist and as the leading literary critic of his time. In his "Dictionary of the English Language" he laid down standards for the use of English and, in his last major work "Lives of the Poets", for English comparative literature. With a number of contemporaries, including Reynolds, Burke and Goldsmith, he founded the Literary Club in London in 1764. He died in 1784 and is buried in Westminster Abbey.

Samuel Johnson (1709–1784)

Inigo Jones, who was born in London, was a landscape painter, scenic artist and architect who was profoundly influenced by Italian models (especially those of Palladio) during journeys to Italy. As a result, it is no surprise that many of the buildings he designed during his period as general building inspector from 1615 to 1649 are in stark contrast to conventional English styles of the period. His most famous work was the Banqueting House in Whitehall, and he also designed the first of London's "Squares" in Covent Garden. Unfortunately, almost all of his most ambitious project, the restoration of St Paul's Cathedral, was destroyed in the Great Fire of London in 1666.

Inigo Jones (1573–1652)

Marlowe, the most important English dramatist before Shakespeare, was born in Canterbury and spent a promiscuous life, mostly in London. He introduced blank verse into English drama and composed solemn plays including the "Jew of Malta" (which provided Shakespeare with "Shylock"), "Dr. Faustus" (which Goether used as one of his sources) and "Edward II". To escape the plague in London Marlowe settled in Deptford, where he was killed in a pub brawl.

Christopher Marlowe (1564–1593)

Thomas More, the son of a lawyer, later a judge, attended St Anthony's, considered the best school in London, the University of Oxford and Lincoln's Inn in London. Among his friends was Erasmus of Rotterdam who often visited him. In 1516 his novel "Utopia" appeared, in which the traveller Raphael Hythloday describes the ideal conditions existing in the fictional state of Utopia, a stark contrast to those then

Thomas More (1477–1535)

Famous People

Thomas More

Florence Nightingale

Virginia Woolf

pertaining in England or France. More's work was a great success and was soon translated in several languages. More wrote speeches for Henry VIII, whose confidant he became, was given important posts and acted as intermediary between Henry and his Lord Chancellor Wolsey. In 1523 he was elected Speaker of the House of Commons and in 1529 he finally succeeded Wolsey as Lord Chancellor. His quarrel with the king came when Henry wanted to divorce Catherine of Aragon and More, a fervent Catholic, was unable to agree. After the break between England and the Catholic Church, More resisted the marriage of Henry with Anne Boleyn. Finally, he also stood out against the Oath of Supremacy by which Henry was recognised as the head of the Anglican Church. In April 1534 he was thrown into the Tower and sentenced to death in July 1535. He was given five days to reconsider his position but refused to take the oath and was executed. Pope Pius XI canonised him in 1935.

Florence
Nightingale
(1820–1910)

When Florence Nightingale, who was born in Florence, was a young woman she was already recognised as an expert in public health. When the Crimean War broke out in March 1854 she immediately went to Turkey where she ran the field hospital of Scutari. A little later her main interest shifted from actual nursing to the organisation of medical care for the British army, and she became general inspector of nursing in the military hospitals. Largely on her initiative, the Army Medical School was founded in 1857. In 1860 she set up the Nightingale School for Nurses in London, the first school of nursing in the world. Until her death in 1910 she lived in London where she continued her work with ruthless energy, in spite of being largely bed-ridden and going blind in 1901.

Marie Tussaud
(1761–1850)

Madame Tussaud was born Marie Grosholtz. In 1794 she inherited from her uncle, from whom she learnt the craft of modelling in wax, his two collections of wax figures. During the French Revolution she was imprisoned as a Royalist and forced to make wax moulds from the heads newly cut off by the guillotine In 1795 she married the engineer François Tussaud, but in 1902 she and her two sons left him and came to England with numerous wax figures. For 33 years she travelled the country displaying her waxworks until finally settling in Baker Street in London. The most famous personalities of her age allowed her to model them; the originals can still be viewed at the famous waxworks.

Edgar Wallace
(1875–1932)

Perhaps more than any other writer, Edgar Wallace from Greenwich has painted the picture of London in his thrillers. Fog, darkness, polished asphalt streets, figures seen in the half-light, a cry in the darkness

– all these greet the readers of his thrillers such as "The Green Archer", "Traitor's Gate" or "The Dead Eyes of London". These stories, which are both detective and mystic tales, were filmed in Germany in the 1960s and were a great box-office success. His portrayal of London, as if it was all like Soho where it is wise to be ever on one's guard, is unforgettable.

Virginia Woolf's house in the London district of Bloomsbury was the meeting-place of the "Bloomsbury Group", a circle of writers, publishers and intellectuals – including E. M. Forster, Victoria Sackville-West, John Maynard Keynes and Lytton Strachey. Virginia Woolf came from a wealthy and cultured London family; after her marriage to the publisher Leonard Woolf she set up with him the Hogarth Press and worked as a critic on the Times Literary Supplement. She was also an essayist, a diarist and an author of novels which, especially in the 1920s, made her one of the most celebrated English authoresses. She committed suicide after her house was destroyed by a bomb during the Second World War.

Virginia Woolf
(1882–1941)

After completing his studies Christopher Wren became Professor of Astronomy at Gresham College in London in 1657. Here a circle of academics, started by him in 1660, was the predecessor of the Royal Academy. In 1661 he became Professor of Astronomy at Oxford. It was here that he began to interest himself in architecture and finally he found his true vocation in 1666 when he became general architect of reconstruction after the Great Fire. Altogether he designed 53 churches in London, Greenwich Hospital and the Chelsea Royal Hospital. His masterpiece, however, is the reconstruction of St Paul's Cathedral, where he is buried beneath the inscription; "lector, si monumentum requiris circumspici" ("reader, if you seek a monument, look around you").

Christopher Wren
(1632–1723)

History of London

Pre- and early history and the Roman period

There is evidence that there were inhabited settlements and small villages on both banks of the Thames during the New Stone Age. These people were followed by Celtic tribes, to whom the name "London" may be attributable, being formed from the Celtic words "ilyn" (pond or lake) and "dun" (a fortified place).

A.D. 43
Beginnings of Roman rule

In A.D. 43 the Celts found themselves confronted by the Romans. Their army under the Emperor Claudius conquered Britain, established it as a new "colonia" garrisoned by four legions, and developed the trading station of Londinium on the north bank of the Thames. The Celts resisted, of course, but eventually had to bow the knee to the Romans, even though the army of Queen Boadicea burnt down the first Roman settlement in A.D. 61 only for it quickly to be rebuilt. The Romans built a forum and a Temple of Mithras as well as the first (wooden) bridge across the Thames. In the centuries that followed Londinium became a thriving Roman town even though overshadowed by Eboracum (York) and Verulamium (St Albans). From A.D. 200 onwards the town was enclosed by a wall 6m/20ft high and up to 2m/7ft thick, the route of which still more or less marks the boundary of "the City". The growing importance of Londinium was shown by the fact that, in the reign of the Emperor Diocletian, it was made the capital of one of the four Roman provinces in Britain.

449: end of Roman rule

However, by 410 the heyday of Roman London was past. The legions were moved to Germania and in 449 Britain was abandoned entirely by Rome and Londinium fell into decay.

Middle Ages

Saxons

After the Roman withdrawal Jutes, Angles and Saxons occupied the country. The last-named built a harbour named Lundenwic outside the Roman walls; from this developed a settlement which in 796 became the capital of Anglo-Saxon Kingdom of Essex and remained so after the unification of the Anglo-Saxon kingdoms under Egbert, King of Wessex, in 872.

886: rebuilt by Alfred the Great

In 851, however, Danish Vikings sailed up the Thames and destroyed Lundenwic. It was not until 35 years later that the old Londinium was re-settled under Alfred the Great; thereafter it enjoyed a revival and until the 10th c. it developed into the largest and richest town in England.

Danes

Between 1016 and 1066 there was period of Danish rule which had far-reaching effects on the development of the capital. Under King Cnut (Canute) London replaced Winchester as the capital of England, and his successor Edward the Confessor moved his residence to Westminster, thus creating the two centres around which London was to grow into one city.

1066: Battle of Hastings – Norman rule

After his victory at Hastings in 1066 William the Conqueror (William I) was crowned in Westminster Abbey, when he promised to preserve the traditional rights of London. As a visible sign of his power he built the White Tower.

1176: first stone bridge over the Thames

The centuries that followed were a period of economic prosperity, as shown by the growth of the city and increased building activity – in 1176 Peter de Colechurch replaced the original wooden bridge with the first stone bridge across the Thames – as well as in a growing confidence among merchants.

The latter formed guilds and a form of civil administration for the city; in 1189 Henry Fitzailwyn was chosen by the representatives of the guilds to be the first Lord Mayor of London. The crown became obliged to grant the citizens of London certain rights. In the reign of Henry I London was established without any doubt as the capital of the realm and asserted its independence and right of self-government as a kind of city republic, subject only to the king. Richard I ("Lionheart") granted the citizens of London a charter establishing their rights over traffic on the Thames. The highlight of these successes was the Magna Carta of 1215, in which King John ("Lackland") recognised the right of the guilds to elect the Lord Mayor annually. Finally, from 1376 onwards the Common Council, which had acted as an informal point of contact between the Lord Mayor and the Aldermen of the Wards since the 13th c., began to meet regularly. At the end of the 14th c. it became an official establishment elected by the citizens, although peasants and those having no possessions had no such rights. The latter's displeasure was one of the additional factors leading up to the Peasants' Revolt of 1381, led by Wat Tyler, against the poll tax imposed to pay for the war against France, and which later showed itself again in the uprising led by Jack Cade in 1450.

1189: first Lord Mayor

The accession of Henry VII to the throne in 1485 marked the beginning of the Tudor dynasty and the end of the Middle Ages in London.

Under the Tudors and Stuarts

The 16th c. saw the city's economic growth accelerated by the establishment of the first trading companies and by the founding of the London Stock Exchange by Thomas Gresham in 1565. By the end of the century London was the most important trading centre of the known world, with a population of 200,000. During this period England seceded from the Catholic church and the Anglican church was founded by Henry VIII. The latter also had some impressive edifices built, such as those at Greenwich and Hampton Court, and invited Holbein and other artists to the city.

1565: founding of the Stock Exchange

The 17th c. began peacefully enough – William Shakespeare's Globe Theatre had been built on the South Bank in 1599 – but soon became one of the most turbulent eras in the history of London.

The abortive attempt by Guy Fawkes to blow up Parliament in 1605 was but a prelude to the looming power struggle between the Puritan Parliament and the Catholic Stuarts who had been on the throne since 1603.

1605: Gunpowder Plot

London soon became the centre of the political disputes which developed into open civil war in 1642, ending in victory for Cromwell and the execution of Charles I in front of the Banqueting House in 1649. After the republic known as the Commonwealth had lasted for eleven years the Stuarts were restored to the throne in 1660 in the person of King Charles II. Scarcely had peace returned to London when the Great Plague claimed 100,000 victims in the city in 1665.

1649: execution of Charles I

One year later another catastrophe occurred. On the morning of September 2nd 1666 a fire broke out in a bakery in Pudding Lane, which soon spread to the whole city and lasted for four days and nights. It devastated four-fifths of the city, destroying 13,200 houses and 84 churches. 100,000 people were rendered homeless. Terrible though it was, the Great Fire did at least provide the opportunity for London to be rebuilt and some of the dreadful medieval slums removed. Sir Christopher Wren was appointed as general architect in charge of the rebuilding. He re-designed St Paul's Cathedral and by the time of his death in 1711 had built 52 other churches. In spite of all these catastrophes London remained at the centre of world trade and by the end of the 17th c. its population had increased to 500,000.

1666: Great Fire

The Great Fire of London, 1666

Industrial Revolution and Victorianism

In the 18th c. London developed along relatively quiet lines. With the growth of the Empire Britain eventually became the world's major maritime power. London, with its port, profited considerably from this and its increasing prosperity showed itself in the form of magnificent buildings, wide asphalted streets and a lively world of theatres. In 1760 the old walls were pulled down and the city extended out as far as Westminster. The introduction of manufacturing heralded the beginning of the so-called Industrial Revolution, and even more people were attracted to London. In 1801 the first official census produced a population figure of 860,035, making London the largest city in the world. With the increasing population came greater social problems, which became exacerbated as the 19th c. progressed. By 1828 the Port of London had expanded to become the largest in Britain, while the establishment of the London Metropolitan Police in 1829 may be regarded as a sign of the growing social unrest.

1837: Queen Victoria comes to the throne

1863: first underground train

Queen Victoria came to the throne in 1837, and during her long reign London enjoyed the most extensive programme of municipal building in its history. In 1836 the first railway train had run from London Bridge to Greenwich, and the construction of further lines and later the underground railway – in 1863 the Metropolitan Line between Paddington and Farringdon came into operation – had a most sustained influence on the changing face of the city. Now even the lower wage-earners could live further away from their place of work. A broad suburban belt grew up which gradually stretched out from the city and took in the surrounding villages. Steam power enabled the docks and factories along the Thames to develop quickly, leading to a need for greater work-forces and attracting large numbers of workers from abroad, especially from Europe. Charles Dickens described in vivid detail the problems which this caused. The Crystal Palace, built to house the Great Exhibition of 1851, symbolises the great 19th c. faith in progress. Buildings and streets dating from this period

Kings and Queens

Anglo-Saxon and Danish kings

Alfred the Great	871–899
Edward the Elder	899–924
Athelstan	924–939
Edmund	939–946
Edred	946–955
(Note: the above five kings ruled only parts of England)	
Edwy (Eadwig)	955–959
Edgar	959–975
Edward the Martyr	975–978
Ethelred II (the Unready)	978–1016
Edmund Ironside	1016
Cnut (Canute) the Great	1016–1035
Harold I (Harefoot)	1035–1040
Hardicnut	1040–1042
Edward the Confessor	1042–1066
Harold II (Godwinson)	1066

Norman kings

William I (the Conqueror)	1066–1087
William II (Rufus)	1087–1100
Henry I (Beauclerc)	1100–1135
Stephen	1135–1154

House of Plantagenet

Henry II (Curtmantle)	1154–1189
Richard I (Lionheart)	1189–1199
John (Lackland)	1199–1216
Henry III	1216–1272
Edward I	1272–1307
Edward II	1307–1327
Edward III	1327–1377
Richard II	1377–1399

House of Lancaster

Henry IV	1399–1413
Henry V	1413–1422
Henry VI	1422–1461

House of York

Edward IV	1461–1483
Edward V	1483
Richard III	1483–1485

House of Tudor

Henry VII	1485–1509
Henry VIII	1509–1547
Edward VI	1547–1553
Mary I	1553–1558
Elizabeth I	1558–1603

House of Stuart

James I	1603–1625
Charles I	1625–1649

Commonwealth and Protectorate

Oliver Cromwell (Protector)	1653–1658
Richard Cromwell (Protector)	1658–1659

House of Stuart

Charles II	1660–1685
James II	1685–1688
William III (of Orange) and Mary II	1689–1702
Anne	1702–1714

House of Hanover

George I	1714–1727
George II	1727–1760
George III	1760–1820
George IV	1820–1830
William IV	1830–1837
Victoria	1837–1901

House of Saxe-Coburg

Edward VII	1901–1910

House of Windsor

George V	1910–1936
Edward VIII	1936
George VI	1936–1952
Elizabeth II	from 1952

remain as evidence of the wave of enthusiasm for change which swept the city – the Houses of Parliament, Trafalgar Square, Victoria Embankment, Regent Street and Shaftesbury Avenue. When Queen Victoria died in 1901 London had 4·5 million inhabitants and was the undisputed metropolis of the world.

The first half of the 20th c. was dominated by the two World Wars. The losses suffered by London in the First World War as a result of air-raids **20th century**

– the first Zeppelin attacks were in 1915 – were relatively small, namely, 700 dead and 2000 injured, but in the Second World War, as a result of "The Blitz" in 1940/41 and V1 and V2 raids in 1944/45, more than 30,000 people lost their lives. Scarcely a single bulding in the "City" escaped unscathed; nevertheless, London was able to host the Olympic Games in 1948.

As the British Empire faded after the war so did the importance of London – not only politically but economically, as illustrated most dramatically in the decline of the Port of London and the resultant wave of strikes by factory, port and dock workers in 1968. In an attempt to tackle the growing problems of the city the Greater London Council was formed in 1965 as the main administrative authority, but this body was dissolved in 1986. 1986 also saw a further landmark in the city's history; in October of that year the expansion and reform of the Stock Exchange, the "Big Bang", came into operation, and London became one of the world's major financial centres, on a par with New York and Tokyo. Thus the former port and industrial city became a metropolis of service industries, a feature which has gained further expression since 1982 in the redevelopment and conversion of the dock area to an office quarter and residential area for bankers and stock-brokers.

Against this background, further events took place which brought London into the headlines of the world's press. In 1952 her loyal subjects celebrated the coronation of Elizabeth II in Westminster Abbey, and in 1981 the glittering wedding of Prince Charles and Lady Diana Spencer took place in St Paul's Cathedral. In the 1960s the world of music and fashion chose "swinging London" as its capital. We should not, however, forget the terror caused by IRA attacks in the city, and it is to be hoped that the new peace treaty will prove effective. The defeat of the Conservative government by New Labour and Tony Blair has resulted in a number of marked changes: the new government plans to restore the Greater London Council with its own chairman, and spectacular new buildings are planned for the new millenium. The tragic death of Diana, Princess of Wales may bring the royal family closer to the people. More than 1½ million people streamed into London on the day of Diana's funeral on September 6th 1997 in Westminster Abbey.

London in Quotations

When I behold this town of London, said our contemplative traveller, I fancy I behold a prodigious animal. The streets are so many veins, wherein the people circulate. With what hurry and swiftness is the circulation of London performed. You behold, cry'd I to him, the circulation that is made in the heart of London, but it moves more briskly in the blood of the citizens: they are always in motion and activity. Their actions succeed one another with so much rapidity that they begin a thousand things before they have finished one, and finish a thousand others before they may properly be said to have begun them.

They are equally incapable both of attention and patience, and tho' nothing is more quick than the effects of hearing and seeing, yet they don't allow themselves time either to hear or see; but, like moles, work in the dark and undermine one another.
Amusements Serious and Comical, 1700

Thomas Brown
(1663–1704)

If a man had the art of the second sight for seeing lies, as they have in Scotland for seeing spirits, how admirably he might entertain himself in this town, by observing the different shapes, sizes and colours of those swarms of lies which buzz about the heads of some people.
Examiner, No. 15, November 9th 1710

Jonathan Swift
(1667–1745)

The buildings are very fine; it may be called the sink of vice, but for her hospitals and charitable institutions, whose turrets pierce the skies, like so many electrical conductors averting the very wrath of heaven . . . An Englishman is cold and distant at first; he is very cautious even in forming an acquaintance . . . The women are not quite so reserved; they consult their glasses to the greatest advantage . . .

Edmund Burke
(1729–97)

You may depend on it, all lives out of London are mistakes, more or less grievous – but mistakes.
Letter to Lady Grey, November 19th 1837

Sydney Smith
(1771–1845)

If you wish to have a just notion of the magnitude of this city, you must not be satisfied with seeing its great streets and square, but must survey the innumerable little lanes and courts. It is not in the showy evolutions of buildings, but in the multiplicity of human habitations which are crowded together, that the wonderful immensity of London consists.
(*July 5th 1763*)

Dr Samuel
Johnson
(1709–84)

When a man is tired of London he is tired of life; for there is in London all that life can afford.
(*September 20th 1777*)

I have passed all my days in London, until I have formed as many and as intense local attachments as any of you mountaineers can have done with dead nature. The lighted shops of the Strand and Fleet Street; the innumerable trades, tradesmen and customers, coaches, waggons, playhouses; all the bustle and wickedness round about Covent Garden; the watchmen, drunken scenes, rattles; – life awake, if you awake, at all hours of the night; the impossibility of being dull in Fleet Street; the crowds, the very dirt and mud, the sun shining upon houses and pavements, the print-shops, the old bookstalls, parsons cheapening books, coffee-houses, steams of soups from kitchens, the

Charles Lamb
(1775–1834)

pantomimes –London itself a pantomime and a masquerade – these things work themselves into my mind, and feed me without a power of satiating me.
Letter to Wordsworth, January 30th 1801

William
Wordsworth
(1770–1850)

Earth has not anything more fair:
Dull would he be of soul who could pass by
A sight so touching in its majesty;
This City now doth, like a garment, wear
The Beauty of the morning; silent, bare,
Ships, towers, domes, theatres and temples lie
Open unto the fields, and to the sky;
All bright and glittering in the smokeless air.
Sonnet composed upon Westminster Bridge

Nathaniel
Hawthorne
(1804–64)

I had found it better than my dream; for there is nothing else in life comparable (in that species of enjoyment, I mean) to the thick, heavy, oppressive, sombre delight which an American is sensible of, hardly knowing whether to call it a pleasure or a pain, in the atmosphere of London. The result was that I acquired a home-feeling there, as no-where else in the world; though afterwards I came to have a somewhat similar sentiment in regard to Rome; and as long as either of those two great cities shall exist, the cities of the Past and of the Present, a man's native soil may crumble beneath his feet without leaving him altogether homeless upon earth.
"Our Old Home", 1863

George Bernard
Shaw
(1856–1950)

This place is rather wonderful at night with its post in the skies and its panorama of the river from St Paul's to Westminster. When the roads are black wet and the embankment lights and car headlights are pouring floods of gold down them there is really nothing like it in the world.
Letter written from his flat in Whitehall Court to the actress Molly Tompkins

Baedeker's
"London" (1901)

London Docks. east of St Katherine's Docks, were constructed in 1809 at a cost of £4,000,000 and cover an area of more than 48ha/120 acres. They have three entrances from the Thames and spaces for 400 ships, not including lighters; there is warehouse space for 260,000 tons of freight and cellarage for 121,000 pipes of wine (700,000 hecto-litres/15,400,000 gallons). On any one day more than 3,000 people are employed here in shifts, gathering in the morning at 6am at the main entrances. They are men of all kinds and from all parts of the world – white, black, brown – who are keen to earn their living by working. Strong arms and a willingness to work are the only necessary qualifications. The freight – foodstuffs, tea, coffee, sugar, tobacco, etc. – is piled up in the warehouses, the apparently inexhaustible supplies of wine in the cellars, the cargoes from the ships on the quays and wharves: animal skins, timber and every other conceivable commodity which the countless barrels, bales and boxes can contain are a more vivid picture of the huge trade and wealth of London than all the figures and accounts.

John Galsworthy
(1867–1933)

On all quarters is the queer adventurous amalgam called London. Soho is perhaps least suited to the Forsyte spirit . . . Untidy, full of Greeks, Ishmaelites, cats, Italians, tomatoes, restaurants, organs, coloured stuffs, queer names, people looking out of upper windows, it dwells remote from the British Body Politic.
The Forsyte Saga

Sightseeing Tours

The recommendations below are intended to help those whose first visit it is to London and who have only a short time at their disposal to plan their stay in the city in the most rewarding way. The sights and places in **bold** type are described in more detail in the A to Z section of this guide.

Note

The visitor who has only a few hours in London but nevertheless wishes to see the most important sights is advised to join an organised city tour (see Practical Information, Sightseeing)

Short visits

Tours and walks

This longish walk leads from Westminster through the City to the Tower and takes in many of London's best-known sights. It should be timed so as to arrive at Horse Guards by 10am, in order to see the changing of the guard.

Tour 1

The walk begins at Westminster underground station, the exit from which is near "Big Ben", the clock-tower of the ★★**Houses of Parliament**. The Parliament buildings can be seen at their best from Westminster Bridge. From there proceed via Parliament Square, bedecked with flags, to ★★**Westminster Abbey**; time permits just a brief glance inside – a proper visit should be reserved for another day. Returning to Parliament Square, now stroll up ★★**Whitehall**, the government quarter. The road leads past the Cenotaph, Downing Street, Banqueting House and Horse Guards to one of London's focal points, ★★**Trafalgar Square**, with Nelson's Column in the centre, the ★★**National Gallery** on its north side and ★**St Martin-in-the-Fields** on the east. From the square be sure to look down Whitehall for a view of **Big Ben**. Now continue north-eastwards along the **Strand** in the direction of the City, just before Waterloo Bridge can be found Somerset House, which houses the ★★**Courtauld Gallery**. From here make a detour north to ★**Covent Garden**, where a rest can be made. Return to the Strand by way of Bow Street where the boundary of the City is marked by the Temple Bar Memorial with the large stone statue of a griffin in the centre of the street. At this spot a narrow archway on the right opens into the courtyards of ★**The Temple**. Behind Temple Bar begins **Fleet Street**, traditionally the centre of British journalism, although most newspapers have now moved to other sites. Fleet Street leads into Ludgate Hill, from where there is a view of ★★**St Paul's Cathedral** some way apart. Leaving the cathedral behind proceed along Cannon Street to its junction with Victoria Street and thence north-east to Bank underground station. Here is the heart of London's financial world with the **Bank of England** and the ★**Royal Exchange**, and on one side **Mansion House**. The official residence of the Lord Mayor. The final stage of the tour begins at Bank Station via Threadneedle Street or **Lombard Street** to Leadenhall Market, then along Gracechurch Street to the ★**Monument** and thence into Lower Thames Street past the Custom House to the ★★**Tower** and ★**Tower Bridge**.

This tour leads away from the busy city centre to the somewhat quieter districts of Holborn and Bloomsbury. It begins in the world-famous and noisy ★**Piccadilly Circus** and thence into the streets of ★**Soho**. Here, stroll through Chinatown and Garrard Street and then up Frith Street to Soho Square – and retrace your steps along these streets and others in the evening! From Soho Square walk a short distance along New Oxford Street and then follow the signs to the ★★**British Museum**. Those who prefer to

Tour 2

see just the highlights of the museum can compile their own brief programme from the description on page 53; those wishing to spend more time here should while away the remainder of the day in the museum or else put the visit off to another day if time permits. In either case, two more possibilities present themselves after visiting the museum. Those who prefer peace and quiet should walk to Gray's Inn (and perhaps make a detour to Dicken's House) and past Staple Inn, the only preserved Elizabethan inn in London, and along Holborn to ★**Lincoln's Inn**, where ★**Sir John Soane's Museum** will also be found. If you decide against this detour, proceed from the British Museum along Bloomsbury Avenue and via New Oxford Street to Shaftesbury Avenue, which leads across the theatre-land of the West End and back to ★**Piccadilly Circus**.

Tour 3

This tour begins in ★**Piccadilly Circus**, from where Regent Street, the main shopping mile of the West End, sweeps round and enters Oxford Circus in busy Oxford Street, with more shops and department stores. Now turn west and continue past Selfridges store to the north-eastern corner of ★★**Hyde Park**, marked by Marble Arch and Speakers' Corner. The route to take through Hyde Park is a matter of individual choice, but in any event arrange to leave it again at **Hyde Park Corner** in order to walk along Constitution Hill or through Green Park to ★**Buckingham Palace**. From the Palace you can now stroll through the wonderful ★**St James' Park** or else go straight along the **Mall** to Carlton House Terrace and then up the steps and past the Duke of York Column to Waterloo Place. The tour now turns in the opposite direction – through the quarter of London's famous gentlemen's clubs – back to ★**St James' Palace**, one of the few Tudor buildings remaining in London. To complete the tour, return to ★**Piccadilly Circus** along one of the exclusive shopping streets in the St James' quarter.

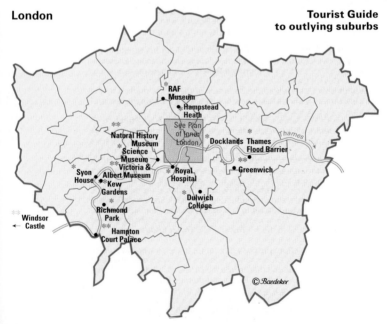

London

Tourist Guide to outlying suburbs

Further recommendations for your stay

It goes without saying that in a giant city like London the three walks described above can cover only a very small part of all that the metropolis has to offer.

Places not to be missed

So, for example, visitors simply must acquaint themselves with the Kensington and Knightsbridge districts – on the one hand for the museums, above all the ★★ **Victoria and Albert Museum** and the ★★ **Natural History Museum** (one of the great attractions for children), and on the other because of the opportunities for shopping: anyone who has not visited Harrods has not seen London!

Another extremely interesting trip is to ★★ **Greenwich**, with its National Maritime Museum and the Royal Observatory. The best way is to begin this trip is on the Docklands Light Railway through ★ **Docklands** and underneath the Thames by the Greenwich Foot Tunnel, returning to the city centre by boat on the Thames.

The sightseeing programmes described above can easily fill five days in London without leaving much spare time. For those with more time or whose interests lie elsewhere here are some other suggestions: In addition to the ★★ **National Gallery**, those interested in paintings will find much to interest them in the ★★ **National Portrait Gallery** and, above all, in the ★★ **Tate Gallery**; history enthusiasts will find a rich source of material in the ★ **Imperial War Museum** and the ★ **Museum of London**. The ★ **Science Museum** and the ★ **Royal Air Force Museum** are meccas for the technologically minded. The list given under "Museums" in the Practical Information section of this guide will provide further suggestions.

Additional suggestions

Finally, one can escape the noise and bustle of the city and make an excursion to the suburbs. In addition to ★★ **Greenwich**, as mentioned above, visitors can enjoy the magnificent parks and greenhouses of ★ **Kew Gardens** or the majestic quiet surroundings of ★ **Hampton Court Palace**. Those desirous of seeing the summer residence of the Royal Family should visit ★ **Windsor Castle**.

One of the many stalls hoping to attract the visitor on a sightseeing tour

Plan of inner city with tours and walks

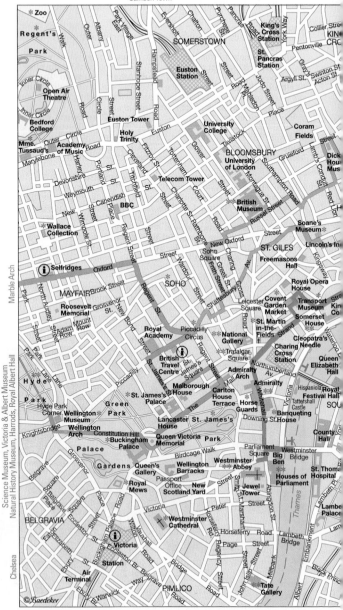

Plan of inner city with tours and walks

London

250 m
750 ft

Tour 1

Tour 2

Tour 3

Road
City
St. John St.
Myddelton St.
FINSBURY
Percival St.
Central Street
Goswell Road
Old Whitecross Street
Golden Lane
Bunhill
Flow
City
Road
New North Road
Cropley Street
Pitfield
Street
Curtain
Eastern
Street
Commercial
Hackney Road

Farringdon
CLERKENWELL
Clerkenwell
Road
Gray's
Inn
BORN
Holborn
Staple Inn
Chancery
Lane
Royal Courts
The Temple
Embankment
HMS President
HMS HMS Crysanthemum
Wellington

Royal Britain
St. Lane
Smithfield Bartholomew
Market
National Postal
Museum
Holborn
Viaduct
Station
Criminal
Court
Blackfriars
Station
Bankside Power
Station

Beech Chiswell St.
Barbican Arts and
Conference Centre
Museum of London
London Wall
Guildhall
St. Paul's
Cathedral
Bank
Extension
Cannon
Victoria St.
Upper Thames Street
Thames
Shakespeare Globe
Museum

Broad
Street
Station
Eldon St.
Moorgate
London Wall
CITY OF LONDON
Bank of
England
Royal
Exchange
Mansion
House
Cannon
Street
Station
Southwark
Bridge

Liverpool
Street
Station
Middlesex
Houndsditch
Bishopsgate
Stock
Exchange
Leadenhall St.
Royal
Lloyd's
Leadenhall
Market
Fenchurch
Eastcheap
Monument
Custom
House

Minories
St. Katharine's Dock Greenwich Docklands

All
Hallows
Tower

National
Theatre
Museum of
the Moving Image
BANK
Waterloo
Station
Old Vic
Lower Marsh
Kennington

Blackfriars
Waterloo
Junction
Union
Street
The Cut
Waterloo Road
Borough Road
St. George's
Cathedral
George's
Imperial
War Museum
Road

SOUTHWARK
Southwark
Southwark
Cathedral
London
Bridge
Tooley
Street
London Dungeon
London
Bridge
Station

HMS Belfast
Tower
Bridge

LAMBETH
Road
Road

Elephant &
Castle Station
New Kent Road
NEWINGTON
Borough High Street
Dover
Taband Street
Harper Road
Long
Weston St.
Tower
Grange
Wyatt
Abbey Street
Druid
Tooley St.
Road
Kennington Park Road
Crampton
Street
Walworth Road
Rooney
Street
East
Pages
Old
Kent
Road
Willow Walk
Dunton Road

**Sights
from A to Z**

★ All Hallows-by-the-Tower   K 3

Location
Byward Street
EC3

Underground station
Tower Hill

All Hallows, the church of the Toc H Christian fellowship founded in 1922, is the oldest church in London. It was consecrated in the 7th c., rebuilt in the 13th–15th c., badly damaged by bombing in the Second World War and restored in 1957. The undercroft dates from the 14th c., while the brick tower (1658) is an example of Cromwellian ecclesiastical architecture. The spire was added in 1959. It was from this tower that Samuel Pepys, whose home was near by, watched the Great Fire of 1666. All Hallows itself was saved from the conflagration by Admiral Sir William Penn, father of the founder of Pennsylvania, who gave orders for the surrounding houses to be blown up. Inside the church remains of a Saxon arch dated A.D. 675 and incorporating Roman stone can be seen on the south wall. Two crosses also date from that period. Other notable features are the statues of St Ethelburga and Bishop Lancelot Andrewes (the latter baptised in the church in the 16th c.), the pulpit (1670) and a 16th c. Spanish crucifix in the south aisle. The new font (1944) is carved from stone from Gibralter.

All Hallows-by-the-Tower

Wellington Memorial and Bank of England

Undercroft

The Undercroft Museum (open: Mon.–Fri. 11am–4.30pm) contains a model of Roman Londinium and various exhibits from Roman and Saxon times including a Roman mosaic pavement with a font cover ascribed to Grinling Gibbons. The parish register records the baptism (1644) of William Penn, founder of Pennsylvania, and the marriage of John Quincy Adams, sixth President of the United States.

Memorial Chapel

In the Memorial Chapel is a crusading altar which originally stood in Richard I the Lionheart's castle in northern Palestine. There is also an exceptionally fine collection of 14th–17th c. memorial brasses.

◀ *Panorama of the City of London with new commercial buildings and dome of St Paul's*

Near by is another church of considerable interest. Opposite All Hallows, on the other side of Byward Street, Seething Lane – where Samuel Pepys lived and worked – leads north to St Olave's Church, which was dedicated to the Norwegian king, Olaf. Built in about 1450 it was one of the few City churches spared by the Great Fire. St Olave's was Samuel Pepys's parish church and there is a commemorative plaque to him by the south wall. In 1672 Pepys commissioned from John Bushnell a bust of his wife Elizabeth who lies buried here. The pulpit is the work of Grinling Gibbons. Noteworthy too are the tombs of the brothers Paul and Andrew Bayninge, of James Deane, his wife and three children, and of Andrew Riccard, head of the East India Company.

St Olave's

All Souls   F 3

All Souls (1822–24) is doubly remarkable, being the only church in London built by John Nash (1752–1835), and taking a most unusual form with a circular portico and a tower surrounded by a ring of freestanding columns. The slender spire was intended as a vertical feature contrasting with the stuccoed arcades of the old Regent Street; today however the effect is largely ruined by the walls of Broadcasting House.

Location
All Souls Place,
W1

**Underground
station**
Oxford Circus

Bank of England   J 3

At the time of the Napoleonic Wars the Bank of England was famously caricatured by James Gillray as "The Old Lady of Threadneedle Street", a name which has stuck ever since. The bank was originally incorporated as a private company by royal charter in 1694 on the suggestion of a Scot, William Paterson, to help finance the war against Louis XIV of France; it is therefore the second oldest central bank in the world after that of Sweden. It was brought under government control only in 1946. As "guardian of the national currency" the Bank of England is responsible for the amount of money in circulation, withdrawing old banknotes and issuing new ones (though not in the case of Scotland which issues its own). The Bank also influences the level of interest rates in accordance with instructions from government. The nation's gold reserves are kept in its vaults, a fact which has proved a source of endless fascination to crime writers.

The building was at first single-storeyed, the architect being Sir John Soane (1753–1837); construction, begun in 1788, was completed only in 1833. Between 1924 and 1939 the Bank was radically remodelled by Sir Herbert Baker; he preserved Soane's façade and Corinthian columns while erecting a new seven-storey edifice behind them. The statues above the main entrance are by Sir Charles Wheeler.

Visitors are admitted only to the banking hall and then only by prior arrangement.

Location
Threadneedle
Street, EC2

**Underground
station**
Bank

Entry to the Bank of England Museum (entrance in Bartholomew Lane) is free. The museum records the history of the Bank and illustrates its functions. In addition to coin and banknote collections there is also a reconstruction of the former Stock Office designed by Soane in 1793, a modern dealing desk and inter-active video displays (open: Mon.–Fri. 10am–5pm).

Bank of
England Museum

Barbican Centre   J 2

Plans for the redevelopment of this area some ten minutes' walk north of St Paul's Cathedral, between Aldersgate Street and Moorgate Street, a bombsite since 1940, were under discussion as early as 1952. Although a scheme was submitted by the architects Chamberlin, Powell and Bon in 1959, it was

Location
Barbican, EC2

Underground stations
Moorgate,
Barbican,
St Paul's

1971 before work started and another decade before the Queen finally opened the Barbican Centre, in March 1982. The name Barbican (= a towered outwork of a city wall) recalls the Roman and medieval fortifications which once stood on the site.

The development comprises flats for more than 6000 people (including three tower-blocks about 394ft/120m high) with an integral arts and conference centre. Lawns, a lake, fountains and terraces soften the impact of the buildings. In addition to the arts and conference facilities the Barbican Centre also houses the Guildhall School of Music and Drama, a girls' secondary school, the economics faculty of the City University and the Music Performance Research Centre (open to anyone wishing to attend live recordings of concerts, operas, etc.). The only pre-war build-

St Giles

ing still standing is the restored St Giles' Church, originally built in 1390 and the burial place of John Milton.

Arts and Conference Centre

The chief attraction, however, is undoubtedly the arts and conference centre. The Barbican Hall (for concerts and conferences), which has 2026 seats, is the permanent home of the London Symphony Orchestra; the Barbican Theatre with 1166 seats is the London base of the Royal Shakespeare Company. In addition there is a studio theatre ("The Pit") holding 200, a lovely conservatory, an art gallery with a sculpture court, municipal lending library, seminar rooms, three cinemas and two large exhibition halls (the Blue Exhibition Hall and Red Exhibition Hall on the other side of Beech Street).

Information

For programme information tel. (0171) 628 2295/9760; box office (0171) 638 8891. Free tickets are sometimes available for concerts at lunchtime on weekdays and at weekends.

HMS "Belfast"   K3

Location
Morgan's Lane,
Tooley Street, SE1

Underground stations
London Bridge,
Tower Hill

Opening times
Mar.–Oct. daily
10am–6pm;
Nov.–Feb.
10am–5pm

HMS "Belfast", part of the Imperial War Museum (see entry), lies moored a short distance upstream from Tower Bridge (see entry). The 11,500-ton warship, the last heavy cruiser to be built for the Royal Navy, came into service in 1939. Just a few months later she was severely damaged by a German mine in the Firth of Forth and did not become operational again until November 1942. Subsequently she played an important role as an escort to Russia-bound convoys and especially in the battle of the North Cape in December 1943 which ended with the sinking of the German pocket battleship "Scharnhorst". In June 1944 the Belfast provided naval support for Allied troops in the D-Day landings. After the Second World War she was stationed in the Far East when she last fired her guns in anger, during the Korean War. She was withdrawn from service in 1963.

Today she is a museum ship open to the public; there is access to all seven decks including to the engine room, galley, bridge and gun turrets. Audio-visual and sound effects plus specially created smells recreate the experience of what life was like for her crew.

Bethnal Green Museum of Childhood   L2

Location
Cambridge Heath
Road, E2

Underground station
Bethnal Green

Opening times
Mon.–Thur.,
Sat. 10am–5.50pm,
Sun. 2.30–5.50pm

The National Museum of Childhood, a branch of the Victoria and Albert Museum (see entry), opened in 1872 in an unusual Victorian building of iron, glass and brick. It contains one of the largest toy collections on public view in the world, a paradise for children and adults alike.

All the exhibits are delightful – toy soldiers, teddy bears, the many kinds of doll, particularly engaging are the dolls' houses and the huge array of board and other games. You can also explore the process of growing up in childhood displays showing baby equipment, nursery furniture, children's dress and teenage fads and fashions.

The last heavy cruiser of the Royal Navy: H.M.S. "Belfast"

British Library   G2

Location
Euston Road
St Pancras Station

After the Bibliothèque Nationale in Paris the British Library is the most richly endowed in Europe. Established in 1972 by Act of Parliament, it was formed by amalgamating a number of important existing libraries. Chief among them was that of the British Museum which, since 1757, has enjoyed the right to receive a copy of every publication printed in Great Britain. The original basis of the collection was formed by bequests from Sir Robert Cotton, Robert Harley, Sir Hans Sloane and Charles Townley, together with the old Royal Library made over to the British Museum by George II in 1757; George III's library was acquired in 1823. The printed book department contains more than 12 million volumes, to which some 60,000 are added every year. The manuscript department holds in excess of 70,000 volumes and 100,000 documents and papyri; the Oriental book and manuscript department has over 35,000 manuscripts and 250,000 printed books. Immense storage problems in the old rooms in the British Museum (see entry) led to new, purpose-built premises being constructed near St Pancras Station; these were designed by Colin St John and handed over in 1997.

Underground
Station
Kings Cross

The exhibition rooms contain the library's showpiece exhibits – incunabula and historical, literary, scientific and musical manuscripts which were previously on display in the British Museum. The most outstanding of these are two of the four original copies of the Magna Carta of 1215. There are also manuscripts by, among others, Charles Dickens and Laurence Sterne, the first score of Handel's "Messiah", Lord Nelson's last letter to Lady Hamilton and the Beatles' song "Yesterday" in Paul McCartney's own hand. Then there are handwritten notes by Alexander Fleming on his discovery of penicillin, Isaac Newton's initial obser-

Exhibition
rooms

53

The main façade of the British Museum

vations on the force of gravity, and a sample of mirror-writing by Leonardo da Vinci. On display, too, are a number of priceless illustrated bibles and books of hours including the Lindisfarne Gospels, as well as a manuscript belonging to Bishop Eadfrith of Lindisfarne which dates from the early 8th c.

The east wing of the Museum houses the Museum's famous circular Reading Room where such notable figure as Karl Marx, George Bernard Shaw and Mahatma Gandhi once studied. Built at the suggestion of Sir Anthony Panizzi, Director of the Library at that time, the room was designed by Sydney Smirke, and completed in 1857.

Great Court
Reading room

Following the removal of the British Library to new premises, the Great Court and Reading Room are being completely refurbished. The architect Sir Richard Rogers will cover the courtyard with a glass roof, thus creating a new room incorporating different levels, and link the whole to the British Museum by means of a bridge. It is hoped that the extension will be completed by the new millennium. Visitors will then find here inter alia an education centre, the African Gallery (containing mainly exhibits transferred from the Museum of Mankind), the main entrance, a café and all other service facilities. The Reading Room will return to its original 1857 layout and will in future house a reference library and the Museum's new multi-media access system named COMPASS.

✶✶British Museum G2

Location
Great Russell
Street, WC1

With seven million visitors a year the British Museum is London's greatest tourist attraction. Its collections are amongst the finest in the world, covering the art and antiquities of Egypt, Assyria, Babylonia, Greece, the Roman Empire, Southern and South-East Asia, China, and countries of

The "Elgin Marbles"

Europe. The Museum continues for the time being to house the British Library.

A number of private collections formed the original basis of the Museum: a collection of medieval manuscripts belonging to Sir Robert Cotton (1570–1631); similar collections belonging to Robert Harley, Earl of Oxford (d. 1724) and his son; the Royal Library (begun in Tudor times); and most important of all, the collection of the scientist Sir Hans Sloane (1660–1753) whose bequest led to the establishment of the Museum by Act of Parliament in the year of his death. Money for a building was raised by means of a lottery and in 1759 Montague House (1675) was acquired. Within a few decades the collection had grown considerably and it was decided to demolish Montague House to make way for new premises. The Neo-Classical building, designed and begun by Robert Smirke in 1823, was completed by his brother Sydney in 1843. The principal façade is 403ft/123m long with a colonnade of 44 Ionic columns. The King Edward VII Building on the north side dates from 1907–1914; the Duveen Galleries were added in 1938.

Until the autumn of 1997 the British Library was housed within the Museum. Its removal to new premises will open the way for new projects within the Museum which should be completed by 2003, the year of its 250th anniversary. The main area affected will be the Great Court; as a result of these changes it should be possible for the ethnographic collections to be returned from the Museum of Mankind.

Exhibits of Outstanding Importance

Comprising at present an estimated 6.5 million items, the Museum's collections are so extensive that only a fraction can be exhibited at any one

Underground stations
Russell Square, Holborn, Tottenham Court Road

Opening times
Mon.–Sat. 10am–5pm, Sun. 2.30–6pm

Guided tours
Information in the main hall

Re-furbishing plans

British Museum

GROUND FLOOR

1 Cyclades in the Bronze Age
2 Bronze Age Greece
3/4 Archaic Greece
5 5th c. B.C. Greece
6 Bassae (mezzanine)
7 Neride Monument
8 Sculptures from the Parthenon
9 Caryatids
10 Payava Tomb
11 Late Grecian Vases (mezzanine)
12 Mausoleum of Halicarnassus
14 Hellenistic World
15 Greek and Roman sculpture
16 Khorsabad
17 Assyria
19/20 Nimrud
21 Nineveh
25 Egyptian sculpture
26 Assyrian sculpture
28 Temporary exhibitions
29 Grenville Library
30–32 Closed
33 Art of S and SE Asia, China, Japan and Korea
33a Amaravatic sculpture
33b Temporary exhibitions
33c Ancient Mexico
34 Art of Islam (downstairs)

BASEMENT

77 Greek and Roman sculpture
78 Classical inscriptions
79–80 Early Greek sculpture
81 At present closed
82 Ephesus
83 Rome
84 Townley Room
85 Portrait collection
86/87 Lecture rooms
88 Biblical Archaeology/Temporary exhibitions
88a/89 Assyrian

time; even to view these would take several days. Visitors must therefore be selective, guided by their own particular interests. The plan on p.56 shows the general layout of the Museum though the precise arrangement of exhibits may vary from time to time. Only one or two items of outstanding importance can be mentioned here.

Room 8 Sculptures from the Parthenon	This room houses the famous "Elgin Marbles", from the Parthenon in Athens, brought to London by the Earl of Elgin at the beginning of the 19th c. They include the "Horse of Selene" from the east pediment. Of the original group of four horses drawing the chariot of Selene (goddess of the moon), a further two are in Athens and the fourth is lost. The largest surviving section of the Parthenon frieze can also be seen.
Room 9	Further objects found in Athens, including a Caryatid from the Erechtheion of the Acropolis.
Room 12	The central exhibit displays finds from the Halicarnassus Mausoleum and from the Temple of Artemis in Ephesos.

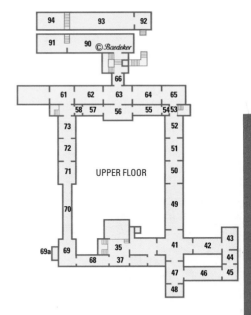

These rooms are devoted to unique treasures of the Assyrian period. Room 17 houses reliefs depicting a lion hunt from the reign of Assurbanipal. Further reliefs from the Nimrud and Nineveh palaces may be seen in other rooms, as well as the imposing figures of winged bulls with human heads from the Sargon palace in Khorsabad and a black obelisk relating the deeds of Shalmaneser III.

Rooms 17–26
Assyrian Lion
Hunt Reliefs

Of special interest here are the colossal bust of Rameses II from Thebes-West and the Rosetta Stone, found in 1798 at Rosetta in the Nile Delta by the members of the Napoleonic Expedition to Egypt. It was this slab of black basalt dating from 195 B.C. and bearing a trilingual inscription (in Egyptian hieroglyphs, demotic script and Greek translation) that enabled the French archaeologist Jean-François Champollion to become the first person to decipher Egyptian hieroglyphics.

Room 25

Rosetta Stone

Lindow Man, whose 2000-year old mummified body is displayed here, was probably a victim of ritual sacrifice before being dumped in a Cheshire bog.

Room 37
Lindow Man

This room contains exhibits from the Sutton Hoo Treasure: weapons, jewellery and coins dating from the 7th c. found in the grave of an Anglo-Saxon king at Sutton Hoo, Suffolk.

Room 41

The 12th c. chess pieces carved from walrus tusks are of particular interest. They originate from the island of Lewis in the Hebrides.

Room 42

The Mildenhall Treasure, a hoard of Roman silver tableware dating from the 4th c. A.D., was found by a farmer while ploughing in Mildenhall, Suffolk in 1942. Of the 34 pieces, the most impressive is "The Great Dish", a large silver dish embossed with figures of Bacchus, god of wine, Hercules, and other figures from Roman mythology. In the centre

Room 49

Mildenhall
Treasure

The Reading Room in the former British Library, now housed in new premises

Rooms 60–62 Egyptian mummies	of the dish a bearded mask, probably representing the sea god Oceanus, is encircled by nymphs riding on sea monsters. The famous collection of mummies will not be fully on view to visitors until the spring of 1999, as they are being overhauled and restored. Until then a few of the major exhibits can be seen in Room 61.
Room 70/71 Portland Vase	Among the many Roman exhibits, rooms 70 and 71 which focus on life in ancient Rome are outstanding. Items on display include the Portland Vase (named after the Dukes of Portland), an exquisite example of Roman artistry in glass and dating from the 1st c. B.C.

Brompton Oratory (Church of the London Oratory of St Philip Neri) D4

Location Brompton Road SW7	Brompton Oratory is the London church of the Oratorians, a Catholic order founded in Rome by St Philip Neri in 1575 and introduced into England in 1847 by Cardinal Newman. A statue of Newman faces the street.
Underground station South Kensington	The Italian Renaissance-style Oratory was built between 1881 and 1884, the dome being added in 1896. The interior is notable for the magnificence and breadth of the nave (the third largest in England, exceeded only by Westminster Cathedral (see entry) and York Minster), as well as
Opening times daily 6.30am–8pm	for its rich decoration. Particularly worthy of note, apart from the Carrara marble figures of the Apostles which for 200 years stood in Siena Cathedral, are: the monumental Renaissance altar in the Lady Chapel, the altarpiece of which came from the Dominican church in Brescia; the altar in St Wilfred's Chapel, with an altarpiece from Maastricht Cathedral; the marble decoration of the chapels; and a number of mosaics.
★Concerts	The Oratory has a particular reputation for organ recitals, and for fine choral music.

Buckingham Palace F4

Buckingham Palace is known all over the world as the London residence of the British Royal Family, though it has only been such since 1837 when, on her accession to the throne, Queen Victoria moved there from St James's Palace (see entry). When the sovereign is in residence, attended by a staff of 300, the royal standard flies over the Palace.

The Palace stands on what at one time was the site of a mulberry garden planted by James I. Later Queen Anne gave the land to the Duke of Buckingham who erected a comparatively modest brick building on it. In 1762 this was purchased by George III for his bride Charlotte Sophia. In 1825 George IV commissioned John Nash, the court architect, to alter and enlarge the Palace, but the project became so expensive that Nash was dismissed. The work continued under Edward Blore and was completed in 1837. The east wing facing The Mall (see entry), and with it the balcony where, on special occasions, Members of the Royal Family traditionally appear, was added in 1846. The east front was given its present Neo-Classical aspect by Sir Aston Webb in 1913, during the reign of George V.

Buckingham Palace was opened to the public for the first time in the summer of 1993, the proceeds going towards the restoration of Windsor Castle (see entry), parts of which had been severely damaged or destroyed by fire. Nineteen of the Palace's more than 600 rooms are open to the public for several weeks each summer; they include the State Dining Room, the Throne Room, and the unusually richly endowed Picture Gallery. The twelve rooms in the north wing making up the Royal Family's private apartments are for obvious reasons kept closed. Nor should visitors expect to see any members of the family whose custom it is to spend this part of the summer at Balmoral Castle in Scotland.

Location
The Mall, SW1

Underground stations
St James's Park,
Victoria,
Green Park

Viewing
Aug./Sept.
daily
9.30am–4.30pm

Tickets: tel:
0171-321-2233

The Victorian Monument in front of Buckingham Palace

Queen's Gallery

The Queen's Gallery, in the former chapel attached to the Palace, is used for changing exhibitions of items from the Royal Collection, one of the finest art collections in the world (open: daily 9.30am–4.30pm).

Victoria Monument

In front of the Palace stands a memorial to Queen Victoria designed by Sir Aston Webb, with sculptures by Sir Thomas Brock. It portrays Queen Victoria surrounded by allegorical figures: Victory, Endurance, Courage, Truth, Justice, Science, Art and Agriculture.

✳ Changing of the Guard

Summer:
daily 11.30am;
Winter:
every second
day 11.30am

A visit to Buckingham Palace should if possible be timed to coincide with the colourful ceremony of the Changing of the Guard which, weather permitting, takes place at the times indicated in the margin. At about the same time a troop of the Household Cavalry, having completed sentry duty at Horse Guards (see Whitehall), ride past the Palace on the way back to their regimental quarters in Hyde Park.

Guard duty at the Palace is shared between the five regiments of Royal Guards: the Scots Guards (founded in 1642), the Coldstream Guards (1650), the Grenadier Guards (1656), the Irish Guards (1900) and the Welsh Guards (1913). All wear the distinctive bearskins and bright red tunics.

Guards Museum

The Guards Museum in nearby Wellington Barracks stirringly documents the history of these famous regiments (Birdcage Walk; open: daily, 10am–4pm, closed mid-Dec. to Jan.).

✳ Royal Mews

Open Wed.,
for other times
tel. 0171-839-1377

The coaches, barouches and carriages, among them a State Landau, belonging to a long line of British monarchs, can be seen in the Royal Mews, situated at the south-east corner of the Palace gardens. Several of the coaches are still used for State occasions today, and the horses which pull them are stabled here too (though it is not always possible to see them). The fleet of royal vehicles is housed in a building designed in 1826 by John Nash, built around a courtyard planted with trees.

One of the most splendid is the Gold State Coach, built originally for George III and used at coronations from 1820 onwards; the harnesses, etc. are said to be the most beautiful in the world. Also on display are the Irish State Coach, bought by Queen Victoria in 1852 and used in the State Opening of Parliament, and the Glass Coach, acquired by George V in 1910 and now the coach in which the bridal couple traditionally ride at royal weddings. Garaged in the Mews as well as the coaches are the fleet of royal cars, Rolls Royces and Bentleys emblazoned with the royal coats of arms.

Charterhouse   H2

Location
Charterhouse
Square, EC1

Underground
station
Barbican

Opening times
Apr.–July
Wed. 2.30–4.15pm

Originally the burial ground for victims of the Black Death in the late 1340s. Charterhouse derives its name from the Carthusian mother house (Chartreuse), an offshoot of which was founded in London in 1371 by Sir Walter de Manny, an officer in Edward III's army. Following dissolution of the priory under Henry VIII – between 1535 and 1537 the prior and fifteen monks were executed for insubordination – the property passed through various hands, including those of John Dudley, Duke of Northumberland (also executed, in 1553) and Thomas Howard, Duke of Norfolk (executed for conspiracy in the Ridolfi plot to put Mary Queen of Scots on the throne). Finally, in 1611, it was purchased by Thomas Sutton, who founded a hospital and a school, the latter destined to become one of the leading public schools in the country. The school moved in 1872 to its present location on a hill above Godalming in Surrey. Meanwhile Charterhouse continues to provide a home for gentlemen pensioners. To qualify they must be bachelors or widowers over 60 and of limited means.

Viewing

The buildings, damaged in the Second World War, have since been carefully restored. The gate-house (15th c.) opens into Master's Court with, on the south-east side, walls surviving from the original priory church. On the north side the Great Hall, built in the 16th c. with stone from the old monastic buildings, is today the dining hall. The Library (17th c.) adjoins the cloister enclosed in 1571. The Great Chamber is a magnificent room with richly decorated stucco ceiling and old Flemish tapestries. The chapel contains several features of interest, in particular the tomb of Thomas Sutton, founder of the hospital and school. Outside are some attractive gardens.

Chelsea
C–E 5

Centuries of rural slumber ended for Chelsea in the 16th c. when Henry VIII built a country mansion (long since demolished) in the then Thames-side fishing village. He was followed in this by Sir Thomas More (see Famous People), who lived there for many years, bringing with him all the trappings of high politics, and later by a succession of distinguished scientists, artists and writers including Joseph Banks, Algernon Charles Swinburne, Oscar Wilde and Thomas Carlyle. It was they who made Chelsea what it is today – an attractive residential borough popular with the more prosperous. In the 1960s and 70s it temporarily surrendered its air of genteel tranquillity, becoming for a brief period in those heady days the centre of Swinging London, where Mary Quant opened her clothes shop in King's Road and the mini-skirt was born.

Location
south-west of the City

Underground station
Sloane Square

King's Road
D/E 5

The name "King's Road" is a relic of the years from 1719 to 1830 when access was restricted to holders of a royal pass and ordinary folk were kept out. From Sloane Square, haunt of the young, well-heeled upper-class set nicknamed "Sloane Rangers", King's Road runs south-westwards across

Echoes of Swinging London

the whole breadth of the borough, lined along its route with pubs, restaurants and interesting shops, many of them selling antiques. Here and there the 60s and 70s spirit of nonconformity still lives on, though increasingly threatened with extinction by the milling crowds of tourists and shoppers and, particularly at weekends, the fumes from cars and buses locked in traffic jams.

Chelsea Old Town Hall

Chelsea Old Town Hall (built 1887) is well known to antique collectors as the venue for the Chelsea Antiques Fair. Held twice a year in spring and autumn the Fair is one of the world's most prestigious. The Town Hall makes a fine setting for the many beautiful items on display – furniture, carpets, china, glass, silver, jewellery, pictures and books. All must be certified as genuine antiques i.e. dating from before 1830.

Antique markets

There are also three largish permanent antique markets, in each of which an assortment of dealers offer a wide range of wares: Antiquarius (No. 37 King's Road); Chenil Galleries (Nos. 181/183); and Chelsea Antique Market (No. 237).

★Cheyne Walk

Just beyond Chelsea Antique Market, Old Church Street runs south to the Thames Embankment and Cheyne Walk between the little park called Roper's Garden and Chelsea Old Church Street. Immediately to the right of the park stands Crosby Hall, remnant of a Bishopsgate mansion built in the 15th c. by Sir John Crosby, a wool merchant, and burnt down in the 17th c. The Great Hall, which alone escaped the fire, was moved from the City to this site beside the Thames in 1910 (not open to the public). Beyond can be seen a number of delightful 17th and 18th c. houses, among them Lindsey House (96–100 Cheyne Walk), now the London base of the Oratorians. The artist James McNeill Whistler lived at No. 101 and J. M. W. Turner at No. 119.

Crosby Hall

Lindsey House

Chelsea Old Church

Go leftwards from the park to reach Chelsea Old Church, founded in the 12th c. and altered several times thereafter. Badly damaged in the Second World War, it was completely restored between 1954 and 1958. Inside, the two chapels and some tombs are of interest. The More Chapel was restored by Sir Thomas More in 1528; his first wife is buried there. The two Renaissance capitals were probably the work of Hans Holbein, a close friend of More's. Note also the inscription in which More asks to be buried next to his wife, a request destined to remain unfulfilled – following his execution, after which his head was displayed impaled on a stake on London Bridge, More's body was disposed of at the Tower. The Lawrence Chapel was the scene of Henry VIII's secret marriage to Jane Seymour a few days before the official marriage ceremony.

The majority of the memorials and tombs date from the 17th and 18th c. They include the tomb of Lady Jane Cheyne, by Bernini, on the north wall (1699); a figurative group depicting Sir Thomas Lawrence, his wife and eight children in the Lawrence Chapel; and in the same chapel the tomb of Sarah Colville (1632). A plaque in the More Chapel commemorates the writer Henry James who lies buried here. The tomb of the celebrated scientist Sir Hans Sloane can be seen in the south-east corner of the churchyard. There are services at 8am Thursdays, noon Fridays, and 8, 10 and 11am on Sundays.

Albert Bridge

From the church forecourt with its seated figure of Sir Thomas More, there is a view of the elegant Albert Bridge (1873).

Old Church to the Royal Hospital

Carlyle's House

Proceed east along Cheyne Walk towards the Royal Hospital, passing on the way a number of noteworthy buildings. Branching off the Walk a short distance beyond Chelsea Old Church is Cheyne Row, where admirers of British literature can visit the home of Thomas Carlyle (1795–1881), the

Scottish historian and essayist (No. 24; open: Apr.–Oct. Wed.–Sun. 11am–5pm).

Just a little further along Cheyne Walk itself is the site, now occupied by No. 19-26, of Henry VIII's original Tudor mansion, built in 1537 and demolished in 1753. Among those who lived there were Anne of Cleves, Henry's daughter Elizabeth (soon to be queen), Lady Jane Grey and later, Sir Hans Sloane.

Henry VIII's Tudor mansion

On the right, with an entrance in Swan Walk, off the Royal Hospital Road lies the Chelsea Physic Garden. Laid out in 1673 as a herb garden by the Society of Apothecarys, who used it for instructional purposes, the garden had a profound influence on the world economy. It was the source of cotton seed planted in Georgia and tea plants were introduced to India from China by one of its ex-curators, Robert Fortune. There is a replica statue of Sir Hans Sloane who leased the land in perpetuity as a physic garden (open: Apr.–Oct, Mon.–Sat. 2–5pm, Sun. 2–6pm).

Chelsea Physic Garden

Continue for a further short distance to the National Army Museum. Its collection of paintings, weaponry, uniforms and documents illustrates the history of the British soldier during war and peace from the creation of the Yeomen of the Guard in 1485 to the present day (open: daily 10am–5.30pm; admission free).

National Army Museum

*Royal Hospital Chelsea

E5

The Royal Hospital is not a medical establishment but a home for war veterans, founded for that purpose by Charles II in 1682 (the idea was probably taken from Louis XIV of France who, in 1670, had equipped the Hôtel des Invalides in Paris for similar use). The Hospital continues to provide accommodation for 400 "Chelsea Pensioners", ex-soldiers over the age of 65 with an Army pension or war disability pension.

The original buildings were designed by Sir Christopher Wren (see Famous People); an extension was added by Robert Adam (1765–82) and the complex was completed by Sir John Soane in 1819.

Opening times
Mon.–Sat.
10am–noon
and 2–4pm;
Sun. 2–4pm

Great Hall of the Royal Hospital

The Hospital is entered through the London Gate in Royal Hospital Road. The principal attraction in the main building is the magnificent panelled dining-room known as the Great Hall, its walls adorned with royal portraits and colours captured during wars with America and France. At the western end is a fine equestrian portrait of Charles II. The chapel, preserved in very much its original state, contains a painting of the Resurrection (1710) by Sebastiano Ricci.

Great Hall and Chapel

A colonnaded portal opens into Figure Court, in the centre of which stands a bronze statue of Charles II, a masterpiece by Grinling Gibbons. On

Figure Court

Founder's Day (the nearest convenient date to Oak Apple Day, May 29th) the statue is decked with oak boughs (commemorating Charles's escape from capture after the Battle of Worcester by hiding in an oak tree) and the pensioners are reviewed on parade in their scarlet uniforms. Benches are set around the court, on which the old soldiers sit and relax. They still wear the traditional uniform dating from the Duke of Marlborough's time – scarlet frock-coats on formal occasions and dark blue overcoats at other times, with a tricorn hat or peaked cap and full decorations.

Museum

A museum in the Hospital's east wing documents its history (open: as hospital except closed Oct.–Mar.).

Royal Hospital Gardens

The Royal Hospital Gardens stretch down to the Thames Embankment and are adorned with a number of cannon, some of them captured from the French at the Battle of Waterloo. Every year in May the Gardens are the venue for the famous Chelsea Flower Show.

Commonwealth Institute   B4

Location
Kensington High Street, W8

Underground stations
High Street Kensington,
Holland Park

Opening times
daily 10am–5pm

The Commonwealth Institute, "centre for Commonwealth education and culture", is the successor of the old Imperial Institute founded on the occasion of Queen Victoria's Golden Jubilee in 1887 to foster understanding of and between the countries and peoples of the Empire and Commonwealth. The Institute's modern building (1962) south of Holland Park houses permanent exhibitions illustrating the historical, social and cultural development of the 40 countries of the Commonwealth. An art gallery and cinema are attached to the Institute. Anyone planning a visit to a Commonwealth country can brief themselves in advance with the aid of the books and journals in the very comprehensive library (open: Tues.–Fri. 11a–4pm, Sat. –4.45pm). There is also an information bureau which will answer questions relating to any visit. The Institute shop sells Commonwealth products.

★★ Courtauld Institute Galleries   G3

Location
Somerset House
Strand, WC2

Underground stations
Temple,

Opening times
Mon.–Sat.
10am–6pm
Sun. 2–6pm

★ **Somerset House**

The Courtauld Gallery houses valuable art collections bequeathed over the years to the University of London, and in particular the bequest by Samuel Courtauld (1865–1947) of his collection of French Impressionist and post-Impressionist paintings, the most important such collection anywhere outside France.

Other major benefactors include Lord Lee of Fareham (a collection of Italian Renaissance works and British portraits), Count Antoine Seilerne, whose special interest was in Renaissance and Baroque paintings (the Princes Gate Collection), and Robert Fry (British and French artists of the late 19th-early 20th c.).

In 1990 the Galleries moved into new premises in Somerset House, formerly government offices though the Royal Academy (see entry), the Royal Society, and the Society of Antiquaries were all previously accommodated there. Indeed it was for this purpose that George III commissioned Sir William Chambers to build Somerset House (1777–86) on a site earlier occupied by a 16th c. mansion belonging to Edward Seymour, Lord Protector of England and first Duke of Somerset. While Chambers' long building of Palladian aspect has its main entrance in the Strand, the imposing main façade, almost 656ft/200m in length with three colonnaded porticoes, faces the Thames (it is seen to best advantage therefore from Waterloo Bridge). During construction the ground level arcades on the Victoria Embankment (see entry), intended for market stalls, were flooded several times, the

Somerset House

Manet: "Bar in the Folies Bergères"

King's College

central arch acting as a flood gate. The East Wing (now the premises of London University's famous King's College) and West Wing were added in the 19th c.

Exhibition of paintings

The paintings occupy the eleven rooms of Somerset House, including the Great Room which was the first purpose-built exhibition space in London.

The collections are displayed according to period, but are rehung at times of special exhibitions. There are major works by Renaissance artists Botticelli, Veronese, Lotto, as well as Cranach's "Adam and Eve". There is also an important group of Rubens, including oil sketches for the "Deposition from the Cross" in Antwerp Cathedral, and a fine collection of Tiepolo oil sketches, and the only full length portrait by Goya in Britain.

Manet:
"Bar at the Folies Bergères"

The highlight undoubtedly is the treasure-house of Impressionist and Post-Impressionist paintings. Among these are Manet's famous "Bar at the Folie Bergères", Renoir's "La Loge", van Gogh's "Self-Portrait with Bandaged Ear", eight paintings by Cezanne, as well as masterpieces by Monet, Gauguin, Modigioni, Seurat and Degas.

St Mary-le-Strand

The church of St Mary-le-Strand occupies a site in the centre of the Strand opposite Somerset House. A masterpiece of Baroque architecture, the church was built in 1714–17 by James Gibb. The beautiful linear proportions are relieved on the exterior by the graceful spire and in the interior by an unusual coffered ceiling constructed on the Italian model.

★ Covent Garden   G 3

Location
Covent Garden
WC2

Underground stations
Covent Garden,
Charing Cross,
Leicester Square

Covent Garden is one of the liveliest places in London. At weekends in particular, acrobats and buskers entertain the busy throng.

The name "Covent Garden" reflects its origins in a medieval convent garden. Edward VI granted the land to John Russell, First Earl of Bedford, whose descendant, the Fourth Earl, embarked on an ambitious programme of development. When in 1631 he commissioned Inigo Jones (see Famous People) to lay out London's first square, the architect responded with a design based on his idea of an Italian piazza. Of the original buildings only St Paul's Church now remains. From 1670 the square was London's flower and vegetable market until, in 1832, the market moved into the newly built Central Hall (still in existence). Relocation of the market in 1974 led to a bitter dispute between the municipal authorities and local people concerned to preserve the familiar aspect of the quarter and find other uses for the old market halls and warehouses. Though controversial plans to extend the Royal Opera House did in the end go ahead, the market halls were saved. Central Hall has been turned into shops and cafés; Jubilee Hall is used for markets (an antique market on Mondays and general markets on other days).

★ Royal Opera House

The Royal Opera House, on the north-west side of the square, started life as the Theatre Royal, Covent Garden, founded in 1732 by John Rich. The present building was erected in 1858 to plans by E. M. Barry. It is the third theatre to stand on the site, its predecessors having burned down (in 1808 and 1856). It is now the home of The Royal Opera and The Royal Ballet. For the site immediately to the south of the Opera House, adjoining the Piazza, Barry designed a combined market and concert hall (the Floral Hall), now used for storing scenery.

The Royal Opera House is to close for extensive refurbishment in the summer of 1997 until autumn 1999, after which the Floral Hall will return to use as a public foyer.

Bow Street
Police Station

The Neo-Classical façade of the Royal Opera House opens onto Bow Street almost exactly opposite the site of the former Bow Street Police Station. It was here in the 18th c. that Henry Fielding established London's first police force, the famous Bow Street Runners.

Covent Garden, the old flower and vegetable market. Shops and cafés in Central Hall

The Theatre Museum on the north-east side of the Piazza (entrance in Russell Street) contains an assortment of original exhibits illustrating all aspects of Britiish theatrical life – from classical drama and comedy to variety, cabaret, opera, musicals, puppet shows and the circus. Guided tours, performance and make-up demonstrations are included in the admission.

Theatre Museum

Beyond the Theatre Museum, a short distance further along Russell Street, stands the Theatre Royal, Drury Lane, opened in 1663 by a company called "The King's Servants". It was the scene of many first performance of plays by John Dryden and others. Charles II was a regular patron, able to enjoy not only the plays but the company of his mistress Nell Gwynne. The original building was destroyed by fire, as were the two which succeeded it. The present theatre, designed by Benjamin Wyatt, was built in 1812. Regular theatregoers claim Drury Lane is haunted by a ghost, said to appear from the left-hand wall before floating across the auditorium (guided tours: Mon.–Sat. from 10.30 am, Sun. from noon).

Theatre Royal Drury Lane

★London Transport Museum

The London Transport Museum, dedicated to the history and technology of the capital's transport system, occupies the east corner of the square. In 1993 the museum was completely refurbished, expanded and re-organised and brought up to date. Whereas before the old vehicles were simply lined up, labelled and described, today's visitors enjoy the benefits of the very latest presentational techniques.

Opening times
Sat.–Thur.
10am–6pm;
Fri. 11am–6pm

The exhibition starts with the 19th c. and continues up to the present day. There are numerous actual examples, as well as models, of London's famous red double-decker buses, everything from a horse-drawn bus of 1870 to a 1930s trolley-bus and from an 1882 horse-drawn train to a 1910 tram. Much space is devoted to London's speediest mode of transport, the

A piece of nostalgia in the London Transport Museum

"Tube". An actor in tunneller's garb explains, in a reconstruction of a section of tunnel, the difficulties and dangers of digging through the London substrata. There are carriages and railcars and a simulator offering visitors the experience of "driving" a tube train through the tunnels beneath London's streets.

Touch-screens are used to explain the exhibits. Changing exhibitions drawn from the museum's 100,000-item photograph and poster collection are mounted in the Frank Pick Gallery; the Ashfield Gallery features cartoons of every imaginable kind on the subject of buses and trams; and the Harry C. Beck Gallery, named after the man who devised the first plan of the Underground, shows all the stages of its evolution through to the present one. London's biggest engineering project, an extension of the Jubilee Underground Line (due for completion in 1998), is explained in a special exhibition. There are also plans for a children's museum.

St Paul's Church

"The handsomest barn in England"

"The handsomest barn in England" was how Inigo Jones described the church he designed in 1633 for the west side of his square and which today stands opposite Central Hall. His comment arose from the fact that the Earl of Bedford, who indeed wanted to see a church on the site, claimed not to be able to afford anything "better than a barn". It is popularly known as the "back-to-front" church. Flying in the face of tradition Jones wanted to have the altar at the west end, but the church authorities would have none of it. He was therefore obliged to close up the columned portico facing the piazza, originally intended as the entrance, and replace it with a doorway at what is actually the rear of the church. Located as it is in London's theatre-land, St Paul's has naturally enough become "the actors' church". Many notable 18th and 19th c. Londoners are buried there, including many actors and actresses – only Westminster Abbey and St Paul's Cathedral (see entries) can claim greater distinction in this respect. As a result, as well as the carved wreath by Grinling Gibbons above the west door (1721), there are several interesting monuments and memorial tablets. Among those commemorated are Grinling Gibbons himself, the playwright Noël Coward, actor Boris Karloff and actress Vivien Leigh.

★Docklands

To the east of the City lies the largest area of London to be redeveloped in the last fifteen years, the disused "up-stream docks" of Wapping, Limehouse and Poplar, Surrey Docks, the Isle of Dogs and Royal Docks, which between 1967 and 1981 ceased operation one by one. Until the 1960s the Docks formed the economic centre of Britain, handling cargo from all over the world; but they quickly lost their status when port facilities were moved further down the Thames. The old docks fell into disrepair and the East End became an increasingly depressed area.

Under the blanket title of "Docklands" this area has been developed into a European business centre and development will continue into the new millenium at a cost of over £25 billion. In addition to modern industrial and business premises and hotels with a workforce of 115,000, it provides recreation areas and housing for 115,000 people, and schools. Leisure craft and windsurfers now monopolise wharves and basins where ocean-going ships once unloaded their cargoes.

The project has faced criticism from many different quarters. Some condemn Docklands for pandering to the interests of big business to the detriment of poorer sections of the community. To alleviate the situation the government has increased its community support through the "London Docklands Development Corporation" (LDDC), who in total have spent £178 million on new and replacement housing and general improvements. In addition the LDDC have invested a total of £116 million in enhancing community facilities, including improvements to education and training (with new schools and colleges), health, leisure and recreation, amenities and the environment.

After much of the construction work had been completed, many of those who had earlier invested vast sums in the project in a heady atmosphere bordering on euphoria, found their fingers badly burned. Recession in 1989 brought the virtual collapse of the London share market, with the consequence that hundreds of thousands of square feet of new office space remained unlet. Happily the situation has since improved with at present 72% of available commercial and industrial space let, and more and more companies are relocating from the City to the Docks. And for the residents of Docklands the infrastructure is steadily improving with the provision of new shopping facilities and restaurants, etc., though the City and West End remain far more popular for an evening out.

Access
Docklands Light Railway

Until the extension to the Jubilee Line opens in 1998, the principal link with the inner city will continue to be the Docklands Light Railway (DLR). The railway which started running in 1987 is administered by the London Underground. It runs east from the Bank and Tower Gateway where it has connections with the Bank and Tower Hill Underground stations respectively, and runs through Docklands to Island Gardens, and beyond Docklands east as far as Beckton. It also runs northwards from Island Gardens to Stratford to join the Underground again. The computer-controlled trains are driver-less during the week, but at weekends staff on the trains will point out the sights on both sides of the line.

Between Tower Gateway and Poplar stations the line follows the route of one of the earliest railways in the capital, the London and Blackwall, constructed in 1840 and linking the City with the Port of London. A stretch of the line running in the other direction follows the route of the Northern London Railway, built in the mid 19th c. to provide transport to

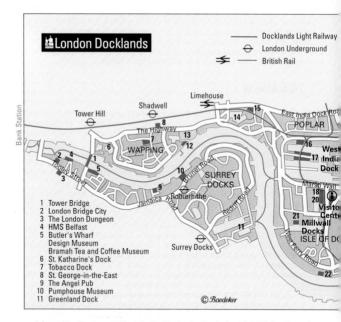

1 Tower Bridge
2 London Bridge City
3 The London Dungeon
4 HMS Belfast
5 Butler's Wharf
  Design Museum
  Bramah Tea and Coffee Museum
6 St. Katharine's Dock
7 Tobacco Dock
8 St. George-in-the-East
9 The Angel Pub
10 Pumphouse Museum
11 Greenland Dock

and from the East and West India Docks to the industrial Midlands and North. Between Poplar and Island Gardens the DLR is elevated where it passes over the docks. It then follows the line of the old Millway Extension Railway, laid out in 1868, on which some of the trains were horse-drawn.

Riverboats

Docklands can of course also be reached by river. Excursion launches operated by various companies ply mainly between Westminster, Charing Cross and Tower Piers and Greenwich (see entry) from where there is access to the DLR terminus at Island Gardens via the Greenwich Foot Tunnel. Between March and November there is a service from Westminster Pier to the Thames Barrier, calling in at Greenwich Pier on the way. (See also Practical Information – Boat Trips.)

Information

The Docklands Visitor Centre (open: Mon.–Fri. 8.30am–6pm, Sat., Sun. 9.30am–5pm), situated at Lime Harbour on the Isle of Dogs, has an exhibition on the Docklands redevelopment project. Guided tours can be arranged, tel. (0171) 512 1111.

Surrey Docks

Surrey Docks extend along the south bank of the Thames from London Bridge (see entry) eastwards to Greenland Dock on the bend of the river at Rotherhithe. There were wharves here as early as the 14th c., handling cargoes of wood and grain. It was from Rotherhithe that the "Mayflower" set sail for Southampton and Plymouth to take the Pilgrim Fathers to North America.

Butler's Wharf

To the east of Tower Bridge the old warehouses on Butler's Wharf, along with the old Anchor Brewery, have been transformed into an exclusive shopping and residential complex, and has become London's gastronomic centre with up-market restaurants and Sir Terence Conran's Chef School where the country's top chefs come to perfect their skills. Some impression

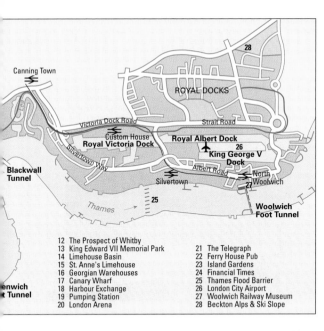

12 The Prospect of Whitby
13 King Edward VII Memorial Park
14 Limehouse Basin
15 St. Anne's Limehouse
16 Georgian Warehouses
17 Canary Wharf
18 Harbour Exchange
19 Pumping Station
20 London Arena
21 The Telegraph
22 Ferry House Pub
23 Island Gardens
24 Financial Times
25 Thames Flood Barrier
26 London City Airport
27 Woolwich Railway Museum
28 Beckton Alps & Ski Slope

of what the area must have been like in Victorian times can be gained from Shad Thames, the street behind Butler's Wharf.

At the end of Butler's Wharf a new building overlooking the Thames houses the Design Museum. On display are everyday articles of all kinds, from vacuum cleaners to coffee cups and cars, graphically illustrating how function determines form and how form changes over the years and decades. On the ground floor there is a pleasant bar; the museum shop sells modern designer products (open: Mon.–Fri. 11.30am–6pm, Sat., Sun. noon–6pm).

★ Design Museum

The Bramah Tea and Coffee Museum, in Maguire Street, downstream from Butler's Wharf, records how these popular beverages were first brought to London and where and from what they were drunk. Tea and coffee tasting (open: daily 10am–6pm).

Bramah Tea and Coffee Museum

Acclaimed in its day as a masterpiece of engineering, the Thames Tunnel was constructed by Marc Brunel in 1843, linking Wapping and Surrey Docks. The old pumphouse is now a museum (open: first Sunday of the month 11am–3pm).

Pumphouse Museum

A good walk upstream from the Pumphouse Museum along riverside walks, the Angel, a pub with a history dating back to the 15th c., offers flagging sightseers a well-earned break (101 Bermondsey Wall East).

The Angel

Wapping, Limehouse and Poplar

Wapping, Limehouse and Poplar docks extend along the north bank of the Thames from Tower Bridge (see entry) to the Blackwall Tunnel. The docks had already made their mark on the area in the 16th c. and reached their

In the Design Museum

The Dickens Inn and the old lightship "Nore"

peak in the 18th and 19th c., handling rice, tobacco and wine. This booming commerce contrasted sharply with the poverty and crime rife among the inhabitants; public executions were held at Wapping's Execution Dock.

Gaily dressed sailing ships celebrated the opening of St Katharine's Dock near Tower Bridge in 1827. Its future became uncertain, however, when the size of sailing vessels increased beyond its capacity. The redevelopment of St Katharine's Dock served as a pilot scheme for the dockland area, and was completed without sacrificing its original character. A number of fine old warehouses were renovated and converted into, for example, the Dock Master's House, the Dickens Inn by the Tower pub (in a building from 1800) and the Italian-looking Ivory House (used originally for storing ivory). New buildings, concealed behind old façades, now accommodate institutions such as the World Trade Centre. Saved from becoming a slum, St Katharine's Dock has been transformed into a lively new quarter while retaining its old charm.

St Katharine's Dock

The dock provides berths for more than 200 privately-owned craft and a base for the Yacht Club. Two historic ships are also moored there: the lightship "Nore" and the steam tug "Challenge", both built in 1931.

Historic Ships

The warehouse at Tobacco Dock, built in 1811, stored tobacco and fleeces under its roof, wine and rum in its cellar. It is currently being developed as a factory outlet shopping centre. On the quayside are replicas of two ships of the type that once delivered tobacco and wine to the dock; the "Sea Lark" operates as a children's crèche and "The Three Sisters" is to be converted to a floating pub.

Tobacco Dock

A little to the north of Tobacco Dock can be seen the tall tower of St George-in-the-East. The exterior is much the same as when it was erected in 1714–26; the interior was destroyed by bombing in 1941 and has been completely rebuilt. Further north, a mural on No. 236 Cable Street commemorates the "Battle of Cable Street" of Oct. 11th 1936 when the East Enders clashed with the Fascist Oswald Mosley and his supporters.

St George-in-the-East Cable Street Mural

First opened in 1502, the Prospect of Whitby (east of Tobacco Dock at 57 Wapping Wall) is the oldest Thames-side public house.

The Prospect of Whitby

St Anne's Limehouse (1712–24), the area's principal church, had its interior rebuilt in 1851 after a fire (open: afternoons).

St Anne's, Limehouse

Nicholas Grimshaw's "Financial Times" Building, of glass, steel and aluminium construction, is one of the many modern buildings in the area to receive widespread critical acclaim. (Printing of the "Financial Times" in this building will cease in March 1996.)

"Financial Times" Building

Isle of Dogs

The Isle of Dogs, at one time marshland occupying a wide bend in the river, lies at the heart of the Docklands redevelopment. Its famous East and West India Docks bore the names of the colonies from whence their cargoes originated. Because of its concentration of wharves and shipping companies, in the mid 19th c. the Isle of Dogs became the centre of London's heavy industry.

The redevelopment has given the area an entirely different aspect, transforming it into a high-tech office and residential quarter abounding with innovative architecture – apartment blocks such as "The Cascades" designed by Piers Gough, the South Quay Plaza office suites by John Outram, the Pumphouse in Stewart Street and the controversial Canary Wharf.

Oasis of Post Modern: Millwall Docks and Canary Wharf

Georgian warehouses

The buildings on the north side of the West India Docks most northerly basin are the oldest surviving multi-storeyed warehouses in London, dating from Georgian times (built 1802-03). There are plans to create a new Docklands Museum in these warehouses with dock-related artefacts from the Museum of London (see entry).

Canary Wharf

Canary Wharf, situated between two of the West India Docks basins, is the most ambitious development in Docklands. Backed by Canadian investment, it comprises an office, shopping and residential complex incorporating 11.8 million sq.ft/1.1 million sq.m of office space, dominated by the 800ft/244m tower block designed by Cesar Pelli, the tallest tower in Great Britain. Much of the office space remains unlet, however, resulting in the tower being nicknamed the "London Space Centre". However, the Music 100 Exhibition should help in this respect.

Millwall Dock

Reconstruction of the area around Millwall Dock is now also complete. The most prominent features are the steel and glass buildings of South Quay Plaza and the Harbour Exchange. The London Arena is a new multi- purpose hall with seating for 12,000. Oppposite it stands the Docklands Visitor Centre (see above).

Island Gardens

Island Gardens, on the southern tip of the Isle of Dogs, offers fine views of Greenwich (see entry), which can be reached from the Gardens via the Greenwich Foot Tunnel.

Royal Docks

The Royal Docks lie to the east of Bow Creek, mouth of the River Lea. The Victoria Dock was opened in 1855 and the Albert Dock in 1880, attracting the chemical, cable and food industries. Industrialisation cost lives, 73 people being killed in 1917 in an explosion at a dynamite factory. In 1922 the King George V Dock, last to be built, was opened. There are plans for a major exhibition centre, known as "Ex Cel", to open in 1998. Also planned is a new business park and university campus.

The end of 1987 saw the first commercial flights from London City Airport ("STOLport" = Short Take Off and Landing airport). Situated between the Royal Albert and King George V Docks, 6 miles/10km or so from the inner city, it handles only smaller short take-off aircraft and is used mainly by business-men and women. It operates flights to thirteen near European destinations.

London City Airport

The North Woolwich Railway Museum is housed in the former North Woolwich station, with exhibits from the Great Eastern Railway founded in 1839 (open: Mon.–Fri. 10am–5pm, Sun. 2–5pm).

Woolwich Railway Museum

Ski enthusiasts can practice their technique on an artificial ski slope built on a waste site north of the Royal Docks.

Beckton Alps & Ski Slope

★Thames Barrier

The largest movable flood barrier in the world, straddling the Thames south of the Royal Docks, came into operation on May 8th 1984. This marvel of technology, 520m/1706ft long, was built at a cost of about £750 million. Nine piers sunk deep into the river bed support the ten steel gates. Powerful hydraulic rams move the gates into position, a process which takes a full 30 minutes.

Location
Unity Way, Woolwich, SE18

British Rail
Charlton, from Charing Cross (then 20-minute walk)

Eight smaller barriers have also been constructed at various points downstream, closing off some of the river's tributaries. Together they

The Thames Barrier

Docklands

Riverboats
ThamesBarrierPier
fromWestminster
PierorGreenwich
Pierfrom
Mar.toOct.

Opening times
Mon.–Fri.
10a–5pm,
Sat. and Sun.
10.30a–5.30pm

protect large areas of Essex and Kent from potentially catastrophic flooding. The Thames Barrier was deemed necessary because the gradual sinking of eastern England and greater frequency of violent storms in the North Sea and English Channel have brought a substantially increased risk of inundation by the sea. In the view of many British experts even larger flood barriers will be required within a few decades.

The Visitors' Centre features a most absorbing audio-visual presentation illustrating the construction and operation of the Thames Barrier. Boat trips run from Barrier Gardens Pier to the sluice-gates.

★Dulwich Picture Gallery

Location
College Road
SE21

**Underground
station**
Brixton,
then P4 bus

British Rail
West Dulwich
from Victoria,
North Dulwich
from London
Bridge

Opening times
Tues.–Fri.
10am–5pm,
Sat. 11am–5pm,
Sun. 2–5pm

Dulwich Village, barely 4 miles/6km south of central London, still retains something of a village atmosphere with its handsome Georgian villas, tollhouse (the only surviving example in London), park and college. The "College of God's Gift" as its founder called it, was endowed in the early 17th c. by Edward Alleyn (1566–1626), a wealthy Shakespearean actor and Master of the King's bears, for the benefit "of six poor men and six poor women".

It was here in 1817 that the first public picture gallery in London was opened, in a building designed by Sir John Soane which, on account of its overhead lighting, became the model for many such galleries. The nucleus of the gallery – apart from some rather undistinguished paintings by Alleyn himself – was formed from a collection of paintings belonging to a Frenchman, Noël Desenfans, who bequeathed it to his friend, the painter and collector Sir Francis Bourgeois in 1807. The decision to open the valuable collection to the public was made soon afterwards by Sir Francis and Desenfans' widow. The collection embraces works by Dutch artists (including Rembrandt, J. van Ruisdael and Aelbert Cuyp), portraits by 17th and 18th c. British painters (Sir Peter Lely, Sir Godfrey Kneller, William Hogarth, Thomas Gainsborough, Sir Joshua Reynolds, George Romney and Sir Thomas Lawrence), and paintings by Italian (Raphael, Paolo Veronese, Guercino, Canaletto, Giovanni Battista Tiepolo and others), Flemish (Peter Paul Rubens, Anthony Van Dyck, David Teniers), Spanish (Bartolomé Murillo, etc.) and French (Antoine Watteau, Nicolas Poussin, Le Brun) masters. The, to modern eyes, congested arrangement of the paintings reflects 19th c. taste.

The Desenfans and their friend Bourgeois lie in their sarcophagi opposite the main entrance, in Soane's Mausoleum, at the centre of the gallery.

Fleet Street   H3

Location
extending from
Trafalgar Square
to Ludgate
Circus

**Underground
stations**
Blackfriars,
Temple
"Street of Ink"

Fleet Street owes its name to the River Fleet which formerly flowed here and which, like all the streams in the London of that time, did duty as a sewer. It was soon built over.

Until a few years ago Fleet Street was the hub of the British newspaper world. The first printing press was set up here at the end of the 15th c., and the first daily newspaper, the "Daily Courant", appeared in 1702. Though the buildings of the various publishing houses with their editorial offices and print rooms can still be seen, they now house insurance companies and brokers, a consequence of changing methods of newspaper production. The introduction of modern technology rendered the old Fleet Street premises redundant as publishers of the "old school" gave way to cost-conscious businessmen convinced of the gains in efficiency to be made by building new offices and works. Today most newspaper groups have their headquarters in the newly redeveloped Docklands (see entry). Fleet Street, the so-called "Street of Ink", is no longer synonymous with the British press.

A griffin adorns the Temple Bar Memorial (1880) marking the entrance to Fleet Street – a continuation of the Strand – on the boundary of the City and Westminster. The memorial stands on the site of Temple Bar Gate, designed by Wren in 1680, on which decapitated heads used to be displayed. By tradition the sovereign always halts here prior to entering the City, awaiting the Lord Mayor's permission to proceed.

The Griffin on the Temple Bar Memorial

Temple Bar

Now the Royal Bank of Scotland, No. 1 Fleet Street, "at the sign of the Marigold", was once occupied by Child's Bank, the oldest bank in London. Founded in 1671 there is a splendid description of it in Charles Dickens's "A Tale of Two Cities" (1859): "It was an old-fashioned place, moreover, in the moral attribute that the partners in the House were proud of its smallness, proud of its darkness, proud of its ugliness, proud of its incommodiousness . . . in a miserable little shop, with two little counters, where the oldest of men made your cheque shake as if the wind rustled it, while they examined the signature by the dingiest of windows, which were always under a shower-bath of mud from Fleet Street, and which were made the dingier by their own iron bars proper, and the heavy shadow of Temple Bar."

Notable buildings

Child's Bank

The tavern room known as Prince Henry's Room at No. 17 Fleet Street (opposite Chancery Lane) has a fine Tudor timber ceiling emblazoned in the centre with the arms of Henry, Prince of Wales (son of James I); the room is crammed with mementoes of Samuel Pepys (open: Mon.–Sat 11am–2pm).

Prince Henry's Room

Also among Fleet Street's numerous historic buildings are two 17th c. pubs: "Ye Olde Cheshire Cheese" (haunt of a number of great writers) and "Ye Olde Cock Tavern" (once a popular meeting place for pressmen and printers); also the church of St-Dunstan-in-the-West which boasts a contemporary statue of Queen Elizabeth I on the south wall. The Temple (see entry) is a world in itself.

Ye Olde Cheshire Cheese · Ye Olde Cock Tavern

The buildings which belonged to the big newspaper groups in the days when Fleet Street symbolised the British press include: the former offices of the Daily Mail between Bouverie Street and Whitefriars Street; the Daily Mirror in Fetter Lane; Express Newspapers on the corner of Shoe Lane; and the Daily Telegraph at 135 Fleet Street. Still at 85 Fleet Street are the offices of the Reuters news agency and Associated Press.

Newspaper publishing houses

From 1748 to 1759 Samuel Johnson (see Famous People) lived in Gough Square (No. 17), a little to the north of Fleet Street. Here he wrote, among other things, his famous dictionary. The house, a fine example of a grand Georgian town house, is filled with memorabilia of this extraordinary critic and man of letters (open: May–Sept. Mon.–Sat. 11am–5.30pm, Oct.–Apr. till 5pm).

Dr Johnson's House

Gray's Inn   G/H2

Location
Gray's Inn Road
WC2

Underground station
Chancery Lane

Gray's Inn is one of the four Inns of Court which have the exclusive right of admitting lawyers to practise as barristers in the English courts. The others are the Middle and Inner Temples, both housed in the Temple (see entry), and Lincoln's Inn (see entry). Gray's Inn is said to have been in existence as early as the 14th c. (though this is the subject of dispute). It takes its name from the former owners of the site, the Lords de Gray. The buildings, damaged during the Second World War but wonderfully well restored, are set in delightful gardens.

The main entrance is from High Holborn, through a 17th c. archway. Visitors are free to walk through the external parts of the Inn, but permission is needed for access to the inside of any of the buildings including the magnificent Great Hall, where in 1594 Shakespeare's "Comedy of Errors" was performed for only the second time. Applications to visit any of the buildings must be made to the Under-Treasurer, The Honourable Society of Gray's Inn, Treasury Office, 8 South Square, London WC1R 5EU; however as all the buildings are in constant use most of the time, permission is rarely granted except to specialist groups. Most visitors content themselves with a walk in the gardens (open during the lunch hour), scene of many a duel, and a quick look round South Square, graced by a statue of the philosopher and statesman Francis Bacon (see Famous People), the most illustrious member of the Inn, who lived here from 1576 to 1626.

★Staple Inn

In High Holborn, just opposite the end of Gray's Inn Road, is the distinctive half-timbered façade of Staple Inn, once a wool merchants' house and premises, and afterwards lodgings for student lawyers at Gray's Inn. Built in 1586 on the site of a much older inn, Staple Inn is now the only remaining Elizabethan half-timbered house in central London (albeit restored).

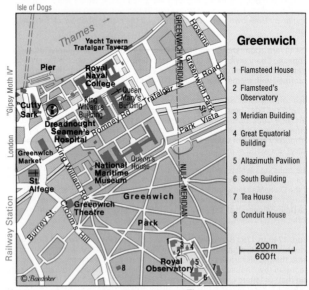

The tea clipper "Cutty Sark" ▶

★★ Greenwich (See map page 78)

Docklands Light Railway
Island Gardens (via Greenwich Foot Tunnel)

British Rail
Greenwich, Maze Hill from Charing Cross and London Bridge

Riverboats
Greenwich Pier from Charing Cross Pier, Tower Pier and Westminster Pier

Greenwich, one of London's most historic suburbs, lies 6 miles/10km downstream from London Bridge on the south bank of the Thames; it definitely warrants a visit. It is familiar of course throughout the world for its Observatory, the "fixed star" of navigators everywhere, whose clocks are set to Greenwich Mean Time and who measure longitude from the Greenwich Meridian. Greenwich is truly a Mecca for anyone seeking a real insight into the history of navigation; but it is also considerably more besides – an altogether delightful place with rich Royal and architectural heritage and lovely parks to enjoy. This was no doubt one of the reasons why the British government has decided to celebrate the new millenium in a giant leisure park to be built here (see Introduction, Architecture and the History of Art, Architecture at the end of the 20th c.)

There are several ways to get to Greenwich: by water aboard an excursion launch or riverboat; via the Docklands Light Railway (DLR) to the terminus at Island Gardens, Isle of Dogs, and from there under the Thames on foot through the Greenwich Foot Tunnel (built 1902); or by British Rail from Charing Cross Station or London Bridge. Perhaps the best idea of all is to go via the DLR and Foot Tunnel (pausing before entering the tunnel to admire the famous view, captured by Canaletto, of the Royal Naval College across the river), and to make the return journey by boat and so see Docklands (see entry) to advantage as it goes gliding by.

★ "Cutty Sark"

The "Cutty Sark" was the last and best known of the old tea clippers which, in the 19th c., plied the "tea route" between Britain and China

Royal Naval College Greenwich

bringing tea and spices to Europe. Built in Dumbarton, Scotland in 1869, she was the finest and fastest sailing ship of her day, capable of a speed of 17.5 knots. She made her record voyage in 1871, covering the distance from Shanghai to London in 107 days; in 1889 while on voyage to Sydney she actually overtook the steamship "Britannia". The name Cutty Sark, meaning "short shirt", was taken from Robert Burns's "Tam O'Shanter", in which poem the witch Nannie pulls off the tail of Tam's grey mare – as depicted on the ship's figurehead. The "Cutty Sark" was brought to her berth in the dry dock in Greenwich in 1954 and subsequently restored. The lower deck contains a delightful collection of old figureheads as well as drawings and memorabilia of the tea clipper's voyages to China, India and Ceylon.

Opening times
Mon.–Sat.
10am–6pm,
Sun. noon–6pm
(winter till 5pm)

Close by the "Cutty Sark" lies "Gipsy Moth IV", the 54ft/16m ketch in which in 1966/67 the 65-year old yachtsman Sir Francis Chichester sailed single-handed round the world. The circumnavigation took him 274 days, 226 of them at sea. He was knighted for his achievement. "Gipsy Moth IV" is open to the public at certain times of the year (enquiries, tel. (0181) 858 3445), but its exterior can always be seen from a viewing platform.

"Gipsy Moth IV"

★Royal Naval College

Within a few yards of the "Cutty Sark" are the grounds of the Royal Naval College, its buildings those of the former Greenwich Hospital. The College closed down in 1997, and the buildings are now used by Greenwich University. The site on which it stands is laden with history. The first of several palaces here was erected by Edward I (1272-1307); in 1428 Humphrey, Duke of Gloucester built Bella Court, which Henry VII converted and renamed Placentia Palace, his favourite residence and that of other Tudor monarchs and, up until the start of the Civil War in 1642, of the Stuart kings also. Henry VIII was particularly closely associated with Greenwich and its palace. Here he was born, from here he ruled England

Old paddle-steamer "Reliant"

for 20 years, here he married Catherine of Aragon and Anne of Cleves and signed Anne Boleyn's death warrant. His daughters Mary I and Elizabeth I, were born in the palace. Henry established Royal docklands at nearby Deptford and Woolwich, and at the latter in 1512 attended the launch of the first four-masted ship, the "Great Harry". During the Civil War the palace fell into disrepair and was eventually demolished. It was replaced by the present buildings and endowed by Queen Mary II in 1694 as a hospital for seamen on the model of the Royal Hospital Chelsea (see entry). Charles II had commissioned a new palace from John Webb earlier but, work had been halted by lack of funds. Sir Christopher Wren's scheme for the new hospital incorporated Webb's partly-completed building. Wren himself supervised the early stages of construction, though it was 1751 before the hospital was finished.

Viewing

Two sections of the Royal Naval College are open to visitors – the Painted Hall in the King William wing and the Chapel in the Queen Mary wing (open: daily 2.30–5pm).

Painted Hall (King William building)

The Painted Hall in the south-west block (King William building, 1707), was originally the refectory and is still in use as a dining room; the decoration to which it owes its name is by Sir James Thornhill and was completed in 1727. The ceiling depicts William and Mary as peacemakers, triumphing over tyranny in the person of Louis XIV of France. The Royal Astronomer John Flamsteed is portrayed in the south-west corner.

Chapel (Queen Mary building)

The Chapel in the south-east block (Queen Mary building) was designed by Wren but after the interior and dome were totally destroyed by fire in 1779 was rebuilt by James "Athenian" Stuart. The altarpiece, "St Paul after the Shipwreck at Malta", is by Benjamin West. The pulpit, lectern and font were carved in the naval dockyard at Deptford.

★★National Maritime Museum

Opening times
Daily
10am–5pm

South of the Royal Naval College are the buildings of the National Maritime Museum, the largest maritime museum in the world. The immensely impressive collection covers Britain's association with the sea from prehistoric, Roman and medieval times to today, including the history of the British Navy from Tudor and Stuart times through the Napoleonic Wars to the Second World War and Falklands War. The museum is housed in two wings on either side of the Queen's House and connected by a colonnade. The wings were constructed between 1805 and 1816 and until 1933 were occupied by the Royal Hospital School for the sons of seafarers. The museum opened in 1937.

N.B.

In addition to the maritime history collection the National Maritime Museum administered the Queen's House, and the Old Royal Observatory. The exhibitions in the National Maritime Museum are at present in process of rearrangement, as a consequence of which some galleries may be temporarily closed. This work should be completed by the summer of 1999. A combined ticket gives access to all three sites, although visitors to the Old Royal Observatory may purchase a single ticket.

Figurehead from H.M.S. "Ajax"

Maritime history collection

The paintings in the museum form a small art gallery in their own right. among them are seascapes by Van de Velde, J. M. W. Turner and Muirhead Bone, and portraits of famous seafarers by leading artists such as Godfrey Kneller,

Peter Lely, William Hogarth, Joshua Reynolds, Thomas Gainsborough and George Romney.

The museum shop is near the entrance to the ground floor. A few steps lead down to a department dealing with seafaring in general. The adjoining room charts the voyages of discovery of James Cook, with some fine pictures by William Hodges (1744–97), who accompanied Cook on his second voyage. On the left is the new department dealing with 20th c. maritime history, including the Merchant Navy, the First and Second World Wars, the Falkland and Gulf Wars. Deafening battle noises and realistic command posts complete the scene. The next room deals with the other end of the time-scale, covering marine archaeology in Great Britain and the building of sailing ships. This leads the visitor on to the main room, Nelson's Hall, which offers an overview of the history of ship and boat building together with a fine collection of figureheads. In the centre of the hall lies the paddle steamer "Reliant", built in 1907.

★State Barges

Neptune's Hall leads into the Barge House which holds four elaborately decorated barges, two of which were used to convey royalty on the Thames – one built in 1732 for Frederick, Prince of Wales, and the other in 1689 for Queen Mary II. The remaining two barges belong to the Admiralty.

Middle floor

The rooms on the middle floor deal with naval battles with the United States of America, merchant shipping in the 18th c. and the wars against revolutionary France in the 18th and 19th c. The newly-equipped section devoted to Lord Nelson contains such memorabilia as the uniform in which he died at the Battle of Trafalgar in 1805.

Upper room

The main themes of the rooms on the upper floor are the voyages of discovery and the elevation of England to the status of a powerful seafaring nation between 1450 and 1700, all illustrated by a number of original exhibits. One particularly fine section deals with the construction of ships of war between 1650 and 1850. A model was first made for their approval. A number of such models including those of the "Royal George" and the "Bellona" are on display and show the meticulous precision and attention to detail which went into their making.

Newly opened is the "All Hands" gallery which enables visitors, especially children, to experience for themselves, inter-actively, just how hard a seaman's life used to be and what skills were required.

★★Queen's House

Opening times
Daily
10am–5pm

Queen's House, a Palladian mansion designed by Inigo Jones – imitated but never equalled by many another house of the period – is a masterpiece of Classical architecture, notable for its symmetrical proportions, harmonious details, and finely executed marble floors, wrought-iron balustrades and carved and painted ceilings. The house, begun in 1616, was originally commissioned by James I as a residence for his wife Anne of Denmark. Planned as an annexe to the Placentia Palace, then still in existence, construction halted in 1619 following Anne's death. In 1629 Charles I revived the project, employing Jones to complete the house for his queen, Henrietta Maria. Having fled the country during the Civil War, Henrietta Maria returned to the palace after the Restoration of the Monarchy in 1660. With Greenwich Park for its garden, the Queen's House is the epitome of a royal residence. It is now restored to its former splendour after renovation lasting six years and costing £5 million.

Tour

The tour of Queen's House begins in the basement with a display of silver treasures from the National Maritime Museum (including a gold chain, 8.5m/28ft long, presented to Admiral William Penn). The history of the house itself is also documented. On the ground floor the Great Hall is cube-shaped and of appropriate Palladian dimensions. Access to the upper floor is by the Tulip Stairs (so-called even though the epony-

★Tulip Staircase

mous flowers appear in fact to be lilies). This superb feature, designed by Inigo Jones, was the first cantilevered spiral staircase in England. On the upper floor visitors can roam through the King's Apartments, which history ensured were never used, and the Queen's Apartments, which Henrietta Maria did ultimately occupy if only for a few years. From the Queen's Apartments another beautiful staircase with wrought-iron balustrade descends to the Orangery.

Greenwich Park

A place
to relax

To the south of the National Maritime Museum lies Greenwich Park, originally palace gardens laid out for Charles II by Le Nôtre, landscape gardener to Louis XIV. Dominated by the Old Royal Observatory ensconced on its hill, the park (open: dawn to dusk) is a popular place of relaxation for Londoners and tourists alike.

★**Old Royal
Observatory
Opening times**

Daily
10am–5pm

Flamsteed House, designed by Wren and bearing the name of John Flamsteed, the first Astronomer Royal, stands beautifully situated within the Park. From the terrace there is a magnificent view over Queen's House and the Royal Naval College, across a sweeping bend in the Thames, to Docklands (see entry) and the Canary Wharf tower in the far distance.

For almost three hundred years Flamsteed House was the home of the Royal Observatory, founded by Charles II in 1675 to foster safer navigation. In 1967 the Observatory was moved to Herstmonceux in Sussex and subsequently, in 1990, to Cambridge. On a mast topping one of the towers of Flamsteed House is a red time ball which drops from the top of its pole at 1 o'clock precisely every day, a device originally installed in 1833 to enable vessels in the river to regulate their chronometers. Navigation and time-keeping remain the principal themes inside Flamsteed House. On display are a collection of instruments including three of John Harrison's original chronometers, the first time-pieces of sufficient reliability and accuracy to be of navigational use. The solution to the problem of determining longitude, for which a reward of £20,000 was offered by the Admiralty in 1714, is clearly explained. Four rooms in the house are still furnished as they were when John Flamsteed lived there.

Meridian
Building

A prerequisite of any method of determining longitude is the designation of a zero meridian to serve as a fixed point of reference for navigational purposes. The exact position of longitude zero, which divides the eastern from the western hemisphere, is marked by a steel rod set in the floor of the Old Royal Observatory's Meridian Building; step over the rod and you step from one hemisphere to the other! The building also houses an interesting collection of old astronomical instruments. Among them is the Transit Circle, a large device constructed in 1851 by George Airy, the seventh Astronomer Royal, by means of which he was able to define the zero meridian with even greater accuracy than before. His definition was officially adopted in 1884 for use world-wide by an international conference held in Washington D.C. The prime meridian line, to give its full name, is also the determinant of the world's time. On the outside wall of the building an electro-magnetic clock shows Greenwich Mean Time, on which the International Time Zone system is based, and by which times around the world are calculated.

Great Equatorial
Building

The Great Equatorial Building is comparatively modern, the original of 1893 having been destroyed during the Second World War. It is easily recognised by its dome housing the largest optical telescope in Britain (28in./71cm). A video presentation explains its capabilities.

Another domed building, the red-brick planetarium, opened in 1965, has a regular programme of shows throughout the year.

Planetarium

Built in 1700–20, Ranger's House, in the south-west corner of the Park, contains an interesting collection of portrait paintings (mainly full-size portraits by a 17th c. artist, William Larkin) and a fine collection of musical instruments (open: in summer daily 10am–6pm, in Winter Wed.–Sun. 10am–4pm).

Ranger's House

Greenwich Town

For those with time and energy to spare there remains Greenwich town itself. Its church of St Alfege, built by Nicholas Hawksmoor in 1714, stands on the site of an older church erected by the Danes on the spot where St Alfege was murdered in 1012. Its successor preserves some wall decorations carved in wood by Grinling Gibbons.

St Alfege

The town's attractive old covered market (weekends) is nowadays largely given over to the sale of craftwork.

Greenwich Market

One unusual attraction is the Fan Museum (12 Crooms Hill), the only one of its kind in the world, with its collection of over 2,000 fans dating from the 17th c. to the present day (open: Tues.–Sat. 11am–4.30pm, Sun. noon–4.30pm).

Fan Museum

The Trafalgar Tavern, right by the river, offers a welcome opportunity to rest weary limbs. Opened in 1837 – replacing an earlier inn called the "George" – it has scarcely changed. Charles Dickens and William Makepeace Thackary both visited here, and Dickens made the inn the setting for a wedding party in his novel "Our Mutual Friend". At one time the British cabinet met in the Nelson Room on the first floor for a whitebait supper, the tradition has been revived in recent years.

Trafalgar Tavern

★Guildhall

J3

The Late Gothic Guildhall, home of the Corporation of London and meeting-place of its Court of Common Council, dates from 1411 (though the only surviving parts of the original building are sections of the outer walls, Great Hall and Crypt). Badly damaged in the Great Fire of 1666, the rebuilt hall and later additions, including the Neo-Gothic-style south front erected in 1789, suffered severely in an air-raid in 1940. The building was restored inside and out after the Second World War.

Location
Gresham Street
EC2

Underground stations
St Paul's, Bank

In February 1988 during excavations in the porch, remains of a Roman amphitheatre dating from the 1st c. a.d. were discovered, extending beneath the medieval building. Traces of London's medieval Jewish quarter also came to light.

Opening times
Mon.–Sat.
10am–5pm;
May–Sept.
also Sun.
10am–5pm

The porch, with the coat of arms of the City of London (motto "Domine dirige nos", "Guide us, O Lord"), leads into the Great Hall. Here, every third Thursday at 1pm, the Court of Common Council meet to discuss municipal business. Open to the public, the meetings are attended by the Mace and Swordbearer, Treasurer, Aldermen and Councilmen of the City of London, arrayed in all their finery. Likewise public events are the election of the Sheriff, a picturesque and colourful ceremony held annually on June 24th, a dais being erected for the purpose at the east end of the Great Hall, and the swearing in of the new Lord Mayor, another grand annual occasion conducted with much traditional pomp and ceremony (see Baedeker Special p.15). For admission to meetings or further information apply direct to the Guildhall or to any tourist information office (see Practical Information).

Great Hall

Guildhall

The Guildhall

The Great Hall is also used for official receptions and banquets, being closed to the public for two to three days preceding and following.

Tour

The Great Hall is over 151ft/46m long, 49ft/15m wide and 95ft/29m high. Its timber roof, destroyed in 1940, was rebuilt after the war by Sir Giles Scott with stone arches. Around the hall are banners bearing the arms of the twelve great "livery companies", the old city guilds. They are, clockwise: the Grocers, Fishmongers, Skinners, Haberdashers, Ironmongers, Clothworkers, Vintners, Salters, Merchant Taylors, Goldsmiths, Drapers and Mercers. Their arms are also painted on the cornices. The windows are inscribed with the names of the Lord Mayors.

The west end is occupied by a minstrel's gallery; this end also has a fine oak screen and figures of Gog (right) and Magog (left). Along the south wall are statues of William Pitt the Younger and Lord Mayor Beckford, followed by a canopied oak dresser housing the City mace and sword, the Royal Fusiliers' Memorial and the only surviving 15th c. window. Along the north wall are statues of Sir Winston Churchill, Admiral Lord Nelson, the Duke of Wellington and William Pitt the Elder, Earl of Chatham. The two galleries are for the use of the press and the Lady Mayoress. The east end of the hall has fine oak panelling. On a dais are the seats occupied by the Aldermen of the Court of Common Council.

Crypt

Under the Great Hall is the 15th c. East Crypt (restored), with one of the finest medieval groined vaults in London. It can be visited as part of a tour as can the Western Crypt (restored), the site of the first Guildhall (1042–66). The vaulting of the Western Crypt is also found in four city churches of 1200.

Guildhall Art Gallery

Originally founded in 1670, the Guildhall Art Gallery, to the east of the Great Hall, has existed on its present site since 1886.

Guildhall Library

A visit to the Guildhall Library is essential for anyone with an interest in the history of London. It has a unique collection of London prints and more than 140,000 volumes on the history of the city. Among its most treasured possessions are first folios of plays by Shakespeare, a map of London dated 1591, and a deed of purchase of a house bearing Shakespeare's signature.

The library also houses a rare collection of 700 clocks belonging to the Worshipful Company of Clockmakers. At least five centuries of clock-making are represented (open: Mon.–Sat. 9.30am–5pm).

Guildhall Clock Museum

Hampstead

Hampstead is a charming place. In bygone days this pretty north London suburb with lots of open spaces, woods and ponds, was favoured by those seeking relative peace and quiet, among them artists and writers including such famous names as John Keats, John Constable, Robert Louis Stevenson, D. H. Lawrence, George Orwell and Elias Canetti. Sigmund Freud and Charles de Gaulle also lived in Hampstead. The delightful Hampstead Heath encircling the highest point in London (476ft/145m), features in many paintings, including some by Constable.

Location
north-west
of the City, NW3
Underground station
Hampstead

The steep streets of Hampstead Village are full of places of interest: old shops and houses in Flask Walk and Well Walk; one of London's finest Georgian terraces in Church Row; and hospitable pubs like Jack Straw's Castle (12 North End Way), not itself very old but standing on a historic site where, during the Peasants' Revolt in 1381, the rebel Jack Straw rallied support before marching on the city of London.

Hampstead Village

Nor is Hampstead short of museums. Burgh House (1703) in New End Square charts the history of Hampstead (open: Wed.-Sun. noon-5pm; excellent caféteria). The beautifully furnished Fenton House, built in

Burgh House

Fenton House

1693, is one of the oldest in Hampstead. In addition to lovely gardens and a fine display of porcelain, it boasts an unrivalled collection of old keyboard instruments, all in immaculate condition and used from time to time for concerts of Baroque chamber music (open: Apr.–Oct. Mon.–Wed. 2–5pm, Sat., Sun. 11am–5pm; weekends only in March). The house where John Keats lived for a while contains memorabilia of the poet (open: Apr.–Oct. Mon.–Fri. 10am–1pm and 2–6pm, Sat.10am–1pmand2–5pm, Sun. 2–5pm only; Nov.–Mar. Mon.–Fri. 1–5pm, Sat. 10am–1pm and 2–5pm, Sun. 2–5pm only). A short distance outside Hampstead Village proper is another address of particular interest (20 Maresfield Gardens). Here Sigmund Freud

Keats House

Freud Museum

Kenwood House (see page 88)

made his home after fleeing from Austria in 1938. The house, which Freud also used as his consulting rooms and which contains his library, is now a museum. The psychoanalyst's famous couch is always a great focus of interest (open: Wed.–Sun. noon–5pm).

Hampstead Heath

Hampstead's "park", better known as the Heath, is situated on the north side of Hampstead Village. Here visitors can relax at a concert beside Concert Pond or enjoy a dip in Kenwood Pond (women only), Highgate Pond (men only) or Hampstead Pond (mixed bathing). Afterwards thirst can be quenched with a pint of best beer at the 18th c. Spaniard's Inn (Spaniard's Road), once a favourite haunt of the highwayman Dick Turpin. Anyone with an interest in art should make a special point of seeing

★ Kenwood House

Kenwood House (1616). The interior, designed and furnished by Robert Adam in 1765–69 for the Earl of Mansfield, boasts an outstanding collection of paintings belonging to Lord Iveagh, including works by Vermeer, Rembrandt, Reynolds, Turner and Gainsborough (open: Apr.–Sept. daily 10am–6pm, Oct.–Mar. till 4pm only). But Hampstead Heath is famous above all for its magnificent views over London; from the high pointest, Parliament Hill, the city lies spread out at your feet.

★★Hampton Court Palace

Location
East Molesey
Surrey,
15½ miles/25km
south-west of
London

Hampton Court, considered by many the finest of Britain's royal palaces, is situated to the south-west of London in a magnificent setting on a bend of the River Thames. It was built between 1514 and 1520 as a private residence for Cardinal Wolsey (1475–1530). When Wolsey fell from favour – having failed to secure papal blessing for Henry VIII's divorce from Catherine of Aragon – he forfeited his position and his possessions were seized. Henry took Hampton Court for himself and immediately set about enlarging it,

Hampton Court Palace

erecting the Great Hall and the buildings around Fountain Court. All Henry's wives apart from Catherine of Aragon lived in the palace as queen; the ghosts of his third and fifth wives, Jane Seymour and Catherine Howard, are said to haunt it. Elizabeth I loved Hampton Court and was staying here when news came of the defeat of the Spanish Armada. Charles I also lived at Hampton Court, both as king and as Cromwell's prisoner. The first major alterations to the palace were carried out in the reign of William and Mary. While the ranges comprising the west side of the Tudor palace remained largely untouched, those on the east side and around Fountain Court, incorporating the present State Apartments, were remodelled in the Renaissance style by Wren. The palace has been open to the public since 1838. (Open: mid Mar.–mid Oct.: Tues.–Sun. 9.30am–6pm, Mon. 10.15am–6pm; Mid Oct.–mid Mar.: Tues.–Sun. 9.30am–4.30pm, Mon 10.15am–4.30pm. The Tudor Tennis Court and Banqueting House only open mid Mar.–mid Oct.)

British Rail
Hampton Court
from Waterloo

Riverboats
Hampton Court
Bridge

The State Apartments are entered from Clock Court, access to which is through Anne Boleyn's Gateway. The great astronomical clock, which Henry VIII had made for St James's Palace in 1540, was only brought to Hampton Court in the 19th c. Approached via the King's Staircase with its superb wall paintings by Antonio Verrio, the State Apartments are embellished throughout with the work of major Baroque artists – wood carvings by Grinling Gibbons, frescoes by Antonio Verrio, wrought-ironwork by Jean Tijou and marble-work by John Nost. Among the numerous paintings from many different periods are some by Tintoretto in the King's Drawing Room and by Godfrey Kneller in the Queen's Guard Chamber. Adjoining the Queen's Apartments to the west are the old Tudor Royal Lodgings: the Chapel Royal, built in Wolsey's time and redecorated by Wren; the Haunted Gallery, frequented it is said by the ghost of Catherine Howard; and, most magnificent of all, the Great Hall, built between 1531 and 1536, with its hammerbeam roof and 16th c. Flemish tapestries depicting the story of

Interior

Hampton Court Palace

State Apartments

1 King's Staircase
2 King's Guard Chamber
3 Wolsey Rooms
4 King's First Presence Chamber
5 King's Second Presence Chamber
6 Audience Chamber
7 King's Drawing Room
8 William III's State Bedroom
9 King's Dressing Room
10 King's Writing Closet
11 Queen Mary's Closet
12 Queen's Gallery
13 Queen's Bedroom
14 Queen's Drawing Room
15 Queen's Audience Chamber
16 Public Dining Room
17 Prince of Wales's Presence Chamber
18 Prince of Wales's Drawing Room
19 Prince of Wales's Bedroom
20 Prince of Wales's Staircase
21 Queen's Private Chapel
22 Queen's Bathing Closet
23 Queen's Private Dining Room

24 Queen's Private Dressing Room
25 King George II's Dressing Room
26 King George II's Private Chamber
27 Cartoon Gallery
28 Communication Gallery
29 Wolsey Closet
30 Cumberland Suite
31 Queen's Staircase
32 Queen's Guard Chamber
33 Queen's Presence Chamber
34 Haunted Gallery
35 Royal Pew
36 Chapel Royal
37 Great Watching Chamber
38 Horn Room
39 Great Hall
40 Great Kitchen
41 Wolsey's Kitchen

a Entrance to the Kitchen and
  the King's Wine Cellar
b Entrance to the Renaissance
  Picture Gallery

Abraham from cartoons by Bernaert van Orley. Wolsey's Closet still has its original furnishings.

Kitchens and cellars	Some idea of what was involved in provisioning a palace of this size, with 500 or more mouths to feed, can be gained from the scale of the kitchens, brewery-cum-beer cellar and wine cellar.
Tudor Tennis Court	One of the palace's more unusual features is a Real Tennis court dating from Tudor times and still in regular use.
Renaissance Picture Gallery	This gallery (entrance in the south-west corner of Clock Court) contains a fine collection of paintings including works by Correggio, Parmigianino, Tintoretto and Lucas Cranach ("Judgment of Paris").

The Food Hall in Harrods

Thorough exploration of the park and gardens requires time. But be sure to see the Kings' Privy Garden, the Fountain Garden (laid out in the reign of William of Orange), the Tudor and Elizabethan Knot Garden, and the Broadwalk designed by Wren. The gardens are at their loveliest in mid May when the flowers are in full bloom. Two major attractions not to be missed are the gigantic 200-year old Great Vine, planted in a hothouse beside the Thames by the landscape gardener Capability Brown and famous even then; and the equally famous Hampton Court maze, ever-popular with children, laid out in its present form in 1714.

Park

Perhaps the biggest surprise of all, however, awaits those entering the Lower Orangery, overlooking the Thames. For inside is a masterpiece of European art, Andrea Mantegna's (1431-1506) great cycle of nine huge paintings "The Triumph of Caesar", purchased by Charles I in 1629.

Lower Orangery

★Harrods

D4

With the exception of the Tower of London, the British Museum, Buckingham Palace, Westminster Abbey and Big Ben, Harrods, the department store established by Charles Henry Harrod in 1849, is the most visited attraction in London; not to see it is certainly a pity. Mr Harrod's original modest shop has grown into a national institution with 1,200,000sq.ft/111,500 sq.m of sales floor and 4000 employees proudly maintaining the company motto "All things for everyone everywhere". Harrods now belongs to the Egyptian Mohamed al-Fayed, father of the late Dodi, who was a friend of Diana, Princess of Wales. A visit to Harrods is an experience and an event rolled into one. Fortnum & Mason may outdo it in elegance – unlike their Piccadilly rivals, Harrods employees do not wear tail coats to work – but the temple to consumerism in the Brompton Road has its own inimitable style. Indeed Harrods is no longer just a very grand department store; it is something

Location
87-135 Brompton Road,
Knightsbridge, SW1

Underground station
Knightsbridge

to be seen in its own right. What more than anything distinguishes Harrods from its rivals is that Harrods supply everything; and what they do not have they will order, even the proverbial white elephant! This unswerving willingness to oblige is a tradition much appreciated by wealthy Londoners, including the Royal Family, and explains why the green-liveried Harrods delivery vans are so often to be seen drawing up at their doors.

It would be quite misleading to think, however, that Harrods is only for the rich: "all things for everyone" remember is the motto! But there's no denying that luxury is Harrods' main attraction and the principal reason why crowds of foreign visitors push their way through its doors under the watchful eye of the security staff. Conditional on no shorts or skimpy tops, no slung rucksacks, and no photographs, they are free to wander wide-eyed through the store; through the Egyptian Hall with its costliest of furnishings, the vast perfumerie, the expensive gifts for men, and the sports department supplying the very best in clothing and equipment for the cricketer, golfer and polo player (not to mention the odd pair of trainers as well). Then there is the toy department (everything from marbles to a scaled-down Ferrari for some lucky child), the school uniform department (very British), and any one of nearly 300 others. Most magnificent of all are the Victorian food halls on the ground floor. It would be an insult to refer to them as "the food section". These opulantly decorated halls are more of a cathedral to fine food. There can be few who fail to succumb to temptation before the mouthwatering selection of dozens of Italian salamis, French cheeses and English biscuits. What more delightful than to leave Harrods' food halls with a bulging carrier bag to partake of luncheon on the grass in nearby Hyde Park.

★Highgate Cemetery

Location
Swain's Lane, N6

Underground station
Archway

This best known of London's cemeteries, situated in the elegant north London suburb of Highgate, a little to the east of Hampstead (see entry), was laid out in 1839 and is still in use. After many years of neglect the west side has been restored by the Friends of Highgate Cemetery. With its overgrown graves it is a haunting but also an enchanting place. Here can be seen the entire gamut of Victorian monumental sculpture, from the tomb of Julius Beer, proprietor of the "Observer", modelled on the Mausoleum at Halicarnassus, to memorials inspired by the tombs of the Egyptian kings along what is known as "Egyptian Avenue". Among the more than 160,000 people who lie buried in Highgate are many major figures including the physicist Michael Farraday, the novelist George Eliot, the philosopher Herbert Spencer and the actor Ralph Richardson. Most famous of all is Karl Marx, whose final resting place is on the east side of the cemetery.

Access

Only the east side has unrestricted access (eastern entrance: Apr.–Oct. Mon.–Fri. 10am–5pm, Sat and Sun. 11am–5pm; Nov.–Mar. till 4pm), access to the Victorian west side being by guided tour only (western entrance: Mar.–Oct. Mon.–Fri. noon, 2pm, 4pm, Sat. and Sun. hourly 11am–4pm; Nov. Mon.–Fri. noon, 2pm, 3pm, Sat. and Sun. hourly 11am–3pm; Dec.–Feb. Sat. and Sun. hourly 11am–3pm). Both are closed on 25 and 26 December and during funerals. Permission is required to take still photographs and video cameras are forbidden.

★★Houses of Parliament (Palace of Westminster) G4

Location
Parliament Square, SW1

The Houses of Parliament, seat of the House of Commons and the House of Lords, are officially known as the Palace of Westminster, recalling the fact that they occupy the site of a former royal palace built originally by Edward the Confessor and enlarged by William Rufus who, in 1097–99, also built Westminster Hall. The palace was almost completely destroyed by a cata-

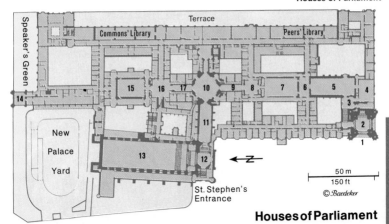

Houses of Parliament

1 Royal Entrance	7 House of Lords	12 St Stephen's Porch
2 Victoria Tower	8 Peers' Lobby	13 Westminster Hall
3 Norman Porch	9 Peers' Corridor	14 Clock Tower (Big Ben)
4 Robing Room	10 Central Lobby	15 House of Commons
5 Royal Gallery	11 St Stephen's Hall	16 Commons' Lobby
6 Prince's Chamber		17 Commons' Corridor

strophic fire in 1512 when only Westminster Hall, the 14th c. St Stephen's Chapel, and crypt survived. Until 1529 when Henry VIII acquired the neighbouring Whitehall Palace, the Palace of Westminster was a royal residence. In 1547 it became the seat of Parliament, the Commons meeting in St Stephen's Chapel and the Lords in a hall at the southern end of Old Palace Yard. In 1605 a group of Roman Catholic conspirators led by Guy Fawkes tried to blow up the Houses of Parliament in what became known as the Gunpowder Plot; to this day, before the State Opening of Parliament, the vaults beneath the Palace of Westminster are searched by Yeomen of the Guard in their traditional uniform.

The present Houses of Parliament – in Neo-Gothic style to harmonise with the nearby Westminster Abbey (see entry) – were built between 1840 and 1888 to the design of Sir Charles Barry. Though officially opened in 1852, building was finally completed only in 1888. Badly damaged by bombing during the Second World War, the Commons Chamber was rebuilt between 1948 and 1950 in the original style.

At the north end of the Houses of Parliament stands the clock tower known as Big Ben, the most celebrated London landmark after Tower Bridge, recognised the world over. Though used to refer to the clock tower as a whole, "Big Ben" is actually the name of the bell which chimes the hours. Weighing 13½ tons, it is possible it took its name from Sir Benjamin Hall, a member of Parliament who was Commissioner of Works from 1855–58 and whose name was on the side of the first bell that cracked. The tower was completed in 1859, is 320ft/97.5m high, with a flight of 334 steps leading up to the clock, the dials of which are almost 23ft/7m in diameter and the minute hands nearly 14ft/4.2m long. The chimes of Big Ben became known throughout the world when the BBC adopted them as its time signal, in 1923.

The architectural counterpoint to Big Ben at the southern end of the Palace of Westminster is the Victoria Tower, the largest and tallest square tower in the world. Built in 1858 it is 75ft/23m square and 335ft/102m tall. When Parliament is sitting the Union Jack flies from the top of the tower.

Underground Station
Westminster

Big Ben

Victoria Tower

The Houses of Parliament: Heart of British Democracy

Jewel Tower

The Jewel Tower, across Old Palace Yard from the Victoria Tower, is one of the few surviving remnants of the medieval Palace of Westminster. Now a museum, it was built in 1366 by Henry Yvele as a repository for the king's private wealth (as distinct from the Crown Jewels and public treasury), continuing in that use until the death of Henry VIII. From the early 17th c. it was used to store the records of the House of Lords and between 1869 and 1938 was occupied by the Weights & Measures Department of the Board of Trade. Badly damaged during the Second World War the tower was afterwards restored (1948–56) to its original appearance. The small vaulted rooms now house an exhibition on the Palace of Westminster past and present (open: Apr.–Sept. daily 10am–6pm, Oct.–Mar. 10am–1pm and 2–4pm).

Westminster Bridge

The best view of the Houses of Parliament is gained from Westminster Bridge, which crosses the river from the foot of Big Ben. Designed by Thomas Page and constructed in 1856–62, it replaced an old stone bridge which was the second to be built across the Thames, only London Bridge (see entry) being older. A sculptural group opposite Big Ben depicts the East Anglian Queen Boadicea.

Admission

Attending sessions

The Palace of Westminster can be visited only by arrangement with a Member of Parliament; even then the Royal Chambers remain closed to the public. When Parliament is in session however (mid Oct. to July), it is possible to attend debates in the House of Lords and the House of Commons. Admission times: House of Lords: Mon.–Wed. from 2.40pm, Thur. from 3pm, Fri. from 11am; House of Commons: Mon.–Thur. from 4.15pm,

(some Wed. from 9.30am), Fri. from 9.30am (if there is a sitting). Intending visitors should arrive in good time and wait at the St Stephen's entrance on the west side. Having been issued with an appropriate pass from the Admission Order Office in St Stephen's Hall, they will be conducted to the Strangers' Gallery of the respective House.

The Royal Entrance, a 52ft/16m-high doorway to the Victoria Tower, is used by the sovereign on ceremonial occasions such as the State Opening of Parliament (an annual event, usually in November).

Royal Chambers
Royal Entrance

From the entrance the Royal Staircase leads up to the Norman Porch, with statues and frescoes of Norman rulers.

Norman Porch

Adjoining the Porch is the sovereign's Robing Room, 59ft/18m long and decorated in the style of the early Victorian period. Notable features include the frescoes, the panelling carved with the badges and coats of arms of successive monarchs, the fireplace made from several different kinds of marble, and the chair of state dating from Queen Victoria's time.

Robing Room

The 118ft/36m Royal Gallery boasts an elaborate ceiling and a frieze with the arms of English and Scottish monarchs. On the walls are two monumental frescoes by Daniel Maclise, "The Death of Nelson" and "The Meeting of Wellington and Blücher after Waterloo". The adjoining Prince's Chamber is the sovereign's anteroom to the House of Lords. The panelled walls are adorned with portraits of the Tudor monarchs and members of their families with, below, bas-reliefs of scenes from their reigns. Opposite

Royal Gallery

Prince's Chamber

the entrance is a white marble statue of Queen Victoria, flanked by figures of Justice and Mercy.

Westminster Hall

Westminster Hall was spared by the fire in 1299 which destroyed the old Palace of Westminster. The 259ft/79m-long, 98ft/30m-high hall was nevertheless rebuilt by Henry Yvele one hundred years later during Richard II's reign. Its most impressive feature is the oak hammerbeam roof (late 14th c.), faithfully restored after being severely damaged during the Second World War.

Westminster Hall has been the scene of some of the great moments in English history. From 1224 to 1892 it was the meeting place of the highest courts in the land and witnessed many famous trials, including those of Richard II (1399), Sir Thomas More (1535) and Charles I (1649). Oliver Cromwell was installed as Lord Protector here in 1653.

St Stephen's Hall

Visitors on their way to attend a parliamentary debate pass through St Stephen's Hall. It stands on the site of the old St Stephen's Chapel where, from 1547 until 1834, the Commons used to meet. The 31m/102ft-long vaulted hall enriched with mosaics depicting the founding of the chapel by King Stephen, contains statues of Norman and Plantagenet kings and queens and of British statesmen of the 17th–19th c.

On entering via St Stephen's Porch a view of Westminster Hall is obtained.

House of Lords
Peer's Lobby

The Peers' Lobby is the anteroom to the House of Lords where members assemble before and after debates. The square chamber has a fine pavement of encaustic tiles. Above the doors are the arms of the six royal houses.

Central Lobby

From the Peers' Lobby the Peers' Corridor leads into the Central Lobby, an elaborately decorated octagonal vestibule with vaulted ceiling 82ft/25m high, situated mid way between the Lords and the Commons.

A sitting of Parliament

The chamber of the House of Lords is sumptuously decorated with red leather benches for the peers, the famous "Woolsack" (recalling the importance of the English wool trade from the 14th c. onwards) on which the Lord Chancellor traditionally sits, and the throne used by the sovereign at the opening of Parliament. The galleries above the throne are for distinguished visitors, those above the north entrance for press and public.

Chamber of the House of Lords

The recesses to the rear of the galleries are embellished with frescoes depicting (south end) scenes from British history and (north end) symbols of Justice, Religion and Chivalry. In the window niches are statues of the barons who in 1215 forced King John to sign the Magna Carta.

The anteroom to the House of Commons where members assemble before and after debates is known as the Commons' or Members' Lobby. The square chamber in Gothic style is adorned with statues of 20th c. statesmen, including bronze figures of Sir Winston Churchill and David Lloyd George. It is entered from the Central Lobby along the Commoners' Corridor.

House of Commons
Commons' or Members' Lobby

The chamber of the House of Commons, destroyed by bombing in 1941, was meticulously restored. The seating arrangement is ideal for debate. At the north end is the chair of black Australian wood occupied by the Speaker, whose responsibility it was in earlier days to "speak" for the Commons in their dealings with the monarch. With contentious matters such as taxation at issue, this could be a hazardous undertaking and to this day a newly elected Speaker is expected to put on a show of reluctance as he or she is led to the chair for the first time.

Chamber of the House of Commons

The members of the governing and opposition parties sit facing each other across the chamber on parallel rows of green benches (nowadays there is insufficient room to seat every member). Between them is the table of the House, on which the mace is placed during sittings of the Commons. On the carpet between the front benches are two red lines, traditionally said to be two sword-lengths apart, originally designed to prevent members coming to blows. Occupants of the front benches today confine themselves to hurling order papers across the floor and noisily expressing agreement or otherwise with fellow members' speeches.

Commons debates are public and since 1989 have been televised, an innovation considered almost revolutionary at the time. The opening of each day's sitting is announced by a cry of "Speaker! Hats off – strangers!", marking the passing of the Speaker's procession – the Speaker attired in a wig and long black robe, preceded by a messenger and Serjeant-at-Arms in knee-breeches carrying the mace, and followed by the Speaker's train-bearer, chaplain and secretary. (The present Speaker is the first woman to hold that office. She is addressed as "Madam Speaker" and continues to wear the official robes but not the wig.) The proceedings begin with a prayer read by the chaplain following which the public are admitted to the Strangers' Gallery.

Proceedings

Hyde Park · Kensington Gardens · Kensington Palace   C–E 3/4

★★ Hyde Park

Hyde Park, having been at different times a royal deer-park, a parade ground and scene of many a duel, is nowadays the place where Londoners relax, enjoying sports of various kinds, picnicking, taking the air, or just doing nothing. A stroll through the park is a pleasure at any time of day, especially in summer. In the morning it is relatively peaceful, with few walkers, horse-riders or joggers on the paths; at lunchtime workers from nearby offices eat their sandwiches on the benches; while in the evening footballers and the sun-hungry take to the grass. "Keep off the grass" signs are non existent.

Location
west of the City

Underground Stations
Hyde Park Corner,
Marble Arch,
Lancaster Gate

V&A Museum

Together with Kensington Gardens which adjoin it to the west, the park forms the largest open space in London; east–west in orientation, 1¼ miles/2km in length and ½ mile/900m across. Originally belonging to Westminster Abbey (see entry), it was taken over by Henry VIII in 1536 and became a royal deer-park. Charles II threw it open to the public in 1635. In the 17th and 18th c. in particular it was the place where wealthy Londoners would drive in their carriages for the express purpose of being seen (despite the considerable risk at one time of robbery). In 1851 Hyde Park was the venue for the Great Exhibition.

The main entrance to the park, at Hyde Park Corner (see entry), is a triple archway by Decimus Burton (1828), with a reproduction of the Parthenon frieze (see British Museum). Near by is a statue of Achilles (by Richard Westmacott, 1822) erected in honour of the Duke of Wellington and cast from French cannon captured by the "Iron Duke". Westmacott modelled his Achilles on the figure of the horse-tamer from the Quirinal in Rome. Close by is a bandstand, where bands play on Sunday in summer. From Hyde Park Corner three roads run through the park. The Carriage Road, to the left, leads to the Albert Memorial in Kensington Gardens; the East Carriage Road, to the right, leads to Marble Arch and Speakers' Corner; and the road in the middle runs west to the Serpentine, the lake which Queen Caroline of Ansbach, wife of George II, created by damming the little river Westbourne. On the south side of the lake is a lido and to the north a bird sanctuary with, next to it, Epstein's figure of "Rima", bird-girl heroine of W. H. Hudson's novel, "Green Mansions". Between the Serpentine and Carriage Road is the sand-strewn bridle-path called Rotten Row – probably a

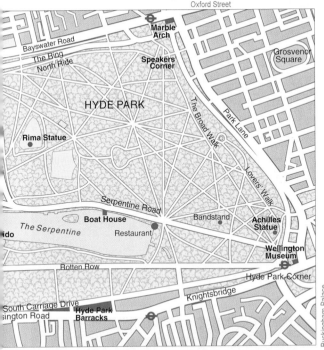

corruption of the French "Route du Roi", this being the route taken by the sovereign when driving from Kensington Palace to Whitehall.

Since 1872 Speakers' Corner in the north-east corner of the park has been a forum of free speech where anyone with a grievance or a mission can find an audience. It is particularly busy on Saturdays and Sunday afternoons when numbers of soapbox orators address large groups of listeners or one or two indifferent bystanders with equal eloquence. The themes are usually religious or political and speakers are frequently exposed to lively heckling. Jomo Kenyatta, first President of Kenya, spoke here in his younger days, and Idi Amin, later notorious as dictator of Uganda, often joined the crowd when he was an NCO in the British army.

Speakers' Corner

Opposite Speakers' Corner, Marble Arch stands on an island in the middle of London's swirling traffic. The huge triumphal arch, designed by John Nash in 1828, was modelled on the Arch of Constantine in Rome. Originally intended for the main entrance to Buckingham Palace (see entry), it was found to be too narrow to admit the state coach and so was moved here in 1851. It stands close to the site of Tyburn, from the 12th c. until 1793, London's place of execution. Criminals were brought here from the Tower or from prison to end on the gallows ("Tyburn Tree").

Marble Arch

Kensington Gardens

Kensington Gardens, once the private grounds of Kensington Palace, begin west of the bridge spanning the Serpentine. In contrast to Hyde Park they

99

A morning ride in Hyde Park

Speakers' Corner

are formal gardens, laid out in 1728–31 by Queen Caroline. They were opened to the public in 1841.

At the far end of the Long Water (Kensington Gardens' continuation of the Serpentine) is an Italian Garden with a pavilion and four ponds. At Lancaster Gate, a little further to the west, there is a small dogs' cemetery established in 1880 by the Duke of Cambridge. Quite the most charming memorial in Kensington Gardens however stands half way down the west side of the Long Water – George Frampton's delightful 1912 statue of Peter Pan. Around the "boy who never grew up" are gathered all his friends from the world of animals and fairy-tale. From there a path leads directly to the Serpentine Gallery (exhibitions of contemporary art; open: daily 10am–6pm; admission free).

★Statue of Peter Pan

Serpentine Gallery

This memorial to Albert of Saxe-Coburg-Gotha (1819–61), prince-consort of Queen Victoria, stands close to the southern boundary of Kensington Gardens. Designed by Sir George Gilbert Scott, it was built in 1863–72 but only unveiled by Queen Victoria in 1876 when the seated bronze statue of Prince Albert was completed. The Queen had originally hoped for a monument in the form of a huge monolithic granite obelisk, to be financed by public subscription. In the event the amount collected was insufficient and the present more modest monument, in the Neo-Gothic style of the period, was built instead. The larger than life-size figure of Prince Albert is located under a richly decorated 190ft/58m-high canopy, holding in his hand the catalogue of the 1851 Exhibition which he had done so much to promote. His gaze is directed towards South Kensington and the great national museums which likewise owe their existence largely to him. Around the pedestal are 178 marble reliefs of artists and men of letters of every period (not a single woman appears among them). At the corners of the pedestal are sculptured groups symbolising Industry, Engineering, Commerce and Agriculture, and at the outer corners of the steps are other groups symbolising the continents of Europe, Asia, Africa and America.

Albert Memorial

By the 1980s the monument had become unsafe due to decay and in 1990 was enclosed by protective scaffolding. After eight years hidden from public view the monument was again revealed in October 1998 following a restoration costing over £11 million. Access to the steps of the memorial is free while a guided tour is also available (infrequent in winter months: tel. 0171 495 0916 for times and charges).

Kensington Palace   C4

Kensington Palace, private residence of the monarch from 1689 to 1760, is situated at the western end of Kensington Gardens. About half the rooms continue to be occupied by members of the Royal Family and by pensioners of the Crown granted "grace and favour" apartments.

Opening times:
daily 10am–4pm

The original house was purchased in 1605 by William III, who commissioned Wren to convert it for use as the monarch's private residence. George I made the palace his official residence, after completion of the rebuilding by Colen Campbell and of the interior by William Kent. After the death of George II the palace reverted to its present use. Here Queen Victoria was born and learned of her accession to the throne; Queen Mary, grandmother of the present Queen, was also born here. William and Mary both died in the palace, as did Queen Anne and George II.

The statue of William III close to the south of the palace was presented to Edward VII by Emperor Wilhelm II of Germany. On the east side there is a memorial to Queen Victoria.

The Orangery (1704), just to the north of the palace, was attributed to Wren but is probably by Nicholas Hawksmoor. Inside are carvings by Grinling Gibbons.

Orangery

Queen of Hearts

There can be no explanation for the scenes which were witnessed between Kensington Palace and Westminster on September 6th 1997. More than one and a half million people lined the route followed by the cortege of Diana, Princess of Wales. London was virtually drowned in a sea of flowers; men and women for whom Diana's life must have seemed like that of someone from another planet dissolved into tears as they bade farewell to the world's most famous lady. The news of her death released a flood of mourning and dismay unequalled in this century even by the death of the late John F. Kennedy. He too was young and well-loved, he too died a pointless death which made him a legend; Diana, however, had already become a legend in her own lifetime and the most public person of the 1990s.

When she married the future king of Great Britain in St Paul's Cathedral on July 29th 1989 she was perhaps not fully ware of what lay ahead. The country needed an heir to the throne and a son was soon born, to be followed by a younger brother, but by then the marriage was in difficulty. Her husband devoted himself to those matters with which the heir to the throne has to concern himself ... official engagements and sporting activities. The photographs and headlines which followed are known only too well. Diana's life became public property and she appeared unable to meet the standards required of the wife of a future king.

In 1992 she revealed her feelings – in confidence, allegedly – to a journalist, who published "Her True Story". She opened her heart in a television interview and did something hitherto regarded as outrageous – she effectively opened the doors of Buckingham Palace to the world and showed that the Windsors were merely mortals. To everyone's amazement she appeared to gain strength from the situation. In December 1992 she and Prince Charles separated and in 1996 the divorce was finalised. However, this did not mean that Diana was free, for she found herself constantly harassed by the paparazzi – right up until that fatal night when life ended against a concrete pillar in Paris.

The warmth and affection for which she craved was given to her by the public at large. She had succeeded in bridging the gulf between herself and the "common people". Her personal misfortunes made her sharing in the troubles and grief of others – those suffering from Aids, victims of mining tragedies, sick children – appear genuinely to come from the heart. On her death, contrary to protocol, Her Majesty Queen Elizabeth personally ordered that the flag over Buckingham Palace should fly at half mast as a sign of mourning, and she also spoke to the British people on the eve of the funeral. Diana will ever remain the Queen of Hearts in the minds of the British people.

The State Apartments on the first floor are open to the public; they are mostly furnished in the style of the 17th and 18th c. There is also a unique exhibition of court dress and other royal robes. There are plans for an exhibition in memory of Princess Diana.

State Apartments

The Queen's Staircase, designed by Wren in 1690, leads to the Queen's Gallery, a room with oak panelling and decorated with royal portraits.

Queen's Gallery

There follows a suite of rooms – dining-room, living room, study and bedroom – used by Queens Victoria, Mary and Anne. All the rooms contain personal possessions of the three queens.

Apartments

Passing through a number of rooms used by Kings William III, George I and George II, the visitor approaches King William's Gallery by way of the King's Grand Staircase, with trompe-l'œil paintings by Kent. The Gallery, 105ft/32m/ long, was designed by Wren in 1694. In it are pictures of 18th and 19th c. London, a ceiling painting by Kent ("Adventures of Ulysses") and woodcarvings by Grinling Gibbons.

King William's Gallery

Of particular interest in the Victorian rooms adjoining are: the blue and gold-domed Cupola Room where Queen Victoria was baptised; the King's Drawing Room with a clock of 1730 representing the "Temple of the Four Monarchies" (Assyria, Persia, Greece and Rome); and the Council Chamber with memorabilia of the Great Exhibition.

Victorian rooms

Hyde Park Corner

E 4

Hyde Park Corner is one of the busiest junctions in London, with roads leading north to Marble Arch and Oxford Street (see entry), south-east to Buckingham Palace (see entry), west to the Royal Albert Hall (see entry) and south-west to Kensington, Brompton (for Harrods, see entry), the Victoria and Albert Museum (see entry) and the Natural History Museum (see entry).

Location
at the south-east corner of the park

Underground Station
Hyde Park Corner

At Hyde Park Corner stands the **Wellington Arch**, a monumental triumphal arch (1828) by Decimus Burton commemorating the Duke of Wellington's (1769–1852) victory at Waterloo. The arch is surmounted by a bronze quadriga (four-horse chariot) with a figure of Peace, placed here in 1912 when the original statue of Wellington was moved.

Wellington Arch
Wellington Monument

At the same time a new memorial to Wellington was erected facing Apsley House (see below) – a bronze equestrian statue of the Duke on his horse "Copenhagen" with, at the corners of the pedestal, figures of a Grenadier Guard, a Scottish Highlander, a Welsh Fusilier and an Inniskillin Dragoon.

There are two other war memorials at Hyde Park Corner: the Royal Artillery War Memorial (1928) and the Machine Gun Corps War Memorial (1927) with a figure of the biblical King David.

War memorials

Apsley House · ★Wellington Museum

Mounted on his bronze steed the figure of the Duke of Wellington gazes towards Apsley House, his London home for many years. The house was built between 1771 and 1778 by Robert Adam for Baron Apsley, later Lord Bathurst. In 1807 it was bought by the Marquess Wellesley, the first Duke of

Opening times
Tues.–Sun.
11am–5pm

The Wellington Arch commemorating his triumph at Waterloo

Wellington's elder brother, from the third Earl of Bathurst and was bought by Wellington from his brother after his victory at Waterloo. The Duke made many changes to the house: originally of red brick, it was refaced with Bath stone in 1828/29 by Benjamin Dean Wyatt, who also added the Corinthian portico and the famous Waterloo Gallery in which the Waterloo Banquet was held annually until the Duke's death. In 1947 Apsley House was presented to the nation by the seventh Duke of Wellington and in 1952 was opened to the public as the Wellington Museum and is a branch of the Victoria and Albert Museum (see entry). Closed latterly for major refurbishment, the house was reopened in the summer of 1995.

There are numerous memorabilia of the "Iron Duke" whose marble bust stands in the entrance hall. Particularly noteworthy among the many works of art are paintings by Velazquez ("The Waterseller of Seville") and Landseer ("The Illicit Highland whisky Still"). The Prussian Dinner and Dessert Service made by the Berlin Porcelain Manufactory and presented to the Duke by King Frederick William III following Waterloo can be seen in the Plate & China Room as well as the great gifts of porcelain from other European monarchs, pieces from vast silver and silver-gilt Services, presentation plate, gold boxes, swords, batons and Napoleon's flags and eagles.

The 90ft/27m long Waterloo Gallery was not only built as a suitable setting for the annual Waterloo Banquet but also to display the First Duke's magnificent collection of paintings, many of which Wellington recovered from Joseph Bonaparte's baggage train following the Battle of Vitoria in 1813 and which were subsequently presented to him by the Spanish king. The paintings had been looted from the Spanish royal palaces by Napoleon's soldiers and included works by Velazquez, Murillo, Rubens, van Dyck, Jan Breughel and Correggio's "The Agony in the Garden". The duke also collected Dutch and Flemish 17th century masters as well as works by contemporary British artists such as Wilkie and Landseer and portraits of his companions in arms. The famous equestrian portrait of the Duke by Goya also hangs in the Waterloo Gallery.

Unquestionably the most impressive of all the exhibits in the museum however is the two times life-size figure of Napoleon by Canova. Removed to London from the Louvre it shows Wellington's adversary wearing only a fig leaf.

★ Imperial War Museum   H 4

The Imperial War Museum was founded in 1920 and moved to its present premises in the old Bethlehem Royal Hospital in Lambeth's Geraldine Mary Harmsworth Park in 1936. Two massive naval guns, barrels pointing skyward, guard the entrance to the domed building. Documenting British military history from the First World War onwards, the collection has recently undergone complete reorganisation.

Location
Lambeth Road SE1

Underground Stations
Lambeth North, Elephant & Castle

HMS "Belfast" (see entry), the Cabinet War Rooms (see Whitehall) and the aircraft museum at Duxford near Cambridge, are all branches of the Imperial War Museum.

Opening times
daily 10am–6pm

The hub of the museum is the large exhibition hall housing aircraft, tanks and artillery from the two World Wars. These include Field Marshal Montgomery's command tank, a German Jagdpanther tank, a British Spitfire, a German Focke-Wulf FW 190, an American P-51 Mustang, a German one-man submarine and German V1 and V2 rockets. St Paul's (see entry) may be spied through a giant First World War periscope.

Large Exhibits Gallery

Visitors enjoy a close-up view of aircraft from the galleries encircling the hall. Also on display is the cockpit of a Lancaster bomber. Paintings from period of the two World Wars can be seen in the upper rooms.

Galleries

Imperial War Museum: Spitfire, FW 190 and a Mustang

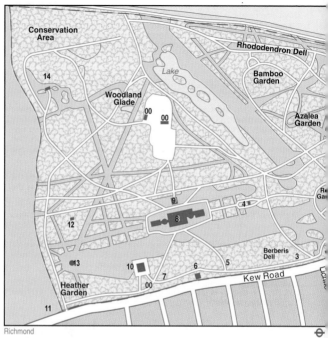

Richmond

1 Victoria Gate Center
2 Temple of Arethusa
3 Temple of Bellona
4 King William's Temple
5 Flag Pole

6 Marianne North Gallery
7 Ruined Arch
8 Temperate House
9 Evolution House
10 Restaurant

11 Lion Gate
12 Chinese Pagoda
13 Japanese Gateway
14 Queen Charlotte's Cottage
15 Palm House

Basement

The basement houses an "Historical Exhibition" which chronicles the First and Second World Wars by highlighting critical events. The impact tends to be lessened however by the excessive zeal shown in gathering together weapons, equipment, decorations and uniforms from every country involved. On the other hand the museum has managed to acquire some unique exhibits e.g. the djellaba (Arab garment) worn by Lawrence of Arabia and a copy of Hitler's will.

The Blitz Experience

"The Blitz Experience", also in the basement, is the recreation of a raid by German bombers during the height of the London "Blitz". Conditions in an air-raid shelter are vividly conveyed, as is the scene in the blazing streets above.

The Trench Experience

"The Trench Experience" similarly evokes conditions in a First World War trench.

Belsen 1945

There is a very moving little section documenting the liberation of the Bergen-Belsen concentration camp by British troops.

Operation Jericho

A flight simulator that gives the impression of flying a Royal Air Force plane on a bombing raid over Europe during the Second World War.

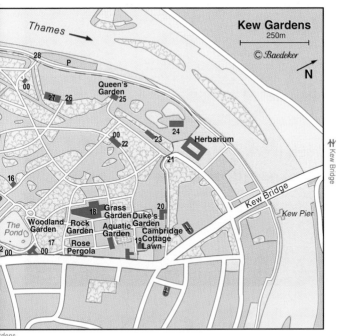

Kew Gardens

Thames →

250m

© *Baedeker*

N

Queen's Garden

Herbarium

Kew Bridge

Kew Pier

Grass Garden Duke's
Garden
The Pond
Woodland Rock Aquatic
Garden Garden Garden Cambridge
Cottage
Rose Lawn
Pergola

'dens

Waterlily House	20 Kew Gardens Gallery	24 Sir Joseph Banks Building
Temple of Aeolus	21 Main Gate	25 Kew Palace
Princess of Wales	22 Orangery &	26 Bakery
Conservatory	Filmy Fern House	27 Cycad House
Alpine House	23 Nash Conservatory	28 Brentford Gate

Uncovers the clandestine world of espionage, intelligence gathering and the work of Britain's special forces from 1909 to the present day.

Secret War

Highlights the many conflicts that have taken place since the end of the Second World War, including the Gulf War and the War in Bosnia (opens June 1996).

Conflicts Since 1945

★★Kew Gardens (Royal Botanic Gardens)

A day in Kew Gardens, officially known as the Royal Botanic Gardens, on the south bank of the Thames south-west of London, should not be missed by any visitor to the capital. Here is escape from the hectic pace of the city, an oasis of greenery and Victorian leisureliness disturbed only by the noise of aircraft approaching nearby Heathrow airport, their flight paths so low as almost to be able to see in through their windows. Beneath its surface tranquillity however, Kew is a hive of research and other activity. Every year some 80,000 plants are examined and identified; specimens and information are exchanged with botanists and botanical institutions all over the world; and more than 44,000 plants are grown – equal to one sixth of all the plant species on earth and including 13 already extinct in the wild and more than 1000 varieties under threat. Here, too, the Brazilian rubber

Location
Kew Road, Kew
Surrey

Underground Station
Kew Gardens

British Rail
Kew Bridge

Riverboats
Kew

Kew Gardens: The Palm House . . .

. . . exotic plants in the Temperate House

tree was adapted to the climate of the Malay peninsula, and the Marquis strain of wheat was developed opening up the prairies of north-west Canada to cultivation. The herbarium contains a collection of over 6 million dried plants and the library has more than 750,000 volumes of botanical literature. Both are open for study purposes.

Opening times
9.30am–6.30pm;
Winter: daily
9.30am–4pm

The gardens were first laid out in 1759 on the initiative of Princess Augusta, mother of George III. Then in 1773, during George III's reign, Joseph Banks, a botanist who accompanied Captain Cook around the world, was put in charge of Kew. At this time countless exotic plants were introduced, the fruit of expeditions to remote parts of the world. Under the guidance of Sir William Hooker, who became Director in 1841, the Royal Botanic Gardens achieved worldwide renown.

The new visitor centre at the Victoria Gate has information about the many activities and facilities available to the public.

Visitor Centre

The two huge Victorian glasshouses, the Palm House (recently restored) and the Temperate House (the largest glasshouse in the world at the turn of this century) were the work of the architect Decimus Burton and engineer Richard Turner and earned great acclaim at the time of their construction. Other features of particular interest in addition to the two glasshouses are the historic herb garden behind Kew Palace, the recently opened Evolution House, and (especially) the Princess of Wales Conservatory with its display of tropical plants in their natural habitat.

Glasshouses

The Marianne North Gallery houses a collection of botanical and other paintings by this Victorian artist.

Marianne North Gallery

The little Kew Palace, officially known as the Dutch House, was occupied by George III during his periods of psychological illness; his wife Charlotte Sophia also died here. The furniture, furnishings and pictures give an impression of the domestic life of the Royal Family in Georgian times (open: May–Sept. daily 11am–5.30pm).

Kew Palace

Queen Charlotte's Cottage, built for the Queen in 1772, was later a favourite residence of Queen Victoria. It stands in a garden which, at Queen Victoria's behest, was allowed to remain in its natural state as an area of woodland (open: Apr.-Sept. Sat. and Sun. 11am-5.30pm).

Queen Charlotte's Cottage

Other charming buildings in Kew Gardens include the Chinese Pagoda, built by Sir William Chambers in 1761, and the Japanese Gateway, copy of a gate in the Nishi-Honganji Temple in Kyoto, brought here from the Anglo-Japanese Exhibition of 1912 and restored in 1995.

Pagoda · Japanese Gateway

Kew Village, the area around Kew Green and Kew Gardens Underground station, should not be missed for its charming 17th and 18th c. houses and St Annes Church (burial place of the painter Thomas Gainsborough).

Kew Village

On the other side of the Thames, across Kew Bridge is Brentford, where apart from Syon House (see entry) there are two museums worth seeing.

Brentford

The Kew Bridge Steam Museum (Green Dragon Lane), easily identified by its tall tower, boasts a remarkable collection of 19th and early 20th c. steam engines, some of astonishing power. Machines like the "100 inch", the world's largest piston steam pump, were used to draw water from the Thames and are kept here in full working order (open: daily 11am–5pm; engines in steam weekends and public holidays). The Musical Museum (368 High Street) is also something quite special; it has no traditional musical instruments, only mechanical ones, including a Wurlitzer (open: Apr.–Jun., Sept. and Oct. Sat. and Sun. 2–5pm; July and Aug. Wed.–Sun. 2–5pm).

*Kew Bridge Steam Museum

Musical Museum

Lambeth Palace   G 4

Location
Lambeth Palace
Road, SE1

**Underground
Stations**
Lambeth North,
Waterloo

Lambeth Palace, for over 700 years the London seat of the Archbishops of Canterbury, stands in delightful grounds on the south side of Lambeth Bridge the next bridge upstream from Westminster Bridge (see House of Parliament). Behind the walls is a complex of domestic buildings, largely medieval and very picturesque. Despite many alterations and restorations, most recently following bomb damage during the Blitz, the house itself, which dates from the late 12th c., preserves its medieval character. Lambeth Palace is the home of the Archbishop of Canterbury and can only be visited by prior arrangement (tel. 0171–928 8282).

A view of the palace is obtained from Lambeth Bridge from where are visible Morton's Tower and the entrance gate dating from Tudor times; behind is the Great Hall and at the north end the Neo-Gothic residential wing.

**Museum of
Garden History**

The redundant church of St Mary-at-Lambeth now houses the Museum of Garden History, chiefly dedicated to the Tradescants, father and son, who were gardeners to Charles I. Both are buried in the graveyard, planted in the manner of 17th c. Admiral Bligh, sometime captain of the "Bounty", is another who lies buried here. There are exhibits on all aspects of garden history (open: 1st Sun. in Mar.–2nd Sun. in Dec. Mon.–Fri. 10.30am–4pm, Sun. 10.30am–5pm).

★ Liberty's   F 3

Location
210–220 Regent
Street, W1

**Underground
Station**
Oxford Circus

Where Harrods (see entry) prides itself on supplying virtually everything, Liberty's has no such pretensions. Quite the opposite in fact. "Not all things, but always the finest" might be Liberty's motto. Ever since 1875 when Arthur Lasenby Liberty first set up shop on the corner of Regent Street and Great Marlborough Street, Liberty's has been known as the leading store in England for fabrics, carpets, furniture and porcelain from Asia and the Orient. It quickly gained a special reputation for its silks, in patterns designed by Liberty's own artists – classic patterns even today. The selection has hardly changed and anyone who is anyone still aspires to a country cottage furnished in Liberty's style. As for tourists, there can be few more cherished souvenirs of London than a Liberty's scarf or tie.

Even if shopping at Liberty's should prove too expensive, do nevertheless pay a visit to the store. The building itself is worth seeing, from the mock-Tudor façade on Great Marlborough Street (main entrance) to the magnificent sales rooms spiralling up round the large inner court. Contributing to the homely atmosphere – typical Liberty's – is the wood panelling, made, naturally, from rather special wood salvaged from HMS Impregnable and HMS Hindustan, the last two wooden ships in service with the Royal Navy.

★ Lincoln's Inn   G/H 3

Location
Chancery Lane
WC2

**Underground
Station**
Chancery Lane

Lincoln's Inn is one of the four great Inns of Court, the others being the Middle and Inner Temple (see Temple) and Gray's Inn (see entry). It was founded in the 14th c. by the Earl of Lincoln as a residential college (inn) for young men being trained in law. Celebrated members of Lincoln's Inn have included Sir Thomas More, Oliver Cromwell, John Donne, William Pitt, Horace Walpole, John Henry Newman, George Canning, Benjamin Disraeli, William Gladstone and Herbert Henry Asquith. The Lincoln's Inn complex is the best preserved of its kind in London. In addition to extensive and beautifully kept gardens it comprises residential buildings, teaching rooms (library, lecture halls, commonrooms), the New Hall (dining-room) and the chapel. Many of the buildings are leased to barristers for use as chambers.

Before visiting Lincoln's Inn permission should be sought from the gate-keeper at the Chancery Lane entrance. There is normally access to the gardens (Mon.–Fri. 9am–6pm) and chapel (Mon.–Fri. noon–2.30pm). The chambers and library can only be viewed as part of a guided tour.

Viewing

The gatehouse (1518) is adorned with the arms of Henry VIII, the Earl of Lincoln and Sir Thomas Lovell. To the left inside the entrance are the Old Buildings, remodelled in Tudor style in 1609; straight ahead lies the Old Hall, and to the right the chapel, built by Inigo Jones in Gothic style in 1623 and radically restored by Wren in 1685. Notable features include the ancient oak pews, the 17th c. Flemish stained glass (restored), the more recent windows with the arms of prominent alumni of the Inn, and the 18th c. pulpit. The open crypt below was for many years a meeting place where barristers and law students would mingle socially and discuss their work. The Old Hall (1491), occupied until 1883 by the Court of Chancery, contains a painting by William Hogarth.

Beyond the chapel stand the New Hall and library (1497) stocked with over 80,000 volumes of law books. The Stone Buildings adjacent to the New Hall are dwelling houses occupied chiefly by barristers. Opening off to the left is New Square (1680) ringed by terraces of identical four-storey buildings.

Behind Lincoln's Inn are the tranquil gardens known as Lincoln's Inn Fields where at lunchtime barristers can be seen enjoying a break from their chambers. In Tudor and Stuart times there were gallows here. Then in 1640 the fields were acquired by a certain William Newton, who erected the first houses. The buildings around the gardens today date mainly from the 18th c. Sir John Soane's Museum (see entry) at No. 13 is a real curiosity and well worth a visit.

Lincoln's Inn
Fields

★ Lloyds of London

K 3

The insurance undertaking Lloyds can look back on a tradition which has lasted for 300 years. It originated in a coffee house owned by one Edward Lloyd, where ship's masters, shipowners and merchants used to meet to arrange insurance for their vessels and cargoes. Lloyds is not an insurance company in the normal sense of the term but an organisation under the auspices of which member agents ("brokers") arrange insurance with "underwriters" acting on behalf of syndicates of wealthy "names", who put up capital and accept unlimited liability.

Location
Lime Street, EC3

Underground Stations
Bank, Monument, Aldgate

Lloyds Tower, opened by Her Majesty Queen Elizabeth II in 1986 and designed by Richard Rogers, architect of the Pompidou Centre in Paris, remains the most striking piece of new architecture in London. The novelty of Roger's design is that the services – lifts, stairs, pipework, etc. – are all on the outside, giving the building a thoroughly bizarre appearance. Only at the Leadenhall Street entrance is any part of the 1928 façade preserved. The clean lines of the fourteen storeyed 250ft/76m-high atrium counteract the otherwise total lack of external homogeneity. Business is conducted in the Underwriting Room, in the centre of which, just as in the old Lloyds Building, stands the so-called "rostrum" with the famous Lutine Bell. Recovered from the French frigate "Lutine", which sank in 1799 with a cargo of silver insured at Lloyds, the bell used to be rung once on receipt of bad news, twice on receipt of good. Nowadays it is rung only on special occasions. Near by is a tall desk on which lies an account book, focus of another traditional practice maintained to this day: whenever a ship insured at Lloyds sinks, the loss is entered in the book, using a quill pen.

Since an IRA bomb was found in the viewing gallery the interior of the building has been closed to the public.

No viewing

Lombard Street

The Lloyds Building

Leadenhall Market

A market has been held in Leadenhall ever since the Middle Ages. Long before that it was the site of Londinium's Roman forum. The present Victorian indoor hall was built by Sir Horace Jones in 1881. The market pub is a popular rendezvous for Lloyds clerks during their lunchbreak.

Lombard Street

Location
City, EC2

Underground Station
Bank

Lombard Street (named after the moneylenders from Lombardy who had their houses here in the 13th c.) has been London's banking and financial centre since medieval times. The street is of interest not so much for its 19th and 20th c. buildings, as for the bank signs hanging above the pavement – continuing a tradition dating from the Middle Ages when illiteracy was rife and the bankers' customers were able to identify them only by their heraldic emblems. Of course, not all the banks in Lombard Street today can claim

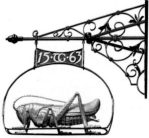

such a pedigree; some of the signs are the same, others more recent. Look out for the sign of the horse (Lloyd's, 1677), the three crowns (Coutts'), the grasshopper (formerly Martin's, 1563), the crown and anchor (National Westminster), the anchor (Williams and Glyn's), the artichoke (Alexander's) and the eagle (Barclay's).

St Mary Woolnoth

Though undistinguished from the outside, a surprise awaits anyone venturing into St Mary Woolnoth (1716–27) at the top of Lombard Street.

Beneath its blue stucco ceiling the interior is a jewel of English Baroque, rightly considered the masterpiece of Wren's pupil Nicholas Hawkesmoor.

London Bridge

"London Bridge is falling down" says the old rhyme. In fact London Bridge has never fallen down, though it has twice been pulled down and replaced by a new bridge. The medieval bridge, the bridge of the rhyme, has long since disappeared and the modern bridge hardly qualifies as a sight at all.

Location
King William
Street, EC3

Underground stations
Monument,
London Bridge

A bridge almost certainly spanned the Thames here in Roman times, remains of supports having been found close to the present bridge. The medieval bridge stood a little further to the east. Until the 18th c. it was London's only Thames crossing. Erected in the late 12th/early 13th c., the bridge was of stone construction, with 20 arches, lined on both sides with houses, shops and even a chapel. Part way across there was a drawbridge, on the south side of which the heads of traitors were publicly displayed (Sir Thomas More's included). The buildings were later removed to make room for recesses in which pedestrians took refuge from the traffic on the narrow carriageway. The London Museum (see entry) has an excellent model of the medieval bridge showing how it must have looked. In 1831 John Rennie replaced the old bridge with a new one of 5 arches, sited a little further upstream. In 1973 this was replaced in turn by the present undistinguished-looking structure. Dismantled stone by stone, Rennie's bridge was sold to an American (who, so the story goes, thought he was acquiring Tower Bridge). Shipped to the United States it was re-erected at Lake Havasu, Arizona.

The waterfront eastwards from London Bridge as far as Tower Bridge and Shad Thames beyond, has been developed as a leisure and shopping complex called "London Bridge City". A steel fountain sculpture, "The Navigators" by David Kemp, makes a striking centre-piece in the attractive arcade known as Hay's Galleria.

London Bridge
City

The old St Mary Overy Dock to the west of the bridge has also been revamped. The schooner "Kathleen and May" and a replica of Sir Francis Drake's "Golden Hind" lie alongside the quay opposite the quaint "Old Thameside Inn". There are proposals to remove the schooner to Ireland and replace it with another boat/ship.

St Mary Overy
Dock

"The Navigators" in Hay's Galleria

The London Dungeon (28–34 Tooley Street) is a gruesome display of the

London Dungeon

more horrific happenings in London and elsewhere from the Middle Ages to the 17th c. – the murder of Thomas à Becket, the Plague, the burning of martyrs at the stake and scenes of torture – accompanied by details of the historical background.

There are two multi-media shows: "Jack the Ripper Experience" allows you to retrace the steps of the notorious Victorian killer while the "Theatre of the Guillotine" recreates scenes of beheading. Many of the wax models are split open and smeared with artificial blood and children may find it rather frightening. There is a restaurant run by a fast food chain (open: daily 10am-5.30pm; Apr.-Sept. until 6.30pm).

Winston
Churchill's Britain
at War Experience

At 64–66 Tooley St. is Winston Churchill's Britain at War Experience where special effects recreate scenes of London during the Blitz of the Second World War (open: daily 10am–4.30pm; to 5.30pm Apr.–Sept.).

★London Zoo   E 1

Location
Regent's Park
NW1

Underground stations
Baker Street,
Camden Town,
then No. 274 bus

Opening times
Summer:
daily
10am–5.30pm
Winter: daily
10am–4pm

Founded in 1826 by Sir Stamford Raffles and Sir Humphrey Davy, London Zoo is among the most pleasant in the world, and with more than 6000 species one of the best-stocked. It is the most popular attraction in the capital. Owned by the Zoological Society of London it is also an internationally respected centre of research. In 1992/93 the zoo's very existence became threatened by a critical shortage of funds, leading to an announcement of intended closure in the autumn of 1993. Aided by private donations and the adoption of a new concept this extreme measure was thankfully averted.

Despite being bisected by the Regent's Canal (see entry) and the Outer Circle around Regent's Park (see entry), the unity of the Zoological Gardens is preserved (there are three bridges over the canal and two pedestrian underpasses beneath the Outer Circle). The main entrance is on the Outer Circle; the zoo can also be entered from Prince Albert Road (North Entrance) and Broad Walk (South Gate). Special attractions include Lord Snowdon's Aviary, "Moonlight World", the "Lifewatch Conservation Centre", the Children's Zoo, the "Animals in Action" show and the sea lions.

Boat trips on
Regent's Canal

Various boat trips are available on Regent's Canal passing through the zoo, departing from Little Venice or Camden Lock (see Practical Information, Boat Trips).

*Madame Tussaud's   E 2

Location
Marylebone Road
NW1

Underground station
Baker Street

Opening times
Mon.–Fri.
10a–5.30pm,
Sat. and Sun.
9.30a–5.30pm

Marie Tussaud (see Famous People), a native of Alsace, came to London from Paris in 1802, bringing with her a collection of wax figures passed down to her by the collection's German-born founder, Dr. Phillippe Curtius. Later the figures formed the nucleus of the waxworks which opened in London in 1835 and which is now famous throughout the world. In recent years Tussaud's has been extensively modernised, including re-arrangement in six sections. The entrance fee is expensive but a ticket which includes admission to the Planetarium (see below) is available at a reduced rate. In the section entitled "Garden Party" visitors encounter such luminaries as Mel Gibson and Elizabeth Taylor in conversation with Arnold Schwarzenegger. The section "200 Years of Madame Tussaud's" consists of an assortment of exhibits ranging from the original key to the Bastille and death masks of people guillotined during the French Revolution to the oldest wax figures in the collection, the "Sleeping Beauty", made in 1765. Major world figures are gathered together in the "Grand Hall" - Henry VIII and his six wives, Queen Elizabeth II and the British Royal Family, Winston

Churchill, and Mahatma Ghandhi. The recently refurbished "Chamber of Horrors" positively revels in torture and execution; as for "Hollywood Legends", the name speaks for itself. Madame Tussaud's newest attraction is an audio-animatronic journey through 400 years of London's history entitled "The Spirit of London".

Adjoining Madame Tussaud's is the London Planetarium, likewise equipped with the very latest technology. Spectacular images of the stars and planets are projected onto the inside of a huge copper dome, with an accompanying commentary (every 40 minutes, Mon.–Fri. 12.20–5pm, weekends from 10.20am). Another of the Planetarium's attractions is an interactive areas which explain the mysteries of the Universe.

London
Planetarium

The Mall   F/G 3/4

The Mall, impressively wide, is today a grand thoroughfare along which the sovereign drives from Buckingham Palace to take part in royal occasions such as the Trooping of the Colour and the Queen's Birthday Parade. It is also itself a venue for military parades and the flag-bedecked route taken by Heads of State and other distinguished foreign visitors on their way to be welcomed by the Queen. For the remainder of the time it is a four lane highway along which London's traffic streams – a far cry from Charles II's intentions when first commissioning it. The Mall in his day was a leafy promenade bordering St James's Park, as in essence it remained until 1911 when Aston Webb laid out the avenue anew, giving it its present dimensions and appearance.

Location
extending from
Admiralty Arch
to Buckingham
Palace

**Underground
station**
Charing Cross

Admiralty Arch (1910) stands at the City end of The Mall. It takes its name from the Old Admiralty building on Horse Guards Parade (see Whitehall). The privilege of driving through the central arch is the sovereign's alone.

Admiralty Arch

Past Admiralty Arch in the direction of Buckingham Palace, a long row of glistening white columns and gables comes into view. These are the two blocks of Carlton House Terrace, built by John Nash in 1827–32 as the replacement for Carlton House which had occupied the site since 1709. Carlton House was the residence of George IV up until his accession to the throne, and was demolished in 1829. The colonnaded portico of the National Gallery (see entry) gives some idea of the scale of Carlton House, having originally belonged to it.

★ **Carlton House
Terrace**

Between the two blocks of Carlton House Terrace a flight of steps leads up to Waterloo Place with, at the top of the steps, a 125ft/38m-high column surmounted by a statue of Frederick, Duke of York. Appointed commander-in-chief of the British army in 1827, the Duke died that same year, discredited on account of his huge debts. It was said wryly at the time that his statue was placed thus high to put him beyond the reach of his creditors.

Duke of York
Column

Once in Waterloo Place, the entrance facades of Carlton House Terrace are in view. The list of occupants makes impressive reading: at No. 5 the Turf Club, No. 6 the Royal Society, No. 12, Nash House, the Institute of Contemporary Art (with 3 galleries of changing exhibitions, 2 cinemas and a theatre; open: Tues.–Sat. noon–1am, Sun. and Mon. noon–11pm; galleries: Sat.–Thur. noon–7.30pm, Fri. noon–9pm), No. 16 the Terrace Club. Further along to the right are Carlton Gardens, from 1940–44 the headquarters of the Free French under Charles de Gaulle (No. 4).

Waterloo Place

Beyond Carlton House Terrace, set some way back from The Mall, stands Marlborough House, now a Commonwealth conference and research centre. It was built by Wren in 1709–11 for Sarah, Duchess of Marlborough, and subsequently much altered and enlarged. During the 19th c. it was the home of the Saxe-Coburg-Gotha family (including Prince Leopold, later

Marlborough
House

The Mall, the approach to Buckingham Palace

Leopold I of the Belgians), and in 1850 became the official residence of the Prince of Wales, occupied in succession by the future Edward VII and future George V. Queen Mary lived here from 1936 until her death in 1953. The house contains magnificent murals by the French painter Louis Laguerre depicting the Duke of Marlborough's victories at Blenheim, Ramillies and Malplaquet during the War of Spanish Succession.

Queen's Chapel

A little further on Marlborough Road branches off The Mall towards St James's Palace (see entry). Note in passing, first the memorial plaque to Queen Mary (1867–1953), and second the Art Noveau fountain, by Sir Alfred Gilbert commemorating Queen Alexandra (1844–1925), wife of Edward VII. Ahead stands the Queen's Chapel, part of St James's Palace. The chapel was built by Inigo Jones for Henrietta Maria, the wife of Charles I, and was the first Classical-Palladian church building in England. It was refurnished for Charles II's marriage to Catherine of Braganza in 1661. A hundred years later it was the scene of another royal wedding when George III married Charlotte Sophia of Mecklenburg-Strelitz. The chapel is open only for Sunday service, at which time it is also possible to admire the woodcarving by Grinling Gibbons and the altarpiece by Annibale Caracci.

Clarence House

Returning to The Mall, the stuccoed front of Clarence House is next to catch the eye, further along on the right. Built in 1828 by John Nash for the Duke of Clarence, later William IV, and much enlarged in the 1870s, the house is today the home of the much-loved Queen Elizabeth the Queen Mother.

Lancaster House

Situated almost at the end of The Mall, one side overlooking Green Park, Lancaster House is nowadays used for government receptions, banquets and conferences. It was begun by Benjamin Wyatt in 1825 for the Duke of York, who died in 1827 before the house was finished, leaving enormous debts. Completed by Sir Robert Smirke and Sir Charles Barry in 1840, it was acquired by the Marquis of Stafford (later Duke of Sutherland), one of the

Duke's creditors, who renamed it Stafford House. In the early 1900s it was presented to the nation by the first Lord Leverhulme as a home for the London Museum and given its present name. It was occupied by the museum from 1914 to 1951. The magnificence of the state apartments once prompted Queen Victoria to remark to her hostess the Duchess of Sutherland, "I have come from my house to your palace". The most impressive rooms are the elaborately decorated Great Gallery with its collection of valuable paintings, the State Dining Room, and the Veronese Room with a ceiling painting by Paolo Veronese.

A short distance north of Lancaster House stands Spencer House, once the residence of the Spencer family whose most famous member is the Princess of Wales. The house has been carefully renovated and is now a fine example of an early 18th c. town mansion. It is the only house of those mentioned here which is open to the public (guided tours, Sun. 10.30am–4.45pm; closed Jan. and Aug.).

Spencer House

Mansion House J 3

The Mansion House is the official residence of the Lord Mayor of London during his one-year term of office. The original plans of this impressive Palladian building were executed by George Dance. The foundation stone was laid in 1739. The 103ft/31m-wide façade has a raised portico supported by six Corinthian columns. On the pediment, sculptures depict London trampling Envy and leading in Plenty, while Father Thames stands by. In 1768, when John Wilkes was elected to Parliament, a mob of his supporters broke the windows and chandeliers of Mansion House, because the lights were not illuminated to celebrate his victory. The Mansion House houses the staff of the Lord Mayor's Office and is a place of work as well as a regular venue for Lord Mayoral and Corporation of London hospitality.

Location
Bank, EC4

Underground station
Bank
Mansion House

Mansion House, official residence of the Lord Mayor

Monument

Admission for organised group tours only is by prior arrangement. Write to the Principal Assistant to the Right Honourable The Lord Mayor, Mansion House, London EC4N 8BH. However, tours are likely to be booked up to a year ahead.

Temple of Mithras

In 1954 exploratory work on the site of Bucklersbury House, an office building in Queen Victoria Street (running south-west from the Mansion House), uncovered remains of a Roman Temple of Mithras, in use for at least 250 years from A.D. 90 onwards. The ground plan has been reconstructed; finds from the excavation can been seen in the Museum of London (see entry).

★ St Stephen Walbrook

A preparation for St Paul's

St Stephen Walbrook, immediately adjacent to the Mansion House on the south side, is the Lord Mayor of London's official church. Built by Wren between 1672 and 1679 it is of particular architectural interest, not least because it appears to have been used by Wren to experiment with the construction of a dome similar to the one he employed later to such good effect on a larger scale at St Paul's. Carried on slender Corinthian columns, the dome of St Stephen Walbrook looks down upon a travertine altar by Henry Moore (1987; disparagingly referred to as "The Camembert"). The pulpit and original altar are by Wren.

★ Monument   J 3

Location
Monument Street
Hill, EC3

Underground station
Monument

This tall column 202ft/61.5m high, known simply as "the Monument", was erected between 1671 and 1677 to commemorate the Great Fire of London in 1666, it stands precisely 202ft/61.5m from the spot in Pudding Lane where the Great Fire started. It was designed by Wren, in consultation with Robert Hooke. A relief on the pedestal depicts the rebuilding of London. Inside what today remains the tallest unsupported Doric column in the world, a spiral staircase of 311 steps ascends to the platform from where a panoramic view of the city is obtained. The column is surmounted by a gilded urn 18ft/5.5m high with, at its apex, a "gilded fireball" (open: Apr.–Sept. Mon.–Fri. 9am–6pm, Sat. and Sun. 2–6pm; Oct.–Mar. Mon.–Sat. 9am–4pm. Last entry, 20 minutes before closing).

St Magnus-the-Martyr

A little way down Fish Street Hill from the Monument stands St Magnus-the-Martyr, today almost completely obscured by new buildings. Documents show a church dedicated to Magnus, a Norwegian prince from the Orkney Isles martyred in 1100, has stood on this spot, close to the north end of the old London Bridge, since at least the latter part of the 12th c. The church from that time was destroyed in the Great Fire, being replaced in 1671–76 with a new building by Wren. The interior is distinguished by its Ionic columns, a pulpit by Wren, and a beautiful sword rest (1708). Henry de Yvele, who contributed substantially to the construction of Westminster Abbey (see entry) and was bridgemaster of London Bridge, is buried in St Magnus.

★ Museum of London   J 2/3

Location
London Wall, EC2

Underground stations
St Paul's Barbican,
Moorgate

The Museum of London, housed in a superbly designed new building in the Barbican area of the City, was opened in 1976. More than 2000 years of London's history are presented chronologically – at least two hours being needed to see round the whole museum.

Roman relics include a wall painting from a bath-house in Southwark and an excellent model of the Roman port of London. There are swords and helmets from the Anglo-Saxon era, and furniture, clothes, documents and

The Monument: commemorating the Great Fire of September 2nd 1666 ▶

Museum of London: The Golden Coach of the Lord Mayor

Opening times
Tues.–Sat.
10am–5.50pm
Sun.
noon–5.50pm

musical instruments from the Tudor and Stuart periods. Imaginative use is made of reconstructions e.g. of a Roman kitchen, a cell from the old Newgate prison, and a shop and offices from Victorian and Edwardian times, these latter with original furnishings etc. There is even an Art Déco lift.

An audio-visual presentation recreates the Great Fire, events on that fateful day in 1666 being relived with the aid of readings from Samuel Pepys' diary. Other displays illustrate the development of local authority services, schools and places of entertainment. The galleries devoted to London in the 19th c. convey a particularly lively and varied impression of the city in its heyday as capital of the British Empire.

The most sumptuous exhibit however is the Lord Mayor's golden state coach. Once a year it leaves the museum to carry the newly installed Lord Mayor through the streets of the City in the procession which is part of the Lord Mayor's Show.

Museum of Mankind

The Museum of Mankind closed its doors to the public on December 31st 1997. When the Great Court in the British Museum (see entry) is reopened in the year 2000 the Museum of Mankind's ethnographical collection will find a new home there.

★★National Gallery   G 3

The National Gallery, its facade filling the whole north side of Trafalgar Square (see entry), possesses one of the most valuable and comprehensive collections of pictures in the world. The Gallery was founded in 1824 when Parliament allocated £57,000 for the purchase of 38 paintings from the famous Angerstein collection. These at first went on show in the Angerstein rooms at 100 Pall Mall, town house of the collector John Julius Angerstein, a City merchant and banker. Numerous other purchases and donations quickly followed, soon making a proper gallery essential, and in 1832 work started on William Wilkins's design for Trafalgar Square. Wilkins's building, completed in 1838, incorporated the huge colonnaded portico from the former Carlton House (see The Mall), demolished in 1829. A constant stream of new acquisitions necessitated enlargement of the Gallery in 1876, at which time the dome was added; further extensions took place in 1887, 1927, 1929 and 1973. In 1952 the entrance vestibules were decorated with mosaics by Boris Anrep in which prominent contemporary figures appeared personifying various virtues. More recently a new annexe was built providing much-needed additional display space, and in 1991 the Sainsbury Wing opened. Designed by American architects Robert Venturi and Denise Scott-Brown and financed by the generosity of the Sainsbury brothers, directors of the supermarket chain, the wing provoked intense public discussion on account of its post-modernist architecture.

Before entering the National Gallery visitors should pause to admire the exceptionally fine view of Trafalgar Square and Whitehall (see entry) from the terrace. Outside the gallery stands a statue of James II by Grinling Gibbons (1686) depicting the king as a Roman emperor, with the inscription "King of England, Scotland, France and Ireland"; also a bronze replica of the Washington statue by Houdon in Richmond, Virginia.

Location
Trafalgar Square
WC2

Underground stations
Charing Cross,
Leicester Square,
Embankment

Opening times
Mon.–Sat.
10am–6pm,
Sun. 2–6pm

Admission free
Wheelchairs
Entrances in
the Sainsbury
Wing and Orange
Street;
wheelchairs
available

The National Galley in Trafalgar Square

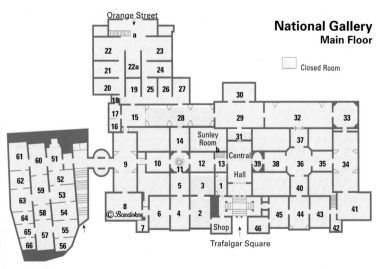

National Gallery
Main Floor

☐ Closed Room

Orange Street

© Baedeker

Trafalgar Square

WEST WING
Painting from 1510 to 1600

4 Dosso, Garofalo
5 Holbein, Cranach, Altdorfer
6 Lotto, Moretto, Moroni
7 Tintoretto, El Greco
8 Michelangelo, Sebastiano, Bronzino
9 Titian, Veronese, Tintoretto
10 Venetian
11 Veronese
12 Gossaert, Bruegel
13 Domenichino frescoes

NORTH WING
Painting from 1600 to 1700

14 Ter Brugghen, Hals
15 Claude and Turner
16 Vermeer, de Hooch
17 Dou, van Mieris
18 Hoogstraten
19 Claude
20 Poussin
21 Van Dyck, Jordaens
22 Rubens
22a Painting in Paris
23 Rubens, Teniers
24 Ruisdael, Hobbema

25 Cuyp, Both
26 Hals, Rembrandt pupils
27 Rembrandt
29 Valázquez, Murillo, Zurbarán
30 State Portraits
32 Caracci, Caravaggio, Guercino

EAST WING
Painting from 1700 to 1920

33 Chardin, Fragonard
34 Reynolds, Gainsborough, Turner, Constable
35 Hogarth, Gainsborough, Stubbs
36 British Portraits
37 Solimena, Giaquinto
38 Canaletto
39 Guardi, Goya
40 Tiepolo
41 David, Ingres, Delacroix
42 Corot, Friedrich
43 Impressionism
44 Van Gogh, Cézanne, Seurat
45 Cézanne, Bonnard
46 Picasso

SAINSBURY WING
Painting from 1260 to 1510

51 Giotto, Leonardo
52 Italian before 1400
53 Italian before 1400, Wilton Diptych
54 Masaccio, Sassetta
55 Uccello, Pisanello
56 Campin, van Eyck, van der Weyden
57 Crivelli, Tura
58 Botticelli
59 Pollaiuolo, Piero di Cosimo
60 Raphael, Perugino
61 Bellini, Mantegna
62 Netherlandish and French
63 German
64 Netherlandish and Italian
65 Antonello, Bellini
66 Piero della Francesca

a Stairs to Gallery A:
   European painting from 1260 to 1920
b Stairs to Galleries B, C, D:
   Temporary exhibitions
   E and G:
   Italian painting

One of the world's major galleries

With more than 2200 pictures the National Gallery offers an almost complete cross-section of European painting from the High Middle Ages to the late 19th c. The greatest treasures are the Collection of Dutch masters and the Italian schools of the 15th and 16th c. The opening of the Sainsbury Wing provided the opportunity for a complete rearrangement of the collection; the practice of grouping into national schools has been abandoned and a new emphasis placed on comparison and connections within periods. An up-to-date plan can always be obtained at the Gallery entrances. Because of the vastness of the collection only a chronological overview of the best-known painters and some of their works can be given here. Outstanding exhibits are highlighted by the use of *italics*.

For those with time available the Micro Gallery in the Sainsbury Wing offers an unusual and utterly intriguing introduction to what for some can seem a daunting, even confusing, array of pictures. Twelve computer terminals provide easily accessed on-line information about each of the paintings found in the Gallery (there are even animations showing how individual works were produced). Accessing the database under any of four headings – individual works, individual artists, genres and periods – allows crystal-clear illustrations to be viewed on-screen in what amounts to a personal tour of the Gallery. Pages from the catalogue and your personally selected Gallery Tour can also be printed out.

★★ Micro Gallery

Sainsbury Wing (painting from 1260 to 1510)

Fra Angelico ("Christ in Majesty"), Duccio, Pisanello, *Masaccio* (*"Mother and Child"*), Giotto, *Paolo Uccello* (*"Battle of San Romano"*), *Piero della Francesca* (*"Baptism of Christ"*), Cosimo Tura, Andrea Mantegna, *Giovanni Bellini* (*"The Doge Leonardo Loredan"*, "Madonna of the Meadow", "Pietà"), Carlo Crivelli, Antonio del Pollaiuolo, Sandro Botticelli, Piero di Cosimo ("Battle of Centaurs and Lepiths"), *Leonardi da Vinci* (*"Madonna and Child with St Anne and John the Baptist"*, the so-called *"Leonardo Cartoon"*), Raphael ("Madonna with Carnations", "The Crucifixion"); *Wilton Diptych* (*"Richard II with his Patron Saints"*, unknown school).

Italian painting

Jan van Eyck (*"The Marriage of Arnolfini"*), Hans Memling ("Altar of Mary"), Dieric Bouts ("Mary with Child"), *Hieronymus Bosch* (*"Christ with the Crown of Thorns"*), Lucas Cranach the Elder ("Portrait of a Young Woman").

Dutch, Flemish and German painting

West Wing (painting from 1510 to 1600)

Michelangelo ("The Entombment"), Pontormo, Andrea del Sarto, Bronzino, Correggio, Giorgione, *Titian* (*"Bacchus and Ariadne"*, "Venus and Adonis"), Tintoretto ("St George and the Dragon"), Paolo Veronese ("Adoration of the Magi"), Giovanni Battista Moroni, Lorenzo Lotto ("Lucretia"), Sebastiano del Piombo; El Greco ("Jesus expels the Money-Changers").

Italian and Spanish painting

Albrecht Dürer (*"The Artist's Father"*), Albrecht Altdorfer ("Landscape with Bridge), *Hans Holbein the Younger* (*"The Ambassadors"*), *Pieter Brueghel the Elder* (*"Adoration of the Magi"*).

German and Dutch painting

North Wing (painting from 1600 to 1700)

Peter Paul Rubens (*"The Straw Hat"*, "Rape of the Sabine Women", "Samson and Delilah"), *Anthony Van Dyck* (*"Charles I on Horseback"*, "The Balbi Children"), Frans Hals ("Man with a Glove"), *Rembrandt van Rijn* (*"Self-portrait"*, "Saskia and Flora", "A Jewish Merchant"), *Jan Vermeer* (*"Lady at the Virginal"*), Pieter de Hooch, Jacob van Ruïsdael ("Landscape"), Carel Fabritius, Gerard Terborch, Meindert Hobbema ("The Avenue, Middelharnis"), Jan Steen ("Two Musicians on a Terrace").

Dutch painting

Diego Velázquez (*"Rokeby Venus"*), Francisco de Zurbarán, Bartolomé Esteban Murillo; Caravaggio ("Boy bitten by a Lizard"): Nicolas Poussin ("The Finding of Moses"), *Claude Lorrain* (*"Psyche outside the Palace of Cupid"*), Louis le Nain, Philippe de Champagne ("Richelieu").

Spanish, Italian and French painting

East Wing (painting from 1700 to 1920)

William Hogarth ("Marriage à la mode"), Sir Joshua Reynolds ("Lady Cockburn and Children"), John Singer Sargent, *Thomas Gainsborough*

British painting

	(*"The Morning Walk"*), *John Constable* (*"The Haywain"*), *J. M. W. Turner* (*"Fighting The Temeraire"*, "View of Margate", "Rain, Steam and Speed").
French painting	*Antoine Watteau* (*"La Gamme d'Amour"*), Jean-Baptiste-Siméon Chardin, *Jean August Dominique Ingres* (*"Madame Moitessier"*), Eugène Delacroix, Honoré Daumier ("Don Quixote"), Gustave Courbet, *Claude Monet* (*"The Water-lily Pond"*, *"Bathers at Grenoullière"*), Edouard Manet, Edgar Degas ("Dancers"), Paul Cézanne ("Les Grandes Baigneuses"), *Georges Seurat* (*"Bathers at Asnières"*), *Henri Rousseau* (*"Tropical Storm with Tiger"*), Auguste Renoir, Vincent van Gogh ("Sunflowers", "Chair and Pipe"), Pablo Picasso.
Spanish and Italian painting	Francisco de Goya ("Duke of Wellington"); *Canaletto* (*"Stone-masons' Yard"* and other Venice scenes), Francesco Guardi, Giovanni Battista Tiepolo ("Entombment of Christ").

★★ National Portrait Gallery G 3

Location
St Martin's Place, Trafalgar Square, WC2

Underground stations
Charing Cross, Leicester Square

Opening times
Mon.–Sat.
10am–6pm,
Sun. noon–6pm

The National Portrait Gallery, founded in 1856, is situated immediately next door to the National Gallery (see entry). The criteria for a portrait's inclusion have more to do with the distinction of its subject than with the quality of the picture as a work of art. No restriction being placed on the form of portrait, the collection includes not only paintings but also drawings, photographs and sculptures, a total of more than 10,000 items depicting leading figures in British public life.

In recent years the gallery's collection of photographs has been substantially enlarged and a series of special exhibitions mounted on particular themes. The arrangement is chronological from the upper floor downwards, the decoration of the room reflecting the particular epoch.

National Portrait Gallery: Elizabeth I and Samuel Pepys

The upper landing on the top floor (Level 4) is devoted to Henry VIII and his predecessors. The exceptional life-size cartoon of Henry VIII by Hans Holbein and a 14th c. portrait of Geoffrey Chaucer, who lived for a time in London, are particularly noteworthy.

Upper floor

Level 4

In three rooms on Level 5 devoted to the 16th c. are portraits of Mary I by Hans Eworth and of Elizabeth I by an unknown artist. The next four rooms (17th c.) contain e.g. a portrait of Shakespeare by John Taylor, miniatures of Walter Raleigh and Francis Drake by Hilliard, and portraits of Charles I and Charles II, the Earl of Arundel (by Rubens) and the famous portrait of Samuel Pepys (by Hayls). Adjoining are eight rooms devoted to the 18th c. with pictures of Christopher Wren, Isaac Newton, the Duke of Marlborough and Robert Walpole (all by Godfrey Kneller), self-portraits by William Hogarth and Joshua Reynolds, Reynold's portrait of Warren Hastings and John Webber's of the explorer James Cook. Completing Level 5 are rooms filled with portraits of late 18th and early 19th c. figures including Lord Byron (in costume), Admiral Lord Nelson and Lady Hamilton, Sir Walter Scott (by Edward Landseer) and the three Brontë sisters by their brother Branwell.

Level 5

On the ground floor, Level 3 is reserved for personalities of the Victorian era – Queen Victoria herself, Cecil Rhodes, Benjamin Disraeli, Henry James (by John Singer Sargent) and a caricature of Oscar Wilde. Among early photographs is one of Thomas Carlyle taken in 1867.

Ground floor

Level 3

Level 2 is devoted exclusively to the 20th c. and features paintings, photographs and sculptures. Subjects range from T. E. Lawrence ("Lawrence of Arabia"), James Joyce, Winston Churchill and John Maynard Keynes to Margaret Thatcher, Mick Jagger and Princess Diana. Portraits of the Royal Family occupy a separate room.

Level 2

Level 1 is devoted to the late 20th c. and features portraits of persons in the media, reflecting both the traditional forms of representation such as oil with portraits of footballer Bobby Charlton, fashion designer Zandra Rhodes, Paul McCartney and the present Queen, and contemporary forms such as television with video portraits of well-known personalities.

Level 1

National Postal Museum

H/J 3

The National Postal Museum, opened in 1966, has a collection of some 350,000 stamps from all over the world, together with artists' drawings, philatelic books and documents on the history of the postal service. The Reginald M. Phillips collection of 19th c. British stamps (covering the development, planning and issue of the world's first postage stamp, a British invention, after Rowland Hill's proposal for uniform Penny Postage from 1837–39), and the Post Office's collection of British and foreign stamps, are particularly impressive.
   The museum is housed in the King Edward Building, west wing of the General Post Office. The Post Office has a vast counters hall well worth seeing in its own right.

Location
King Edward Street, EC1

Underground station
St Paul's

Opening times
Mon.–Fri.
9.30am–4.30pm

★★ Natural History Museum

C 4

Anyone visiting London in the company of children should certainly have the Natural History Museum on their itinerary; it is one of the few museums to have successfully solved the problem of conveying sometimes difficult material both clearly and entertainingly.

Location
South Kensington SW7

On his death in 1753, the scientist Sir Hans Sloane bequeathed his extensive collections to the nation; they became the nucleus of the British Museum. In 1860 the decision was taken to move the scientific collections into premises of their own, and the architect Alfred Waterhouse was commissioned to erect a new museum in Kensington. His vast Romanesque cathedral of a building took seven years to complete, the Natural History Museum finally opening its doors in 1881. The massive façade dominating Cromwell Road is 755ft/230m long, with twin towers 210ft/64m high. The terracotta blockwork of the exterior is embellished with figures of animals, etc. in relief.

Underground station
Cromwell Road,
South Kensington

Opening times
Mon.–Sat.
10am–5.50pm
Sun. 11am–5.50pm

Wheelchairs available

Sir Hans Sloane's original collections, comprising 50,000 books, 10,000 preserved specimens and 334 volumes of pressed plant species, were augmented over the years by thousands of new acquisitions: Joseph Banks, who accompanied Captain Cook around the world, was a particularly avid collector; the artist Sydney Parkinson donated three volumes of his zoological drawings and eighteen volumes of botanical watercolour studies; Charles Darwin also donated many specimens from his expeditions. Today over half a million items are added to the collection every year. Latterly, great effort has been invested in presenting this material in a much more graphic and entertaining way, an objective triumphantly achieved. The museum is now divided into two main parts: the Life Galleries (Cromwell Road building) incorporating the animal, plant and minerals collections; and from July 1996 the Earth Galleries (annexe; alternative entrance in Exhibition Road) forming the world's finest geological collection.

Growth of the collection

Life Galleries

Immediately inside the main Cromwell Road entrance there is an information desk. The imposing Central Hall (straight ahead) has been virtually emptied of exhibits apart from the enormous 85ft/26m skeleton of a diplodocus.

Ground floor

Central Hall

Anyone for whom dinosaurs have come to mean a few large dusty bones obscurely labelled cannot fail to have their interest rekindled by visiting the dinosaur gallery on the left of the Central Hall. Here is the world of Triceratops and Tyrannosaurus rex brought alive again. Videos, robotic models and dioramas are used to explain the evolutionary development, physical characteristics, diet and living habits of these pre-historic giants. Among the highlights are a life-size reconstruction of the head of a carnivorous dinosaur discovered in Britain, and a similarly true-to-scale diorama "America 115 million years ago" in which three robotic deinonychus devour a dead tenontosaurus to the shrill churring of desert crickets.

★★ Dinosaur gallery

Also in this part of the museum is a hall devoted to human biology with a larger than life-size model of the human fœtus. Adjoining are the mammals, not only living species but also fossils, extinct species and mammals exterminated by man. The floor of the hall is taken up with land animals including okapis, platypuses and the "Tasmanian Devil"; aquatic mammals occupy the gallery. A huge life-size cast of a 89ft/27m blue whale hangs suspended from the ceiling.

Human biology
Mammals

Fishes, reptiles and amphibians and marine invertebrates follow in succession, the collection of starfish being especially absorbing.

Fish

Off to the right of the Central Hall, the "Creepy Crawlies" gallery (arthropods; first left) is another of the museum's highlights. Among the many enthralling features in this informative and entertaining section are: the gigantic model of a scorpion; No. 1 Crawley House (with drawers and cupboards which open to reveal the arthropods with which we share our homes); a terrarium with leaf-cutting ants; and a termite mound. Less

★ Arthropods

◀ *Natural History Museum: The Central Hall*

Diorama: "America 115 million years ago"

Ecology

entertaining perhaps but equally informative is the section starting immediately opposite devoted to the ecology of the planet, in particular the balance of nature and the environment. A fascinating insight is provided into the problem of acid rain and the interaction of forest and coastal eco-systems. The opening display at the far end of the gallery features a giant video-wall (quadroscope) illustrating the water cycle of evaporation, precipitation, transpiration, etc.

Birds

Beyond the bookshop, gift shop and restaurant is the Bird Gallery containing among other things preserved specimens of some now extinct species such as the dodo and passenger pigeon. Finally comes a presentation entitled "Land of Sacred Fires" about the oil-rich Caucasus.

First floor
African mammals

Evolution

Minerals
and meteorites

Upstairs on the left are African mammals and a section on the evolution of species (including the latest developments in methods of artificial breeding and gene technology). A special area is devoted to primates with, on the right-hand balcony, a section entitled "Our place in evolution". Always centre of attention here are the remains, nick-named "Lucy", of Australo- pithecus, between 1½ and 5 million years old, discovered in Ethiopia in 1974. In the adjoining gallery are minerals and shells of which the museum possesses some 130,000 specimens (75% of known minerals are represented). One of the most beautiful exhibits is a hand-engraved nautilus shell from Hans Sloane's original collection. A room at the far end of the gallery contains meteorites, among them the huge Cranbourne meteorite from Australia, weighing three tons. Also on display here are specimens of moon rock.

Second floor

The second floor gallery is devoted to the natural history of the British Isles.

Earth Galleries

No less spectacular are the redeveloped Earth Galleries, portraying the earth's history, geology and minerals. A giant lift takes visitors on a journey to the centre of the earth and from the night-sky out into the solar system. State-of-the-art interactive exhibits demonstrate how earthquakes occur and volcanoes erupt, and in the "restless surface" section visitors can experience how wind and weather are constantly changing the face of the earth.

Old Bailey (Central Criminal Court)   H 3

The massive building officially known as the Central Criminal Court but more commonly referred to as the Old Bailey (after the short street in which it stands), is the main criminal court for the City and the Greater London area. Constructed in 1902–07 the Old Bailey became known to people abroad through the film "Witness for the Prosecution" starring Marlene Dietrich and Charles Laughton. The dome is surmounted by a figure of Justice, with her sword and scales, but not blindfolded. Proceedings of the court can be watched from the visitors' gallery; cameras, tape recorders and mobile phones are not allowed (Mon.–Fri. 10am–1pm and 2–4pm).

Location
Newgate Street/
Old Bailey, EC4

Underground stations
St Paul's,
Blackfriars

From the 13th c. until 1902 the site on which the Old Bailey now stands was occupied by Newgate Prison, for many years London's principal jail. Between 1783 and 1868 public executions were carried out at Newgate. Taking place in front of the prison they were considered an unparalleled spectacle and provided excellent business for the landlord of the pub opposite (the "Magpie and Stump", demolished 1988) where special "execution breakfasts" were served on those particular days.

Newgate Prison

★Piccadilly Circus   F 3

Piccadilly Circus, in the 1960s the heart of "Swinging London", is one of the great centres of the city's life. The capital's residents consider it the "hub of the world"; for tourists it is a sight not to be missed. First impressions are none too auspicious: a frenetic, noisy road junction, heavy with traffic fumes from the buses, taxis and other vehicles spewing forth from four major thoroughfares – Regent Street, Piccadilly, Haymarket and Shaftesbury Avenue. The tube station serves two underground lines. Nor is the Circus any quieter after nightfall, the myriad night spots, theatres and cinemas in the surrounding streets making it the heart of the West End world of entertainment, lit by a thousand flashing neon signs.

Underground station
Piccadilly Circus

In the centre of the Circus stands the Shaftesbury Memorial, a bronze fountain (1892) by Sir Alfred Gilbert, commemorating the philanthropic Earl of Shaftesbury. The winged figure crowning it, cast in aluminium, is universally known as "Eros" though in fact representing the angel of charity.

Eros

Near Piccadilly Circus lies the Trocadero Centre, a large modern shopping complex with restaurants, theatres, the Guinness World of Records" laser and video and virtual reality attractions with "Alien War", "Emaginator" and the giant Imax 3-D cinema in "Segaworld". In the London Pavilion, another shopping arcade just across the road, the "Rock Circus" presents a history of Rock and Pop.

Trocadero
Centre · London
Pavilion

Picadilly Circus

★ Piccadilly

Location
extending from
Piccadilly
Circus to Hyde
Park Corner

Piccadilly, the street leading west from Piccadilly Circus, is thought to have taken its name from the "pikadels" (collars) made by a successful 18th c. tailor.

★Fortnum &
Mason

Some of London's finest, most traditional and most typically English shops are found in Piccadilly today, just as they were two centuries ago. One of the most famous is Fortnum & Mason (at number 181), founded in 1707 and noted particularly for its high-class food department (especially its teas, biscuits and jams). The assistants behind the counters wear tail-coats.

**Royal Academy
of Arts**

The Royal Academy of Arts, founded in 1768 under the patronage of George III, has been accommodated since 1869 in Burlington House (opposite Fortnum & Mason), an imposing mansion embellished with a Neo-Renaissance façade. Begun originally in 1664 the building was remodelled several times, the last in 1867–73. The Academy's first president was Sir Joshua Reynolds (1723–92), whose statue stands in the courtyard.

The Royal Academy is a self-governing and self-supporting society of artists with a membership of 50 Royal Academicians and 25 Associates all of whom are either painters, sculptors, graphic artists or architects. Election to the Royal Academy was for long the pinnacle of an artist's career, holding out the prospect of considerable wealth and not infrequently a title. The Academy's art school in Burlington House boasts a most impressive list of distinguished pupils including Constable, Lawrence, Turner and Millais. Every year between June and August the Academy mounts a summer exhibition of work by contemporary British artists. Only work done within the past ten years is eligible; competition for inclusion is fierce. The Royal Academy is perhaps better known abroad, however, for its special exhibitions devoted to a particular period in art.

A special exhibition drawn from the Academy's permanent collection is on view in the Private Rooms on the first floor. The Sackler Galleries, opened in 1991, house a real art treasure, the Michelangelo Tondo. This relief – of the Virgin and Child with the infant John the Baptist, in white Carrara marble – is the only Michelangelo sculpture in Britain. Michelangelo carved it, almost immediately after completing his "David", for the Florentine patrician Taddeo Taddei, in whose family it remained until the early 19th c. In 1823 it was purchased by a well-known British collector, Sir George Beaumont, and presented to the Royal Academy after his death (open: daily 10am–6pm).

Permanent exhibition

Just beyond the Royal Academy lies the entrance to Burlington Arcade, an attractive and very expensive Regency style shopping arcade, built in 1819 for Lord Cavendish. More than 70 small but exclusive shops sell luxury goods to wealthy customers - bespoke shirts, jewellery, cashmere sweaters, hand-made shoes, toiletries, cigars and pipes and the finest tobaccos. Nothing better conveys the ambience of the Arcade than a quotation from the original regulations, still in force: "... a piazza for the sale of haberdashery, clothes and articles which neither look nor smell offensive. It is not permitted to whistle, sing, play a musical instrument, carry a package, nor to unfurl an umbrella." Patrolling "beadles" in top hats and tails ensure that these rules are obeyed.

★Burlington Arcade

On either side of Fortnum & Mason across the road are two more arcades, almost as exclusive: the Piccadilly and Princes Arcades. Both extend from Piccadilly through to Jermyn Street where a string of top class gentlemens' outfitters vie for the custom of the fashion-conscious man.

Jermyn Street

Where better to enjoy afternoon tea – that thoroughly British custom – than in the Palm Court of the Ritz Hotel on the corner of Piccadilly and Green Park. Such an indulgence though is far from cheap! Suit and tie are obligatory.

The Ritz Hotel

Regent's Canal

C–N 1–3

Regent's Canal was dug and opened in 1820, linking the Grand Union Canal to the Port of London. John Nash, architect of Regent's Park, originally intended the canal to be a major landscape feature, cutting right through the centre of the park (see entry); in the event it was made to sweep in a curve around the northern edge, lest the coarseness of the bargees offend the park's more refined residents. The canal starts in Paddington at Little Venice, a pretty, even romantic triangular basin surrounded by terraces of Georgian houses (Underground station: Warwick Avenue). From there it winds its way towards Regent's Park, then on between the animal enclosures of London Zoo (see entry) and past old warehouses to Camden Lock (see entry below). This is by far the most attractive stretch of the canal. Eastwards from Camden Lock the scenery has more specialised appeal, with locks, bridges, basins and lines of antique gas holders, before the canal vanishes into a tunnel beneath Islington Hill, and finally into the Thames. Along this stretch is the London Canal Museum. The London Canal Museum (12/13 New Wharf Road; Underground station: King's Cross) which is accommodated in an old ice-house, documents the history of London's canals (open: Tues.–Sun. 10am–4.30pm).
    There are two ways of seeing Regent's Canal: by boat from either Little Venice or Camden Lock (see Practical Information, Boat trips), or on foot along the tow-path.

Location§ extending from Little Venice (Paddington) to Limehouse Basin in Docklands

London Canal Museum

Camden Lock is one of the most pleasant and certainly one of the busiest spots on the canal (Underground station: Camden Town). One of twelve locks, and a popular meeting-place, its attractions include a well-supported craft market run in conjunction with a pub. Until about twenty-five years

Camden Lock · Camden Town

Camden Lock

ago Camden Town, the district immediately to the east of Regent's Park, was a typical, rather dreary and faceless London suburb. Then it became popular with artists, musicians, students and other members of the "alternative" society. Today it is a vibrant mixture of pubs, clubs and junk, antique and second-hand book and record shops. At weekends in particular vast numbers flock to its colourful flea markets.

Regent's Park   D/E 1/2

Location
Marylebone, NW1

Underground stations
Baker Street,
Regent's Park,
Great Portland
Street

When John Nash was first commissioned by the Crown to develop the Marylebone Fields, he drew up an ambitious scheme for a spacious, landscaped park with splendid terraces of elegant rich man's houses ringing two circular avenues. There was also to be a palace for the Prince of Wales (the future George IV), and numerous grand villas. The proposed Regent's Canal was to be a major landscape feature, cutting through the centre of the park. In the event his plans, drawn up in 1812, were only realised in part; no palace was built, and just eight villas, of which only three survive. The park which Nash intended for an exclusive residential development has become a recreation ground for the people of London, one where they can enjoy a variety of sports including boating (on the artificial lake), tennis and cricket. There are in addition several childrens' playgrounds, an open-air theatre (used in summer for performances of Shakespeare as well as pop concerts) and the beautiful Queen Mary's Garden, a delightful rose garden and rockery as well as Avenue Garden in Victorian style. London Zoo (see entry) occupies a large section of the north end of the park.

On the west side of the park can be seen the tall white minaret of the London Central Mosque, completed in 1978.

Buildings by John Nash

The superb "Nash terraces" around the southern circumference of Regent's Park give a hint of what might have been. They include the

Cumberland Terrace

exceptionally attractive Park Crescent, a semi-circular terrace of houses with colonnaded fronts, situated in the south-east corner at the point where the north end of Portland Place opens onto the park. Completed in 1821 the Crescent is a particularly fine example of its genre. A walk around the Outer Circle reveals other terraces by Nash: York Terrace (1821), west of the Crescent; Chester Terrace, on the east side of the park, boasting the longest unbroken colonnade; and the adjacent Cumberland Terrace (1828) with a fine relief of Britannia on the pediment. Primrose Hill, adjoining Regent's Park on the far side of the canal to the north of the zoo, was raised using earth dug up during construction of the underground system. Now a pleasant park, it offers a good view of the city.

Park Crescent

Outer Circle

Cumberland Terrace

Primrose Hill

A little to the west of Regent's Park, also on the further side of Regent's Canal, lies Lord's Cricket Ground, named after Thomas Lord, a veteran player of the time, who purchased the ground in 1814. To cricket lovers throughout the world, Lords is the Mecca of the game. As headquarters of the Marylebone Cricket Club (MCC) – as well as of Middlesex Cricket Club – Lord's is to cricket what Wimbledon is to tennis and Wembley to football. A museum in the pavilion traces the history of the ground and of this quintessentially English, and to the uninitiated, somewhat complex, game. Among the items on display is the tiny urn holding the legendary "Ashes", the trophy for which the England XI and Australia XI compete in Test series between the two countries and about which feelings always run high. Tours of Lord's, departing daily at noon and 2pm, include a visit to the sacred Long Room, Museum of Cricket, a real tennis court and the cricket school (tel. 0171–266 3825 to check availability).

Lord's Cricket Ground

To any Sherlock Holmes fan, 221b Baker Street, not far from the south-west entrance to Regent's Park, is an address almost as familiar as their own. Callers today will find a Sherlock Holmes Museum, which on closer inspection turns out in fact to be situated between Nos. 237 and 239. Visitors see the great detective's apartment on the first floor, complete with Holmes' violin and distinctive tobacco pouch in the shape of a Turkish slipper (open: daily 10am–6pm). Also find time to visit "Mrs Hudson's" restaurant on the ground floor which serves up delicious Victorian cuisine.

Sherlock Holmes Museum

Richmond

The suburb of Richmond, on the south bank of the Thames south-west of London, is considered one of the "better" places to live, being quiet and preserving something of a rural atmosphere. These attributes were

Location
south-west
of the city

Mr Sherlock Holmes, the consultative detective

The life of the greatest detective of all time, who described himself as a "consultative detective", can be reconstructed only through his own reports and those of his companion and chronicler Dr John H. Watson, who was involved in many of his cases.

Sherlock Holmes was born in rural Sussex, probably in 1854: after leaving school he went to university. In 1881 he was working on an experiment at St Bartholomew's Hospital in London when he first met Dr Watson, who was seeking comfortable accommodation. The two men took lodgings with the widow Mrs Hudson at the now legendary address of 221b Baker Street. Watson describes Holmes as a gaunt, lean man with an incredibly sharp mind and a profound knowledge of all the most curious crimes on record. He was also an outstanding chemist who had gained fame for his treatise on "140 different kinds of cigar ash". On the other hand Holmes had little interest in literature or philosophy – indeed, he could almost be described as an ignoramus in such matters. To help him to think and ponder problems he played the violin and smoked cheap tobacco. The master detective was, to put it mildly, not "compatible" with women, much preferring his bachelor existence with Watson. In the years they shared lodgings Holmes solved numerous extremely complicated cases using his own methods of scientific deduction: a detailed study of clues – seeking all possible explanations – dismissing the impossible – resultant conclusions. In this way he cleared up such criminal cases as the famous "Hound of the Baskervilles" and the first case they dealt with together, "Study in Scarlet", a bestial murder in Lauriston Gardens near the Brixton Road. As in this case, London was the scene of many of his enquiries, one of the most spectacular of which was without doubt the mystery of "The Sign of Four" which Holmes solved after a dramatic steamboat chase on the Thames downstream from Westminster Pier. In 1891 Holmes was on the trail of Professor Moriarty, the "Napoleaon of crime". On May 4th came their dramatic meeting in the Reichenbach gorge near Meiringen in Switzerland, where as they struggled they both fell into the gaping chasm. Holmes, however, was able to save himself by clinging to an overhang. He claimed that he spent the following three years in travelling and research; the *cognoscenti*, however, will know that he visited Sigmund Freud in Vienna to seek a cure for his addiction to morphine. In 1894, to Watson's total amazement, he reappeared in Baker Street and in the years that followed again successfully applied himself to hunting down criminals, ending in 1912 to 1914 when he hunted down the German master spy von Bork and saved the British Empire from ruin.

Nothing is known of dates on which Holmes and Watson may have died; however, anyone writing to their famous address will be informed that Mr Holmes is no longer taking on any cases, as he has retired to Sussex to keep bees. Those wishing to delve into the life of the great detective should visit the Sherlock Holmes Museum (see entry under Regent's Park).

obviously appreciated in the past by the English monarchs, several of whom made their seat here. Edward I initiated the tradition. His 14th c. manor house was the precursor of the 15th c. palace of Shene, replaced later by Richmond Palace, which Henry VII had built in 1501 and in which Henry VIII lived until moving to Hampton Court (see entry). Anne of Cleves was installed in Richmond after Henry had divorced her; Elizabeth I died there. Little has survived of the Tudor palace except the gatehouse bearing its builder's arms (on the left in what is now Old Palace Yard). The Trumpeters' House (1702–04) stands on the site of the palace's Middle Court.

Underground station
Richmond

British Rail
Richmond

Riverboats
Richmond

Richmond Green, once the preserve of the court, is now a pretty open space with 17th and 18th c. houses and traditional pubs ("The Cricketers", built in 1666, and the "Prince's Head"). Maids of Honour Row, four houses built on the instructions of the future George II in 1724 for the use of his wife's ladies-in-waiting, is particularly eye-catching. Between Richmond Green and George Street run several narrow lanes containing some attractive shops.

Richmond Green

Leaving Old Palace Yard proceed past the White Swan in Old Palace Lane to the Thames embankment, then along the riverside to the elegant Richmond Terraces.

Richmond Terraces

From Richmond Hill there is a wonderful view on clear days over the Thames valley, sometimes even as far as Windsor (see entry).

Richmond Hill

★Richmond Park

Extending over some 660ha/2300 acres, Richmond Park is the largest park in the Greater London area. Situated to the south of Richmond, it was enclosed by Charles I in 1637 as a deer-park; numbers of red and fallow deer still roam freely in its well-wooded expanses. The Pen Ponds, excavated in the 18th c., are the haunt of waterfowl of all kinds. On the east side of the park, facing Roehampton, are two public golf courses, and on the west side are attractive footpaths crossing Ham and Petersham Commons. Among the most pleasant features of the park are the Isabella Plantation, a woodland garden laid out in 1831, and Prince Charles Spinney, containing some of the oldest oaks in Britain as well as beech, chestnut, ash and maple.

Bus
No. 65 from Richmond Under-ground station

Near the Roehampton Gate is White Lodge, built by George II as a hunting lodge, and in which the Duke of Windsor (Edward VIII) was born and the Duke of York lived before acceding to the throne as George VI. The house is now occupied by the Royal Ballet's Junior School.

White Lodge

Ham House

Ham House, situated close to the River Thames to the west of Richmond Park, was originally a modest country mansion, built by Sir Thomas Vavasour in 1610. In the mid 17th c. it was inherited by Elizabeth Dysart who, following her marriage to the Duke of Lauderdale, enlarged and remodelled the house in a lavish Baroque style. Today it is the property of the National Trust, preserved very much as it was in the Duke and Duchess's time. The interior is typical of an aristocrat's house of the period; the beautiful gardens perfectly complement the house. Noteworthy is a priceless collection of miniatures, a treasure in their own right.

Bus No. 371 from Richmond Underground station

Opening times
Apr.–Oct.:
Wed. 1–5pm,
Sat. Nov. and Dec. weekends only

★Royal Air Force Museum

Britain's National Museum of Aviation – the Royal Air Force Museum – tells the story of flight and the people who made it possible. The museum

Location
Hendon, NW9

Royal Air Force Museum

Underground station
Colindale

Opening times
daily 10am–6pm

occupies the former factory site and aerodrome of the aircraft pioneer Claude Grahame-White. Grahame-White, a pupil of Louis Blériot, the first man to fly the Channel, established a European flying centre here at Hendon. On display are more than 70 British, US, German and Italian military aircraft, from some of the earliest to some of the latest, making this one of the largest museums of its kind in the world. There is also a comprehensive collection of official records, decorations and technical exhibits.

Aircraft Hall

Bomber Command Hall

The Aircraft Hall, the hub of the museum, houses 35 aircraft, including a Blériot XI (the type used by Blériot for his historic flight), and military aircraft ranging from the legendary Sopwith Camel (1917) and the famous World War II Spitfire, to modern fighters of the 1980s like the vertical take-off Harrier and the Tornado.

Another attraction in the hall is a flight simulator in which visitors can experience the thrill of low-level flying through the Welsh mountains or the bone-shaking discomfort of a First World War biplane.

As the name implies, Bomber Command is the branch of the Royal Air Force responsible for its bomber fleet. In a part of the Aircraft Hall specifically assigned to it are British and US bombers from the First World War up to the Gulf War, mainly from the Second World War; they include an Avro Lancaster and a B-17 Flying Fortress. There are also special features on Air Marshal Arthur "Bomber" Harris, head of Bomber Command during the Second World War, and Sir Barnes Wallis, inventor of the "bouncing bomb" used in the Dambusters raids on the reservoir of the Ruhr.

Galleries

Displays in the galleries trace the history of the Royal Air Force.

Battle of Britain Hall

Fourteen British, German and Italian aircraft which took part in the Battle of Britain in the summer of 1940 are exhibited in the Battle of Britain Hall. Also of interest are a Second World War operations room and air-raid shelter.

Replicas of a Spitfire and a Hurricane in front of the Aircraft Hall

Audio-visual presentations explain the dramatic story of the Battle of Britain, including its effect on the civilian population. The most impressive sight in the museum though is the Sunderland Flying Boat which you are able to go inside.

Royal Albert Hall

C 4

This large concert hall, also used for public meetings, balls and other events, was completed in 1871. Its full name is the Royal Albert Hall of Arts and Sciences, and it is a memorial to Prince Albert, Queen Victoria's husband, who first proposed its construction. The circular building, 690ft/210m in circumference, was designed by two Royal Engineers, Captain Fowke and General Scott, and was hailed by contemporaries as a noble building, worthy of Rome in its golden age. Although originally noted for its poor acoustics – a defect which was later put right – this huge amphitheatre with its great glass dome has become over the years one of London's best-loved concert halls for both classical and popular music. The famous "Proms" (promenade concerts; see Practical Information, Music) take place here every year.

Location
Kensington Gore,
SW7

Underground stations
Knightsbridge,
High Street
Kensington

★Royal Exchange

J 3

The Exchange was founded in 1568 by Sir Thomas Gresham and was granted "Royal" status in 1571 by Elizabeth I. Gresham is commemorated by a statue to the rear of the Exchange and by the weather vane in the shape of a grasshopper, the Gresham family emblem. The building was burnt down in the Great Fire of 1666 and again in 1838. In 1844 Sir William Tite designed the Exchange in its present Neo-Classical form. In the tympanum

Location
Bank, EC3

Underground station
Bank

No visiting

The Bank of England, Stock Exchange and Royal Exchange

pediment is a relief by Richard Westmacott representing trade and the Royal Exchange's charter.

Work on restoring this Victorian edifice took place between 1986 and 1991. The roof level was raised to create new third and fourth floors. In an effort to match the design of the original building, the external walls were clad with Portland Stone and hand carved with intricate classical detail. The building is now occupied by the Guardian Royal Exchange assurance company and is not open to the public.

By tradition it is from the steps of the Royal Exchange that a new monarch is always proclaimed, a declaration of war announced, the conclusion of a peace treaty publicised, and the dissolution of Parliament is proclaimed. There are some tasteful small shops where stockbrokers can buy a tie or have an umbrella repaired. In the forecourt above Bank station some even tinier shops have been set up in what was formerly Britain's oldest public convenience, dating from 1855.

In front of the Exchange stands an equestrian statue of the Duke of Wellington, surprisingly without stirrups.

Stock Exchange

No visiting

Glinting like steel only a short step away from the Royal Exchange is the 110m/360ft tower of the Stock Exchange in Old Broad Street. Founded in 1773 and originally located in Threadneedle Street, the London Stock Exchange quickly developed into the leading institution of its kind in the world; it remains one of the most important. Following reform of the Exchange in 1986 (referred to in the City as the "Big Bang"), the distinction between "broker" (agent) and "jobber" (dealer) was abolished and all the member firms brought under one roof. In the old days business was transacted on the floor of the Exchange in the Great Hall, deals involving massive sums being struck simply on the principle of "dictum meum pactum" (my word is my bond), a motto enshrined in the Exchange's coat of arms. Nowadays all business is done from computer terminals. After a terrorist bomb attack in 1991, the visitor centre was closed and the Exchange is not now open to the public.

★ St Bartholomew-the-Great   H/J 2

Location
West Smithfield
EC1

Underground stations
Barbican,
Faringdon

St Bartholomew-the-Great, the City's oldest parish church, lies partly concealed behind a 16th c. half-timbered passageway on the east side of West Smithfield. The church originally belonged to an Augustinian priory and hospital founded in 1123 by a monk named Rahere, one-time court jester to Henry I, and its first prior (died 1145). Apart from the church, very little of the priory remains. The church had already been enlarged and altered before, at the time of the dissolution in the reign of Henry VIII, the nave was pulled down, leaving the choir to become the parish church. During the 18th c. parts of the church were used as a warehouse, a store, a blacksmith's forge and also a printing works (where in 1724 Benjamin Franklin was aprenticed). These parts were brought back into use for worship when the church was restored during the last century.

Interior

The Norman origins of St Bartholomew's can still be discerned from the horseshoe-shaped arches of the choir and the gallery. The most notable of the features within the church however is the tomb (c. 1500) of the founder, with a fine recumbent figure of Rahere clad in the black robe of an Augustinian canon; at his feet is a crowned angel holding a shield embellished with the arms of the priory. Also of interest are: the alabaster tomb of Sir Walter Mildmay, Chancellor of the Exchequer under Elizabeth I; the early 15th c. font, where the artist William Hogarth was baptised; and the cloister (built 1405, restored in the original style 1905–28), entered via a Norman doorway with 15th c. doors.

Churchyard

The churchyard occupies the site of the demolished nave. The 13th c. gateway was originally the entrance to the south aisle.

Entrance gatehouse to Bartholomew's Church and the Clock Tower

The nearby Smithfield Market is the largest meat market in the capital. **Smithfield**
Since it first opened in 1867, this Victorian indoor market has seen almost **Market**
1000 tons of meat traded every working day. The market area has undergone recent restoration and is worth a visit (an excursion for night owls
only, virtually all business being conducted in the early hours). Afterwards,
breakfast can be taken in one of the pubs – the "Fox and Anchor" perhaps –
specially licenced to serve beer at 6.30 in the morning, this being what the
market traders themselves have for breakfast.

Smithfield (a corruption of "smooth field") has a long tradition as a
market and was the site of the famous St Bartholomew Fair, held here until
1855. Established, like the priory and hospital, by Rahere, the fair was
notorious for its disorderly aftermath which regularly got out of hand (this
being the reason why the fair was eventually closed down). Tournaments
and executions also took place here.

St Bride's   H 3

St Bride's, dedicated to the 6th c. Irish saint known also as St Bridget, is   **Location**
traditionally the parish church of the press, being located not far from Fleet   St Bride's Lane
Street (see entry). The church is first mentioned in the records in the 12th c.   EC4
In total, eight churches have occupied this site; the present building was
restored in 1957 from Wren's original plans for the church of 1701, which   **Underground**
was destroyed in the Second World War. The 230ft/70m tower is the tallest   **station**
of any designed by Wren; almost as soon as it had been built, London's   Blackfriars
bakers began modelling wedding cakes on it. Inside the church are numer-
ous plaques commemorating famous figures from the world of newspapers, the arts and literature who regularly worshipped here. Also
noteworthy are the 16th c. font and the carved oak reredos. The crypt
houses an interesting museum containing a Roman pavement, remains of

earlier churches and an exhibition illustrating the history of St Bride's, its close association with the press receiving special emphasis.

St Clement Danes   H 3

Location
Strand, WC2

Underground station
Temple

Designed by Wren and built in 1681, this famous church on an island site in the centre of the Strand, was gutted by bombing in 1941 during the last war; only the tower by James Gibb (1719) remained unscathed. The church may derive its name from the fact that there was a Danish settlement on the site before the Norman Conquest which was rebuilt several times before Wren's design.

St Clement Danes is the official church of the Royal Air Force. Kept inside the church are Books of Remembrance inscribed with the names of more than 125,000 men and women of the Commonwealth and Allied Air Forces who lost their lives in the Second World War. Inlaid in the floor are more than 800 badges of RAF units and squadrons. There are also memorial gifts from many other countries. The altar and font in the crypt were donated by the Norwegian and Dutch Air Forces. Outside the church stands the controversial memorial to Air Marshal Sir Arthur "Bomber" Harris. A statue in front of the church commemorates the writer Samuel Johnson, who worshipped here.

"Oranges and lemons, say the bells of St Clement"

Long familiar to children from the old nursery rhyme "Oranges and Lemons", the bells of St Clement's still ring out daily at 9am, noon, 3pm and 6pm. The song is thought to derive from a time when, on market days, it was the custom of those delivering fruit and vegetables to Clare market to donate something to the poor children of the parish. Every year in March a special children's service is held at which each child receives an orange and a lemon.

★ St Helen Bishopsgate   K 3

Location
Great St Helen's,
Bishopsgate, EC3

Underground station
Liverpool Street

St Helen Bishopsgate is one of the finest and most interesting churches in the City. First built in the 12th c., it was altered between the 13th and 14th c. and has been preserved mainly in its somewhat unusual 14th c. form. It has two parallel naves of equal size, the northern being reserved originally for the nuns of the convent to which the church belonged, and the southern for the lay congregation. Note in particular the 15th c. stairs by which the nuns would descend to the north nave from the convent for nocturnal worship. The most interesting features in the church however are the tombs, including, in the nun's choir, the sarcophagus of Sir Thomas Gresham (d. 1579), founder of the Royal Exchange (see entry), and next to it the tomb-chest of Sir Julius Caesar Adelmare (d. 1636), advisor to James I; also the canopied tomb of Sir William Pickering (d. 1574), Elizabethan ambassador to France and Spain; the table-tomb of Sir John Crosby (d. 1475) immediately opposite; and the tomb of Sir John Spencer, Lord Mayor of London (d. 1608). The church has been fully restored after the IRA bombing in 1993.

★ St James's Palace   F 4

Location
Pall Mall, SW1

Underground station
Green Park

No visiting

Situated not far from Buckingham Palace (see entry) and just a short distance north of the Mall (see entry), St James's Palace remains a fine example of brick-built Tudor architecture despite later destruction and alteration. It takes its name from a leper hospital dedicated to St James the Less, Bishop of Jerusalem, which stood here from the 12th c. until 1532. The old hospital was pulled down by Henry VIII and replaced by a palace, architect unknown but the ceiling of the Chapel Royal (see below) is

St James's Palace

attributed to Holbein, in which Charles II, James II, Mary II, Queen Anne and George IV were born. After the old palace of Whitehall burnt down in 1698, St James's Palace became the official residence of the monarch until it in turn gave place to Buckingham Palace. Even today the ambassadors of foreign countries are still accredited to "the court of St James".

St James's Palace is also the headquarters of the Queen's Bodyguard, consisting of the Yeomen of the Guard and the Honourable Corps of Gentlemen at Arms. The Yeomen of the Guard, a corps established by Henry VII in 1485, are popularly knowns as the Beefeaters, probably a corruption of the French "Buffetiers du Roi".

Beefeaters

The main relic of the Tudor palace is the turreted gate-house in St James's Street. Guarded by sentries in traditional bearskins, it leads into Colour Court, with a 17th c. colonnade.

Gate-house

In Ambassadors' Court (west of the gate-house; with access from Stable Yard) is the entrance to the Chapel Royal, built in the 1930s (except the ceiling designed by Holbein dated 1540) but with much subsequent alteration. Visitors are admitted to Sunday morning services (11.15am) between October and July. The fine paintings on the coffered ceiling are attributed to Holbein. Other notable features are the royal pew, the Carolean panelling and the richly ornamented roof. The marriages of William and Mary (1677), Queen Anne (1683), George IV (1795), Victoria (1840) and George V (1893) were all celebrated in this chapel.

Chapel Royal

On the north side of Ambassadors' Court stands York House, occupied in 1915–16 by Lord Kitchener and from 1919 to 1930 by the Prince of Wales, later Edward VIII, afterwards Duke of Windsor; it is now the offices of Prince Charles, the Prince of Wales.

York House

Baedeker Special

Members only

No sign on the door, at most perhaps a fleeting appearance of a liveried attendant to admit a gentleman: in Pall Mall and St James' Street one would scarcely know that here beats the very heart of London club life. There is no need for a sign, because members of a club know where they will be able to gain admittance without the assistance of a name plate or such.

The halcyon days of the club were in the 19th c., during the reign of Queen Victoria, when one after another was founded. It was here that a gentleman found refuge. For a membership fee and an annual subscription members could enter a world of their own, eat together in the club dining-room, talk or play cards in the smoking room, read in the library, their every need attended to by devoted servants, all within luxuriant suroundings which few could afford as it all had to be paid for out of one's own pocket. The true gentleman pursued his social life in the club, going home only to sleep, so that the responsibilities of marriage under such circumstances became something of a burden; he had everything he wanted at the club. The logical consequence was that women were never admitted, a rule to which many clubs still adhere even today.

The club offered another invaluable advantage: not just anybody could join – to be exclusively different from the others was (and is) the fundamental aim and *raison d'être* of every club. Waiting lists to join were accordingly very long, and as a result disappointed applicants often founded their own club – again with strict rules of membership – resulting in considerable degrees of animosity between many establishments.

It all actually started in 1693 in White's Chocolate House which, after it had moved to St James' Street, became one of the most expensive coffee and chocolate houses under the manager John Arthur. Mr Arthur offered his customers "gallantry, pleasure and entertainment", which meant in the main gambling for high stakes and betting on the most ridiculous things – for example, in 1750 Lord Arlington placed a wager of 3000 pounds with another gentleman on which of two raindrops would be the first to run down to the bottom of a window. About this time there existed an "inner club" which not every member could enter and which later became *White's Club* at 37–39 St James' Street, the oldest and most exclusive of all the London clubs. George IV, William IV, Edward VII, the Duke of Wellington, William Pitt the Elder and, of course, Beau Brummel, dandy *par excellence*, were all members. White's soon faced competition. In 1760 opponents of Pitt's reform policies, including the Prince of Wales, met in *Brook's Club* at 60 St James' Street. However, the political nature of these two clubs was of comparatively short duration; less than 90 years later members were concerning themselves with more important matters; for example, there were furious arguments about whether smoking should be allowed in White's, where until then only the use of snuff had

---

Pall Mall · St James's Street – London's "Clubland"

Opposite the gate-house lies the junction of St James's Street with Pall Mall. These two thoroughfares are the heart of London's "clubland", home to some of London's most famous clubs, past and present.

Several of the most exclusive are found in Pall Mall (which name derives from "paille-maille", a popular 17th c. game with affinities to cricket and golf). They include the Reform Club (No. 104) and the Travellers' Club (No. 106), both designed by Sir Charles Barry, architect of the Houses of Parliament (see entry); also the United Services' Club (No. 116) by John Nash (see Baedeker Special).

been permitted. With some bad grace and much gnashing of teeth a separate room was finally set aside as a smoking salon, but in spite of this the smoking lobby decided to form their own club, the **Marlborough Club**, where they could puff away to their heart's content in all the rooms.

The Marlborough was founded at a time when clubs were sprouting up like mushrooms. Whether political or social in nature, almost every organisation with a common denominator founded its own club: soldiers founded the **United Services Club** and the **Army and Navy Club**, horse-racing enthusiasts the **Turf Club**. The **Garrick Club**, 15 Garrick Street, founded in 1831 by the Duke of Sussex, was named after a famous actor of the period and was the meeting-place of writers, artists and actors. Its members included Charles Dickens and William Thackeray. Seven years before this the writer and politician John Wilson Croker had established the **Athenaeum Club**; in 1830 it moved to 107 Pall Mall and attracted the intellectual élite of the land. Croker is credited with being the first to introduce into British political life the name of "Conservatives" for the Tory party. The Tories had suffered a disaster in the 1832 elections, and those that were elected lost no time in founding a club in which Conservative values could be preserved; this was the **Carlton Club**, 69 St James' Street, and was named after the Carlton Hotel, its second home. Even today membershp is limited to those who recognise the principles of the Conservative Party – politics and careers are formed here. All Tory leaders from Gladstone onwards have belonged to the Carlton Club. In the same year that the Tories opened the Carlton their political opponents, the Whigs, opened their own club, the **Reform Club**, 104–105 Pall Mall, which has gained literary fame, for it was here that Jules Verne's Phineas Fogg wagered that he could travel round the world in eighty days.

A "gentleman" could, of course, be a member of several clubs, but not of all of them. William Thackeray, for example, belonged to the Reform, the Garrick and the Athenaeum, but he was never able to gain entry to the considerably more snobbish Traveller's Club.

White's, Brook's, the Athenaeum, Carlton, Garrick and Reform are only some of the most glittering names of this great era of the gentleman's club. They all still exist today, but the times in which they governed London society and were amused by all kinds of eccentrics from among their members are now more or less past. On the other hand their influence cannot be too highly regarded: to be a member of the right club can be almost a *sine qua non* for the furtherance of one's career. They are still swathed in a cloak of exclusivity, even though some have shown a pride in appearing to be progressive and have taken quite revolutionary steps to adapt to the 20th century, like the Reform Club, which has admitted women members since 1981.

★ St James's Park · Green Park   F 4

St James's is the oldest and most attractive of London's many parks, a masterpiece of landscape architecture by John Nash, here striving to achieve the unspoiled natural effect of an English country park. The park is known for its magnificent display of flowers, in spring and summer especially. Originally a marshy area of meadowland, it was drained in the reign of Henry VIII and made into a deer-park. James I established a public menagerie with exotic animals and birds (it was the aviaries on the southern side which gave rise to the street-name Birdcage Walk). Advised by the

Location
The Mall, SW1

Underground stations
St James's Park, Green Park

Daffodil time in St James's Park

French landscape gardener Le Nôtre, Charles II then had the park laid out as a formal Baroque garden. Finally, in 1829, Nash, commissioned by George IV, gave the park its present aspect, the epitome of an English landscape garden, transforming Le Nôtre's lineal canal into the curving lake seen today. From the bridge over the lake there are fine views of Buckingham Palace (see entry) to the west, and the rear of Whitehall (see entry) in the east.

Green Park

Immediately north-west of St James's Park lies Green Park, which was also part of Henry VIII's deer-park. Charles II opened it to the public as Upper St James's Park. Little was done to landscape it however, and as a result it remains a grassy expanse dotted with trees; only in spring when the daffodils are out is there much in the way of colour. Many a duel has been fought in Green Park, though nothing there today suggests it.

St John's Gate · St John's Church · Museum of the Order of St John

H 2

Location
St John's Lane, Clerkenwell, EC1

Underground stations
Farringdon, Barbican

The Order of the Hospital of St John of Jerusalem (the Knights Hospitallers), founded in the holy city in the 11th c. and later based successively in Cyprus, Rhodes and Malta, established themselves in England in the 12th c., building a priory in Clerkenwell about 1140. This was largely destroyed during the Peasants' Revolt of 1381 but was rebuilt in 1504. In 1547 the Order was suppressed in England. A move to revive the priory as a Protestant Order in 1840 resulted in the formation of the Order of St John, elevated to a British Royal Order of Chivalry by Queen Victoria in 1888.

Dating from 1504, St John's Gate was the main entrance to the former priory of the Order of St John, of which only it and parts of the priory church survive. The rooms in the gateway were the headquarters of the English branch of the Order, a role they have resumed again today. The Museum of the Order of St John traces the history of the Order in England, who in 1877 founded the St John's Ambulance; it includes some priceless exhibits, notably silverware, armour and paintings (open: Mon.–Fri. 10am–5pm, Sat. 10am–4pm).

The site of the priory church of 1185 is now occupied by St John's Church (1721–23) in St John's Square, which incorporates the choir walls of the old part-12th c., part-16th c. church. Damaged in the Second World War, St John's was completely restored in 1958. Its finest treasure is a 15th c. altar painting depicting the victory of the Knights of St John over the Turks at the seige of Rhodes. Against all odds, the Norman crypt (1140–80) has survived the vicissitudes of the centuries. The gatehouse and crypt can be visited by a tour at 11am and 2.30pm Tues., Fri. and Sat.

★ St Martin-in-the-Fields
G 3

St Martin-in-the-Fields, in the north-east corner of busy Trafalgar Square (see entry), is the royal parish church (hence the royal coat of arms above the portico), as well as the church of the Admiralty (for which reason the White Ensign can be seen flying above the portico on special occasions). There has been a church on this site since at least 1222. The original church was rebuilt in the reign of Henry VIII (1544) and replaced in 1726 by the present one, designed by James Gibb, a pupil of Wren.

Location
Trafalgar Square
WC2

Underground station
Charing Cross

St Martin's is Gibb's masterpiece. With its Corinthian portico and slender 56m/184ft-high steeple it became the model for many churches erected in Britain's North American colonies. Of particular note in the interior are the elliptical ceiling, with plasterwork of Italian workmanship by Artari and Bagutti, supported on Corinthian columns, and the boxes either side of the altar, the royal box on the north side, the Admiralty box on the south. Above the chancel arch are the arms of George I. Among those buried in the church are William Hogarth, Joshua Reynolds and Charles II's mistress, Nell Gwynne.

St Martin-in-the-Fields is perhaps most widely known today for its ministry to London's poor and homeless, a tradition begun by "Dick" Sheppard, vicar of St Martin's from 1914 to 1927. In the spirit of that tradition all the profits from the "Café-in-the-Crypt" go to help the needy.

More than just a church

The "Pearlies" are another London institution with a traditional involvement in charitable works.

The "Pearlies"

With a membership drawn from among East End market traders, the Pearlies gather in St Martin's on the first Sunday in October to celebrate harvest festival. Decked out in suits and dresses embroidered with pearl buttons, they choose a Pearly King and Pearly Queen to "reign" for the coming year.

St Martin-in-the-Fields enjoys one of the finest musical reputations in the world. Since 1726 it has played host to some of the world's greatest musicians including Handel and Mozart. Free lunchtime concerts are given every weekday except Thursday in addition to frequent evening concerts.

Music

A Pearlie collecting for charity

145

The London Brass Rubbing Centre in St Martin's Crypt has 70 or so replica church brasses from which rubbings can be made (open: Mon.–Sat. 10am–6pm, Sun. noon–6pm).

London Brass
Rubbing Centre

There is a well-supported craft and souvenir market in the courtyard of the church.

Craft market

St Mary-le-Bow Church

J 3

The City church of St Mary-le-Bow, with its famous bells, occupies a special place in the affections of Londoners. To be a genuine Cockney, it is said, you must have been born within the sound of Bow Bells. Every morning since the Middle Ages Londoners have awoken to the chimes of the Great Bell of Bow, and every evening at 9pm the same chimes have accompanied them to bed, a twice-daily acoustic affirmation of the City's bounds.

Location
Cheapside, EC2

**Underground
stations**
St Paul's, Bank

The church, originally a Norman foundation and one of London's oldest stone churches, was rebuilt by Wren between 1670 and 1683. It suffered heavy damage during the Second World War and was re-dedicated after extensive restoration in 1964. The name, St Mary-le-Bow, derives from the Norman arches still preserved in the crypt ("bow" being the mason's term for an arch), which Wren employed as a motif in the design of the 239ft/73m steeple, topped by a weathervane in the shape of a dragon nearly 10ft/3m high. Bricks dating from the Roman occupation of Britain are visible in the vicinity of the arches in the 11th c. crypt.

★★St Paul's Cathedral

H/J 3

St Paul's Cathedral, seat of the Bishop of London and "parish church of the British Commonwealth", is the largest and most famous of the City's churches. The place where the present-day cathedral stands was, legend has it, the site of a Roman temple of Diana in the 7th c. of a church. In its day Old St Paul's was one of the richest churches in the world, a great Gothic church with a spire 558ft/170m high. It was badly damaged by fire in 1561, partly rebuilt by Inigo Jones in 1627–42 and finally destroyed in the Great Fire of 1666. The present cathedral, begun in 1675 and completed in 1711, was designed by Sir Christopher Wren, The plan was approved only after long wrangling with the church commissioners, who turned down Wren's first two designs. The result was a compromise between Wren's original idea of a dome and the commissioners' preference for a plan in the form of a Latin cross. (A large model in the crypt shows the cathedral as Wren himself visualised it.)

Location
Ludgate Hill
EC4

**Underground
stations**
St Paul's,
Mansion House

Opening times
8.30am–4pm;
daily
galleries
10am–4.15pm
(special services
or events may
close all or part of
the Cathedral)

Even so, as finally built, St Paul's is Wren's masterpiece, a harmoniously proportioned Renaissance church 558ft/170m long, 246ft/75m wide across the transepts, with two Baroque towers 154ft/47m high and a magnificent dome rising to 364ft/111m. Wren had already studied the constructional problems relating to such a dome, the second largest in the world after St Peter's Rome, in his design for St Stephen Walbrook (see Mansion House).

Guided tours
Mon.–Sat.
11 and 11.30am,
1.30 and 2pm

The west front, with the main entrance, is 197ft/60m long and has a columned portico surmounted by an upper colonnade. The pediment relief of the Conversion of St Paul is by Francis Bird, as are the statue of St Paul above the pediment and the statues of St James and St Peter flanking it. The other sides of the building have ornamentation by Bird, Edward Pierce and Grinling Gibbons.

West front

On either side of the portico are two matching Baroque towers, in the left-hand one of which hangs a peal of twelve bells and in the right-hand

Towers

◀ *St Martin-in-the-Fields*

Choir-stalls of St Paul's

one the heaviest bell in England, Great Paul, weighing almost 17 tons, cast in 1882.

Interior

On entering St Paul's the immediate impression is one of overwhelming size and spaciousness. In addition to being one of the largest church interiors in the world, the absence of tombs and other monuments serves to further heighten the effect, giving rise to an aura of ceremony and celebration.

To the left of the entrance is All Soul's Chapel, which since 1925 has been a memorial chapel to Field Marshal Lord Kitchener (d. 1916).

All Soul's Chapel

The adjacent St Dunstan's Chapel is reserved for private prayer. It has a 17th c. oak screen and a mosaic by Salviati depicting the three Mary's at the tomb of Jesus.

St Dunstan's Chapel

In the north aisle are monuments to the painter Lord Frederic Leighton, to General Charles George Gordon and Prime Minister William Melbourne.

Tombs

Mid way along the north aisle, facing the nave, stands an imposing monument to the Duke of Wellington (d. 1852) by Alfred Stevens. Two groups of allegorical figures represent Valour and Cowardice, Truth and Falsehood. The equestrian statue of the victor of Waterloo by John Tweed was added in 1912.

Wellington Monument

The north transept, with a fine font and statues of Sir Joshua Reynolds and Dr Samuel Johnson, was damaged by a bomb in 1941 and rebuilt in 1962.

North transept

◀ *Dome of St Paul's*

St Paul's Cathedral

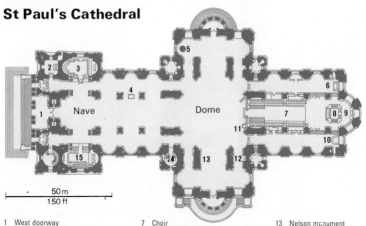

1 West doorway
2 All Souls Chapel
3 St Dunstan's Chapel
4 Wellington monument
5 Font
6 Chapel of Modern Martyrs

7 Choir
8 High altar
9 American Memorial Chapel
10 Lady Chapel
11 Pulpit
12 Steps down to Crypt

13 Nelson monument
14 Steps up to Whispering
   Gallery and Upper Galleries
15 Chapel of St Michael and
   St George

Dome	The highlight of any visit to St Paul's is the sight of the great dome, borne on eight massive double piers with Corinthian capitals, buttressed by four subsidiary piers. The cupola is embellished with eight scenes from the life of St Paul by James Thornhill; the mosaics were the work of Salviati at the end of the 19th c.
Chancel	Before proceeding to the chancel note the beautifully carved wooden pulpit to the right of the entrance to the choir. The ceiling arches and walls of the chancel itself are adorned with glass mosaics by William Richmond. The oak choir-stalls, master-pieces of 17th c. craftsmanship, were carved in the workshop of Grinling Gibbons. The magnificent high altar with its baldacchino (canopy) is modern, designed by Dykes Bower and Godfrey Allen on the basis of sketches by Wren. The wrought-iron screens in the chancel and ambulatory are the work of Jean Tijou, a Huguenot who fled to England.
American Memorial Chapel	Behind the high altar is the American Memorial or Jesus Chapel, with a roll of honour bearing the names of 25,000 American servicemen killed during the Second World War.
John Donne's tomb	In the south choir aisle stands a statue of the poet John Donne, the only monument in the old St Paul's to survive the Great Fire.
Nelson Monument	The vestry is concealed behind the massive south-east double pier. Beyond it, in the south transept aisle, is a particularly fine monument to Nelson by John Flaxman, with allegorical reliefs representing the North Sea, the Baltic Sea, the Mediterranean Sea and the River Nile; the pedestal is inscribed with the names of Nelson's greatest victories – Copenhagen, The Nile and Trafalgar.
Chapel of St Michael and St George	Off the south aisle is the chapel of the Order of St Michael and St George (instituted in 1818), an honour conferred for services to Commonwealth and foreign relations.
Crypt	From the vestry a flight of steps leads down into the crypt, which occupies the whole of the area beneath the cathedral and contains the tombs of

many notable figures including the painters Constable, Turner, Landseer and Reynolds, the scientist Alexander Fleming, and T. E. Lawrence, better known as Lawrence of Arabia. Underneath the south aisle lies the simple tombstone of Sir Christopher Wren himself, with the famous inscription "Lector, si monumentun requiris, circumspice" (Reader, if thou seekst a monument, look around thee). The sarcophagi of Nelson and Wellington can also be seen in the crypt. Nelson's 15th c. marble tomb was, so to speak, third-hand, having been intended for the ill-fated Cardinal Wolsey and then rejected by Henry VIII himself. Nelson's coffin was made of wood from the mainmast of the French flagship "L'Orient", blown up at Abukir Bay.

Wren's tomb

Galleries and Dome

Access to the stairway leading up to the Library and Trophy Room (both not open to the public except by prior arrangement), Whispering Gallery and Dome is through a doorway in the south-west double pier.

Access

143 steps lead up from the south aisle to the Triforium Gallery, where plans, models, etc. of the earlier churches are displayed. At the end of the gallery is the library (not open to the public except by prior arrangement).

Triforium Gallery

The west gallery leads into the Trophy Room. Here Wren's original plans rejected by the church commissioners can be seen, together with other drawings (not open to the public except by prior arrangement).

Trophy Room

The Whispering Gallery runs round the inside of the dome 98ft/30m above the ground. The gallery is so called on account of its remarkable acoustic properties, the slightest sound being clearly audible on the other side of the 48m/158ft-wide dome. From the gallery Thornhill's paintings on the ceiling of the dome can be seen close-to and a breathtaking impression gained of the size and proportions of the nave below.

Whispering Gallery

From the Whispering Gallery a further 117 steps climb to the Stone Gallery on the outside of the dome; 166 steps above that is the Golden Gallery. Both offer superb views of London. The ball on top of the lantern is big enough to hold ten people, though it is not open to the public.

Stone Gallery · Golden Gallery

★ Science Museum

D 4

The extensive collections of the National Museum of Science and Industry, better known simply as the Science Museum, offer an exciting insight into the history and workings of science, both in its pure form and applied in industry, technology and medicine.

Location
Exhibition Road, South Kensington SW7

Models, displays, experimental apparatus and original pieces of equipment illustrate the processes by which theoretical advances are achieved and turned to practical use. Since the opening of the world's first children's gallery in 1933, the museum has always been popular with children, their interest captured by interactive displays, "hands-on" experiments and demonstrations. The museum puts on special exhibitions and a series of events throughout the year, tel. 0171–938 8080 for information.

Underground station
South Kensington

Opening times
daily 10am–6pm,

Tour

The museum occupies seven floors. The basement is an interactive area geared to younger visitors. The Secret Life of the Home gallery demonstrates ingenious household labour-saving devices. The Things gallery,

Basement

aimed at 3–6 year olds, attempts to explain what things do, how they work, etc. The Garden allows self-discovery of simple scientific principles.

Ground floor

Apollo 10
capsule

"Puffing Billy"

On the ground floor the largest of the halls is devoted to the different ways of producing energy; exhibits include Boulton and Watt's steam-engine (1788). Beyond a Foucault's pendulum demonstrating the Earth's rotation lies the Exploration of Space gallery, housing among other things the Apollo 10 Command Module and a reconstruction of the Lunar Excursion Module, a Soviet spacecraft, and numerous rockets. The furthest hall is dedicated to Land Transport and contains a wide array of exhibits ranging from "Puffing Billy" (1813; the oldest locomotive in the world) to Rover's safety bicycle (1888), and an Austin 7 (Britain's first mass-produced car).

First floor

Launch Pad

Food for
Thought

On the first floor, The Launch Pad is an immensely popular section aimed primarily at children, inviting involvement in a variety of scientific experiments. Other galleries include: Telecommunications (telling the story of long distance communications from the 1830s to the present day including one of Alexander Graham Bell's telephones, telegraph equipment dating from 1846, and one of the very first short-wave radio transmitters), Gas (natural gas extraction; model of Murdoch's pioneering gas-works), Agriculture, Meteorology, Surveying, Time Measurement and a section called "Food for Thought" devoted to food and food technology (reconstructions of old shops and a variety of intriguing items such as the oldest surviving tin can, manufactured in 1823). A new gallery on Materials is planned for the spring.

Second floor

Babbage's mech-
anical computer
Shipping

The second floor's many galleries include Chemistry (with Crick and Watson's original model of DNA), Weighing and Measuring, Lighting, Printing and Papermaking (note the 1875 typewriter with the keyboard arrangement still in use today), Petroleum, Chemistry Industry, and Nuclear Physics and Power. Beyond these is Computing Then and Now (including Charles Babbage's mechanical computer of 1847–49). Also a large area is devoted to life on, under and beside water, with an impressive collection of model ships like the 17th c. HMS "Prince".

*A typewriter of
1875 by Sholes
and Gidden*

The Flight gallery has suspended from its roof many pioneering aircraft, including A. V. Roe's triplane (1909) and Amy Johnson's Gipsy Moth, while the Flight Lab examines the principles of flight and includes a hot-air balloon, wind tunnel and computer simulator.

Third floor

Aeronautics

This floor also houses Optics, Heat and Temperature, The King George III Collection, Photography and Cinematography, and the multi-media exhibitions of Health Matters that examines the major characteristics of 20th c. Western medicine.

The fourth and fifth floors are occupied by the Wellcome Museum of the history of medicine (veterinary as well as human). Among many fascinating items are the first functional stethoscope (1818) and experimental equipment used by Louis Pasteur (1860s).

Wellcome Museum

★ Sir John Soane's Museum

G 3

The celebrated architect and collector Sir John Soane (1753–1837) purchased, demolished and rebuilt successively for his own occupation over fifty years Nos. 12, 13 and 14 Lincoln's Inn Fields. The unusual feature of his house and museum is that it remains arranged exactly as it was at the time of Soane's death in 1837 – from the positioning of furniture and works of art to the arrangement of mirrors and coloured and stained glass which Soane used to create "poetic" effects of light and shade within the building. Anyone with a love of classical and 18th–19th century works of art and architecture should certainly include it on their itinerary.

Of the numerous works of art in the collection, the ceiling paintings by Henry Howard in the Library and Dining Room are particularly impressive. The Dining Room also contains a painting by Reynolds and a splendid portrait of Soane by Sir Thomas Lawrence. Soane's "Museum", which

Location
13 Lincoln's Inn Fields, WC2

Underground station
Holborn

Opening times
Tues.–Sat.
10am–5pm

Guided tour
Sat. 2.30pm

In Sir John Soane's Museum

runs across the back of his house, was designed to display antique Roman fragments, sculpture and plaster casts after antique originals, all lit through skylights containing coloured glass. In the adjoining Picture Room, specially designed with folding screens for the display of many more paintings than could normally be shown in a room of the size, hang two celebrated series of Hogarth paintings ("The Rake's Progress" and "The Election": twelve paintings in all). Also in the Picture Room are works by, amongst others, Turner, Fuseli, Prianesi, Calcott and Watteau as well as many grand designs for Soane's architectural schemes rendered in watercolour by Joseph Michael Gandy for exhibition at the Royal Academy. The "Monk's Parlour" in the basement contains medieval casts and works of art whilst the adjoining Crypt contains sculptures by John Flaxman and Thomas Banks. The "Sepulchral Chamber" is a particular attraction. Situated directly below the "Dome" skylight its centrepiece is the magnificent Egyptian sarcophagus of Seti I, father of Rameses the Great, discovered in 1817 in the Valley of the Kings by G. B. Belzoni. On the first floor of No. 13 the Drawing Rooms can be viewed whilst on the second floor is a "Model Room" which may be seen on request. Access to Soane's first house, No. 12 Lincoln's Inn Fields, is via a Link Passage from the ground floor Ante Room. In No. 12 visitors can see the ground floor Breakfast Room, now restored to its 1790s appearance, and can visit the adjoining "Soane Gallery" in which changing exhibitions of drawings from Soane's collection are mounted. The drawings collection, only normally available to researchers by appointment, contains 30,000 works including drawings by Robert Adam, George Dance, Sir Christopher Wren and Sir William Chambers as well as items such as five illuminated manuscripts and two of Reynolds' sketchbooks.

Admission to the museum is free. There is a charge for guided tours except for 22 free tickets available on a first-come first-served basis on Saturdays from 2pm.

★ Soho   F 3

Location
between Oxford Street, Charing Cross Road, Leicester Square, Piccadilly Circus and Regent Street, W1

Underground stations
Piccadilly Circus, Oxford Circus, Leicester Square, Tottenham Court Road, Charing Cross

Soho for many people still conjures up images of vice and iniquity. In fact its reputation as a red light district dates only from the 19th c. and laws against street walking introduced in 1958, combined with a further "clean-up operation" in the 1980s, have reduced this perception to an illusion. Soho today is neither more nor less disreputable than many other districts – like beauty, it is in the eye of the beholder.

In its earliest days Soho was actually a rather aristocratic part of London. Originally one of Henry VIII's many deer-parks (the old hunting cry "So-ho" gave the area its name), the first residents included members of the nobility who built grand town mansions for themselves. When later they moved to more fashionable districts, refugees from mainland European and the East moved in, giving the whole area an ethnic flavour.

Modern Soho represents different things to different people. For the businessman it is a good address, a convenient central location attracting a wide range of businesses: film companies, publishers, sound-recording studios, record companies, importers and exporters and agencies of all kinds. During business hours life in Soho is dominated by the comings and goings of those employed in these multifarious activities.

With its specialised food shops and delicatessens and its restaurants offering an endless variety of cuisine, Soho is also a Mecca for the gourmet. For the adventurous home cook keen to try out foreign dishes, this is the place to come for the more exotic ingredients – in Berwick Street Market for instance, or the shops of Chinatown. Here too are found a multitude of speciality restaurants. People of many nationalities having settled in Soho over the years – Italians, Swiss, Chinese, Indians and many others – the area has built up a reputation for foreign cuisine, at first within the family, then commercially, often in small restaurants comprising no more than a single room. Things have changed considerably from the days when the

Soho Square

clientèle was largely made up of thrifty foreigners and impoverished students; Soho is now a fashionable place to eat and a meal can be quite expensive. There are still plenty of reasonably priced restaurants however, and since they are open for lunch as well as dinner, a meal in Soho can be combined with a stroll through its streets.

As for an evening out, Soho has more to offer theatregoers than almost anywhere else in London, boasting several of the finest theatres in the West End (see Practical Information, Theatre). For many visitors to the capital though, Soho is still a place of dubious entertainments, sex shops and late night shows to be found in, for example, Great Windmill St. Although in recent years the number of such establishments has declined, in this respect as in others Soho has something to offer everyone.

Soho should really be seen both by day and by night. On a daytime visit the best place to start is in Carnaby Street. Synonymous with the Sixties, this one-time haunt of the Flower Generation is now a pedestrian precinct busy with all kinds of shops. Next go to Wardour Street and the church of St Anne's Soho, where Theodore, King of Corsica, lies buried, then up Dean Street, past No. 28, where Karl Marx lived from 1850 to 1856, to Soho Square, an oasis of peace in a notorious district, with its statue of Charles II and mock-Tudor garden-house. A few steps along from Soho Square in Greek Street stands St Barnabas House (built 1746), a relic of life here in grander days. Continue along Greek Street to the junction with Old Compton Street, the real heart of Soho. Any one of its array of pubs, bars, cafés and restaurants would make a good port of call if returning in the evening. Frith Street (parallel to Greek Street) is the home of Ronnie Scott's Jazz Club, the best in London, and just across the road, the Bar Italia. Ahead lies Cambridge Circus and the Palace Theatre (1891) where Anna Pavlova made her London début in 1910. The theatre is now owned by Andrew Lloyd Webber, "king" of the musical, whose "Les Misérables" has been playing to packed audiences there for years. Shaftesbury Avenue, which extends

Soho by day and by night

155

south-west from Cambridge Circus to Piccadilly Circus, lays claim to some of London's most famous theatres, including the Lyric (1888), the Apollo (1901), the Globe (1903), the Queen's (1907) and the Shaftesbury (1911). The Palace, though, is the most delightful of them all. Tickets for this relic of Victorian days are seldom easy to obtain, but it is always worth a try at the Half Price Ticket Booth in Leicester Square (see Practical Information, Theatres).

What better end to an evening than a restaurant in Chinatown – Mr Kong's in Lisle Street perhaps, or Chuen Cheng Ku's in Wardour Street. Though London's Chinese community is 30,000 strong, the area on which their life is centred is surprisingly small, comprising only Gerrard Street (its main throroughfare), Lisle Street and part of Wardour Street. Even so it is a microcosm of China: numerous tiny restaurants with Peking ducks hanging in the window, exotic food shops, bookshops, hairdressers, acupuncturists and even pagoda-shaped telephone kiosks. Cantonese is spoken everywhere. This miniature Chinatown grew up largely in the 1980s when, having up until then been scattered throughout the city, London's Chinese took over the premises left vacant after the authorities cracked down on vice, turning them into restaurants and shops. Prior to the Second World War the Chinese community lived mainly in London's dockland, in Limehouse, E14.

★ **Chinatown – China in miniature**

GERRARD STREET W1
爵 祿 街
CITY OF WESTMINSTER ＊＊＊

Leicester Square is today the heart of London's West End cinema- and theatre-land – something of a contrast to earlier days when Isaac Newton, William Hogarth and Joshua Reynolds were numbered among its residents, the second Earl of Leicester having begun its development by building a house here in 1631. By the 19th c. it was already known for its music halls, replaced nowadays by cinemas such as the Empire and Odeon. In the middle of the pedestrianised square is a small garden laid out by Albert Grant in 1874, its lawns and flower beds a welcome haven in hot weather from the crowded pavements all around. In the centre of the garden stands a large statue of Shakespeare, and opposite it a statue of Charlie Chaplin. Unveiled in 1981 the latter is by far the more unusual of the two.

The Half Price Ticket Booth in Leicester Square sells half-price theatre and show tickets (matinée and evening performances on day of purchase only – see also Practical Information, Theatres).

Leicester Square theatre- and film-goers Mecca

South Bank

G/H 3/4

The opening of the Museum of the Moving Image in 1988 saw the fulfilment of a long-cherished ambition to redevelop and revitalise what was a rather run-down part of the city. Originally the location of a dockyard and workshops, this area on the south bank of the Thames either side of Waterloo Bridge suffered badly from German bombing during the Second World War. At the centre of the modern complex is the Royal Festival Hall, built in 1951 for the Festival of Britain. Since then other buildings have been added: two concert halls (the Queen Elizabeth Hall and Purcell Room), the Royal National Theatre, the National Film Theatre, the Museum of the Moving Image and the Hayward Gallery for modern art. Adjoining to the south are the Jubilee Gardens and County Hall.

Location
south bank of the Thames at Waterloo Bridge

Underground station
Waterloo

Completed in 1976 the Royal National Theatre to the east of Waterloo Bridge is the permanent home of the National Theatre Company, itself founded in 1963 and accommodated in the interim in the historic Old Vic Theatre behind Waterloo Station. Sir Denys Lasdun's massive concrete structure contains three auditoria with a total capacity of 2400, two restaurants, six bars, 135 air-conditioned dressing-rooms, scenery and wardrobe

Royal National Theatre

◀ *Gerrard Street, main street of Chinatown*

stores, offices, workshops and car parking. The company performs in all three theatres: the Olivier, Lyttelton, and Cottesloe.

The Royal National Theatre was established specifically to provide a suitable forum for British drama. Under its first director, Sir Laurence Olivier, the theatre quickly acquired a fine reputation with its comprehensive and varied repertoire performed by a first-rate company. Successive directors have continued that tradition while further extending the scope of the theatre's activities. There are always performances and exhibitions going on in other parts of the building quite apart from the auditoria. These additional performances – pop and folk music, jesters and street theatre, jazz and medieval music, etc. – are extremely popular. Each evening before curtain-up a programme of music is presented in the foyer, ranging from classical music to jazz; many theatregoers now make a point of arriving early so as not to miss it.

On certain days of the week there are also what are called "Platforms" in any one of the theatres. A temporary stage is erected in front of the curtain, on which members of the Royal National Theatre Company or guest artists from the worlds of theatre, music or literature discuss aspects of their art.

Queen Elizabeth Hall

The building to the west of Waterloo Bridge is the Queen Elizabeth Hall, a symphony hall opened in 1967, with seating for 1000. In the same building is the Purcell Room (375 seats), used for chamber music and solo recitals. These are smaller sister venues of the Royal Festival Hall (see entry below).

★Museum of the Moving Image

Opening times
daily 10am–6pm

Situated beneath Waterloo Bridge are the Museum of the Moving Image (or MOMI) and the National Film Theatre. They are closely associated, a fact often reflected in the choice of films shown in the Film Theatre's two cinemas.

The Museum of the Moving Image is one of the most original and best museums in London, great fun for children in particular. Over 50 display areas trace the history of "moving pictures" from their earliest years to the present, television-orientated, day. Visitors find themselves surrounded on every side by excerpts from over 100 films, projected by means of the latest lasar technology. The museum traces the development of cinematography from the earliest Asian shadow projections, Chinese shades, to the invention of the film and the era of silent film. Exhibits include Charlie Chaplin's hat and cane, and sets from Fritz Lang's "Metropolis". There is a comprehensive guide to "talking pictures", including the first films, the British film, cartoons, Western and Horror movies and modern-day sci-fi films such as "ET". The behind-the-scenes work of make-up and costume departments is also illustrated. Completing the exhibition are the history of television and modern video technology. Throughout the museum a particular effort is made to actively involve the visitor; actors dressed in every

A relic of the cinema: Hat and Cane of Charlie Chaplin

kind of costume encourage visitor participation in e.g. acting out a role in a short scene, presenting the news in front of camera, auditioning for a part or trying on stage make-up.

Though not to everyone's taste, the futuristic New Style building of the Hayward Gallery, behind the Museum of the Moving Image, on the west side of Waterloo Bridge, perfectly befits its role as a gallery of modern art. Opened in 1968, the gallery is laid out on two levels; intricate lighting arrangements enable the pictures and objects to be seen at their best, an end to which the design of the interior, with rooms of widely varying size and height, is also intended to contribute. Three open courts provide effective display areas for sculpture.

Hayward Gallery

Opening times
daily 10am–6pm,
Tues. and Wed.
till 8pm during
exhibitions
(closed between
exhibitions)

The Hayward Gallery mainly functions as an extension of the Tate Gallery (see entry), being used to display the latter's collection of modern art. The gallery has no permanent collection but a variety of temporary national and international exhibitions are mounted several times a year.

The Royal Festival Hall, earliest of the South Bank buildings, stands facing the Hungerford rail and foot bridge. Designed by Robert Matthew and J. M. Martin, the Hall was erected for the Festival of Britain in 1951; the façade overlooking the Thames was extensively altered in 1965. The excellent acoustics of the 3097-seat concert hall make it a first-class venue for orchestral and choral works as top London and international orchestras and acclaimed ensembles, plus top contemporary music artistes all perform here.

Royal Festival Hall

The Royal Festival hall is also home to the Voice Box, one of the city's top venues for literature events, and the Saison Poetry Library which houses the most comprehensive collection of 20th c. poetry in the UK.

On the west side of Hungerford Bridge lie the Jubilee Gardens, established in 1977 to mark Queen Elizabeth II's Silver Jubilee. A memorial in the gardens honours British members of the International Brigade in the Spanish Civil War.

Jubilee Gardens

There are plans to build on the edge of the County Hall Gardens a giant wheel as part of the millenium celebrations: it will be the largest in the world, 500ft/151m high with 60 heated cabins.

Millenium Wheel

Beyond the Jubilee Gardens rises the nine-storeyed Neo-Renaissance style building known as County Hall. Begun in 1912 and completed in 1932, this huge edifice with more than 1500 rooms was the headquarters of the Greater London Council. After the GLC was abolished the building stood empty for years. Now the London Aquarium has taken it over and offers visitors a fantasy journey into the underwater world, with sharks being the major attraction. There are also inter-active displays and guided tours (open: daily 10am–6pm).

County Hall

The riverside terrace in front of County Hall affords a splendid prospect of Westminster Bridge and the Houses of Parliament (see entry).

★Southwark Cathedral

J 3

Southwark Cathedral, near the south end of London Bridge (see entry), is the mother church of the Anglican diocese of Southwark, covering most of London south of the Thames. Westminster Abbey apart, it is London's finest Gothic church. Tradition has it that the site was originally that of a convent, named Mary of the Ferry after the eponymous founder, a ferryman's daughter. In the 9th c. the convent became a house of Augustinian canons. In 1106 Gifford, Bishop of Winchester, erected a large Norman church known as St Mary Overie (St Mary Over the River); later destroyed by fire, it was rebuilt in 1220 in the Gothic style under Bishop Peter de Rupibus. From this period date the lower part of the

Location
Montague Close
SE1

Underground station
London Bridge

otherwise 15th c., 180ft/55m tower, the crossing, the choir and the ambu-latory. The nave, added later in the 13th c., was rebuilt in 1469 and, after a partial collapse in 1838, was re-erected in Gothic style by Sir Arthur Blomfield in 1890–96. The church was elevated to cathedral status for the new diocese of Southwark in 1905.

Tour of the Interior

The Cathedral is entered by the south-west door, to the left of which can be seen a length of 13th c. arcading. In front stands a monument to the victims of a 1989 Thames pleasure boat disaster.

Roof

At the west end of the north aisle are a number of interesting carved wooden bosses from the 15th c. roof. Among the subjects are a pelican feeding her young on her own blood (a popular symbol of self-sacrifice) and Judas Iscariot (wearing a kilt) being devoured by the Devil.

Also in the north aisle is a 12th c. Norman doorway which at one time gave access to the cloister. Under the sixth window is the tomb of the poet John Gower (1330–1408) who enjoyed the patronage of both Richard II and Henry IV. A friend of Geoffrey Chaucer, following the loss of his sight Gower retreated to the Priory of St Mary Overie where he died. The life-size effigy lies recumbent, head supported on Gower's three books – "Speculum Meditantis", "Vox Clamantis" and "Confessio Amantis".

North aisle

Tomb of
John Gower

The north transept dates from the 13th c. though the arches are Norman. In it are three interesting monuments: a memorial to Joyce Austin (d. 1626) by Nicholas Stone; a monument to Lionel Lockyer (d. 1672), a quack doctor whose miracle-working pills (supposedly made from sun-beams) earned him a great reputation in his own day; and, beneath a canopy, the beautifully carved bust of Richard Blisse (d. 1703), an vestry-man of the church.

North transept

The Harvard Chapel, originally the Chapel of St John the Evangelist, was given its present name after restoration in 1907. It commemorates John Harvard, baptised in this church in 1607, who emigrated to America and became the benefactor of the now world-famous Harvard University. The chapel is entered from the north choir aisle; further Norman work can be seen to the left of the altar. Also to the left of the altar are the arms of Harvard University, presented to the cathedral by Harvard stu-dents; to the right are the arms of Emmanuel College, Cambridge, of which John Harvard was a member.

Harvard Chapel

An unusual stilted arch gives access to the choir ambulatory, which again contains a number of interesting monuments. The Trehearne monument shows John Trehearne, "gentleman portar" to, and favourite of, James I, together with his family. Trehearne and his wife hold a tablet the inscription on which quaintly records the king's regret that Death could not be persuaded to spare him his servant. In the corner nearing the retrochoir is the late 13th c. effigy of a knight, finely carved in oak – one of the few such effigies surviving from that period. Set into the choir wall is the tomb of Alderman Richard Humble and his two wives.

North ambulatory

The choir and retrochoir are among the oldest Gothic work in London. The choir itself was built about 1220; the High Altar screen dates from 1520. On the north side of the sanctuary are the bishop's throne and on the south stalls for the suffragan bishops. Behind the High Altar is the 13th c. retrochoir (vaulting several times restored). By the monument is a 16th c. oak chest, a masterpiece of inlay work and expressive carving. At the east end of the retrochoir are four chapels: St Andrew's Chapel; St Christopher's Chapel; the Lady Chapel and the Chapel of St Francis and St Elizabeth of Hungary (built at the same time as the main choir and a superb example of the Early English Style).

Choir

Retrochoir

◀ *Southwark Cathedral: largest place of worship on the south bank of the Thames*

South ambulatory	The south ambulatory contains the heavily restored tomb of Bishop Lancelot Andrewes (d. 1626), one of the team of translators who produced the Authorised Version of the Bible.

South transept

In the south transept, built in about 1310 in Gothic style, are the arms and cardinal's hat of Henry Beaufort, half-brother to Henry IV; also busts of Sir Frederick Wigan (d. 1907), a former Cathedral Treasurer, John Bingham (d. 1625), a church vestryman and Richard Benefield one of the original cast of Webster's "Duchess of Malfi".

Shakespeare Monument

The south aisle boasts two modern memorials to William Shakespeare, the Shakespeare Window and a monument dating from 1912. The Bard's brother Edmund (d. 1607), and Lawrence Fletcher, who together with Shakespeare and the actor Richard Burbage rented the Blackfriars and Globe Theatres, are buried in the cathedral. The window by Christopher Webb depicts characters from Shakespeare's plays.

Near Southwark Cathedral

Borough Market

Just a few yards from the cathedral, squeezed in under the railway viaduct leading to London Bridge Station, are the halls of Borough Market (built 1851), where vegetables and fruit are sold. The market is mentioned in a document of 1276.

★George Inn

South of the railway viaduct in Borough High Street stands the George Inn (1676), one of the few surviving wagoners' inns to retain its galleried yard (or rather one side of it). Still in business, the George is a splendid place to rest weary limbs.

Old Operating Theatre Museum

Documents show that there was already a hospital in what today is St Thomas Street, in the 12th c. Though St Thomas's Hospital was moved to a site further west in 1862, the old gynaecological operating theatre-cum-lecture hall has been preserved in the garret of St Thomas's Church, offering a salutary glimpse of surgical conditions and methods in the 18th c. (open: Mon–Fri. 10am–4pm).

Clink Exhibition

Clink Street runs parallel with and close to the Thames just to the west of Southwark Cathedral. It takes its name from the dungeons of the palace of the Bishop of Winchester which formerly stood there; The surrounding area of Bankside formed the notorious "Liberty of the Clink", famous (and infamous) for its medieval "stewes" (brothels) and taverns, and the bear gardens and theatres of Elizabethan London. The Clink Prison and the Liberty are the subject of the Clink Exhibition (1 Clink Street; open: daily 10am-6pm).

The Anchor

There has been an inn called the Anchor on Bankside (by the river beyond the railway bridge at the western end of Clink Street) from at least the late 17th c. The present pub, its building dating from the 18th c., possesses a pleasant riverside terrace.

Shakespeare's Globe Theatre and Exhibition

Just a short walk south of the Anchor, in present-day Park Street, a memorial to Shakespeare marks the site of the original Globe Theatre, "headquarters" of the Bard's troupe of players. On New Globe Walk is a reconstruction of the Globe Theatre which has been built using materials, techniques and craftsmanship similar to the original building. Open-air, summer performances of the Bard's plays commenced in the summer of 1997. Nearby, the Globe Exhibition explains the history of the original Globe, May–Sept. daily 9am–12.15pm and 2–4pm, Oct.–Apr. daily 10am–5pm.

The Strand

The Strand, one of the busy main thoroughfares linking London's West End and the City, takes its name from a pathway along the Thames, long since disappeared having been swallowed up first by the gardens of grand mansions built a little way up from the river, and later by the embankment itself.

Despite the constant traffic, a walk along The Strand brings rich rewards, not least in the shape of old established shops, pubs and hotels, many of which were founded in the 19th c. when The Strand was *the* London pleasure mile.

Walking east along The Strand from Trafalgar Square, the Adelphi Theatre, opened in 1806 and renovated in the Art Déco style in 1930 showing Andrew Lloyd Webber's musical "Sunset Boulevard", is seen on the left beyond the junction with Bedford Street. A little further along on the other side of the road stands the famous Savoy Hotel. When it opened in 1889 it set new standards in comfort, being the first hotel to have electric light and a bath to every room. Right next to it is Simpsons in the Strand, an equally famous and long-established restaurant where real English roast beef and Yorkshire pudding is a speciality (nowhere served better, but almost certainly served cheaper elsewhere). Also near the Savoy Hotel, set back a little from the road, is the Savoy Chapel, officially known as the Queen's Chapel of the Savoy. As the chapel of the Duchy of Lancaster it is a private chapel of the sovereign, the Duchy having become attached to the Crown through the succession of the 2nd Duke to the throne as Henry IV.

The chapel (and the hotel) stand on site of the Savoy Palace, razed to the ground during the Peasants' Revolt of 1381. The Late Perpendicular chapel was built between 1505 and 1511 under Henry VII and Henry VIII and after the interior was gutted by fire in 1864 was restored in the same style. It is

Location
extending from
Trafalgar Square
to the Temple
Bar Memorial, WC2

**Underground
stations**
Charing Cross,
Aldwych, Temple

**A walk along
the Strand**

Savoy Hotel

Savoy Chapel

Royal Courts of Justice in the Strand

the Chapel of the Royal Victoria Order, membership of which is in the personal gift of the sovereign.

Aldwych

Across Lancaster Place (leading to Waterloo Bridge), Somerset House, home of the Courtauld Institute Galleries (see entry) and the University of London's King's College, lies on the right. Opposite, branching left off The Strand, is the sweeping arc of Aldwych, on which are situated India House (1928–30) and Bush House (1925–35), the latter the headquarters of the BBC's World Service. The Strand itself continues past the Baroque church of St Mary-le-Strand and Australia House (1912–18) to the junction with the eastern end of Aldwych. Ahead the road divides to pass either side of St Clement Danes (see entry), a short distance beyond which, on the left, are

Royal Courts of Justice

seen the Royal Courts of Justice (1882), otherwise known as the Law Courts, a magnificent Victorian building with close to 1000 rooms. It is here that civil actions are heard, criminal cases being dealt with at the Central Criminal Court, or Old Bailey (see entry). Across the road at No 210, two Chinese figures and a gilded lion above a doorway announce the entrance

Twinings

to Twinings, a tea shop of centuries-old tradition, extending back almost 300 years to Tom's Coffee House, opened here in 1708. It contains a small museum covering the history of Twinings (open: Mon.–Fri. 9.30am–4.30pm). Just a few yards further on, the Temple Bar Memorial marks the boundary between Westminster and the City, and with it the end of The Strand.

Detour to the Victoria Embankment

On reaching Lancaster Place there is the opportunity for a short detour to the Victoria Embankment, alongside the Thames, to see Cleopatra's Needle, a few hundred yards upstream from Waterloo Bridge. Although

Cleopatra's Needle

this pink granite obelisk 43ft/13m high and weighing 180 tons is indeed Egyptian, it has no connection with Cleopatra. Presented to Britain in 1819 by the Turkish Viceroy in Egypt, Mohammed Ali, it was brought to London only in 1878 (surviving a stormy voyage during which six seamen lost their lives), and was set up here on the Victoria Embankment. The people of the capital immediately christened it Cleopatra's Needle, by which name it has been known ever since.

The obelisk is one of a pair erected at Heliopolis in about 1500 B.C.. In contrast to its companion, now in New York's Central Park, the London one has suffered less from pollution and is much better preserved. The hieroglyphic inscriptions on the obelisk glorify the deeds and victories of Tuthmosis III and Rameses II the Great. Across the road from the Needle are the

Embankment Gardens

little Embankment Gardens embellished with a gate which once belonged to York House, former London seat of the Bishops of York. Built originally for the Duke of Buckingham in 1626, it is known as York Water Gate, having stood at first directly at the waterside. Looking upstream towards Westminster, note the massive post-modern arch of the shopping precinct built over Charing Cross Station.

★ Syon House · Syon Park

Location
Brentford, Middlesex

Underground stations
Gunnersbury, then No. 237 or No. 267 bus to Brentlea

Syon House, which stands in its own park just across the Thames from Kew Gardens (see entry), was originally a monastery founded in the 15th c. in the reign of Henry V. In the 16th c. the estate passed into the ownership of the Duke of Somerset, from which time the house was gradually transformed into one of the architectural jewels on the periphery of London, especially from the point of view of its internal architecture. The chief credit for this lies with Hugh Smithson, Duke of Northumberland, who in the 18th c. engaged two of the day's most talented men in their spheres, Robert Adam to redesign the rooms and Capability Brown to lay out the park. Adam created five rooms – the Great Hall, Ante-Room, State Dining Room, Red Drawing Room and Long Gallery – the only such Neo-Classical interior in the vicinity of London, with Roman-style columns, a variety of statues, antique furnishings and fine wall-coverings (open: Apr.–Sept. Wed.–Sun. 11am–5pm, Oct. Sun. only).

Syon Park

Syon House is surrounded by a magnificent park extending over 54 acres/22ha and containing the exceptional Great Conservatory, erected in 1820–27 by Charles Fowler; his design is said to have influenced Joseph Paxton, architect of the Crystal Palace. Near the south entrance to the park there is a rose garden (open: daily 10am–6pm).

Also in the park is a butterfly house in which tiny "Essex Skippers" flutter alongside giant South American Owlet Moths with a wing span of up to 8in./20cm. In a separate section insects such as crickets and various species of poisonous spider are kept in a naturalistic setting (open: summer daily 10am–5pm, winter daily 10am–3.30pm).

London Butterfly House

★★Tate Gallery

G 5

The Tate Gallery, one of London's largest art collections, was opened in 1897 in a Neo-Classical building designed specially for it by Sidney R. J. Smith, overlooking the Thames at Millbank. The gallery was paid for by the sugar magnate and art collector Sir Henry Tate, whose object in presenting it to the nation, together with 65 paintings by British artists from his own collection, was to lay the foundations of a national collection of important British paintings. Today the collection is arranged according to two principal themes: the evolution of British art from the 16th to the 20th c., in which are included works by Turner exhibited separately in the Clore Gallery; and modern art in an international context. For the year 2000 there are plans to move the 20th c. works to a new gallery in the Bankside Power Station.

Location
Millbank, SW1

Underground station
Pimlico

Opening times
daily
10am–5.50pm,

**Admission free
(charge for major exhibitions)**

To allow the public access to as many of the Gallery's huge number of art treasures as possible, up to 30 rooms are re-arranged every year. Any changes to the rooms containing the older British paintings (Rooms 1–10) are however likely to be small; visitors can thus be confident of seeing the most important British works. A plan of the current exhibition and details of

N.B.

William Hogarth: "O the Roast Beef of Old England"

any temporary exhibitions can be obtained at the information desk. On Saturdays and Sundays in the Auditorium there are video presentations on the subject(s) of the temporary exhibitions and the artists represented in the gallery.

British art

The oldest item in the British collection is John Bettes' painting "Man in a Black Cap" (1545). The 17th c. is represented by Anthony Van Dyck ("Lady of the Spencer Family"), William Dobson ("Endymion Porter", 1643/45) and Francis Barlow ("Monkeys and Spaniels"). Also in this British section are numerous drawings and engravings by William Blake ("Newton", 1795/1805), portraits by Peter Lely, works by William Hogarth ("O the Roast Beef of Old England/The Gate of Calais", 1748), landscapes by Thomas Gainsborough, Joshua Reynolds, Richard Wilson and George Stubbs ("Mares and Foals") and works by Edwin Landseer and Henry Fuseli. Best known of all are the landscapes of John Constable ("Chain Pier Brighton", 1826/27). Artists from the 19th c. include John Everett Millais ("Christ in the House of His Parents", 1849/50) and James Abbot McNeill Whistler ("Nocturne in Blue and Gold: Old Battersea Bridge", 1872/75). Among the modern artists are Stanley Spencer ("Resurrection, Cookham"), Francis Bacon (Triptychon) and David Hockney ("Mr. and Mrs. Clark Perry").

Sculpture

The collection of modern sculpture contains works by Auguste Rodin ("The Kiss"), Aristide Maillol, Ivan Meštrović, Jacob Epstein and Henry Moore.

International modern art

The Tate's collection of modern foreign painting includes works by the French Impressionists and post-Impressionists, among them Paul Cézanne, Edgar Degas, Claude Serrain, Paul Gauguin, Henri Rousseau, Henri de Toulouse-Lautrec and Marc Chagall; Cubists such as Georges Braque ("Mandolin", 1909/10) and Fernand Léger, and among later works, Picasso's "Reclining Nude with Necklace" (1968). The abstract art movement is represented by e.g. Wassily Kandinsky's very important

Sculpture Gallery of the Tate Gallery

"Cossacks" (1911), the Dadaists and Surrealists by Giorgio de Chirico ("The Uncertainty of the Poet", 1913), Max Ernst ("Celebes", 1921), Paul Klee, Salvador Dali and Joan Miró. There are also examples of Expressionism, Pop-Art (Andy Warhol: "Marilyn Diptych"; Roy Lichtenstein: "Whaam!"), Minimal Art and Conceptual Art. Contemporary artists include Joseph Beuys, Mark Rothko ("Seagram Murals", 1958/59), Tony Cragg ("On the Savannah", 1988) and Lucian Freud ("Standing by the Rags", 1988/89).

The Clore Gallery, first stage of a comprehensive rebuilding programme, was opened in April 1987. The two-storeyed building, named after the benefactor, the art patron Sir Charles Clore, was designed by the Scottish architect James Stirling. In it are exhibited works, including water-colours, by J. M. W. Turner (1775–1851), all of them from the Turner Bequest.

Clore Gallery

J. M. W. Turner

★ The Temple H 3

Almost abreast the spot in Fleet Street (see entry) where a large griffin crowning the Temple Bar Memorial marks the boundary between the City and Westminster, a small archway leads off southwards into the enchanting and sometimes confusing maze of alleyways and wonderful Georgian buildings known as the Temple. Charles Dickens caught its atmosphere exactly in "Barnaby Rudge": "There are, still, worse places than the Temple, on a sultry day, for basking in the sun, or resting idly in the shade. There is yet a drowsiness in its courts, and a dreamy dullness in its trees and gardens; and those who pace its lanes and squares may yet hear the echoes of their footsteps on the sounding stones, and read upon its gates in passing from the tumult of the Strand or Fleet Street, 'Who enters here leaves noise behind'. There is still the plash of falling water in fair Fountain Court . . ."

Location
Fleet Street, EC4

Underground station
Temple

Oliver Goldsmith is buried in the churchyard of the Temple Church

In the 12th and 13th c. the Temple was the headquarters in England of the Templars, an order of knighthood founded in Jerusalem in 1119. Following the dissolution of the order in 1312, the property fell to the Crown and was given to the Earl of Pembroke. After his death it was granted to the Knights of St John who, in 1346, leased it to a group of professors of common law. Ever since then the Temple has remained in the hands of the legal profession, accommodating two of the four Inns of Court whose sole prerogative it is to admit lawyers to practice as barristers in the English courts. It is situated in convenient proximity to the Royal Courts of Justice, which stand almost opposite on the north side of the Strand (see entry).

Middle Temple

The Temple is entered from Fleet Street through a handsome Wren gateway. To the west of Middle Temple Lane are buildings of the Middle Temple, the members of which have included such notable figures as Sir Thomas More, Sir Walter Raleigh, John Pym, Henry Fielding, Thomas de Quincey, W. M. Thackeray and R. B. Sheridan.

Middle
Temple Hall

The Middle Temple Hall was built in 1572 in the reign of Elizabeth I as a dining and assembly hall. After suffering severely from bomb damage during the Second World War, it was restored in the original style; it still preserves much of the original panelling, a carved screen of Elizabethan style, a magnificent double hammerbeam roof, armorial glass and a serving table made from the timbers of Drake's "Golden Hind". The large windows bear the coats of arms of Middle Templers who were members of the House of Lords; among the paintings in the hall is an equestrian portrait of Charles II by Godfrey Kneller. The first performance of Shakespeare's

Barristers and Solicitors

The English legal system comprises two separate professions, those of barrister and solicitor. The barrister is a lawyer (or attorney) qualified to plead for a client at High Court level, and can also write opinions on the prospects of a case before trial; however, he has no direct contact with the client. The solicitor, on the other hand, does have such direct contact but cannot appear before the High Court and must therefore fully brief a barrister on behalf of his client.

Barristers study at one of the four Inns of Court in London – Middle Temple, Inner Temple (see entry for Temple in both cases), Lincoln's Inn (see entry) and Gray's Inn (see entry); on successful completion of their training they are "called to the Bar". The "Inns" were established in the reign of Edward I, when the ecclesiastical bearers of office in the public courts were replaced by civil lawyers and judges. Each Inn occupies a large building complex which, in addition to rented offices and large gardens, includes the actual academic premises such as a library and lecture rooms together with student accommodation, dining rooms and a church.

To become a barrister each student must attend one of these Inns and pass the necessary examinations. A further prerequisite for this qualification springs from the British love of tradition; each student wishing to become a barrister must dine in the Hall of his Inn on at least three evenings during each term, and continue to do so for twelve such terms.

Each Inn is managed by a committee known as the Benchers. All High Court judges automatically become Benchers, while leading barristers first have to be elected to the committee. The chairman is always the oldest Bencher, known as the Treasurer, and is elected annually. This Treasurer is also the person who each semester "calls" the successful candidates "to the Bar" during an evening known as "call-night".

"Twelfth Night" took place here on February 2nd 1601. Judges and barristers still lunch in the hall, as do students during term (open: Mon.–Fri. 10am–noon and 3–4.30pm, Sat. 10am–4pm).

The Hall overlooks Fountain Court, which leads to Garden Court and the Middle Temple Gardens from where a gate opens onto the Embankment.

Fountain Court

A little less than half-way along the east side of Middle Temple Lane lies the entrance to Pump Court (1680), with access to the Inner Temple.

Pump Court

Inner Temple Hall, the dining and assembly hall of the Inner Temple, was destroyed by bombing in 1941 and rebuilt in 1952–55. It too has stained glass windows emblazoned with the arms of former members of the Inn. At the west end are a vaulted room and crypt dating from the 14th c. (opening times as for the Middle Temple Hall).

Inner Temple

Inner Temple Hall

The Inner Temple Gardens, reaching down to the Thames, are not open to the public. In them are still grown the white and red roses which, according to tradition, were plucked here at the commencement of the Wars of the Roses (1455) which plunged England into 30 years of civil war. The roses became the emblems of the houses of York (white) and Lancaster (red).

Inner Temple Gardens

Across the court from Inner Temple Hall stands the Temple Church, which serves both Inns. The original Norman church ("The Round", 1185), circular in plan in imitation of the Church of the Holy Sepulchre in Jerusalem, was enlarged in 1240 by the addition of a rectangular chancel in the Early English style. The entire church was renovated by Wren in 1682. The circular interior and chancel are both distinguished by clustered columns of Purbeck marble. The church contains fine recumbent marble figures of Templar knights dating from the 12th and 13th c., one of which is believed to be of William Marshall, Earl of Pembroke (d. 1219), brother-in-law of King John and Regent for Henry II.
   The Temple Church is used for the marriages of members of benchers' families, as well as for memorial services for benchers recently deceased.

Temple Church

★ marble figures

Oliver Goldsmith (1728–74) is buried in the churchyard.

Churchyard

Thomas Coram Foundation for Children

G 2

In 1739 Captain Thomas Coram, master mariner, trader and co-founder of the North American colony of Georgia, established a foundling hospital for the care of abandoned children. He sought donations from prominent people, among them William Hogarth who painted a portrait of Coram and persuaded fellow artists to contribute pictures to the foundation as a means of raising money for its charitable works. Among the most notable of its patrons was Georg Friedrich Handel.
   In 1926 the children's home moved to Berkhamstead but the gallery (Foundling Hospital Art Treasures) remained in London. It is housed in the Foundation's Brunswick Square headquarters in a building erected in 1937. The collection includes paintings by Hogarth, Reynolds, Gainsborough and Millais, a cartoon after Raphael or Studio, and various items connected with the history of the hospital. Among memorabilia of Handel, who was a friend of Coram and choirmaster to the hospital, are a score of the "Messiah" in the composer's own hand and the keyboard from his organ.

Location
40 Brunswick Square, WC1

Underground stations
Russell Square, King's Cross

Opening times
Mon.–Fri.
9.30am–4pm
(currently only open by special arrangement due to possible refurbishment)

★ Tower Bridge

K 3

Tower Bridge, magnificent monument of Victorian engineering and architecture, is the best known London landmark after Big Ben. Designed by Horace Jones and engineered by Sir John Wolfe Barry, it was begun in 1886

Location
Whitechapel, EC1

View of Tower Bridge and the Thames

Underground station
Tower Hill

Opening times
Apr.–Oct.:
daily
10am–5.15pm
Nov.–Mar.:
daily
9.30am–4.45pm

and completed in 1894. The blue and white colour-scheme was introduced in 1977; prior to that the ironwork was painted battleship grey.

The bridge is a complex structure. The principal features are the two matching Victorian-Gothic towers, 213ft/65m high, supported on massive piers the foundations of which are sunk 25ft/7.5m into the bed of the Thames. Each is linked to its respective bank by an 269ft/82m chain suspension bridge. Between the towers is a central lifting span, with a clearance of 29ft/9m above Trinity high-water level when closed, consisting of two bascules ("see-saws") with a combined weight of over 2000 tons. High level walkways, 141ft/43m above the river, enable pedestrians to cross even when the bridge is raised – though nowadays they have to pay for the privilege. The electrically operated lifting mechanism installed in 1975, allows the bascules to be raised in just 90 seconds for the passage of large ships. The bridge opens several times a week – hardly comparable with the fifteen or so times a day it used to open before new docks were constructed downstream.

The history of Tower Bridge, including how it was built and how it works, is told in an exhibition inside the bridge. From the high-level walkways between the towers, visitors can also enjoy panoramic views of the Thames and London. In addition, the magnificent steam engine rooms are kept in working order and can be seen as part of the tour.

★★Tower of London   K 3

Location
Tower Hill, EC3

Underground station
Tower Hill

The Tower of London, former citadel and prison where prisoners of state were held, is situated on the eastern edge of the City just outside the limits of the old city walls. The forbidding, irregularly-shaped complex of buildings surrounded by a crenellated wall and deep moat (dry since 1843), is historically the most important building in England and the most visited of

A queue waiting to enter the Tower

London's many tourist attractions. Visitors must be prepared for long queues in the high season and at weekends – unless tickets have already been purchased at an underground station.

A fortress probably already stood at this point on the north bank of the Thames in Roman times. The present Tower was built by William the Conqueror after the Battle of Hastings, not only to protect London but to subdue its citizens and to enable a watch to be kept on shipping in the Thames. William's original tower, erected in about 1078, is today known as the White Tower. The fortress was enlarged and strengthened in the 12th c. and again in the 13th and 14th c.; it was restored in the 19th c.

The Tower was a stronghold which was many times besieged but never taken. It was also a royal palace (up to the time of James I), a prison (still used during the last war, when one of its inmates was Rudolph Hess), a mint (until the opening of the Royal Mint nearby in 1810), a treasure vault (it still safeguards the Crown Jewels), an observatory (until the establishment in 1675 of the Royal Observatory at Greenwich; see entry), and for five centuries (until 1834) housed the royal menagerie.

The history of the Tower reflects the history of England. Many who figure prominently in the country's history have suffered confinement there, among them King David II of Scotland (1346–57), King John the Good of France (1356–60), King James I of Scotland (1406–07), Charles, Duke of Orleans (1415), the Princess Elizabeth, later Queen Elizabeth I (1554), Sir Walter Raleigh (1592, 1603–16, 1618) and William Penn (1668–69). Many famous people, too, have been executed or murdered within its walls, including Henry VI (1471), the Princes in the Tower – the young Edward V and his brother the Duke of York (1483), Sir Thomas More (1535), Henry VIII's second and fifth wives, Anne Boleyn (1536) and Catherine Howard (1542), Thomas Cromwell (1540), Lady Jane Grey, the "Nine Days Queen" (1554), and the Duke of Monmouth (1685). The last executions carried out in the Tower took place during the Second World War, when a number of spies were shot.

Opening times
Mar.–Oct.
Mon.–Sat.
9am–6pm,
Sun. 10am–6pm
Nov–Feb
Mon.–Sat.
9am–5pm,
Sun. 10am–5pm
(Last admission
1 hour earlier)
N.B.
Tickets may
also be
purchased at
underground
stations

171

Tower of London

★Ceremony of
the Keys

The Tower is guarded by the Yeoman Warders, a company of 38 ex-servicemen who proudly wear the traditional Tudor uniform (for which reason they are often confused with the Yeomen of the Guard (see St James's Palace) and thus incorrectly referred to as "Beefeaters"). Among their duties is the ceremonial closing of the gates each evening, the 700-year-old Ceremony of the Keys, at which the Chief Warder presents the keys of the Tower to the Resident Governor. Special passes are required to attend the ceremony (apply in writing to: The Ceremony of the Keys Clerk, Waterloo Block, HM Tower of London, EC3N 4AB). The ceremony begins nightly at 9.40pm; visitors with passes are admitted at 9.30pm at the main entrance.

The Ravens
in the Tower

While the Yeomen Warders are charged with the security of the Tower, the eight ravens kept within the precincts bear an even greater responsibility, at least if legend is to be believed; should they ever leave, so it is said, the Commonwealth will collapse. That danger is minimised by clipping their wings and doing everything possible to protect them. During the last war the British government took special measures to ensure their safety from German bombs.

A Yeoman

The layout

Occupying an area of more than 18 acres/7ha, an irregular pentagon in shape, the Tower comprises an Outer Ward and an Inner Ward with historic buildings. The Outer Ward is surrounded by a wall with six towers and two bastions, probably built by Edward I in the 14th c.; it is separated from the Inner Ward by a wall with thirteen towers, dating from the time of Henry III.

The entrance to the Tower is in the south-west corner, formerly the site of the Lion Tower, in which the royal menagerie was housed from the 14th c. until 1834.

Outer Ward

Middle Tower
Byward Tower

Seen first on entering are the Middle and Byward Towers, at the outer and inner ends respectively of the stone bridge across the moat. Both were built in 1307 during the reign of Edward I. The Byward Tower (from "byword", or password) incorporates guardrooms and machinery for raising and lowering the portcullis.

Bell Tower

Immediately beyond the Byward Tower stands the Bell Tower, built in about 1190 under Richard I. The ramparts between the Bell Tower and the Beauchamp Tower to the north of it, are known as Princess Elizabeth's Walk, the future Elizabeth I having exercised there while imprisoned in the Bell Tower by her half-sister Mary.

Medieval
Palace

Edward I's medieval palace was only recently opened to the public (in 1993). The Great Chamber, Throne Room and a hall are furnished with appropriate reproductions.

Traitors' Gate

Continuing east along the narrow Outer Ward between the two circuit walls, there is a view of Traitors' Gate opening onto the Thames. In the days when the river was the principal means of transport between the royal palace at Westminster and the Tower, prisoners sentenced at Westminster were brought to the Tower by boat, entering through Traitors' Gate.

St Thomas's
Tower

The tower above Traitors' Gate is called St Thomas's Tower. Built by Henry III in 1242, it contains a small chapel dedicated to St Thomas Becket.

The White Tower and Traitor's Gate from the Thames

The Bloody Tower, in the wall of the Inner Ward opposite St Thomas's Tower, was built by Richard II. It was in this tower in 1483 that Richard of Gloucester, later Richard III, imprisoned his two young nephews following the death of their father Edward IV. Secretly murdered, their skeletons were uncovered in the White Tower some two hundred years later. Sir Walter Raleigh, the great Elizabethan seafarer-explorer, was held in the Bloody Tower for thirteen years; here too Henry Percy, Duke of Northumberland, took his own life.

Bloody Tower

Immediately adjoining the Bloody Tower is the massive bulk of the Wakefield Tower, built, as was St Thomas's Tower, by Henry III. The last of the Lancastrian kings, Henry VI, is believed to have been murdered in a vaulted room in this tower in 1471. The tower is also sometimes referred to as the Record Tower, having served as a state archive up until 1856. The Crown Jewels were kept in it until 1968. Near the exit is a cage for the eight ravens on whose continued presence the fate of the Commonwealth rests – or so legend has it. The tower was formerly adjoined by the Great Hall in which Anne Boleyn was tried.

Wakefield Tower

Towards the eastern end of the south outer wall are three more towers: the Cradle Tower, a 14th c. water-gate; the Well Tower, with vaulting dating from the reign of Henry III; and the Develin Tower.

South outer wall

Two bastions built by Henry VIII, Brass Mount Battery in the north-east corner and Legge's Mount Battery in the north-west corner, reinforce the impregnability of the outer walls

Bastions

An opening in the walls between the Cradle and Well Towers gives access from the Inner Ward, through the Outer Ward, to Tower Wharf. Originally constructed in 1228, it is from Tower Wharf that royal salutes are fired on occasions such as the accession or coronation of the monarch, or a royal birth. The firing of these salutes is the privilege of the Honourable Artillery

Tower Wharf

173

Company, Britain's oldest military unit, originally formed by Henry VIII in 1537 as the Fraternity of St George. The Honourable Artillery Company also provide the guard of honour when the sovereign makes an official visit to the City.

Inner Ward

The entrance to the Inner Ward is through under the Bloody Tower. The ward is dominated by the White Tower standing in the centre; on the north side are Waterloo Barracks, where the Crown Jewels are now displayed; to the west lie the Queen's House, Tower Green, the site of the execution block, the Beauchamp Tower and the Chapel Royal of St Peter ad Vincula; to the east is the Regimental Museum of the Royal Fusiliers.

Queen's House

Queen's House is an attractive half-timbered Tudor house in which Anne Boleyn spent her last days before execution and where the trial of Guy Fawkes was held. Now the residence of the Governor of the Tower, it is not open to the public.

Yeoman Gaoler's House

Next to it is the Yeoman Gaoler's House, a 17th c. building of rustic style. On ceremonial occasions the Yeoman Gaoler still wears the traditional goaler's uniform and carries the executioner's axe.

Site of block

A small square formed from granite sets marks the site on Tower Green where the execution block stood. Beheadings were normally carried out with an axe, but in Anne Boleyn's case, Henry VIII gave special dispensation for the use of a sword. The majority of executions took place not in the Tower but on nearby Tower Hill. Only Anne Boleyn, Catherine Howard, Lady Jane Grey, the Countess of Salisbury and Robert Devereux, Earl of Essex and Jane, Viscountess Rochtard, lost their heads within the precincts of the Tower itself.

Beauchamp Tower

The Beauchamp Tower is named after Thomas Beauchamp, Earl of Warwick, who was imprisoned here in the reign of Richard II (1397–99). The three-storeyed semicircular tower was built in 1199–1216 and was principally used as a prison. The walls have inscriptions carved in the stonework by former prisoners, among them Lady Jane Grey's husband Lord Guildford Dudley, and his father and brothers. Lady Jane Grey's own carving "Jane" can still be seen.

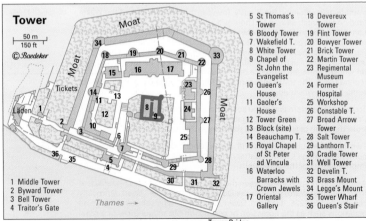

Tower

50 m
150 ft

© Baedeker

Tickets
Läden

1 Middle Tower
2 Byward Tower
3 Bell Tower
4 Traitor's Gate

Moat

Thames →

5 St Thomas's Tower
6 Bloody Tower
7 Wakefield T.
8 White Tower
9 Chapel of St John the Evangelist
10 Queen's House
11 Gaoler's House
12 Tower Green
13 Block (site)
14 Beauchamp T.
15 Royal Chapel of St Peter ad Vincula
16 Waterloo Barracks with Crown Jewels
17 Oriental Gallery
18 Devereux Tower
19 Flint Tower
20 Bowyer Tower
21 Brick Tower
22 Martin Tower
23 Regimental Museum
24 Former Hospital
25 Workshop
26 Constable T.
27 Broad Arrow Tower
28 Salt Tower
29 Lanthorn T.
30 Cradle Tower
31 Well Tower
32 Develin T.
33 Brass Mount
34 Legge's Mount
35 Tower Wharf
36 Queen's Stair

Tower Bridge

The Chapel Royal of St Peter ad Vincula takes its name from the day on which it was consecrated, the festival of St Peter in Chains. Probably built about 1100, it was altered in the 13th c., and rebuilt after a fire in 1512. It contains monuments to some former Governors of the Tower.

Many of those executed in the Tower or on Tower Hill also lie buried here, including Sir Thomas More (executed 1535), Anne Boleyn (1536), Thomas Cromwell (1540), Catherine Howard (1542), Admiral Lord Seymour of Sudeley (1549), Lord Somerset (1552), John Dudley, Earl of Warwick and Duke of Northumberland (1553), Lady Jane Grey and Lord Guildford Dudley (1554), Robert Devereux, Earl of Essex (1601), James Fitzroy, Duke of Monmouth (1685) and Simon, Lord Fraser of Lovat (1747).

Waterloo Barracks, extending along the whole of the north side of the Inner Ward, were built in 1845 for the Royal Fusiliers, who occupied them until 1962. Today the barracks house the Crown Jewels (see below).

Along the north wall of the Inner Ward, behind Waterloo Barracks, are five towers: the Devereux Tower, the Flint Tower, the Bowyer Tower (in which the Duke of Clarence is said to have been drowned in a barrel of wine), the Brick Tower and the Martin Tower.

The Regimental Museum of the Royal Fusiliers, on the east side of the Inner Ward, boasts a collection of trophies and memorabilia of this historic regiment. Next to it is the former hospital.

The adjacent building, at one time workshops was the New Armories, but this is now closed.

The wall of the Inner Ward behind the east range of buildings is fortified with three towers, the Constable Tower, the Broad Arrow Tower and the Salt Tower (in which in 1561 Hugh Draper was imprisoned for sorcery). Further round the corner, on the south side, stands the Lanthorn Tower.

Chapel Royal of St Peter ad Vincula

Waterloo Barracks

North wall of the Inner Ward

Regimental Museum

Workshop

East wall of the Inner Ward

✦✦Crown Jewels

In 1994 the Crown Jewels were moved to a new display area in Waterloo Barracks, the old underground vault in which they were kept being unable

Photography prohibited

St Edward's Crown

to accommodate the ever-increasing tourist numbers.

Almost without exception the regalia date from 1660 or later, the old Crown Jewels having been either sold or melted down during the Commonwealth.

Chief among the many notable items in this unique collection are:

St Edward's Crown, of pure gold, made for the coronation of Charles II and still used in the coronation ceremony.

The Imperial State Crown, made for Queen Victoria's coronation in 1837. It was remade with practically the same stones for George IV in 1937 and today worn by Queen Elizabeth II for the State Opening of Parliament and other important official occasions. It is set with more than 2800 diamonds and other precious stones,

Highlights

including the huge balas ruby presented to the Black Prince by Pedro the Cruel of Castile in 1367 and said to have been worn by Henry V at the Battle of Agincourt, and one of the two "Stars of Africa" cut from the Cullinan Diamond, the largest diamond ever found; and, at the back of the crown, the "Stuart Sapphire", said to have descended from the crown of the Scottish King Alexander II.

Imperial State Crown

The Imperial Indian Crown, made in 1911, set with an emerald weighing more than 34 carats, together with over six thousand diamonds.

Queen Elizabeth, the Queen Mother's Crown, graced by the world's most celebrated diamond, the legendary 106-carat "Koh-i-noor" (Mountain of Light), owned by the Raja of Lahore, Runjit Singh, until appropriated by the British following the seizure of the Punjab in 1849. The crown was made in 1937 for the then Queen Elizabeth, now the Queen Mother, on the occasion of the coronation of her husband King George VI.

The Royal Sceptre, with the second of the two "Stars of Africa", the largest cut diamond in the world, weighing 530 carats.

The gold St Edward's Staff (sceptre), weighing 3lb 9oz/1.74kg, has many legends associated with it. For instance it is reputed to contain a fragment of the True Cross.

Notice also the silver christening font in which royal infants are baptised; and the gold ampulla and anointing spoon (the only piece surviving from the pre-Restoration Crown Jewels).

White Tower

Oldest part of the Tower

Rising above the other buildings, in the centre of the ward, stands the original Norman stronghold, the White Tower, so called on account of the white Caen stone from which it was built. It now houses a collection of arms and armour. The tower, which replaced two bastions erected by King Alfred in 885, was begun in 1078 for William the Conqueror by Gundulf, later Bishop of Rochester; it was continued by William Rufus and completed by Ranulph Flambard in about 1100. Flambard later became the first of a long line of prisoners to be incarcerated in the Tower; among those who shared his fate were James I of Scotland (1405) and Sir Walter Raleigh. In 1674, nearly two centuries after the murder of the young Edward V and his brother Richard, who were imprisoned by their uncle in the nearby Bloody Tower, the skeletons of two young boys, thought to be Edward and Richard, were discovered beneath an outside staircase leading to the first floor.

The White Tower is of four storeys and stands 92ft/28m high, with walls up to 16ft/5m thick. The little cupolas on the corner turrets were added in the 17th c. The exterior was restored by Wren.

Arms and armour

The inside of the tower, little changed from Norman times, is a fine example of this style of fortress architecture.

Nelson's Column in Trafalgar Square ▶

Most of the Royal Armouries collection formerly displayed in the White Tower have been moved to a new museum in Leeds, Yorkshire. What remains is currently being re-interpreted only using pieces relevant to the Tower of London. New catering facilities are also being installed.

Chapel of
St John
the Evangelist

The Chapel of St John the Evangelist in the south-east corner of the White Tower was built in about 1080. With its sturdy circular piers topped by simple capitals and rounded arches in the apse, it is one of the best-preserved examples of Early Norman ecclesiastical architecture in England.

Tower Hill Pageant

Close by the Tower on Tower Hill Terrace, the Tower Hill Pageant, a branch of the Museum of London (see entry) tells the story of the city of London and its port. Automated vehicles transport visitors past tableaux depicting London from Roman times to the present day, complete with sound and smell effects and commentary in seven languages. An archaeological museum exhibits finds from the Thames waterfront (open: daily 9.30am–4.30pm; to 5.30pm Apr.–Oct.).

★★ Trafalgar Square   G 3

Location
Westminster, WC2

Underground
station
Charing Cross

Like Piccadilly Circus (see entry), Trafalgar Square is a place where crowds congregate. There, however, the similarity ends, Trafalgar Square being much more handsome, with an altogether greater harmony of architecture. Traditionally a venue for political and other rallies, it is also, in the summer months especially, a popular meeting-place for Londoners and tourists from all over the world. Each Christmas, ever since World War II, a giant Christmas tree is erected in the square, a gift from the people of Norway. And on New Year's Eve a vast crowd always gathers to see in the New Year, marked by the chimes of Big Ben and the singing of "Auld Lang Syne" – something truly to be experienced.

The square, named in commemoration of Nelson's victory over the French and Spanish fleets at Trafalgar in 1805, was designed by John Nash. Started in 1829, it was completed by Sir Charles Barry in 1851. Barry contributed the North Terrace in front of the National Gallery (see entry), from where there is a superb view down Whitehall (see entry) to the Houses of Parliament and Big Ben (see entry).

Nelson's Column

The central feature of the square is the 184ft/56m-high Nelson Monument (Nelson's Column), constructed in 1840–43 by William Railton on the model of one of the columns in the temple of Mars Uthor in Rome. It is topped by a 16ft/5m-high statue of Horatio Nelson. Before hoisting him into position for the first time, fourteen stone-masons celebrated completion of the column by dining on the platform. On the base of the monument are four bronze reliefs cast from captured French cannon, depicting Admiral Nelson's naval victories at Abukir Bay in 1798 (north side), Copenhagen in 1801 (east side), Cape St Vincent in 1797 (west side) and Trafalgar (averting an invasion of Britain by Napoleonic troops). This latter relief depicts the great admiral's last moments and bears the words of his famous signal: "England expects that every man will do his duty".

The four huge bronze lions at the corners were modelled by Sir Edwin Landseer in 1868. The two fountains were designed by Sir Edwin Lutyens but only installed in 1948.

Monuments

Other notable monuments in the square include: a statue of Henry Havelock, who in 1857 led British troops in the relief of Lucknow in northern India during the Indian Mutiny (east); an equestrian statue of George IV (north-east); statues of Generals Gordon of Khartoum (between the fountains) and Charles James Napier, conqueror of Sind (west); and on a traffic island facing Whitehall, an equestrian statue of Charles I by Le Sueur dating from 1633. It stands on the original site of Charing Cross, the final cross of twelve erected in 1290 by Edward I along the route of the funeral cortège of Eleanor his queen.

Charing Cross

Set into the parapet on the north side of the square is a brass plate inscribed with Imperial Standards of length (foot, yard, etc.). A curious account attaches to the origin of the yard, said to represent the distance from the tip of the nose to the tip of the outstretched fingers of a king whose identity is now lost in oblivion.

Imperial Standards of Length

Buildings of interest other than the National Gallery (see entry) and the church of St Martin-in-the-Fields (see entry) are Canada House, seat of the Canadian High Commissioner, on the west side of the square, and South Africa House on the east side. Exits on the south side of the square lead south-west beneath the imposing Admiralty Arch into The Mall (see entry), south into Whitehall (see entry), and south-east into The Strand (see entry); and on the north side of the square north between the National Gallery and St Martin-in-the-Fields to Leicester Square and Soho (see entry), and west into Pall Mall.

Canada House
South Africa House

★★Victoria and Albert Museum

D 4

The idea for a museum of applied art and fine craftmanship, to be a source of inspiration and instruction to budding craftsmen, came from Prince Albert, Queen Victoria's husband and consort. Exhibits from the Great

Location Cromwell Road, South Kensington SW7

View of the Gamble Room

Victoria and

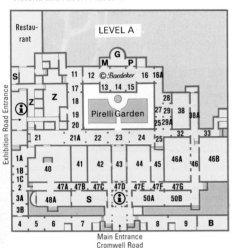

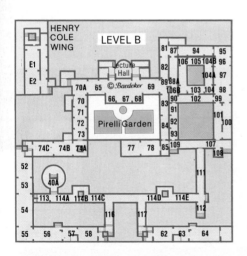

LEVEL A (Ground floor and Basement)

1–7	17th and 18th c. European furniture
8–9	19th c. European and American art
11–20	Italian Renaissance art
21–22	17th c. European art
23–24	12th–15th c. European art
25	15th–16th c. Spanish art
27–29	Northern Europe
32–33	Tapestries
38–39	Changing exhibtions
40	Clothing from 17th c. to the present
41	Indian art
42	Islamic art
43	Medieval Treasury
44	Chinese art
45	Japanese art
46	Forgeries and copies
46A	Copies of North-European sculpture
46B	Copies of Italian sculpture
47A–E	Indian sculpture
47F–G	Chinese and Korean sculpture
48A	Cartoons by Raffael
50A–B	English architecture and sculpture
B	Pictures and slides
M	Morris Room
G	Gamble Room
P	Poynter Room
S	Museum shop

LEVEL B (1st floor and mezzanine)

40A	Musical instruments
52–58	English furniture and craftwork in 16th–18th c.
62–64	English stone- and woodcarving
65–69	Silver work
70A–73	20th c. silver work
74	Gallery of the 20th c.
77–78	National Art Library
81–82	Metal work
83–84	Church silver
87–88A	Arms and armour
89	Copper and brass articles

Underground station
South Kensington

Opening times
Mon. noon–5.50pm
Tues.–Sun.
10am–5.50pm

Exhibition of 1851 formed the nucleus of the collection when the Museum of Manufacturers first opened in Marlborough House (see Bethnal Green Museum of Childhood) in 1852. Five years later it moved to South Kensington. The foundation stone of the present building, designed by Aston Webb, was laid by Queen Victoria in 1899, at which time the museum was renamed in honour of the Queen and the Prince Consort. The "V & A" as it is affectionately known, was opened officially by Edward VII in 1909 as a national museum of fine and applied art. With its wealth of material from many periods and countries, it ranks as one of the foremost art museums of the world. The sheer size of the collection, however, can make it seem

Albert Museum

90	Arms and armour
91–93	Jewellery and precious stones
94	Carpets
95–102	Textile collection
103–106	Design in 20th c.
107	Textiles
108	Fans
109	Embroidery
111	Ships and engraved glass
112	Modern work in glass
113–114E	Wrought iron
116–117	Coloured glass

LEVEL C (2nd mezzanine)

118–120	Victorian art
121	Regency art (1810–1820)
122–126	English furniture and craftwork (1750–1820)
127–128	French ceramic and enamel work
129	Chinese work in glass and stone
131	Glass

LEVEL D -2nd floor)

133	Islamic ceramics
134–138	Ceramic- and stoneware
139–140	18th and 19th c. English porcelain
141	Tiles and bricks
142	European porcelain and enamel work
143–145	Ceramics and porcelain from the Far East

HENRY COLE WING

Level 1	Museum shop
Level 2	Prints, Frank Lloyd Wright Gallery. European Ornamental Gallery
Level 3	Changing exhibitions
Level 4	European painting, Gainsborough transparencies and miniature portraits
Level 5	Prints and Drawings
Level 6	Watercolours and paintings by Constable

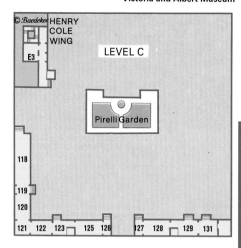

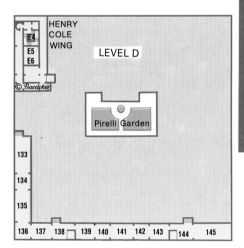

bewildering, hundreds upon hundreds of exhibits filling gallery after gallery. To set out to see everything in a single day is a hopeless undertaking.

Suggested tours

The exhibits are arranged under two heads: Art and Design, which brings together masterpieces in every field of art, according to style, period and country of origin; and Materials and Techniques, which groups objects together according to the materials used, so that their versatility can be appreciated. The V & A itself has drawn up five different itineraries covering

The layout:
Art and Design ·
Materials and
Techniques

181

all the principal galleries and the most famous of the exhibits – the Gloucester candlestick, the Raphael cartoons, the Great Bed of Ware, the Ardabil carpet, Tipoo's Tiger, and Roubiliac's monument to Handel (Room 50). Be sure to include also the Morris Room, Gamble Room and Poynter Room at the rear of Level A. These three richly decorated rooms once housed the first museum restaurant in England.

Europe in the Middle Ages and Renaissance

★ Gloucester candlestick

This tour is confined to Level A, concentrating on the rooms around the Pirelli Gardens. The highlight occurs right at the start with the Medieval Treasury (Room 43) containing the ivory Symmachorum Diptych (c. 400), the Eltenburg reliquary (Cologne, 1180), the 12th c. Gloucester candlestick, a 13th c. Flemish silver hand-reliquary and sculptures including a 14th c. French Madonna with Child. Rooms 26–29a on the right of the Pirelli Gardens are devoted to Medieval Art North of the Alps, among the finest pieces being a kneeling angel by Tilman Riemenschneider (c. 1500), stained glass from the Heiligbloedkapel (Chapel of the Holy Blood) in Bruges, a Virgin with Child by Veit Stoss, and the Nuremberg beaker in the shape of a castle (1475–1500). Rooms 12–21a to the rear and left of the Pirelli Gardens are dedicated to the Italian Renaissance. The highlight of this entire section however is Room 48a, containing the Raphael cartoons (closed until end of October 1996), executed in 1515–16 and representing the designs for the tapestries in the Sistine Chapel in the Vatican.

★★ Raphael cartoons

Europe in the modern period

The second tour begins on Level A but also includes some rooms on Level B. Rooms 1–7 display furniture and items of decorative art from 1600 to 1800, e.g. Sèvres porcelain and a cupboard by the famous French cabinet-maker Charles Boulle. Rooms 8 and 9 have similar work from the 19th c., including a chair and cupboard which belonged to Napoleon, and furniture belonging to the Viennese Secessionists Adolf Loos and Otto Wagner. Before proceeding to Level B take a look into Rooms 46A and B known as the Cast Courts, housing a collection of plaster casts of masterpieces of classical sculpture such as Michelangelo's David and Trajan's Column (in two halves). Rooms 52–54 on Level B contain a wealth of English craftmanship from 1500 to 1650, including a desk belonging to Henry VIII and Catherine of Aragon, a miniature of Anne of Cleves by Hans Holbein, and a clock belonging to James I. Much the largest exhibit is the huge 12ft/3.6m-square bed from the White Hart Inn at Ware, a masterpiece of English cabinet-making to which reference is made in Shakespeare's "Twelfth Night".

★ Great Bed of Ware

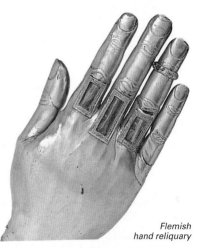

Flemish hand reliquary

Asia

A series of rooms on Level A are devoted to Asian Art. In addition to large exhibits such as the 1m/3⅓ft-high bronze head of a Buddha from the Tang Dynasty (700–900), the T. T. Tsui Gallery of Chinese Art (Room 44), immediately to the right of the Medieval Treasury, has exquisite small items such as a jade box in the shape of eight geese, dating from the Quing Dynasty

*Tipoo's
Tiger*

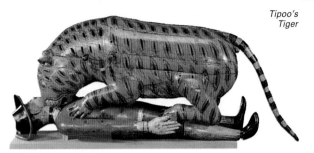

(1750–1820). The next room (Room 45) houses the Toshiba Gallery of Japanese art, with e.g. a collection of Netsukes, a 13th c. Buddha and a complete suit of Samurai armour made in 1850. On the left of the Medieval Treasury, Rooms 42 and 47c contain a magnificent display of Islamic art including the celebrated Ardabil carpet, made in 1539–40 for Safi-al-Din, founder the Safavid dynasty. The V & A's collection of Indian art (Rooms 41 and 47a/b) is the largest outside the sub-continent, with superb carpets, wonderful ivories, bronzes such as an 11th c. Shiva, and Tipoo's Tiger, a wooden hand organ in the shape of a tiger mauling a British officer. It was commissioned by Tipoo Sahib, Sultan of Mysore, at the end of the 18th c. and when played emits the tiger's roar and cries from the hapless victim.

★ Ardabil carpet

★ Tipoo's Tiger

Displayed in Room 40 (Dress Collection) are European fashions 1600 to the present day, from the V & A's costume collection. Stairs lead directly up to Room 40A (Level B) which houses musical instruments, including a cembalo made in the workshop of Jerome in Bologna in 1521, and a collapsible violin (1665) for dancing teachers. Elsewhere on Level B the jewellery collection (Rooms 91–93) has many interesting pieces, among which a 7th c. gold necklace from Ireland deserves special mention.

Costume, musical instruments and jewellery

The V & A possesses the world's largest collection of works by John Constable, which can be seen in Rooms 603–620 in the Henry Cole Wing (not to be missed). In the same wing Room 406 (Level 4) contains delightful English and Continental portrait miniatures, mainly from the 16th and 17th c.

John Constable ·

Miniatures

Three special galleries must also be mentioned: the Glass Gallery (opened in 1994), housing the National Collection of Glass; the Ironwork Gallery (also opened in 1994), with a range of ironwork made during the present century; and the 20th Century Gallery focusing on the development of household and consumer product design from 1900 onwards.

Special galleries

For those in search of well-earned refreshment, the New Restaurant on the ground floor of the Henry Cole Wing can be recommended. As well as being very pleasant it offers a good selection of dishes.

Restaurant

★ Wallace Collection   E 3

The Wallace Collection, one of the most valuable art collections ever presented to the nation by a private individual, is accommodated in 25 galleries on the ground and first floors of Hertford House, which was originally built for the Duke of Manchester in 1776–88. Despite extensive subsequent alteration, the house is still able to convey an excellent impression of the appearance of a great town mansion of the period.

    Principal credit for the collection itself lies with the fourth Marquis of Hertford who, resident mainly in Paris, built upon his forebear's passion for art in amassing an outstandingly fine set of paintings. His son Richard

Location
Hertford House,
Manchester
Square, W1

**Underground
stations**
Baker Street,
Bond Street

Wembley Stadium

Wallace (1818–90) added further to the collection, which was bequeathed to the nation by his widow and opened to the public in 1900. Since that time nothing has been changed, for it was a condition of the bequest that the collection should be kept intact, "unmixed with other objects of art". The collection contains an extraordinarily wide range of works of the highest quality in many different genres.

Viewing

Many of the rooms have pieces by the celebrated French furniture makers Boulle (1642–1732), Cressent (1685–1768) and Riesener (1734–1806), as well as Sävres porcelain, bronzes, and Italian majolica including the exceptional "Bath of the Maidens" (1525) by Giorgio Andreoli.
   In Rooms 5–8, European and Oriental arms and armour.

Paintings

Superb miniatures – including a portrait of Holbein by Horenbout – in Rooms 20 and 21; also numerous outstanding paintings, among them Lawrence's "George IV" and "Countess of Blessington" in Room 1, works by Clouet and Foppa in Rooms 3 and 4, religious paintings by Murillo in Rooms 12 and 19, and views of Venice by Canaletto and Guardi in Rooms 13 and 14. Rooms 15 to 19 are the highlight of the gallery, with 17th c. Dutch and Flemish masters – Rubens ("The Holy Family", "Isabella Brandt", "Landscape with Rainbow"), Rembrandt ("The Good Samaritan"), van der Neer, van Noort, Cornelis de Vos, Brouwer, Metsu, Jan Steen, Terborch, von Cuyp, van Ostade, van Ruisdael, van de Velde, Frans Hals

**★Frans Hals
"Laughing
Cavalier"**

("The Laughing Cavalier"), Van Dyck (Portrait of King Philip and his Wife). Also Velàzquez ("Lady with a Fan"), Titian ("Perseus and Andromeda"), Rosa ("Landscape with Apollo and the Sybils"), Reynolds, Gainsborough ("Mrs Robinson"), Philippe de Champaigne (religious subjects). With the exception of works by Joshua Reynolds, the paintings in the remaining rooms are almost exclusively French; they include pictures by Fragonard, Watteau ("Resting from the Hunt", "Lady at her Toilet", Vigée-Lebrun ("Comte d'Espagnac"), Nattier, and Greuze ("Mademoiselle Sophie Arnould").

Wembley Stadium

Location
Empire Way,
Wembley,
Middlesex
7–1/2 miles/12km
north-west of
central London

Wembley Stadium, the "mecca of national and international football", is situated in North London, on a site which was laid out from 1920 onwards for the British Empire Exhibition. The stadium was inaugurated in 1923 having taken scarcely a year to build. Designed to accommodate 125,000 spectators, a crowd of more than 200,000 packed the arena and terraces for the opening match. Today it is an all-seater stadium with a capacity of 80,000. Spared demolition in 1927, Wembley has been the scene of many great sporting occasions. Every year on the second Saturday in May, the stadium hosts the FA Cup Final, climax of the English football season.

**Underground
station**
Wembley Park
Wembley Stadium
Tours

There are daily tours of the stadium, except on days of major events, operating on the hour between 10am and 4pm (in winter until 3pm).
   Neasden underground station (linked with Wembley Park underground) is the stop for the otherwise deserted Neasden district and the Swaminarajan Hindu Temple (54–62 Meadow Gath, Brentfield Road), the largest Hindu church outside India. This miracle in marble was financed by Hindus living in Britain and built using their own labour.

**Swaminaragan
Hindu Temple**

Wesley's Chapel and House   J 2

Location
49 City Road, EC1

John Wesley (1703–91) was founder of the Protestant sect whose members were called "Methodists" on account of their pious and methodical life-style. In 1778 he established in London the simple chapel which is still the movement's mother church. Despite the plain brick exterior, the interior is very handsome.

**Underground
stations**
Moorgate, Old Street

Wesley is buried in the graveyard behind the Chapel. His house (next door) has been furnished as a memorial; it contains the preacher's books, furniture and personal effects – including an electrical appliance for curing melancholy which he himself made. Adjoining is a museum tracing the history of Methodism.

Opening times
Mon.–Sat.
10am–4pm, Sun.
after the
11 o'clock service

★★Westminster Abbey   G 4

Westminster Abbey – officially the Collegiate Church of St Peter in Westminster, with a Dean and Chapter appointed directly by the Crown – is one of the greatest tourist attractions in London. First and foremost however it is a church, drawing large congregations to its services. Since 1066, when William the Conqueror was crowned here, Westminster Abbey has been the place of coronation of every subsequent sovereign except Edward VI and Edward VIII. In addition, commencing with the burial of Edward the Confessor in 1066, virtually every monarch up to George II (d. 1760) was interred here too. The Abbey also contains the tombs of numerous prominent national figures, many more being honoured with memorials.

An Anglo-Saxon church dedicated to St Peter is said to have stood on this site as long ago as the early 7th c. Named "Westminster" to distinguish it from "Eastminster" (St Mary-of-the-Graces), the original church was destroyed by the Danes. Edward the Confessor built anew on the same spot, having chosen it for his burial place. Edward's Norman church was later rebuilt by Henry III in a style influenced by French Gothic, but only the nave was completed during his reign.

Following a devastating fire in 1298, parts of the abbey were rebuilt by Henry Yvele in 1388 working from the 13th c. plans. The vaulting of the nave was completed by Abbot Islip in 1506. The Gothic-style west front with its two 68m/223ft towers (1735–40) was the work of Nicholas Hawksmoor, a pupil of Wren. A masterpiece of Gothic architecture, Westminster Abbey is 512ft/156m long, 200ft/61m wide across the transept, and has the highest Gothic nave in England (111ft/34m).

Location
Broad Sanctuary
SW1

Underground stations
Westminster,
St James's Park

Opening times
Nave and
Cloisters:
Mon.–Sat.
Wed. to 7.45pm
8am–6pm,
Quire (choir),
Transepts,
Royal Chapels:
Mon.–Fri.
9.20am–4pm,
Sat.
9.20am–2pm
and 3.45–5pm

Nave

The Abbey is entered by the west door. It contains numerous monuments, statues and memorials. Those of particular interest are listed below.

On the right of the entrance is St George's Chapel, formerly the baptistery, and now dedicated to those who fell in the First World War. To the left of the memorial to Franklin D. Roosevelt is a 14th c. portrait of Richard II, probably the oldest surviving portrait of an English monarch.

St George's
Chapel

The south aisle contains: a tablet commemorating Lord Baden-Powell (d. 1914), founder of the Scout movement; the Abbot's Pew, a small oak gallery erected by Abbot Islip in the 16th c.; a collection of 18th c. busts of British officers; a bust of the theologian Isaac Watts (d. 1748); and memorials to the founder of Methodism John Wesley (d. 1791), Godfrey Kneller, the only painter immortalised in Westminster Abbey (d. 1723; memorial constructed to his own design), the Corsican national hero Pasquale Paoli (d. 1807), William Thynne, translator of the Bible (d. 1584), and Andrew Bell, pedagogue (d. 1832; commemorative relief).

South aisle

Immediately ahead on entering, set in the pavement a few paces from the doorway, is the Tomb of the Unknown Warrior, commemorating all those killed in the First and Second World Wars; beyond is a memorial stone to Sir Winston Churchill (d. 1956). Other slabs in the nave mark the graves of architects Sir Charles Barry (d. 1860), Sir Gilbert Scott (d. 1878), G. E. Street (d. 1881) and J. L. Pearson; the African missionary-explorer David Livingstone (d. 1873); engineers Robert Stephenson (d. 1859) and Thomas Telford (d. 1834); Lords Clyde (d. 1863) and Lawrence (d. 1879) and Sir James Outram (d. 1863), who distinguished themselves in the Indian Mutiny; and statesmen Andrew Bonar Law (d. 1923) and Neville Chamberlain (d. 1940).

Nave

Westminster Abbey

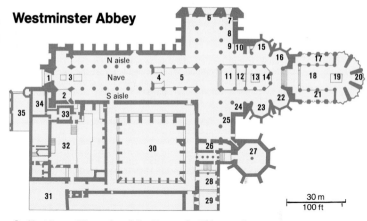

Collegiate Church of St Peter in Westminster

1　West doorway
2　St George's Chapel
3　Tomb of Unknown Warrior
　　and Churchill memorial
4　Organ loft
5　Choir
6　North doorway
7　St Andrew's Chapel
8　St Michael's Chapel
9　Chapel of St John the
　　Evangelist
10　Islip Chapel
11　Sanctuary

12　High altar
13　St Edward's Chapel
14　Henry V's Chantry Chapel
15　Chapel of St John the Baptist
16　St Paul's Chapel
17　Tomb of Elizabeth I
18　Henry VII's Chapel
19　Tomb of Henry VII
20　RAF Chapel (Battle of Britain
　　Memorial Window)
21　Tomb of Mary Queen of Scots
22　St Nicholas's Chapel
23　St Edmund's Chapel

24　St Benedict's Chapel
25　Poets' Corner
26　St Faith's Chapel
27　Chapter House
28　Chapel of the Pyx
29　Westminster Abbey
　　Museum
30　Cloisters
31　Dean's Yard
32　Deanery
33　Jericho Parlour
34　Jerusalem Chamber
35　Bookshop

Above the portal in the north aisle is an allegorical memorial to William Pitt the Younger (d. 1806), shown delivering a speech with History listening on the right and Anarchy enchained on the left. Other important monuments on this side of the choir screen commemorate William Wilberforce (d. 1833), one of the principal opponents of the slave trade; statesman Charles James Fox (d. 1806); the poet Ben Jonson (d. 1637); the composers Orlando Gibbons (d. 1625), Henry Purcell (d. 1695) and William Croft (d. 1727), the latter two being organists at the Abbey; and the scientist and explorer Charles Darwin (d. 1882). A window is dedicated to the engineer Isambard Brunel (d. 1859). On the left side of the entrance to the choir stands the black sarcophagus of Sir Isaac Newton (d. 1726).

North aisle

Transept

The central "nave" of the north transept, known as Statesmen's Aisle, has on its east side a fine memorial to Admiral Sir Peter Warren (d. 1752) on the ambulatory screen; in front is the tomb of William Gladstone (d. 1898), with next to it a memorial to Sir Robert Peel (d. 1850). On the west side of the Aisle are memorials to Warren Hastings (d. 1818), Governor-General of India; Lord Mansfield (d. 1793), judge and statesman; and William Pitt the Elder (d. 1778). The whole of the east side of the transept is taken up by three chapels: the Chapel of St Andrew, with the tomb of Lord Norris

North transept

◀ *Westminster Abbey*

(d. 1801); the Chapel of St Michael, with the tombs of J. Gascoigne Nightingale (d. 1752) and his wife (d. 1734); and the Chapel of St John the Evangelist, with the tomb of Sir Francis Vere (d. 1608), an officer of Elizabeth I.

Quire (choir) and sanctuary	The Quire (choir), occupying the same position as the choir of Edward the Confessor's earlier Norman church, extends across the transept into the nave. The sanctuary in front of the altar, where the crowning of the sovereign takes place, has a mosaic pavement (usually covered), brought to London from Rome in 1268. To the left are three particularly beautifully-worked tombs: of Edmund Crouchback (d. 1296), founder of the House of Lancaster; of Aymer de Valence, Earl of Pembroke (d. 1324); and of Aveline, Countess of Lancaster, Edmund Crouchback's wife (d. 1273).

On the right-hand side of the sanctuary are oak sedilia (seats for the clergy), thought to stand above the grave of the 7th c. Saxon king Sebert. In the north-west corner of the ambulatory can be seen the marble monument to General Wolfe, killed at Quebec in 1759. The reredos (by Sir Gilbert Scott, 1867) is embellished with a glass mosaic of the Last Supper by Salviati, and fine sculptured figures.

South transept and ★ Poets' Corner	In the south transept, west side, are a relief for the actor David Garrick (d. 1779); a memorial to the author W. M. Thackeray (d. 1863); and, higher up to the left, Roubiliac's statue of Handel. The south and east walls, particularly the latter, are lined with statues and memorial plaques to British poets. Among those commemorated by a monument or a bust in what has come to be known as Poet's Corner are Sir Walter Scott (d. 1832), Oliver Goldsmith (d. 1774), John Gay (d. 1732), author of the Beggars' Opera; William Shakespeare (d. 1616), John Dryden (d. 1700), H. W. Longfellow (d. 1882), Geoffrey Chaucer (d. 1400), Percy Bysshe Shelley (d. 1822), Lord Byron (d. 1824), Robert Burns (d. 1796), Robert Browning (d. 1889), Charles Dickens (d. 1870), Alfred Lord Tennyson (d. 1892), Lewis Carroll (d. 1898), Rudyard Kipling (d. 1936), Dylan Thomas (d. 1953) and T. S. Eliot (d. 1965).
St Faith's Chapel	On the south side of the transept is the entrance to St Faith's Chapel, with two 16th c. Brussels tapestries.

Royal Chapels

North ambulatory Islip Chapel	The tour of the Royal Chapels begins on the left of the sanctuary with the two-storeyed structure housing the tomb of Abbot Islip (d. 1532) who in 1506 completed the vaulting of the nave. The chapel's upper storey is now a memorial to the Medical Corps.
Chapel of St John the Baptist	Adjoining is the Chapel of St John the Baptist, containing the tomb of Thomas Cecil, Earl of Exeter (d. 1622). The space on the left was reserved for his second wife; she however declined to be buried there, the place of honour on his lordship's right having already been taken by her predecessor.
Chapel of St Paul	The next chapel is the Chapel of St Paul, in which can be seen the tombs of Sir Roland Hill (d. 1879) who introduced the Penny Post; Lord Cottington (d. 1652), Chancellor of the Exchequer to Charles I; and James Watt (d. 1819).
★★ **Lady Chapel**	Twelve black marble steps lead up to the Lady Chapel adjoining the apse. This magnificent structure, almost a church within a church, was built in 1503–19 by Robert Vertue, Henry VII's master mason. The nave of the chapel is a supreme example of Perpendicular architecture, with a profusion of rich sculptured decoration and beautiful fan vaulting.

The tomb of Henry VII and his queen in the centre of the chapel was the work of the Florentine sculptor Torrigiani. The recumbent figures of Henry (d. 1509) and Elizabeth of York (d. 1502), whose marriage united the Houses of Lancaster and York and brought to an end the Wars of the Roses, are of bronze gilt. James I, George II and Edward VI are also interred in the chapel. Ranged along the sides of the chapel are the carved stalls of the Knights Grand Cross of the Order of the Bath, whose colourful banners hang suspended from the walls.

In the chapel's north aisle is Innocents' Corner in which are buried James I's two daughters, Sophia who lived only three days and Mary two years. Near by is a small sarcophagus containing the bones of Edward IV's two sons murdered in the Tower (see entry). Also in this aisle are the tombs of Elizabeth I (d. 1603) and her predecessor Mary Tudor (d. 1558).

Innocents' Corner and the tomb of Elizabeth I

Of the five small apsidal chapels, the second on the right contains the marble tomb of the Duke of Montpensier (d. 1807), brother of King Louis-Philippe; adjoining at the east end is the Royal Air Force Chapel, dedicated to the fallen of the Battle of Britain, with a fine memorial window; the chapel adjacent to it on the left houses the tombs of John Sheffield, Duke of Buckingham (d. 1723), and Anne of Denmark (d. 1618), wife of James I; the chapel next to the north aisle contains the tomb of George Villiers, Second Duke of Buckingham. Until 1661 Oliver Cromwell and some of his officers were also buried there.

Notable among the monuments in the south aisle of the main chapel are those of Lady Margaret Douglas (d. 1577), daughter of Queen Margaret of Scotland, here shown with her seven children kneeling around the sarcophagus; the recumbent figure of Mary Queen of Scots, beheaded in 1587; and the life-size figure of General George Monk, Duke of Albemarle (d. 1670), who restored the Stuarts to the throne. Buried here in the royal vault are Charles II, William II and his wife, and Queen Anne and Prince George of Denmark, Anne's husband.

Tomb of Mary Queen of Scots

Immediately ahead on leaving the Chapel of Henry VII lies the Chantry Chapel of Henry V. Above the tomb-chest with its recumbent figure of the king are a saddle, helmet and shield, believed to be those worn by Henry at the Battle of Agincourt. The head of the effigy was stolen during the Reformation.

Chantry Chapel of Henry V

The Henry V Chantry Chapel leads to St Edward's Chapel, built over the apse of the older church. In the centre is the wooden shrine of Edward the Confessor (d. 1066) and his wife, which has been robbed of its original decoration. It was built in 1269 on the orders of Henry III and for a long time was a place of pilgrimage. Against the screen separating the chapel from the sanctuary stands the old oak Coronation Chair of Edward I, beneath which the Stone of Scone lay for 700 years. This block of sandstone from the west coast of Scotland was the symbol of the power of the Scottish princes; it was considered to have been Jacob's pillow and that on it had rested the head of the dying St Columba in the Abbey of Iona. Edward I brought the stone to London in 1296 after vanquishing the Scots. Not until 1996 was it finally sent back to Scotland. Many monarchs have since been crowned on the old chair, which on these occasions is placed in the sanctuary and decorated with gold brocade. Next to the Coronation Chair can be seen the Sword of State and the shield of Edward III.

★★**St Edward's Chapel**

Coronation Chair · Stone of Scone

Notable tombs around the sides of the chapel include (from the right, starting at the chair): the simple tablet of Edward I (d. 1308); the porphyry tomb of Henry III (d. 1272) with rich mosaic decoration; the tomb of Queen Eleanor (d. 1290), first wife of Edward I, with an inscription in old French; the tomb of Philippa of Hainault (d. 1369), wife of Edward III; the marble tomb of Edward III (d. 1377); the small tomb of Margaret Woodville (d. 1472), nine-month old daughter of Edward IV; and the tomb of Richard II (murdered in 1399).

The first chapel in the south ambulatory is dedicated to St Nicholas. In the centre stands the marble tomb of Sir George Villiers, first Duke of Buckingham (d. 1606) and his wife. For 350 years Catherine de Valois, wife of Henry V, lay buried beneath this tomb before being re-interred in the Chantry

South ambulatory

Chapel of St Nicholas

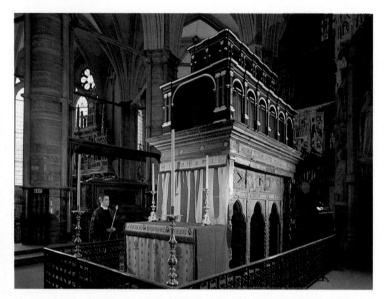

The wooden shrine of Edward the Confessor

Chapel of Henry V. Among the other monuments is a notable one to Elizabeth, Duchess of Northumberland (d. 1776); her memorial (on the right) is a masterpiece by Robert Adam and Nicholas Read.

Chapel of St Edmund

Outstanding among the many tombs in the adjacent Chapel of St Edmund is that of William de Valence, Earl of Pembroke and half-brother to Henry III (killed in battle at Bayonne in 1296). The effigy is covered with gilded copper plates and decorated with Limoges enamel. Also of interest are the tomb of Eleanor de Bohun, Duchess of Gloucester (d. 1399), here represented as a nun; the alabaster tomb of John of Eltham (d. 1334), second son of Edward II; and the tomb of Edward Talbot, Earl of Shrewsbury (d. 1617) and his wife.

Chapel of St Benedict

The Chapel of St Benedict in the south-west corner of the ambulatory contains, among others, the marble tombs of Simon Langham (d. 1376), Abbot of Westminster and Archbishop of Canterbury; in the centre, the tomb of Lionel Cranfield, Earl of Middlesex (d. 1645), chancellor to James I; and the tomb of Anne of Cleves, fourth wife of Henry VIII.

Cloisters · Brass Rubbing Centre

The cloisters, entered via a doorway at the east end of the south aisle, date from the 13th and 14th c., though it may be that a part of the walls is Norman. As well as a cafè there is a Brass Rubbing Centre where rubbings can be made of some of the many tombs seen in the cloisters (open: Mon.–Sat. 9am–5pm).

To the west of the cloisters is a range of buildings including the Deanery, Jericho Parlour and Jerusalem Chamber (where, in 1413, Henry IV died).

Jerusalem Chamber

The Jerusalem Chamber has lovely 16th c. tapestries and ceiling paintings.

Chapter House · Pyx Chamber · Abbey Museum

The Chapter House, reached from the east cloister, was the meeting-place of the king's Great Council in 1257 and of Parliament from 1282 to 1547. It was subsequently used as an archive until 1865. It is an octagonal chamber 66ft/20m across, probably built by Henry of Reims (1245–55). The vaulting is supported on a single pier of clustered shafts (a copy of the original pier by Sir George Gilbert Scott, set during the restoration of the Chapter House in 1866). Other features worth noting are a Roman sarcophagus, the well-preserved 13th c. pavement, the ornamental tracery of the six windows, and the circular tympanum of the doorway, with figures of Christ in Majesty, the Virgin and angels (13th c.). On display is Edward the Confessor's founding charter.

Opening times Apr.–Sept. Daily 10am–6pm; Oct.–Mar. Daily 10am–4pm;

The Chapel of the Pyx (Pyx Chamber) was originally a sacristy in Edward the Confessor's church and boasts the oldest altar in the abbey. It later became a royal treasury in which was kept the "pyx", a chest containing the trial-plates of gold and silver used in the annual test of the coinage.

Pyx Chamber

The Norman undercroft, part of Edward the Confessor's church, now houses the Westminster Abbey Museum, with old seals and charters, 14th and 15th c. chests, architectural fragments and the coronation chair of Mary II. There is also a most unusual collection of wax funeral effigies, which at one time were placed inside the abbey beside the appropriate tomb. They include figures of Charles II, Elizabeth I, Mary II, William III, the Duke of Buckingham and Admiral Lord Nelson. The wooden figure of Edward III is the oldest wooden effigy of a monarch in Europe.

Abbey Museum

Near Westminster Abbey

The Neo-Tudor gatehouse diagonally opposite the abbey's west door, stands near to the site of the former bell tower and sanctuary wherein anyone might find refuge from their pursuers. Edward V was actually born in the sanctuary, his mother having fled to safety there. The one-time existence of the sanctuary is reflected in local street names such as Broad Sanctuary and Little Sanctuary.

Sanctuary

Behind the gatehouse lies Dean's Yard, once a place of relaxation for the monks. From the cloisters of the Abbey there is access to the College Garden, said to be one of the oldest gardens in England (open: Tues. and Thur. only). In July and August brass band concerts take place in the garden on Thursdays between 12.30 and 2pm. Westminster School, one of the country's leading public schools, is first mentioned in 1239 as a monastic school; it was refounded by Elizabeth I in 1560. Former pupils include John Dryden, John Locke, Ben Jonson, Christopher Wren, Warren Hastings and Winston Churchill. Every Christmas there are performances in Latin in the old monastic dormitory (now the school hall), and on Shrove Tuesday the school observes the ancient Pancake Greaze, at which boys scramble for a pancake thrown by the school cook, with a guinea as prize for the boy who comes away with the largest piece. (The widespread custom of Tossing the Pancake sprang up in the 18th c.; its origins are no longer known.)

Dean's Yard · College Garden · Westminster School

Middlesex Guildhall, a Renaissance-style building erected in 1913, faces onto Parliament Square. Memorial panels in the entrance hall, with the signatures of King George of Greece, Queen Wilhelmina of the Netherlands and King Haakon of Norway, commemorate the use of the court-rooms by the Allies during the last war as military and naval courts.

Middlesex Guildhall

St Margaret's, a church in the shadow of the great Westminster Abbey, was founded in the 11th c. by Edward the Confessor and rebuilt between 1488 and 1523 by Robert Stowell for the Westminster wool merchants. Since Palm Sunday 1614 when members of the Puritan-dominated House of

St Margaret's

Commons worshipped here for the first time, it has been the parish church of the Commons. It is also the scene of many a fashionable wedding, Winston Churchill being among those to have married here.

St Margaret's is especially notable for the Flemish stained glass in the east window, presented by Ferdinand and Isabella of Spain on the occasion of the marriage of Prince Arthur, elder brother of Henry VIII, to Catherine of Aragon. By the time the glass reached London, Arthur had died and Henry had married his widow, whereupon the glass was sent to Waltham Abbey. It was installed in St Margaret's only in 1758, after Parliament had purchased it.

Other features of interest are the altarpiece, the centre panel of which is a carving of the "Supper at Emmaus", copied from Titian's picture; 16th and 17th c. memorial brasses (including one to Sir Walter Raleigh, the founder of Virginia, who is believed to have been buried here following his execution); and Elizabethan and Jacobean monuments.

★ Westminster Cathedral   F 4

Location
Ashley Place
SW1

Underground station
Victoria

Westminster Cathedral, seat of the Cardinal Archbishop of Westminster, is the principal Roman Catholic cathedral in Britain, rivalled only by the Cathedral of Christ the King in Liverpool. It was designed in the early Christian Byzantine style by the architect John Francis Bentley. Constructed between 1895 and 1903, it is brick-built, 394ft/120m long, and crowned by four domes.

The cathedral is entered from the Piazza which faces Victoria Street. Inside, next to the gift shop, is an elevator leading to the 273ft/84m high campanile, St Edward's Tower, which affords extensive views over London (tower open: Apr.–Nov. daily 9am–5pm; Dec.–Mar. Thur.–Sun. 9am–5pm).

Interior

Near the entrance are two columns of red Norwegian granite, symbolising by their colour the Precious Blood of Christ to which the cathedral is dedicated. By the left-hand column is a bronze figure of St Peter, a copy of the famous statue in St Peter's, Rome.

Nave

The nave is the highest (109ft/34m) and widest in England (60ft/18m). The decorative scheme is complete to the gallery level, with mosaics intended for the upper walls and domes to be provided by future generations. Even in its unfinished state, the nave is immensely impressive on account of its size and decoration (mosaics, over 100 differently coloured marble facings, etc.). The galleries over the aisles are borne on marble columns from the same quarries in Greece which supplied marble for the great St Sophia Basilica in Istanbul. The capitals, all different, are of white Carrara marble. The great cross which hangs from the arch at the east end of the nave is 33ft/10m long, with painted figures and (on the back) the Mater Dolorosa. The 14 Stations of the Cross by the sculptor Eric Gill are especially renowned.

Chapels

On a tour of the chapels the eye is caught in particular by the splendour of the mosaics. Among the chapels of special note are: St George's Chapel, with the tomb of the martyr St John Southworth, "parish priest of Westminster", hanged at Tyburn in 1654; the Chapel of St Thomas of Canterbury (also known as the Vaughan Chantry) in the north transept, with a fine effigy of Cardinal Vaughan who oversaw the building of the cathedral; the Chapel of St Patrick and the Saints of Ireland with, in the niches, the badges of the Irish regiments which fought in the Great War; the Chapel of St Andrew (patron saint of Scotland), having a beautiful marble floor; and the Chapel of St Gregory with a fine marble and gilt bronze screen opening into the baptistery. The Lady Chapel is wonderfully adorned in marble and mosaics and is the richest of all those in the cathedral.

The high altar in the sanctuary has a baldachino (canopy) supported on marble columns; to the left is seen the Archbishop's Chair. The highly acclaimed cathedral choir sing from the apse behind the high altar.

Altar

Behind the Lady Chapel steps lead down to the crypt (St Peter's Chapel), which houses a collection of treasured relics, including a mitre which belonged to St Thomas à Becket and a fragment of the True Cross.

Crypt

★★Whitehall
G 3/4

Whitehall is synonymous with the UK's central government, the great ministries of state and other government offices being concentrated along its length together with that of its extension, Parliament Street, and the streets on either side. The name preserves the memory of the old Whitehall Palace, which once covered the area between Trafalgar Square and Westminster Bridge bounded on one side by the Thames and on the other by St James's Park. The palace had its roots in the 13th c. when the land passed to the archbishops of York, whose London seat, York Place, originally stood there. It was in his capacity as Archbishop of York that Cardinal Wolsey laid hands on it and began enlarging the house. Following Wolsey's fall, Henry VIII took the property for himself and immediately set about transforming the house into a royal palace, building among other things a banqueting hall, a tournament ground and the Holbein Gate, a large gatehouse with Renaissance elements, not far from where the Cenotaph now stands. James I hatched even more ambitious plans, the realisation of which he entrusted to Inigo Jones and John Webb; in the end however only the Banqueting Hall was built. In 1698 fire broke out destroying virtually all the palace buildings apart from the Banqueting Hall. They were never rebuilt.

Location
Westminster, SW1

Underground stations
Westminster,
Embankment,
Charing Cross

From Trafalgar Square to Parliament Square

Proceeding south along Whitehall from Trafalgar Square (see entry), the Admiralty is seen on the right. The older part was built by Thomas Ripley in 1723–26, while the domed building to the rear was added between 1895 and 1907.

Admiralty

Branching off Whitehall opposite the Admiralty is the street known as Great Scotland Yard, where in the 16th c. the kings of Scotland had a palace. The fame of the street owes less to this however, than to its connection with London's Metropolitan Police, for which force "Scotland Yard" is all but a synonym. Founded by Robert Peel in 1829, the force had its first headquarters here and has kept the name ever since. Each time police headquarters have moved, first in 1890 to the Embankment and again in 1967 to their present address in Victoria Street, not far from Westminster Abbey (see entry), the new premises have been given the name New Scotland Yard.

Scotland Yard

Further down on the left, on the other side of Whitehall Place, stands the Old War Office, an irregularly-shaped building now containing offices of the Ministry of Defence. The Ministry's monumental main block lies behind Banqueting House, on Horse Guards Avenue, and extends to the Victoria Embankment on the Thames. Over the building fly the regimental standards of British army regiments while in front are statues of Sir Walter Raleigh, Field Marshal Lord Montgomery of Alamein and others. A fragment of Henry VIII's Whitehall Palace wine cellar is preserved in the basement.
  Other relics of the old palace can be seen in the Ministry of Defence gardens at the Embankment end of Horse Guards Avenue; they include

Old War Office

Ministry of Defence

The Old War Office and Banqueting House (right)

Inspection of the Queen's Life Guards – a tourist attraction

part of Queen Mary's Terrace with riverside steps and a jetty built in 1691 by Wren.

Facing Horse Guards Avenue across Whitehall is the building known simply as Horse Guards, designed by William Kent in 1753. Finely proportioned and set around a small forecourt with an archway and two stone sentry-boxes, it stands on the site of the former palace guard-house. Today it is occupied by still more government offices.

Horse Guards

The principal attraction at Horse Guards is not so much the building but the sentries on duty in front of it. The three troopers from the Household Cavalry, one on foot and two mounted, keep watch by the gate and sentry-boxes with stoic sangfroid, unperturbed by the tourists milling round them. The Household Cavalry is comprised of two different regiments, the Queen's Life Guards, who wear scarlet tunics and white plumed helmets, and the Blues and Royals, who wear blue tunics and red plumed helmets. The Life Guards originated as a cavalry unit forming Charles I's bodyguard during the Civil War; the Blues and Royals (formerly the Royal Horse Guards) as a troop of Cromwellian cavalry. The changing of the guard, which takes place in almost all weathers, is a great tourist attraction (be sure to take up position in good time). The return ride to regimental headquarters, 1½ miles/2½km away in Hyde Park Barracks, is carefully arranged so that the troopers pass by Buckingham Palace at almost exactly the time of the changing of the palace foot guard. There is also a short ceremonial dismounting of the mounted sentries daily at 4pm which spectators are welcome to watch.

★Changing of the guard
Mon.–Sat. 11am, Sun. 10am

Behind Horse Guards, between it and St James's Park (see entry), is the large open expanse of Horse Guards Parade where, every June on the Queen's official birthday, the colourful military spectacle of Trooping the Colour takes place (see Practical Information, Events).

Horse Guards Parade

Opposite Horse Guards stands Banqueting House, the only part of the old Whitehall Palace to have survived intact. Designed by Inigo Jones (see Famous People) for Charles I and erected in 1619–22, it was London's first Palladian building and affords a supreme example of the style. The orderliness of arrangement typical of Palladianism is very much in evidence – horizontally in the rows of windows along the length of each storey and the alternating segmental and triangular pediments distinguishing the lower; vertically in the attached Corinthian and Ionic columns of the centre bays and the pilasters on either side. A frieze of garlands and an open balustrade round off the elegant design.

★**Banqueting House**

The building is the third on this site. Its two predecessors – one of which was demolished and the other destroyed by fire – were used for court banquets and receptions; the present building serves similarly for royal and official functions. But the Banqueting House was by no means used only for banquets, etc. and in earlier days was the scene of many historic events. It was in the old Banqueting House that in 1533 Henry VIII married Anne Boleyn and where he died in 1547; and it was from there that his daughter Elizabeth was taken to imprisonment in the Tower. The history of Inigo Jones's "new" Banqueting House is inextricably linked with that of the Stuarts. It was through one of its windows that Charles I stepped to face execution on the scaffold erected outside (marked today by the bust of Charles I by Le Sueur above the door); and his "successor" Oliver Cromwell lived and died (1658) within its walls. It was in the Banqueting Hall that Parliament invited Cromwell to assume the mantle of king, and where, after the Restoration, the members swore loyalty to Charles II. It was here too that in 1689 William of Orange was offered the crown.

A staircase leads up to the Banqueting Hall, a double cube 125ft/38m long 59ft/18m across and 59ft/18m high, the only division being a small gallery

Banqueting Hall

Charlies, Robin Redbreasts and Bobbies

"**W**anted: a hundred thousand men as constables in London. The following need NOT apply: those who are not yet sixty, seventy or eighty years of age, blind in one eye and unable to see much with the other, lame in one or both legs, deaf as a post, with an asthmatic cough enough to cut one in half, quick as a snail and so strong that they are unable to lock up a burly old washerwoman after she has finished doing the washing".

Always friendly, sometimes amusing: London's Bobbies are a landmark of the city. They owe their name and existence to Sir Robert Peel.

This "situations vacant" advertisement – tongue in cheek of course – appeared in a London newspaper in 1821, hitting out at the pathetic state of the London police, or rather what purported to be the police, for to tell the truth there were no such officers for the whole of London, only some somewhat dubious patrolmen operating in some of the boroughs, mainly in the City. London could blame this state of affairs on the fact that the latest universally applicable law regulating the police was the Statute of Winchester, dating from 1285 but still valid, at least in principle. Under this law, every male person between the ages of 15 and 60 was obliged "to carry arms in order to safeguard the peace". In a special law applying to London it was laid down that every free citizen and taxpayer must do guard duty at night – if he refused he would have to pay a fine or go to prison. Many cunning "free citizens" of London avoided this obligation by hiring substitutes, mainly old men, cripples and the unemployed. These, however, brought a strange concept of duty to the task, because they soon became known for their laziness, stupidity, brutality and drunkenness on duty – no wonder, then, that they ended up by not officially earning a single penny. However, the city councillors were concerned about public safety, and therefore, in 1603, the office of city marshal was created, as the head of the police, with one under-marshal and six marshalmen under him. However, there was but little change as far as the quality of the force was concerned, and a further law of 1663, shortly after Charles I came to the throne, merely resulted in the police constables being given a new nickname, the "Charlies". In fact, the reverse of what the law intended actually happened, and the security force attracted some shady characters to its ranks. The most dubious and sinister of all was Jonathan Wild, initially a marshal and soon appointed "General Thiefcatcher of Great Britain and Ireland". He ran a racket whereby he arranged to return recovered stolen goods to their owners for a suitable payment – so he employed a veritable army of thieves, pickpockets and street robbers and made a lot of money from this method of "combating" crime. However, in 1725 he was finally unveiled and hanged at Tyburn.

The first attempt to establish a genuine police force was made from 1748 onwards by Henry Fielding, in his capacity as city councillor, and later by his brother John. "Mr Fielding's People" were initially seven intrepid men who hunted down thieves and burglars and went down in London history as the "Bow Street Runners", as they were quartered in a house in Bow Street near Covent Garden. Inspired, perhaps, by their example, in 1782 the City of London installed a force of policemen who were on watch during the day as well as at night and were even given a uniform of sorts in the shape of a blue coat, as blue was regarded as a suitable colour to act as a backcloth to public hangings which the police were obliged to attend. Further armies of police were called into service: in 1798 the Thames Police were formed to combat piracy on the river, and in 1805 the Bow Street Runners became a mounted unit aimed at curbing highway robbery. They patrolled in a radius of 20 miles around London and, because of their red waistcoats, soon became known as "Robin Redbreasts".

But still London lacked an efficient police force capable of serving the whole city – the joke advertisement of 1821 was not made without just cause. On to the scene now strode Sir Robert Peel (1788–1850) who in 1821, when Home Secretary, made his first attempt to improve matters. The City of London in particular initially opposed his plans, and it was not until 1829, when it was offered its own police force, directly responsible to the Lord Mayor and the City Council, that Peel was able to force the Metropolitan Police Bill through Parliament. This created the London Metropolitan Police, a force under the direct control of the Home Secretary, with its headquarters in the building at the rear of No. 4 Whitehall Place, best reached through a courtyard with a name which has now become famous – **Scotland Yard**, the most renowned police force in the world. Initially the force comprised 3000 men, dressed in a blue uniform with a top hat which, for a number of years, they were obliged to wear even when off duty. That soon showed itself to be an unwise requirement, because the new police were anything but popular and as a result some of Peel's "Blue Devils" were murdered or beaten up. In the early years of its existence the Metroploitan Police were required solely to keep law and order, and they also met with competition. In 1839 they absorbed the Bow Street Runners and the Thames Police; later that year the City of London Police was formed, and still exists today. It was not until 1842, after two spectacular cases of murder, that Scotland Yard formed its first criminal investigation department, made up of two inspectors and six sergeants. Gradually the police earned the trust and respect of the public, and when in 1864 they were given the new uniform – a tunic and the famous helmet – they had already earned a considerable reputation which was reflected in the nickname "bobby", after Sir Robert Peel. In the early 1870s the criminal investigation department (C.I.D.) was considerably expanded. Its successes – in spite of such spectacular setbacks as the still unsolved Jack the Ripper murders, which led to the resignation of Police Commissioner Henderson – were to make Scotland Yard famous and tended to cause the general public to forget that the C.I.D. was only a part of the whole Metropolitan Police Force.

The "bobbies" remain popular thanks to their willingness to help anyone who turns to them for assistance, something which is engrained in their tradition. From the beginning they went around unarmed, trusting in the persuasive powers of their words, and that is something which has remained unaltered to this day; in a poll conducted by the police trades union in 1995 79% of the officers asked were against the carrying of arms. Something else too – in older detective novels Scotland Yard detectives were seldom portrayed as heroes, rather as patient plodders or even as fools, as can be seen by reading the tales about Sherlock Holmes, Miss Marple or Hercule Poirot. Perhaps that serves to show that the "Met" regards itself as a collective whole in which each individual carries out his work in unspectacular fashion.

right the way round, supported on Ionic columns. The whole splendour of the hall derives from twelve allegorical ceiling paintings commissioned by Charles I and executed by Peter Paul Rubens with the assistance of Jordaens and other pupils (1635). The central scene depicts the Apotheosis of James I while another symbolises the Union of England and Scotland. Rubens received a fee of £3000 and a knighthood for his work (open: Mon.–Sat. 10am–5pm).

Gwydyr House

Next to Banqueting House stands Gwydyr House, a handsome Georgian building erected as a private residence by John Marquand in 1772. It was the temporary headquarters of the Royal Commission on Local Government and is now the Welsh Office.

Dover House ·
Old Treasury

Across the road the space between Horse Guards and Downing Street is filled by the Scottish Office and old Treasury building, the latter occupied by offices of the First Lord of the Treasury, the Chancellor of the Exchequer, and the Privy Council. It was built by Hans Soane and refaced by Charles Barry in 1847.

Downing Street

Barring the entrance to the adjoining street is a set of heavy iron railings and a gate, guarded by policemen and usually besieged by curious onlookers. This is Downing Street, an inoccuous little cul-de-sac famous throughout the world. No. 10 has been the official residence of the Prime Minister since 1735 when George II presented the house to Sir Robert Walpole who, although the title was not in use at that time, is regarded as having been the first prime minister in the modern sense. No. 11 is the official residence of the Chancellor of the Exchequer, and No. 12 the Government Whips' Office. All three houses were built in the 1680s by Sir George Downing, a diplomat and courtier who contrived to hold office under both Cromwell and Charles II and was knighted by the latter in 1660. From the outside the brick buildings appear modest and surprisingly small; behind the façades however they are actually quite spacious, even rather grand. Neither Downing Street nor any of the houses is open to the public.

Government
Offices

Adjoining Downing Street are the Renaissance-style Government Offices erected in 1868–73 to designs by Sir George Gilbert Scott. The block north of King Charles Street houses the Foreign Office, the Commonwealth Office, the Home Office and the India Office Library (containing over 250,000 volumes on oriental culture and affairs). The block to the south of King Charles Street accommodates the Treasury and other offices.

Cenotaph

The Cenotaph (Greek: "empty tomb"), Britain's memorial to the dead of the two World Wars, stands in the centre of Whitehall opposite the Foreign Office. Designed by Sir Edwin Lutyens, it was unveiled on November 11th 1920, the second anniversary of the 1918 armistice, as a memorial to those who lost their lives in the "Great War". After the last war the inscription was amended so that it now reads "To the Glorious Dead".

The Cenotaph is devoid of religious symbols in recognition of the fact that the dead belonged to many different races and creeds; it bears only the emblems of the services – army, air force, navy and merchant navy.

Every year on Remembrance Day (the second Sunday in November), at 11am, a memorial service is held at the Cenotaph in the presence of the Queen and other members of the Royal Family, Members of Parliament, members of the armed forces and representatives of the Commonwealth and of public life.

★**Cabinet War
Rooms**

At the western end of King Charles Street, between the Foreign Office and the Treasury, is a short flight of steps (Clive Steps) leading down to the Cabinet War Rooms. It was from these 19 rooms situated only a few feet below ground, that the British Cabinet and Chiefs of Staff controlled Britain's destiny during the Second World War. The rooms contain all kinds of memorabilia of that critical time, including the telephone used by Churchill

10 Downing Street . . .

. . .and the Cabinet War Rooms

Winston Churchill and the flags of the Commonwealth in Parliament Square

for his lengthy discussions with President Roosevelt. The Conference Room, Map Room, and even Churchill's simply furnished bedroom, are all excellently preserved (open: Apr.–Sept. daily 9.30am–6pm, Oct.–Mar. daily 10am–6pm).

Parliament Square

At its southern end Parliament Street opens onto Parliament Square immediately west of the Houses of Parliament (see entry). The lawned area in the centre is adorned with the flags of Commonwealth countries and statues of British and US statesmen, that of Churchill being the most impressive.

Wimbledon

Location
south London

Underground station
Southfields

Wimbledon lies about 6 miles/10km south of central London. It is a district of handsome houses with well-tended gardens, and of extensive open spaces, sports grounds and walks. Every year in the last week of June and first week of July it is the venue of the world famous tennis tournament organised by the All England Lawn Tennis and Croquet Club. The town of Wimbledon has a long history; it is believed to have been the site in the first century A.D. of the last Roman settlement in England.

The tennis championships had a somewhat curious beginning. In 1877, when croquet was the only game played here, funds had to be found for the purchase of a much-needed roller for use on the croquet lawns. It was decided to raise the money by holding a tennis tournament, tennis being in those days a new sport rapidly gaining in popularity. The roller at the centre of it all now occupies a place of honour at the Club.

The most successful Wimbledon competitor of all time is neither Boris Becker nor Björn Borg but Hugh Lawrence "Laurie" Doherty who, between 1897 and 1906, won a total of fourteen titles: in the singles from 1902 to 1906 and in the doubles, partnered by his brother Frank "Reggie" Doherty, from 1897 to 1905. Reggie Doherty took the singles title himself four times (1897–1900).

Wimbledon Lawn Tennis Museum

The Wimbledon Lawn Tennis Museum in Church Road was opened in 1977 to commemorate the centenary of the tournament. It has a wealth of interesting material relating to the history of the "white sport". On display are a collection of tennis outfits, rackets, balls, etc., as well as the much-prized Championship Trophies. Wimbledon's holy of holies, the famous Centre Court, can also be viewed (open: Tues.–Sat. 10.30am–5pm, Sun. 2–5pm; open only to those with tickets to the grounds during the Championships. Closed Fri.–Sun. prior to, and the middle Sun., of the Championships. The tea shop opens ½ hour before the museum).

Wimbledon Common

Wimbledon Common offers woodland, lakes and play areas for recreation, as well as 15½ miles/25km of bridle-paths. Other attractions include an old windmill and the 17th c. Southside House, a gentleman's mansion built in 1687 (guided tours: Oct.–May Tues., Thur., Sat. hourly from 2–5pm).

★★ Windsor Castle

Location
Windsor, Berkshire, 22 miles/35km west of London

Anyone on any but the very briefest of visits to London should be sure to make the excursion to Windsor Castle, the largest castle in the world still inhabited. Built on a chalk cliff above the Thames, the Castle dominates the little town of Windsor which, as a hamlet some nine and a half centuries ago, was granted to the monks of Westminster Abbey (see entry) by Edward the Confessor. William the Conqueror then purchased the land in order to erect a fortress on the hill. Construction began in about 1078 at the same time as the Tower of London (see entry) was being built; nothing now remains of the original timber structure. The first stone buildings were erected by Henry I in about 1110; Henry II then replaced the timber palisade with a stone wall reinforced by square towers; Henry III added still more defensive works, including the Curfew Tower. In 1189 the English barons laid siege to the castle, defeating the Welsh forces of Prince John – who some years later, as King John, nicknamed "John Lackland", was forced to sign the Magna Carta at Runnymede, only a short distance from Windsor. Edward III, born in Windsor in 1312, had William the Conqueror's old castle taken down; then, through William of Wykeham, Bishop of Winchester, he had further fortifications and enlargements carried out, including the building of the Round Tower. Under Elizabeth I the north terrace was added.

During the reign of Charles II the picturesque old stronghold was transformed into a comfortable castle home, though little use was made of it by later monarchs until comparatively recent times. Not until George III moved into the Castle in about 1800 was anything further of substance done. It was left to George IV to initiate an extensive programme of restoration under the direction of the architect Sir Geoffrey Wyattville, which continued into the reign of Queen Victoria.

In November 1992 fire broke out in the State Apartments, causing widespread damage. Among the rooms destroyed was St George's Hall. All of the priceless works of art in the royal collection were however saved.

Windsor Castle has served successive monarchs as a summer residence for 900 years. But when The Queen is at Windsor today, her presence signalled by the royal standard flying above the Round Tower. The great

British Rail
Windsor & Eton
Central Station
from Paddington
Station (change at
Slough) –
35 minutes;
Windsor & Eton
Riverside Station
from Waterloo
Station –
50 minutes
Bus
Green Line
704, 705 from
Hyde Park Corner

Opening times
Castle precincts:
Mar.–Oct.:
daily 10am–5.30pm;
Nov.-Feb.:
daily 10am–4pm
tel. information
1753-831118

Royal residence

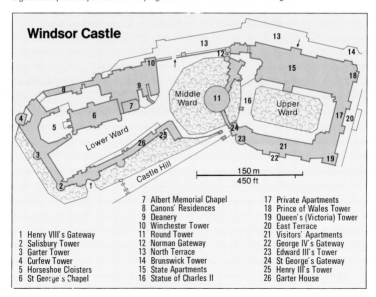

Windsor Castle

150 m
450 ft

1 Henry VIII's Gateway	
2 Salisbury Tower	
3 Garter Tower	
4 Curfew Tower	
5 Horseshoe Cloisters	
6 St George's Chapel	
7 Albert Memorial Chapel	17 Private Apartments
8 Canons' Residences	18 Prince of Wales Tower
9 Deanery	19 Queen's (Victoria) Tower
10 Winchester Tower	20 East Terrace
11 Round Tower	21 Visitors' Apartments
12 Norman Gateway	22 George IV's Gateway
13 North Terrace	23 Edward III's Tower
14 Brunswick Tower	24 St George's Gateway
15 State Apartments	25 Henry III's Tower
16 Statue of Charles II	26 Garter House

Windsor Castle

Windsor Castle from the Thames

complex of buildings making up the castle is laid out around two court-yards, the Lower and Upper Wards, separated by the Round Tower occupying the Middle Ward. St George's Chapel is on the north side of the Lower Ward, the State Apartments on the north side of the Upper Ward.

Lower Ward

Henry VIII's Gateway

The Castle is entered by Henry VIII's Gateway, a monumental gatehouse in the Tudor style giving access to the Lower Ward. On the south side of the court, between the Salisbury Tower and Henry III's Tower, are the former lodgings of the Military Knights of Windsor, an order founded by Edward III.

Horseshoe Cloisters

On the north side of the court, directly opposite the gateway, are the Horseshoe Cloisters, built in the reign of Henry IV and restored in 1871.

Curfew Tower

In the north-west corner of the Horseshoe Cloisters is the entrance to the Curfew Tower, built in 1227 under Henry II and incorporating some of the oldest masonry in the Castle. The front and roof of the tower were renewed in 1863. Within the tower is part of a 13th c. dungeon, with the beginnings of an escape tunnel. Also in the tower is a peal of eight bells, first hung in the 15th c.; the clock, dating from the 17th c., sets off a carillon every third hour.

Canons' Residence

North-east of the Horseshoe Cloisters lies a small courtyard with, on the north side, the Canons' Residence and Chapter Library, both being parts of the Canons' Cloister of 1333.

Winchester Tower

In 1390 Geoffrey Chaucer stayed in the Winchester Tower (in the far north-east corner of this northern group of buildings).

St George's Chapel: Chapel of the Order of the Garter

Immediately north of St George's Chapel lie the very picturesque Dean's Cloisters (1356) and adjacent Deanery. The cloisters contain numerous tombs and statues.

Deanery

On the north side of the Lower Ward stands St George's Chapel, the most noteworthy building in the Ward. It is the chapel of the Knights of the Order of the Garter and thus dedicated to St George, their patron saint. A fine example of Late Perpendicular architecture, the chapel was begun by Edward IV in 1474 and completed by Henry VIII (open: Mon.–Sat. 10.30am–3pm).

★★**St George's Chapel**

Above the main west doorway is a huge window of 16th c. stained glass through which light floods, picking out the popes, kings, princes, military leaders, bishops and saints depicted thereon. The chapel's north and south facades are decorated with the heraldic beasts and shields of the Houses of Lancaster and York: on the south side Lancaster (lion, unicorn, swan, antelope, panther and red dragon), on the north side York (falcon, stag, bull, black dragon, hind and greyhound).

Exterior

The interior is notable for the fine lierne vaulting of the nave (1509) and the fan vaulting of the choir (1506), also for the choir-stalls, in local oak, carved with scenes from the life of St George and the crests of Edward III and the Knights of the Garter. Behind and above the stalls can be seen the coats of arms, banners and swords of 700 knights. In a central vault below the choir are the tombs of Henry VIII, Jane Seymour and Charles I.

Interior

Another vault, known as the Royal Tomb House, extends from below the choir eastwards under the Albert Memorial Chapel. Built in 1240 and altered during Queen Victoria's reign, it contains the tombs of George III, George IV, and William IV. Other interesting tombs and memorials in St George's Chapel include: in the Bray Chapel (now a bookshop) in the south

Honi soit qui mal y pense

In the year 1348 at Windsor Castle Edward III founded The Most Noble Order of the Garter, the highest Order in the kingdom. The occasion was said to have been a banquet at which one of the ladies of the court lost her garter, and Edward picked it up among much laughter and ribald jokes from the courtiers. The king retorted that very soon it would be an honour for his knights to be presented with such a garter. The Order of the Garter was an attempt – on the lines of King Arthur's Round Table – in the later Middle Ages, when the age of chivalry was already showing signs of decline, to establish a select circle of brave men and women who would safeguard the knightly virtues. Only 26 knights and their ladies may belong to this select circle, although this number can be exceeded by the nomination of "extra-knights" by order of the sovereign. The Order is awarded in the course of a colourful ceremony held in the Garter Throne Room at Windsor Castle.

The Insignia of the Order consists of a heavy chain with the sign of "The George", worn on ceremonial occasions, the shoulder band with "The Lesser George", worn on more minor occasions, together with the famous garter of dark blue velvet with the motto *Honi soit qui mal y pense* ("Shame be on him who thinks evil of it"), which the knight wears below the left knee and the lady on the left upper arm. This insignia can be viewed in Room 46 of the British Museum (see entry).

aisle, the tomb of Sir Reginald Bray (d. 1503); in the Beaufort Chapel in the south-west corner, the tomb of the Earl of Worcester (d. 1526) and next to it the tomb of the Duke of Kent, father of Queen Victoria; in the Urswick Chapel, the white marble memorial to Charlotte, daughter of George IV, and diagonally opposite it the tomb of George V and Queen Mary; in the north ambulatory the tombs of George VI (left) and Edward IV (right); in the south ambulatory, the tombs of Edward VII and Henry VI; also the Lincoln Chapel in the south-east corner dedicated to the Earl of Lincoln (d. 1585) and his wife, and the Oxenbridge Chantry (by the choir-screen) with Edward III's sword on the outside wall.

★ Albert Memorial Chapel

Next to St George's Chapel stands the Albert Memorial Chapel, built by Henry VII for his own burial but never thus used (the king being interred instead in Westminster Abbey – see entry). It served James II as a Roman Catholic chapel. The vaults were constructed in the reign of George III. Following the death of Prince Albert in 1861, Queen Victoria had it made into a memorial chapel for her husband. The interior is elaborately decorated with different coloured marble, mosaics, sculptures and stained glass depicting biblical scenes, members of the royal family and relatives of Prince Albert. The Prince Consort's tomb can be seen at the east end, the sarcophagus and recumbent figure of Albert being by Triqueti. To the right of it is the porphyry sarcophagus of the Duke of Clarence, eldest son of Edward VII. At the west door stands a marble statue of the kilted Duke of Albany (d. 1884).

Middle Ward

Round Tower

Between the Lower and Upper Wards rises the Round Tower, erected at the time of Edward III atop the artifical mound on which William the Conqueror had earlier raised a keep. The tower is encircled on three sides by a deep moat. Access is from the north-west corner of the Upper Ward, reached from the Lower Ward by the Norman Gateway (1360) with its flanking crenellated towers. From the platform of the Round Tower, 24m/79ft above the ground, there are panoramic views of the surrounding countryside.

Below the walls of the Round Tower a passageway leads onto the North Terrace, which enjoys magnificent views of the Thames and of Eton on the further bank.

North Terrace

Upper Ward

The Upper Ward, also known as the "Quadrangle", is enclosed to the north by the State Apartments, to the south by the Visitors' Apartments and to the east by the private apartments of the royal family adjoining the East Terrace and gardens. On the west side of the court stands an impressive statue of Charles II, dated 1679.

The State Apartments are open to the public whenever the Royal Family are not in residence (opening times as for the rest of the Castle precincts). The last major alterations to the apartments were made by Geoffrey Wyattville during the first half of the 19th c. Entrance is from the North Terrace.

★★**State Apartments**

Inside the entrance is a gallery which has themed exhibitions – principally drawings and watercolours from the Royal Collection and items from the Royal Photographic Collection.

The Gallery

Seen near by is Queen Mary's Dolls' House (1923), a masterpiece of scaled-down craftsmanship by Sir Edwin Lutyens.

The China Museum with its fine collection of porcelain leads to the Grand Staircase, dominated by Chantrey's statue of George IV and a display of arms and armour (including some made for Henry VIII). The cannon at the head of the staircase are from Borneo.

Grand Staircase

The Grand Vestibule, 46ft/14m long and nearly as high, contains armour, flags and military mementoes such as one of Napoleon's cloaks.

Grand Vestibule

Waterloo Chamber, 98ft/30m long, has carvings by Grinling Gibbons and a giant Indian carpet. On display are portraits of Europe's statesmen who united against Napoleon in 1813 and 1815, including Wellington, Blücher, Castlereagh, Metternich, Pius VII, Czar Alexander I, Canning, Friedrich Wilhelm III of Prussia and Kings George III and IV of Britain.

Waterloo Chamber

To the left is the Garter Throne Room where since George IV's reign the Order of the Garter has been conferred.

Garter Throne Room

Among the finest pieces in the adjoining Rococo-style Grand Reception Room are tapestries with scenes of Jason and Medea and a malachite vase presented by Czar Nicholas I. The tapestries were damaged by fire in 1992 and are currently being restored.

Grand Reception Room

St George's Hall, the Queen's banqueting hall, which was built in the 14th c. at the time of Edward III, was badly damaged by the fire in 1992 but is being restored. There are paintings by Van Dyck, Kneller and Lely of the Stuart and Hanoverian kings.

St George's Hall

The Queen's Guard Chamber contains fine armour, Indian cannon and a golden shield presented to Henry VIII by Francis I of France.

Queen's Rooms

The ceiling paintings of Catherine of Braganza in the Queen's Presence Chamber are the work of Antonio Verrio. The Gobelins tell the story of Esther and Mordecai. Some of the sculptures are by Grinling Gibbons.

The series of Gobelins is continued in the Queen's Audience Chamber; the ceiling paintings are again by Verrio.

The Queen's Ball Room, originally created for Catherine of Braganza by Charles II, was subsequently decorated by George IV exclusively with paintings by Van Dyck, including portraits of Charles I and his family and a self-portrait of the artist. Most of the furniture was made in the 17th c.

The Queen's Drawing Room, formerly a private apartment of the queen, contains a portrait by Van Dyck of Charles I's five children.

King's Rooms

In the King's Closet and the adjoining King's Wardrobe are paintings by Holbein, Rubens and Rembrandt; also the famous triple portrait of Charles I by Van Dyck.

The furnishings of the King's State Bed Chamber, with its paintings by Canaletto and Gainsborough, include a richly ornate 18th c. bed. Whenever there was a need for confidential discussions to take place, they would do so in this room.

The King's Drawing Room is embellished with works by Rubens ("The Holy Family") and Van Dyck ("St Martin").

The final room in the State Apartments is the King's Dining Room, with particularly impressive carvings by Grinling Gibbons and ceiling paintings by Verrio (1678–80); also a portrait of Catherine of Braganza by Jacob Huysmans.

Town of Windsor

With its old half-timbered houses and 17th and 18th c. inns, narrow winding alleyways and cobbled streets, Windsor town centre still preserves a picturesque medieval aspect. The town hall was designed by Wren.

Madame Tussaud's "Royalty and Empire"

In 1897 Queen Victoria celebrated 60 years on the throne. The event is commemorated by an exhibition, "Royalty and Empire", in the old Windsor station. There are wax figures from Madame Tussaud's, old rail carriages and a carriage from the royal train (open: daily 9.30am–5.30pm; in winter until 4.30pm).

Home Park

Home Park borders Windsor Castle to the north and east. In the park are Frogmore House and the Mausoleum where Queen Victoria is buried.

Great Park

Windsor Great Park, extending south of the castle for some 5½ miles/9km, supports a large population of red deer.

Legoland Windsor

Windsor's latest attraction is Legoland, situated a mile or two outside the town towards Ascot on the B3022. This 150 acre/60ha theme park features models of medieval castles, pirate ships, a mini-town, cars and a 30ft/9m tall dinosaur, all made from Lego bricks. (Open: end Mar.–end Sept. daily 10am–6pm, to 8pm in Aug.: Oct.–mid Mar. weekends only). At the centre of the Park is "Miniland" which recreates scenes from European cities such as London, Paris and Amsterdam in astonishing detail from 25 million Lego bricks. There are also five main activity areas, each relating to a different Lego play theme, with interactive rides, shows and play areas: "My Town" recreates a busy harbour town; "Duplo Gardens" is a fantasy-themed area for the younger child; "The Driving School" where children drive electric Lego cars in a mock driving school; "Wild Woods" is a pirate-themed adventure area featuring the biggest rides; and "Imagination Centre" gives you your chance to build your own creation out of Lego.

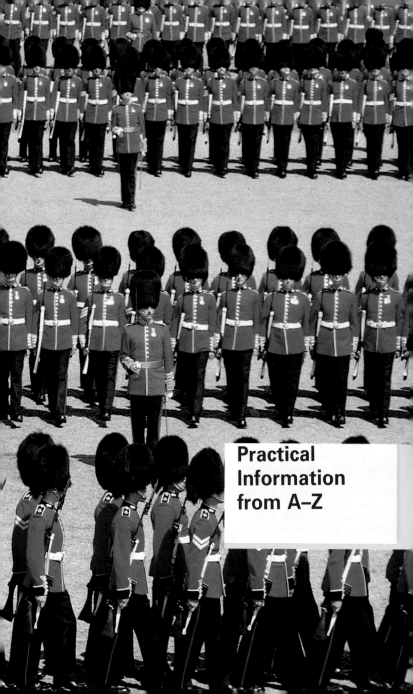

**Practical
Information
from A–Z**

Accommodation

Accommodation
Reservations

London Tourist Board (see Information) operates an Accommodation Bookings Hotline on (0171) 824 8844 for Access/Visa card holders. Bookings for most kinds of accommodation can also be made at Tourist Information Centres (see Information).

Bed and
Breakfast

Bed and Breakfast (B&B) accommodation – either with a family or in a budget guest house – works out cheaper than most hotels, but is less likely to be in central London. Agencies include:

Central London Accommodation, 83 Addison Gardens W14 0DT; tel. (0171) 602 9668, fax 602 5609 (West London)

London Homestead Services, Coombe Wood Road, Kingston-upon-Thames, Surrey KT2 7JY; tel. (0181) 949 4455, fax (0181) 549 5492

Camping

See entry

Hotels

See entry

Youth Hostels

See entry

Addresses

Greater London is divided into postal districts. These postal districts are made up of letters and numbers, with the first letter or two letters indicating the general area and the numbers the exact district, e.g. SW3 represents Chelsea. These postal districts also appear alongside the street names.

E = East   SE = South East
EC = East Central   SW = South West
N = North   W = West
NW = North West   WC = West Central

Air Travel

Airports

Heathrow

London's biggest airport and one of the world's busiest, Heathrow is 15 miles/24km west of the city centre and is the point of entry for most passengers on scheduled flights.

Information

These telephone numbers are all dealt with by one general tel. no. now General information: tel. (0181) 745 7702.

Transfers to
Central London

Underground: about 47 minutes by Piccadilly Line to Piccadilly Circus every 4–7½ mins. (Mon.-Sat. 5.40am–11.40pm; Sun. 6.50am–11.40pm).
  Crowded though it may be, this is still the fastest – and cheapest – way of travelling between the airport and the city centre. It pays to know that Heathrow has two stations for the Underground, one for Terminals 1, 2 and 3, and one for Terminal 4.
Bus: Airbus A1 to Victoria Station every 20–30 mins. (6.40am–10.10pm);
  Airbus 2 to Russell Square via Euston Station every 20–30 mins.

◀ *Trooping of the Colour on the Queen's Official Birthday*

(6.30am–9.55pm). Buses stop at main points along the route, but how long they take (50–80 mins.) depends on the traffic.

All-night bus: N 97 once an hour from Trafalgar Square from 11.55pm to 5am.

Taxi: expensive (around £40–£45) and liable to get held up in traffic. The same applies to taxis and the other airports.

Gatwick airport is about 27 miles/45km south of London and its two terminals take both charter and scheduled flights. A shuttle bus runs between the two terminals. **Gatwick**

Tel. (01293) 535353 Information

British Rail: about 37 mins. by "Gatwick Express" to Victoria Station every 15 mins. (6.20am–10.50pm) or hourly at night; there is a stop at Tottenham Hale with access to the Victoria Line of the Underground. Transfers to Central London

Bus: about 80 mins. by National Express and Flightline 777 to Victoria Station.

Stansted, 37 miles/59km north-east of London, is used for charter flights. **Stansted**

Tel. (01279) 680500 Information

British Rail: 45 mins. by "Stansted Express" to Liverpool Street Station. There is also the Thameslink service to the City, via King's Cross, every 30 mins. (hourly in the evening); journey time 40 mins. Transfers to Central London

Luton airport, 32 miles/51km north-west of London, handles mainly internal and charter flights. **Luton**

Tel. (01582) 405100 Information

British Rail: a bus takes you to Luton Station, then 45 mins. by train to King's Cross Station. Transfers to Central London

Bus: about 75 mins. by Luton & District's 757 to Victoria Station.

London City Airport, London's newest airport, opened in 1987 in the heart of Docklands 10 miles/16km east of the city centre. It mainly serves the business community but also operates scheduled services to Europe and the Channel Islands. **London City Airport**

Tel. (0171) 646 0000 Information

British Rail: North London Line from Silvertown station. Transfers to Central London

Bus: about 30 mins. by a shuttlebus to Liverpool Street Station; or a few mins. by a shuttlebus to Canary Wharf Station then by Docklands Light Railway.

Taxi: about 30 mins.

Airlines

PO Box 10, Heathrow Airport, Hounslow, Middlesex TW2 2JA; tel. (0345) 222 787. British Airways

Antiques

Antique hunters will find London the happiest of hunting grounds, with something for everyone, from the most exclusive of antique emporia (with prices to match) to very cheap junkshops. Something for everyone

Antiques

Top shops

The expensive and very expensive shops are clustered mainly in and around Mayfair's Old and New Bond Street, all in London W1, and include Aspreys, 165–169 New Bond St. (furniture and works of art); Bond Street Antiques Centre, 114 New Bond St.; Christopher Wood's, 141 New Bond St. (Victoriana); S J Philips, 139 New Bond St. (silver); Richard Green, 4 New Bond St. (old masters); Tryon and Morland, 23 Cork St. (Victorian works of art); and close by, at 58 Davies St./1–7 Davies Mews, Gray's Antiques Market. Equally exclusive, St. James, in SW1, has the likes of Spink & Son, 5 King St. The antique furniture shops along Pimlico Road, also in SW1, such as Westenholz at 68 Pimlico Road, are not quite so dear but by no means cheap. Kensington also has a good reputation for antiques, with Kensington Church Street and Christie's salerooms at 85 Old Brompton Road SW7, where items can be had from this famous auction house for quite reasonable prices. Last but by no means least there is Chelsea, with its whole range of shops centred around King's Road, New King's Road and the Fulham Road, where a bargain can still be found in places such as the Lot's Road Galleries at 73 Lot's Road SW10.

Antique and flea markets

London's many markets are a treasure trove for the bargain hunter, with stalls offering everything from genuine antiques to miscellaneous second-hand goods. The main markets of this kind are listed below.

Alfie's Antiques Market, 13–25 Church Street NW8
Underground: Edgware Road; Tues.-Sat. 10am–8pm
London's biggest antiques market, with 370 dealers under one roof

Antiquarius, 131–141 King's Road SW3
Underground: Sloane Square; Mon. –Sat. 10am–8pm
Covered antique dealers' market in Chelsea

Bermondsey (New Caledonian) Market, Bermmondsey Square SE1
Underground: Borough, London Bridge; Fri. 5am–2pm
Early every Friday this is where all the dealers converge south of the Thames at what used to be the old Caledonian Market.

Camden Lock Market NW1; Underground: Camden Town
Sat., Sun. 8am–6pm. Second-hand goods (especially clothes!), records; can get extremely crowded.

Camden Passage Market N1; Underground: Angel
Wed. 10am–2pm, Sat. 10am–5pm. Chiefly Victoriana

Chelsea Antiques Market, 245–253 King's Road SW10
Underground: Sloane Square. Mon–Sat. 10am–6pm
Less upmarket and hence very reasonably priced

Chenil Galleries, 181–183 King's Road SW10
Underground: Sloane Square. Mon. –Sat. 10am–6pm
Also Chelsea, more upmarket, many 18th c. items

Gray's Antique Market, High Road, SE1
Underground: Bond Street, Mon.–Fri. 10am–6pm
20 stands of fine, expensive pieces

Greenwich Antiques Market, High Road SE1
Docklands Light Railway: Island Gardens; British Rail: Greenwich
Sat., Sun. 9am–5pm. Antiques of every quality

Leather Lane, EC1
Underground: Chancery Lane, Mon.–Fri. 10.30am–2pm
More of a junk market, also gramophone records and clothes

Camden Lock Market: the place for second-hand clothes

Portobello Road Market W11
Underground: Ladbroke Grove, Notting Hill Gate. Sat. 8am–5.30pm
Antiques and second-hand market Saturdays only, fruit and vegetable
stalls Mon.–Fri.

Silver Vaults, Chancery House, 53 Chancery Lane WC2; Underground:
Chancery Lane
Mon.–Fri. 9am–5.30pm, Sat. 9am–12.30pm
Old and new silver on sale from 50 dealers

Christie's and Sotheby's, two of the world's top auction houses, are both **Auction houses**
based in London, as are Phillips and Bonhams, and notices of their forth-
coming sales appear in the press. The catalogues are available for
anyone with a particular interest, but it is worth just paying a visit to
their venerable salerooms to take in the atmosphere, especially since
you are not obliged to buy!

Bonham's. Montpelier Street, SW7; tel. (0171) 584 9161

Christie's, Christie's branch at Brompton Road is still running, with the
deleted tel. no. (581 7611) 8 King Street SW1; tel. (0171) 839 9060

Phillips, 101 New Bond Street W1; tel. (0171) 629 6602

Sotheby's, 34–35 New Bond Street W1; tel. (0171) 493 8080

Boat Trips

With a boat trip on the Thames you get to know London from a quite dif- **On the Thames**
ferent perspective. Scheduled services departing every 20 to 30 minutes

from the three Inner London piers and heading downstream for Greenwich and the Thames Barrier and in summer upstream for Kew, Richmond and Hampton Court. The packages on offer include circular trips and evening and dinner cruises. For further details contact:

Visitorcall; tel. (0839) 123432

Piers and destinations

Westminster Pier, Victoria Embankment SW1
Destinations: Tower of London, Greenwich and Thames Barrier. Also in summer to Kew, Richmond and Hampton Court

Charing Cross Pier, Victoria Embankment WC2
Destinations: Tower of London and Greenwich

Tower Pier EC3
Destinations: Greenwich and Thames Barrier

Operators include:
Catamaran Cruises
Charing Cross Pier, Victoria Embankment WC2; tel. (0171) 839 3572

Westminster-Greenwich Thames Passenger Boat Services
Westminster Pier SW1; tel. (0171) 930 4097

On the Regent's Canal

A trip in an old narrow boat on the Regent's Canal, while perhaps enjoying a meal on board, is a much more tranquil affair, and a very pleasant way of travelling from Little Venice (Underground: Warwick Avenue) through Regent's Park to Camden Lock. Trips generally operate daily in summer, weekends only in winter.

Operators include:

Jason's Trip
60 Blomfield Road, Little Venice W9 2PD; tel. (0171) 286 3428

Jenny Wren Cruises
250 Camden High Street NW1; tel. (0171) 485 4433

London Waterbus Company

Little Venice, Blomfield Road W9; tel. (0171) 482 2550

Cafés and Tearooms

Nowadays fast-food outlets and sandwich bars are rapidly gaining ground on London's traditional "caffs", but tearooms, especially those in the grander hotels, continue to remain a bastion of the British way of life for those who prefer to take their afternoon tea English-style. Here you can still get cucumber sandwiches, dainty cakes, scones and jam as part of a set tea for between £7 and £15. Other good places for tea include some of the museum cafés – in the Museum of London or the Victoria and Albert Museum for example – which offer a surprisingly wide range of good quality teas, coffee, cakes and snacks.

Cafés

Bar Italia, 22 Frith Street W1; tel. (0171) 437 4520
In Soho, and London's most popular Italian café.

Café Royal, 68 Regent Street W1; tel. (0171) 437 9090
A venerable establishment whose patrons have included Oscar Wilde and Princess Diana.

Canadian Muffin Co., 5 King Street WC2; tel. (0171) 379 1525
Just the right place for those who know their muffins, be they sweet or
savoury.

Maison Bertaux, 28 Greek Street W1; tel. (0171) 437 6007
Soho's old-established purveyor of pastries – its window display alone
will whet your appetite – sells mouthwatering savouries as well as delicious cakes.

Monmouth Coffee House, 27 Monmouth Street, WC2; tel. (0171) 836
5272
A favourite with coffee-drinkers, with no less than seven types of coffee
on offer.

Pâtisserie Des Amis, 63 Judd Street WC1; tel. (0171) 383 7029
Wonderfully fresh pastries at reasonable prices.

Pâtisserie Valerie, 44 Old Compton Street W1; tel. (0171) 437 3466
One of London's most famous patisseries, with four other branches: 105
Marylebone High Street W1; 8 Russell Street WC2; 215 Brompton Road
SW3; 66 Portland Place W1.

Richoux, 172 Piccadilly W1; tel. (0171) 493 2204
Here smart patrons partake of their coffee in equally smart surroundings, with a correspondingly higher price bracket. Other branches: 41a
South Audley Street W1, tel. (0171) 629 5228; 86 Brompton Road SW3,
tel. (0171) 584 8300; 3 Circus Road NW8, tel. (0171) 483 4001.

Very much a social occasion in some circles, afternoon tea is taken   Afternoon tea
around the hallowed hour of 4 o'clock as compared with high tea which
is much more substantial and can take the place of an evening meal at
around 5 or 6 o'clock.

The Fifth Floor, Harvey Nichols, Knightsbridge SW1; tel. (0171) 235 5250
The tearoom on the fifth floor of Harvey Nichols' "absolutely fabulous"
department store is a London institution, and can offer all the requisites
of a proper afternoon tea at relatively low cost.

Fortnum & Mason, 181 Piccadilly W1; tel. (0171) 734 8040
The same applies to Fortnum & Mason's St James's Restaurant, but
comes rather more expensive. Here motherly waitresses serve afternoon, high and champagne teas.

The Muffin Man, 12 Wrights Lane W8; tel. (0171) 937 6652
English tea and sandwiches come into their own here too.

Afternoon tea at its most refined is to be found in the genteel setting of   Hotel teas
some of London's top hotels, where you are expected to dress – and pay
– accordingly.

Brown's Hotel, 30 Albemarle Street W1; tel. (0171) 493 6020
London's oldest hotel (founded in 1837) is famous for being a legendary
place for afternoon tea.

The Capital, 22 Basil Street SW3; tel. (0171) 589 5171
This smaller hotel's charming tearoom is just the place to relax after
shopping in Harrods.

Claridge's, Brook Street W1; tel. (0171) 629 8860
Tea at Claridge's is served in the foyer so that you can enjoy your opulent setting from the undisturbed comfort of a sofa.

The Ritz, Piccadilly W1; tel. (0171) 493 8181
For afternoon tea in London the Palm Court at the Ritz comes first in every sense and gets booked up weeks in advance.

Savoy, Strand WC2; tel. (0171) 836 4343
The Savoy is a good place for the hungry because, although the price is high, you can help yourself as often as you like.

Camping and Caravanning

Information

The Camping and Caravanning Club
Greenfields House, Westwood Way, Coventry, West Midlands CV4 8JH; tel. (01203) 694995

The following sites are recommended by the Automobile Association.

Crystal Palace

Crystal Palace Caravan Club Site, Crystal Palace Parade SE19; tel. (0181) 778 7155
In south London, via the A205, at the foot of the Crystal Palace television mast.

Chertsey

Camping and Caravanning Club Site, Bridge Road, Chertsey, Surrey; tel. (01932) 562405
South of London, off junction 11 of the M25

Chingford

Lee Valley Campsite, Sewardstone Road E4
tel. (0181) 529 5689
In north London via the A112 from junction 26 of the M25

Edmonton

Lee Valley Leisure Centre Campsite and Caravan, Meridian Way N9; tel. (0181) 345 6666 or 803 6900
In north London signposted from the A10

Hoddesdon

Lee Valley Caravan Park, Dobbs Weir, Essex Road, Hoddesdon, Hertfordshire; tel. (01992) 462090
In north London from the Hoddesdon exit of the A10

Laleham

Laleham Park Camping Site, Thameside, Laleham, Surrey TW18 1SH; tel. (01932) 564149
South of London, off junction 1 of the M3, onto the A308 and Ferry Road

Car Rental

Anyone wanting to rent a car must be over 21 and have held a driving licence for at least 12 months. The major car rental firms have offices or desks at the airports, and can also be contacted on the numbers listed below. Besides these many others are listed under Car Hire in the Yellow Pages and it is always worth shopping around for the best rates. The British Tourist Authority (see Information) also publishes a useful leaflet "Britain: Vehicle Hire" full of helpful advice on the subject.

Avis

(0990) 900500

Eurodollar

(0171) 820 0202

Europcar

(0181) 568 5606

Hertz

(0990) 996699

Budget

(0800) 18 1181

Chemists

See Health Care

Children

London offers so much for children in the way of entertainment and attractions that no child – or grownup for that matter – could complain of boredom or having nothing to do! Everything possible is done to cater for families with children. Under-fives travel free on buses and the Underground, and under-fourteens only pay half-fare; fourteen and fifteen year-olds need to produce a Photocard (see Public Transport – Tickets) to qualify for half fare. Children travel at full fare on buses from 10pm to 0.59am. There are special reduced rates of admission to museums and other attractions for children and families (under fives are normally free), and the major museums go to great lengths to make their exhibits both attractive and instructive for children. Many food outlets have children's menus and some even lay on entertainment during the meal. There are also theatres specially for children. To find out more about where to take children telephone Visitorcall on (0839) 123424.

Children's London

Children love the free spectacle of the Changing of the Guard at Buckingham Palace and Horse Guards Parade, and a sightseeing tour on the top of a double-decker bus is a delight. A boat trip on the Thames and perhaps a narrow boat ride on the Regent's Canal also come high on the list of things to do together. If that is too much you can simply go for a paddle in the Serpentine in Hyde Park. In fact London's parks – Regent's Park, Hampstead Heath (kiteflying), Primrose Hill, Greenwich Park, etc. – offer plenty of fun and space to run and play in. Another favourite pastime is making brass rubbings at centres such as those in Westminster Abbey and St Martin-in-the-Fields.

Activities with children

You can find out what's on for children by ringing Visitorcall on (0839) 123404.

Telephone information

The Bethnal Green Museum of Childhood, London Toy and Model Museum and Pollock's Toy Museum (see Museums) are specially aimed at children. Top of the other museums is undoubtedly the Natural History Museum, especially its dinosaurs and insects, closely followed by the Science Museum which in "Launch Pad" has a special hands-on section for children. There are also plenty of opportunities for hands-on fun in the Museum of the Moving Image – try flying on the magic carpet! – and the London Transport Museum. Also top among children's favourites are Greenwich's tea clipper, the "Cutty Sark", the Tower of London, Tower Bridge, Madame Tussaud's, the London Planetarium and of course London Zoo. Battersea Park south of the Thames opposite Chelsea also has a children's zoo, and there is a children's farm in Crystal Palace Park. For those who enjoy playing soldiers and sailors there is the Imperial War Museum and HMS "Belfast", while the London Dungeon, though not suitable for the very young or more sensitive, caters for the most ghoulish of childish tastes.

Museums and other attractions

Little Angel Marionette Theatre, 14 Dagmar Passage N1
tel. (0171) 226 1787; Underground: Angel
Famous puppet theatre; book in advance

Children's theatre

Polka Children's Theatre, 240 The Broadway, Wimbledon SW19
tel. (0181) 543 8888; Underground: South Wimbledon
Also exhibition of dolls, costumes and props

Cinemas

Puppet Theatre Barge, Blomfield Road, Little Venice W9;
tel. (0171) 249 6876; Underground: Warwick Avenue

Unicorn Theatre for Children, 6 Great Newport Street WC2
tel. (0171) 379 3280; Underground: Leicester Square

Eating out

Eating out with children does not necessarily mean ending up at Pizza Hut or McDonalds. Burger and chips, not to mention lots of other favourite fare, are also on the menu, but against a more interesting background, in places such as:

Hard Rock Café, 150 Old Park Lane W1; tel. (0171) 629 0382
  Planet Hollywood, 13 Coventry Street W1; tel. (0171) 287 1000 (no reservations)
Rock Island Diner, 2nd Floor London Pavilion, Piccadilly Circus W1; tel. (0171) 836 4052
  Smollensky's Balloon, 1 Dover Street W1; tel. (0171) 491 1199
Smollensky's on the Strand, 105 The Strand WC2; tel. (0171) 497 2101

The café-restaurant in the crypt of St Martin-in-the-Fields (Café-in-the-Crypt) is good value for money too; many of the ethnic restaurants are also places where a family can eat out more cheaply.

Shopping

Early Learning Centre, 225 Kensington High Street W8
Toys for little ones

Hamley's, 188–96 Regent Street W1
Five floors of the biggest toy shop in the world

Harrods, 87–135 Brompton Road SW1
Harrods toy department is just as cheap or dear as anywhere else – just steer them clear of the mini Ferrari! Wonderful stuffed toy department

Mothercare, 174 Oxford Street W1
Everything for the mother and baby, not forgetting the tiny tots

Special hotel

Pippa Pop-Ins, 430 Fulham Road SW6; tel. (0171) 385 2458
A hotel which caters specifically for families with children aged from 2 years and over, right down to the babysitting!

For those who want to leave the children behind for once:

Babysitters

Babysitters Unlimited, 2 Napoleon Road, Twickenham;
  tel. (0181) 892 8888
Childminders, 9 Paddington Street W1; tel. (0171) 935 2049
Pippa Pop-Ins (see Special hotel, above) also have a babysitting service for non-residents

Cinemas

A feast for film fans, London has a whole host of cinemas, with the biggest – and most expensive – mainly in the West End. Most Hollywood blockbusters are premièred in London before they get to Continental Europe. It pays to book in advance, especially at weekends.

Première houses

Odeon Leicester Square, Leicester Square WC2; tel. (0181) 315 4215
  Enormous, seats almost 2000
ABC 135 Shaftesbury Avenue WC2; tel. (0171) 836 6279

Picture palaces, cinemathèques

Electric Screen, 191 Portobello Road W11; tel. (0181) 743 0648
  Worth visiting as much for London's oldest remaining art deco foyer as for the film.

Charlie Chaplin Statue in Leicester Square

Everyman, Hollybush Vale, Hampstead NW3; tel. (0181) 743 0648
  London's oldest repertory cinema.
ICA Cinema, Nash House, The Mall SW1; tel. (0171) 930 3647
  Experimental and art house.
National Film Theatre, South Bank SE1; tel. (0171) 928 3232
  British Film Institute's national cinemathèque alongside its Museum of
  the Moving Image; home of the London Film Festival.
Prince Charles, Leicester Place WC2; tel. (0171) 437 8181
  Has the cheapest seats in London; showing recent American films,
  classic revivals and European imports.
Screen on Baker Street, 96 Baker Street NW1; tel. (0171) 935 2772
  Independent and British films.
Screen on the Hill, 203 Haverstock Hill NW3; tel. (0171) 435 3366

Currency

The unit of currency is the pound sterling (£), made up of 100 pence (p). Unit
Bank notes are for £5, £10, £20 and £50, and coins are 1p, 2p, 5p, 10p,
20p, 50p, £1 and £2.

There are no controls on the export or import of sterling or of foreign Controls
currencies.

Most high street banks are open from 9.30am until 3.30 or 4.30pm. Banks
Some also open on Saturday mornings. The banks at Heathrow and
Gatwick airports are open round the clock.

Any bank will take travellers' cheques, Eurocheques, etc., but Travellers'
Eurocheques can only be cashed up to a limit of £100. Remember to cheques, etc.

keep your receipt and record of travellers' cheques separately from the cheques themselves so that the latter can be replaced if lost or stolen.

Credit cards
Most hotels, restaurants and stores accept the major international credit cards. Switch cards, Eurocheque cards and credit cards can also be used for withdrawals at most banks and cashpoints. Keep a note of the number to telephone to put a stop immediately on any of these cards in case they are lost or stolen.

Changing money
The best place to change money is in a bank at the official rate. There are also exchange bureaux in stores such as Harrods, Dickins & Jones, Selfridges, John Barker and Marks & Spencer (Marble Arch and Oxford Street), at major travel agencies such as Thomas Cook, and at many other places, including all major train and Underground stations in central London. Some of these can charge a high commission and give a poor rate, so they are best used only in an emergency.

Customs Regulations

Duty-free items on entry
Member states of the European Union (EU) form a common internal market within which items for personal use are generally free of duty. There are, however, certain guidelines on maximum amounts and for the UK the upper limits for incoming travellers aged over 18 on items purchased elsewhere in the European Union are 800 cigarettes or 400 cigarillos or 200 cigars or 1 kilo tobacco, 10 litres of spirits over 22% proof or 20 litres below 22% and 90 litres wine, plus an unlimited amount of perfume and toilet water and other goods and presents up to a total value of £420.

For items bought in duty-free shops or brought in by visitors from countries such as Australia, Canada, New Zealand, South Africa and the USA the equivalent amounts are 200 cigarettes, or 100 cigarillos or 50 cigars or 250 g tobacco, and 1 litre of spirits over 22% or 2 litres below 22% and 2 litres wine, plus 50 g of perfume, 0.25 litre of toilet water and other goods and presents up to a value of £32.

Re-entry to other countries
The duty-free limits for Ireland, as a fellow member of the European Union, are roughly the same as for the United Kingdom. For other English-speaking countries the duty-free allowances are as follows: Australia 250 cigarettes or 50 cigars or 250 g tobacco, 1 litre spirits or 1 litre wine; Canada 200 cigarettes and 50 cigars and 900 g tobacco, 1.1 litres spirits or wine; New Zealand 200 cigarettes or 50 cigars or 250 g tobacco, 1 litre spirits and 4.5 litres wine; South Africa 400 cigarettes and 50 cigars and 250 g tobacco, 1 litre spirits and 2 litres wine; USA 200 cigarettes and 100 cigars and a reasonable quantity of tobacco, 1 litre spirits or 1 litre wine.

Diplomatic Representation

Australia	High Commission, Australia House, Strand WC2; tel. (0171) 379 4334
Canada	High Commission, 38 Grosvenor Street W1; tel. (0171) 258 6356
Ireland	Embassy, 17 Grosvenor Place SW1; tel. (0171) 235 2171
New Zealand	High Commission, New Zealand House, 80 Haymarket SW1; tel. (0991) 100 100
South Africa	Embassy, South Africa House, Trafalgar Square WC2; tel. (0171) 930 4488
USA	Embassy, 24 Grosvenor Square W1; tel. (0171) 499 9000

Disabled Access

Artsline, on (0171) 388 2227, provides information about the accessibility of arts and entertainment venues.

Holiday Care Service, on (01293) 774535, can advise on the accessibility of hotels and other accommodation.

Tripscope, on (0181) 994 9294, is an information line on the suitability of transport for the disabled.

Special publications giving details of disabled access include "London for All" from the London Tourist Board, "Access to the Underground" from London Transport, and "Access in London" from Access Project, 39 Bradley Gardens, West Ealing, London W13 8HE.

Electricity

Voltage throughout the UK is 240v 50Hz AC and plugs are square-pronged. Overseas visitors will need an adaptor for any electrical appliances they bring with them.

Emergency Services

Call 999

All 999 calls are free – just ring the operator on 999 and say which emergency service you want.

See Motoring

See Health Care

Events

Listings of what's on in London appear in the local and national press (see Newspapers), including London's own daily (except Sunday) paper the "Evening Standard", but the most comprehensive are to be found in the weekly listings magazines, "Time Out" and "What's On In London", both of which come out on Wednesdays. There is also "Events in London" which is published every two months by the London Tourist Board. Visitorcall (see Information) can supply telephone information about events and other happenings.

Calendar of Events (selection)

The London Parade (January 1st): New Year procession headed by the Lord Mayor of Westminster.
West London Antiques Fair mid-January in Kensington Town Hall.
St Paul's Day (January 25th): performance of Mendelssohn's St Paul oratorio in St Paul's Cathedral.
Commemoration of Charles I (last Sunday in January): laying of wreaths before King Charles' statue in Trafalgar Square and service in the Banqueting Hall, Whitehall.
Chinese New Year: Soho late Jan./early Feb.

Events

February	Cruft's Dog Show in Earls Court.
	Pancake-tossing at Westminster School (Shrove Tuesday).
	Stationers' Company service, in ancient robes, in the crypt of St Paul's (Ash Wednesday).
	Trial of the Pyx in Goldsmith's Hall: 13th c. custom for testing coins from the Royal Mint (late Feb./early March).
March	Traditional Oranges and Lemons service in the Church of St Clements.
	Chelsea Antiques Fair in Chelsea Old Town Hall (mid-March).
	Ideal Home Exhibition at Earls Court: Europe's greatest consumer show (mid-March-early April).
Easter	Performance of Bach's St Matthew Passion in St Paul's Cathedral (Tuesday before Easter); repeated in St Bartholomew the Great on Easter Sunday or Monday.
	Royal Maundy ceremony (Maundy Thursday every other year) in Westminster Abbey: ancient ceremony when the Queen, accompanied by the Royal Almoner and Yeomen of the Guard, distributes white leather purses of specially minted Maundy money to deserving men and women equal in number to the age of the monarch.
	Easter procession to Westminster Abbey (Easter Monday).
	London Harness Horse Parade in Battersea Park (Easter Monday).
April	Gun Salute to mark the Queen's birthday (April 21st) in Hyde Park at noon and an hour later at the Tower.
	Rugby League Challenge Cup Final at Wembley Stadium (end of the month).
	Oxford and Cambridge Boat Race (late March/early April).
	London Marathon: Europe's biggest, attracting runners, including the world's best, from all over the world (late April or early May).
May	Football Association Cup Final at Wembley Stadium (2nd Saturday).
	Royal Windsor Horse Show (2nd week).
	Chelsea Flower Show (late May).
June	Royal Academy Summer Exhibition (until mid-August).
	Gun Salute marking the Queen's coronation day (June 2nd).
	Trooping the Colour, Horse Guards Parade, and gun salute to mark the Queen's "official birthday" (Saturday nearest June 11th).
	Gun Salute marking Prince Phillip's birthday (June 10th).
	Derby Day at Epsom Racecourse (early June).
	Royal Ascot race meeting (mid-June).
	Election of the Sheriff of the City of London: grand ceremony in the Guildhall (June 24th).
	Lord's Test Match, Lord's Cricket Ground, St John's Wood.
	Service of the Order of the Garter, St George's Chapel Windsor: attended by the Queen and other Knights of the Order with picturesque procession dating back to the 14th c. and including the Household Cavalry and Yeomen of the Guard.
June/July	Covent Garden street theatre festival.
	Wimbledon Lawn Tennis Championships, All England Lawn Tennis Club: the world's top tennis event.
July	City of London Festival.
	Vintners' Company procession from Vintners' Hall to St James Garlickhythe Church, preceded by their Wine Porter acting as a roadsweeper to ensure them a safe path (mid-July).
	Dogget's Coat and Badge Race: annual rowing match for Thames watermen on or near August 1st upstream from London Bridge to Chelsea Bridge, instituted in 1715 by actor Thomas Dogget to mark the accession of George I.

Swan Upping: the swans on the Thames traditionally belong to the Crown and the Dyers' and Vintners' Companies, whose representative process up the river counting the swans and marking the cygnets.

Royal Tournament at Earls Court (2nd half of the month).

BBC Henry Wood Promenade Concerts, Royal Albert Hall (late July to mid-September).

Gun Salute to mark the Queen Mother's birthday (August 4th).   August

Notting Hill Carnival: Europe's largest street festival, organised by London's West Indian community (late August).

Battle of Britain Day: fly-past over London commemorating the air battle   September for Britain in the Second World War (September 15th, 11am–noon).

Chelsea Antiques Fair in Chelsea Old Town Hall.

Last Night of the Proms: spectacular final concert of the Henry Wood Promenade Concerts in the Albert Hall (late September).

Costermongers' Harvest Festival: service in St Martin-in-the-Fields for   October the coster pearly kings and queens at 3.30pm on the first Sunday. The "pearlies" get their name from the mother-of-pearl buttons sewn all over their outfits, a custom dating from the late 19th c. when cockney costermongers adopted this way of showing their pride in their community despite their poverty.

Trafalgar Day parade and service: ceremony by Nelson's Column commemorating Nelson's victory at the Battle of Trafalgar (October 21st).

Quit-rent ceremony at the Law Courts: performance of the ancient ceremony of rendering the quit-rent services due to the Crown by the Corporation of the City of London (late October).

State Opening of Parliament: the Queen travels from Buckingham Palace   November in the Irish State Coach to deliver her speech in the House of Lords marking the opening of the new session of Parliament; gun salutes in Hyde Park and the Tower (early November).

London to Brighton Veteran Car Run: starting from Hyde Park Corner (early November).

Guy Fawkes Night: bonfires and fireworks mark November 5th, the date of the Gunpowder Plot in 1605 when Guy Fawkes and his fellow conspirators tried to blow up the Houses of Parliament.

Mayor-making ceremony in the Guildhall: colourful inauguration ceremony for the new Lord Mayor of London on the Friday before the Lord Mayor's Show.

Lord Mayor's Show: procession of floats from the Guildhall to the Law Courts headed by the new Lord Mayor who is then presented to the Lord Chief Justice representing the Crown (2nd Saturday).

London Film Festival (2 weeks mid-month).

Remembrance Day: red poppies are worn to commemorate the fallen and wreaths are laid in a service at the Cenotaph in Whitehall (2nd Sunday).

Carol services, some with readings from Charles Dickens, in various   December churches from mid-December onwards.

Tower of London church parades: parade and inspection of the Yeomen warders (Sunday before Christmas).

Christmas tree and carols in Trafalgar Square.

Christmas service in Westminster Cathedral.

New Year's Eve revelry in Trafalgar Square.

Excursions

There are several very interesting places within a 60-mile/100km radius of London which are well worth visiting if you have the time to spare.

Excursions

They are well served by public transport or you can join an organised tour on a day trip; a list of operators is available from London Tourist Board and the British Travel Centre (see Information).

Arundel

Location: about 50 miles/80km south of London
How to get there: train from Victoria Station
Arundel, on the South Downs, is one of the South-east's most attractive towns, and is dominated by its castle, home to the Dukes of Norfolk, which also contains a museum.

Ascot

Location: 17 miles/28km west of London
How to get there: train from Waterloo Station
Ascot racecourse, not far from Windsor Castle, is where the cream of society gather for Royal Ascot week in June when the ladies' hats are as much the object of all eyes as the horses. On Gold Cup Thursday the Royal Family travel from Windsor in their open carriages.

Brighton

Location: about 50 miles/80km south of London
How to get there: train from Victoria Station
Famous for its wonderful Victorian pier and exotic Regency Royal Pavilion, Brighton is a charming and fashionable South Coast resort.

Cambridge

Location: 60 miles/90km north of London
How to get there: train from Liverpool Street or King's Cross
World-famous university town with medieval colleges, churches and several excellent museums. The lovely college grounds, gardens and parks along the riverside make up the beautiful "Backs".

Canterbury

Location: about 47 miles/75km south-east of London
How to get there: train from Victoria Station
Medieval Canterbury's great attraction is its historic Cathedral to which pilgrims have flocked down the centuries.

Crystal Palace Park, National Sports Centre

Location: Penge SE19, 7 miles/11km of the city centre
How to get there: train from Victoria Station or Charing Cross
Crystal Palace gets its name from Sir Joseph Paxton's great iron and glass palace built for the 1851 Great Exhibition. Brought here in 1854 from Hyde Park, it was one of the sights of London until it burnt down in 1936. Its site is now filled with the National Sports Centre and a park boasting a plaster collection of prehistoric monsters, all that remains of the Great Exhibition.

Eton

Location: 22 miles/35km west of London
How to get there: train to Windsor and Eton Central Station from Paddington Station (change at Slough) or to Windsor and Eton Riverside Station from Waterloo Station.
The town of Eton, close to Windsor Castle (see A–Z), owes its fame to its select boys' public school founded by Henry VI in 1440, considered to be one of England's finest. Famous old boys include Henry Fielding, William Pitt, Shelley, Gladstone and the Duke of Wellington. The red-brick school buildings frame two courtyards and consist of the Lower School, built between 1624 and 1639, and the Upper School, built between 1689 and 1692. The school chapel, built in Perpendicular style in 1441, contains some beautiful late 15th c. frescoes of the life of the Virgin.

Oxford

Location: about 57 miles/90km north-west of London
How to get there: train from Paddington
One of the world's oldest and most celebrated universities, some rank Oxford as second only to London in terms of historical and architectural importance. The ancient colleges, cathedral, gardens and High Street are particularly worth seeing. Blenheim Palace, seat of the Duke of

Marlborough and birthplace of Sir Winston Churchill, lies 7½ miles/12km to the north.

See A–Z

Windsor Castle

Food and Drink

British food and drink certainly no longer deserves the doubtful reputation it used to have. Anyone prepared to cast their national prejudices aside will find that the traditional English fare served in many pubs and restaurants is as tasty as it is satisfying. If, however, your tastes do not run to the likes of roast beef and Yorkshire pudding or steak and kidney pie there are also plenty of international eating places to chose from.

Meals

Some hotels still serve early morning tea in your room for a small service charge, although there is an increasing tendency to provide tea and coffee-making facilities en suite.

Morning tea

The classic full English breakfast consists of fruit or cereal followed by variations on bacon and eggs, sausages, tomatoes, fried bread and baked beans or mushrooms, accompanied by toast and marmalade or jam and a pot of tea or coffee. A light Continental breakfast is also usually an option.

Breakfast

Lunch is usually at around 1 o'clock and is often a light meal, particularly if it follows a filling English breakfast. Most people nowadays tend to have a snack of some kind or a sandwich.

Lunch

The evening meal in hotels and restaurants is referred to as dinner, as opposed to supper, with four or more courses and the expectation that diners are suitably dressed for the occasion.

Evening meal

Typical British Dishes

Supposedly invented by John Montague, the fourth Earl of Sandwich, during a break from the gaming tables in the 18th c., the sandwich has become an English institution like afternoon tea or the traditional pub. The original slice of meat between two pieces of white bread has since taken on many different guises, and, as sold in innumerable sandwich bars, pubs and hotels, comes with all kinds of fillings between all kinds of bread, often freshly made to suit your own particular requirements.

Sandwiches

Starters range from chilled fruit juice, melon, grapefruit cocktail, pâté and various kinds of potted meat, to preparations of fish and shellfish such as prawn cocktail, smoked salmon, mackerel or eel, crab salad, potted shrimp, cockles, winkles, and oysters, including "angels on horseback" (oysters rolled up in bacon, grilled and served on toast).

Starters

Soup is another favourite starter, with plenty of choice ranging from simple vegetable soups, tomato, chicken and mushroom soups, to excellent fish soups.

Soup

With its island coastline Britain is famous for the quality of its fish, including cod, rock salmon and plaice – the staple fish of "fish and chips" – and such fishy delicacies as crab, lobster, salmon and Dover sole.

Fish

Although less meat is eaten than formerly, British meat is of top quality. The "roast beef of Old England" is still a favourite, usually accompanied

Meat

by gravy and Yorkshire pudding, with mustard or horseradish sauce. Steak and salt beef or silverside are also still popular. Lamb tends to come with mint sauce or redcurrant jelly, and is also delicious as lamb chops. Pork chops are another favourite, while roast pork should come with crispy crackling and apple sauce. You can also get tasty pork sausages and excellent sliced ham. Steak and kidney can either be in a pie, with a crust, or in a pudding case of suet pastry. Other meat dishes include cottage pie, Irish stew and Cornish pasties, but Welsh rabbit, despite its name, is actually a form of melted cheese on toast.

Poultry and Game	Chicken is popular as a white meat, often simply roasted with stuffing; duck and goose are less common, although goose or chicken are often also served at Christmas as an alternative to the traditional roast turkey. Wild game, such as grouse from Scotland, is usually only available in season. Like pheasant and partridge, grouse tends to be served wrapped in bacon and accompanied by cabbage and game chips. Other game includes jugged hare and venison.
Side dishes	Meat is usually accompanied by fresh vegetables. These include potatoes (roast, mashed, boiled or chipped), peas, cabbage, broccoli, carrots, etc. Other traditional accompaniments include Norfolk dumplings and Yorkshire puddings.
Sweets	Britain boasts a whole range of sweets and puddings. Traditional desserts made with cream include syllabub, gooseberry fool, and sherry trifle. Steamed puddings, a truly British speciality, usually have a suet dough base and range from jam roly-poly and treacle pudding to that highlight of the festive season, the Christmas pudding.
Cheese	The best British cheeses are Stilton, Cheddar, Cheshire, Leicester, Double Gloucester, Wensleydale and Caerphilly.

Drink

Beer	In a pub customers mainly drink beer and the request is for "a pint (or half a pint) of bitter". Just as driving on the left is typically British, so is the traditional pint of "best bitter". Unlike the rest of Europe, who went over to making the paler, lager-type beers in the mid-19th c., Britain still brews its beer known as "bitter" by top fermentation with the addition of hops, tending to make it much stronger than most Europeans and non-Europeans are used to. Despite its name, bitter can be quite sweet and fruity. It takes a number of different forms and because it has to mature is usually served unchilled and without much foam to bring out the subtle variations in flavour. Classic versions include bottled "pale ale", "real ale", a keg bitter which has been further matured in the barrel, "mild", a dark-brown beer from the barrel, and "brown ale", another dark beer but a bottled version. "Strong ales" are somewhat stronger.
Stout	Stout is a strong, dark, sweet ale brewed in Ireland from black malt, a bitter served with a creamy head of foam and most widely represented by the traditional Guiness, but other good names include Murphy's, Beamish and, from Scotland, Gillespie's.
Lager	Lager, the kind of chilled pale beer favoured by Americans and the rest of Europe, is now as popular as other beers and on sale everywhere.
Sherry and port	The traditional apéritif is a sherry, which in Britain is of an excellent quality. Port is classically drunk after dinner or with the Stilton – British shippers take the bulk, and the best, of Portugal's output.
Whisky	Choosing a whisky can be an art in itself, but suffice to say you will never go wrong with a Scotch single malt; Irish whiskies also have a well-deserved reputation. Purists take their whisky straight – no water, no ice.

Galleries

London has a great many commercial galleries and their exhibitions (except "special exhibitions") are normally free of charge. Most of the older-established galleries – offering top quality art but at top prices – are in Mayfair in the streets off Old and New Bond Street such as Cork Street, a stronghold of modern art, and in South Kensington and St James's, especially Duke Street. Many of the newer galleries have also established themselves in the East End and around Notting Hill's Portobello Road.

Details of exhibitions can be found in the daily press or specialist publications such as "Art Review" and "Art and Artist" or weekly what's on listings in "Time Out" and "What's on in London".

Chris Beetles, 10 Ryder Street SW1; tel. (0171) 839 7429   **Old Masters**
  (illustrations and caricatures)   **and 19th c.**
Fine Art Society, 148 New Bond Street W1; tel. (0171) 629 5116
Johnny van Haeften, 13 Duke Street SW1; tel. (0171) 930 3062
Derek Johns, 12 Duke Street SW1; tel. (0171) 839 7671
Maasallery, 15a Clifford Street W1; tel. (0171) 734 2302
  (specialists in Victorian art)
Mathaf Gallery, 24 Motcomb Street SW1; tel. (0171) 235 0010
  (Oriental art)
Tryon and Swann Gallery, 23 Cork Street W1; tel. (0171) 734 2256
Wood Christopher Gallery, 141 New Bond Street W1; tel. (0171) 135 9141

Belgrave Gallery, 53 Englands Lane NW3; tel. (0171) 722 5150   **Modern art,**
  (abstract art)   **young artists**
Curwen, 4 Windmill Street W1; tel. (0171) 636 1459
Angela Flowers Gallery at London Fields, 282 Richmond Road E8;
  tel. (0181) 985 3333
Frith Street, 60 Frith Street W1; tel. (0171) 494 1550
Laure Genillard, 38a Foley Street W1; tel. (0171) 436 2300
Annely Juda, 23 Dering Street W1; tel. (0171) 629 7578
Karsten Schubert Contemporary Arts, 42 Foley Street W1;
  tel. (0171) 631 0031
Lisson Gallery, 67 Lisson Street NW1; tel. (0171) 724 2739
Piccadilly Gallery, 16 Cork Street W1; tel. (0171) 629 2875
Raab Gallery, 9 Cork Street W1; tel. (0171) 734 6444
Saatchi Collection, 98a Boundary Road NW8; tel. (0171) 624 8992
Todd, 1–5 Needham Road W11; tel. (0171) 792 1404
Waddington Galleries, 11/12 and 34 Cork Street W1;
  tel. (0171) 437 8611 (main gallery for modern art)

Photographers' Gallery, 5 and 8 Great Newport Street W2;   **Photography**
  tel. (0171) 831 1772
Special Photographers' Company, 21 Kensington Park Road, W11;
  tel. (0171) 221 3489

Getting to London

The fastest way to get to London is usually by air, although nowadays   **By air**
for travellers from Paris and Brussels Eurostar (see below) can prove quicker and more convenient from city centre to city centre. Direct daily flights operate in and out of Heathrow and Gatwick (see Air Travel) from cities all over the world, including Atlanta, Boston, Chicago, Dallas, Los Angeles, Montreal, New York, San Francisco and Toronto in North America, and there are several flights a week from Sydney, Melbourne, Perth and Auckland.

Health Care

By rail   For visitors arriving in London by rail from Europe the main departure points are Paris, Brussels and Amsterdam. Trains onward from the ferry ports arrive at Liverpool Street Station from Harwich and Victoria Station from Dover, Folkestone, Ramsgate, Sheerness and Newhaven.

Eurostar   The newest and most spectacular method of getting to London by rail is to travel via the Channel Tunnel (Eurotunnel) by Eurostar. This high-speed train, reaching speeds of up to 186mph/300km ph, gets under the Channel in less than 35 minutes. Departing from either Paris Gare du Nord or Brussels Gare du Midi, services arrive 3 hours and 3¼ hours later respectively at London's Waterloo International station. Certain trains additionally call at Lille and Calais in northern France and Ashford (Kent) on the British side. With some of the special rates this can work out cheaper than travelling by air.

By car   To get to London by car visitors from mainland Europe can either travel through the Channel tunnel on Le Shuttle (see below) or by ferry:

FERRY PORTS	DURATION	COMPANY
Hook of Holland–Harwich	6½–7 hrs. (day)	
	8½–10 hrs. (night)	Stena Line
Vlissingen (Holland)–	8 hrs. (day)	Eurolink
Sheerness	9½ hrs. (night)	Ferries
Ostend–Ramsgate	4 hrs.	Sally Line
Ostend–Ramsgate	1 hr. 35 mins. (hydrofoil)	Sally Line
Dunkirk–Ramsgate	2½ hrs.	Sally Line
Boulogne–Folkestone	55 mins. (catamaran)	Hoverspeed
Calais-Dover	1¼ hrs.	P & O
Calais-Dover	1½ hrs.	Stena Line
Calais–Dover	35 mins. (hovercraft)	Hoverspeed
Calais–Dover	45 mins. (catamaran)	Stena Line
Calais-Dover	1½ hrs.	Sea France
Dieppe–Newhaven	4 hrs.	Stena Line

Le Shuttle   Le Shuttle, the Eurotunnel's car-carrying rail service, departs every 15 minutes (every 1 hour 15 minutes between midnight and 6am) and takes just 35 minutes (45 minutes between midnight and 6am). During the journey from Calais to Folkestone you can either stay in your car or stretch your legs in the transporter coach. You pay on arrival at the loading terminals which are directly connected to the motorways at either end: the A16, via junction 13, in France, and the M20, via junction 11a, in Britain.

Routes to London   Harwich–Colchester–Chelmsford–London: 70 miles/113km (A12)
Dover–Canterbury–Rochester–London: 70 miles/112km (A2); the A2 is also the route to London from Ramsgate and Sheerness
Folkestone–Maidstone–London: 77 miles/124km (M20)
Newhaven–Brighton–Crawley–London: 63 miles/101km (A23/M23)

Reservations   It is wisest to book in advance for any kind of sea crossing, whether by ferry or tunnel. This can be done through most travel agents.

By coach   The main coach company offering scheduled services from European cities to London is Eurolines, a division of National Express. These terminate in London at Victoria Coach Station. Further details are available from: Eurolines, 52 Grosvenor Gardens, Victoria SW1W 0AU; tel. (0171) 730 8235.

Health Care

National Health Service   Britain's National Health Service provides medical care free of charge for nationals of European Union, most other European countries and certain other countries such as Australia and New Zealand, but only on an emergency basis for other visitors who should therefore ensure they have some form of health insurance to cover them during their stay.

Ambulance: call 999
Emergency Doctor: Doctorcall (0181) 900 1000
Emergency Dental Care: (0191) 955 5000

Emergencies

New Charing Cross Hospital, Fulham Palace Road W6;
tel. (0181) 748 2040

Accident and
emergency units

Chelsea and Westminster Hospital, 369 Fulham Road SW10;
tel. (0181) 746 8000

Middlesex Hospital, Mortimer Street W1; tel. (0171) 636 8333

Royal Free Hospital, Pond Street NW3; tel. (0171) 794 0500

St Bartholomew's Hospital, West Smithfield EC1; tel. (0171) 601 8888

St Mary's Hospital, Praed Street W2; tel. (0171) 725 6666

St Thomas's Hospital, Lambeth Palace Road WC1; tel. (0171) 928 9292

University College Hospital, Gower Street WC1; tel. (0171) 387 9300

Great Ormond Street Children's Hospital, Great Ormond Street WC1;
tel. (0171) 405 9200

Children

Paddington Green Hospital for Children, Paddington Green W2;
tel. (0171) 723 1081

Moorfields Eye Hospital, High Holborn WC1; tel. (0171) 836 661

Eyes

Guy's Hospital, St Thomas Street SE1; tel. (0171) 405 7600

Poisoning

Chemists who dispense prescriptions (for which a charge has to be paid) are often in a special section of a larger pharmacy or drugstore. Some of the larger chains of chemists have London branches with late-night opening hours.

Chemists

Bliss, 5 Marble Arch W1; tel. (0171) 723 6116 (9am–midnight)
50 Willesden Lane NW6; tel. (0171) 624 8000 (9am–midnight)
Sloane Square SW1; tel. (0171) 730 1023
Boots, 44 Regent Street, Piccadilly Circus W1; tel. (0171) 734 6126
   (Mon.–Fri. 8.30am–8pm, Sat. 9am–8pm, Sun. 11am–6pm)
   75 Queensway W2; tel. (0171) 229 9266
   (Mon.–Sat. 9am–10pm, Sun. 5–10pm, Summer opening 2–10pm)

Day and night
service

Hotels

The fact that London is one of the world's most expensive cities is reflected not least in its hotel prices. Clearly anyone not travelling on a tight budget can stay at one of the luxury hotels, some of which are among the most famous in the world, with so much to offer by way of atmosphere and service that it would be a shame just to treat them as overnight accommodation. But anyone looking for a good inexpensive hotel should not go below £70 for a double room and should also be sure to book well ahead. On the other hand there is scarcely any risk of being unable to find a hotel if you arrive without having booked, provided you are prepared to pay more if necessary, or to put up with

Book well ahead

poorer facilities. In the peak season, though, it can prove more difficult. Bookings can be made direct with the hotels or through a travel agent.

Finding accommodation

For holders of Access and Visa cards there is London Tourist Board's Accommodation Bookings Hotline (tel. (0171) 932 2020; Mon.–Fri. 9am–5.30pm).

Help with finding a hotel is also on hand at London's Tourist Information Centres (see Information) where staff make on-the-spot bookings, or for general advice dial Visitorcall on (0839) 123 435. The agency London Hotels (tel. (0171) 454 5000; Mon. –Fri. 9am–8pm, Sat. 9am–4pm) will also book for you, sometimes under their very reasonable last-minute tariff – however you will only know in which hotel just before you arrive.

Hotel list

The brochures "Where to Stay in London" (charge), a guide to hotels, guest houses and bed and breakfast and "London Accommodation for Budget Travellers" (free), a list of selected, reasonably-priced hotels, can be obtained from the London Tourist Board and BTA (see Information).

Classification

Hotels inspected annually by the London Tourist Board are classified according to the range of facilities and services you can expect. These classifications start with "Listed" and go up to "Five Crowns" – the more crowns, the wider the range.

The Automobile Association (AA) has its own grading system based upon stars, from "one star" to "five stars", with recognition of excellence within a star-rating signified by red stars. This roughly corresponds to the crown system. All hotels listed below are AA-appointed. A star (★) signifies a red star hotel.

The prices indicated below are average prices for a double room in their category; they are only a rough guide and may vary considerably (especially upwards in the de luxe category). As a rule only a (modest) continental breakfast is included; there is usually an extra charge for full English breakfast. All prices are subject to 17% VAT (value added tax). At many hotels it is worth asking about bargain group and weekend arrangements, especially in the holiday months of July and August.

Classification	Average price for a double room
5 Crowns/5 Stars: de luxe or luxury	over £200
4 Crowns/4 Stars: first class	£150–200
3 Crowns/3 Stars: very good	£100–150
2 Crowns/2 Stars: good	£70–100
1 Crown/1 Star: modest	£40–70
Listed: basic	£20–40

Hotel selection

Most of the hotels listed below are in the West End or in Kensington and Knightsbridge, within easy reach of London's main sights.

Luxury hotels

★Claridge's, Brook Street W1; tel. (0171) 629 8860, fax (0171) 499 2210; 192 r., bar, restaurant, business service. One of London's most elegant addresses, truly aristocratic and above all discreet.

★The Connaught, Carlos Place W1; tel. (0171) 499 7070, fax (0171) 495 3262; 90 r., bar, restaurant, in the old-style British tradition, 1897 carved oak: discretion is of paramount importance and the guests' wishes are sacrosanct. The best chance of getting a reservation is through a polite letter – but regular patrons get preference over allcomers.

★The Dorchester, 53 Park Lane W1; tel. (0171) 629 8888, fax (0171) 409 0114; 244 r., bar, three very good restaurants, parking, fitness suite, business service. Lavish use was made of marble in 1900 when it was built and this was carried on in the 1990 refurbishment. Magnificent view over Hyde Park.

The Dorchester: an excellent London hotel

Forty Seven Park Street, 47 Park Street, Mayfair W1; tel. (0171) 491 7282, fax (0171) 491 7281; 52 suites, bar, restaurant, business service. Every suite has French bronzes, chandeliers and wood panelling. Best of all, the hotel is over top restaurant La Gavroche, and you can order from your room.

Four Seasons, Hamilton Place, Park Lane, W1; tel. (0171) 499 0888, fax (0171) 493 6629; 227r., Bar, restaurants. The elegant rooms are furnisbed to a high standard and there is a fitness suite for the guests.

Grosvenor House, Park Lane W1; tel. (0171) 499 6363, fax (0171) 493 3341; 366 r., bar, restaurants (including top restaurant Nico at Ninety), parking, swimming pool, fitness suite, business service. A giant in the de-luxe class and famous as a venue for grand social occasions and parties – the Great Hall holds 1500. View over Hyde Park.

Hotel Inter-Continental, 1 Hamilton Place, Hyde Park corner W1; tel. (0171) 409 3131, fax (0171) 493 3476; 458r., health and fitness suites. The hotel is popular with international travellers and is renowned for its Le Soufflé restaurant that offers English, French, Italian and Oriental cuisines.

★Hyde Park, 66 Knightsbridge SW1; tel. (0171) 235 2000, fax (0171) 235 4552; 185 r., bar, restaurants Mandarin Oriental. parking, fitness centre. Edwardian hotel overlooking Hyde Park. Rooms have period furnishings.

The Ritz, Piccadilly W1; tel. (0171) 493 8181, fax (0171) 493 2687; 131 r., bar, restaurant, parking, business service, garden terrace. One of the flagships of London's hotel business, situated directly on Green Park. All the rooms are furnished in Louis XVI style; if a stay there is beyond your means you can at least take tea in the Palm Court.

★The Savoy, Strand WC2; tel. (0171) 836 4343, fax (0171) 240 6040; 207 r., bar, very good restaurant, the Savoy Grill, parking, rooftop swimming pool, fitness suite, business service. A legendary Victorian hotel with art deco foyer, where tea is served in the afternoons. Some bathrooms with magnificent old-fashioned (but not old!) fittings. Rooms with a river view cost extra.

The Waldorf, Aldwych WC2; tel. (0171) 836 2400, fax (0171) 836 7244; 292 r., bar, restaurant, business service. This illustrious name, now part of the Forte chain, has undergone a multi-million pound refurbishment.

First-class hotels

★Athenaeum, 116 Piccadilly W1; tel. (0171) 499 3464, fax (0171) 493 1860; 156 r., bar, restaurant, business service. Not without reason does this hotel bear the same name as the nearby Gentleman's Club – pure elegance, attentive service. Meet for tea in the Windsor Lounge.

The Beaufort, 33 Beaufort Gardens SW3; tel. (0171) 584 5252, fax (0171) 589 2834; 28 r., bar, business service, health club. Very elegant, intimate hotel, a short step from Harrods; only Harry, the hotel cat, is allowed to interrupt the service.

★Capital, Basil Street, Knightsbridge SW3; tel. (0171) 589 5171, fax (0171) 225 0011; 48 r., bar, restaurant, parking. Small and exclusive hotel with the personal touch.

★Goring, 15 Beeston Palace, Grosvenor Gardens SW1; tel. (0171) 396 9000, fax (0171) 834 4393; 76 r., bar, restaurant, parking. This Edwardian hotel has been run by three generations of Gorings with discreet but attentive service.

Halcyon, 81 Holland Park W11; tel. (0171) 727 7288, fax (0171) 229 8516; 43 r., bar, restaurant, parking, business service. Magnificent belle-epoque establishment, opulently furnished.

Tower Thistle, St. Katharine's Way E1; tel. (0171) 481 2575, fax (0171) 488 4106; 803 r., bar, restaurant, parking, business service. Large modern hotel by Tower Bridge.

Very good hotels

★Abbey Court, 20 Pembridge Gardens, Kensington W2; tel. (0171) 221 7518, fax (0171) 792 0858; 22 r., bar, business service. Small, quiet country-house style hotel for guests who value excellent service.

Academy, 17–21 Gower Street WC1; tel. (0171) 631 4115, fax (0171) 636 3442; 40 r., bar, restaurant, garden. Georgian town house not far from the British Museum.

Basil Street Hotel, 8 Basil Street, Knightsbridge SW3; tel. (0171) 581 3311, fax (0171) 581 3693; 89 r., bar, restaurant, business service. Family-run country-style hotel, very convenient for Harrods. Especially popular with the ladies, with its women-only Parrot Club.

Mostyn, 4 Bryanston Street W1; tel. (0171) 935 2361, fax (0171) 487 2759; 121 r., bar, restaurant and 24-hour room service. Listed Georgian hotel with recently redecorated bedrooms. Close to Marble Arch.

Royal Trafalgar Thistle, Whitcomb Street WC2; tel. (0171) 930 4477, fax (0171) 925 2149; 108 r., bar and restaurant. Informal hotel in the Thistle chain. Centrally located for West End theatres.

Rubens, Buckingham Palace Road SW1; tel. (0171) 834 6600, fax (0171) 828 5401; 180 r., bar and restaurant. Formerly a hostel for debutantes visiting Buckingham Palace, now an elegant hotel with views over the Royal Mews.

Sherlock Holmes, 108 Baker Street W1; tel. (0171) 486 6161, fax (0171) 486 0884; 125 r., bar, restaurant and 24-hour room service. A comfortable hotel containing memorabilia associated with Sherlock Holmes.

Clarendon, 8–16 Montpelier Row, Blackheath SE3; tel. (0181) 318 4321, fax (0181) 318 4378; 193 r., bar, restaurant and parking. Busy hotel overlooking the heath.

Comfort Inn, 22–32 West Cromwell Road, Kensington SW5; tel. (0171) 373 3300, fax (0171) 835 2040; 125 r., bar and restaurant. Bright, modern hotel conveniently positioned for Earl's Court, popular with business guests and tourists alike.

Hotel Ibis, 30 Stockwell Street, Greenwich SE10; tel. (0181) 305 1177, fax (0181) 858 7139; 82 r., bar, restaurant and parking. Modern hotel in the heart of historic Greenwich. Bedrooms are functional but well equipped.

Hotel Ibis Euston, 3 Cardington Street NW1; tel. (0171) 388 7777, fax (0171) 388 0001; 300 r., bar, restaurant and parking. Busy hotel adjacent to Euston Station. Breakfast is self-service.

Regent Palace, Glasshouse Street, Piccadilly W1; tel. (0171) 734 7000, fax (0171) 734 6435; 950 r., bars, restaurants (carvery and brasserie) and games room. A large hotel with comfortably appointed bedrooms.

Information

British Tourist Authority Overseas

The British Tourist Authority (BTA) is responsible for providing tourist information overseas and has offices in the following English-speaking countries:

8th Floor, 210 Clarence Street, Sydney,
New South Wales 2000; tel. (02) 267 4555, fax (02) 267 4442

Australia

Suite 450, 111 Avenue Road, Toronto, Ontario M5R 3J8;
tel. (416) 925 6326, fax (416) 961 2175

Canada

Suite 305, 3rd Floor, Dilworth Building, corner Customs/Queen Steets, Auckland 1; tel. (09) 303 1446, fax (09) 377 6965

New Zealand

18–19 College Green, Dublin 2; tel. (1) 670 800

Republic of Ireland

Lancaster Gate, Hyde Lane, Hyde Park, Sandton 2196 (personal callers); PO Box 41896, Craighall 2024 (postal address);
tel. (011) 325 0343, fax (011) 325 0344

South Africa

Suite 1510, 625 North Michigan Avenue, Chicago, IL 60611 (personal callers only);
Suite 450, World Trade Center, 350 South Figueroa Street, 7th Floor, 551 Fifth Avenue, New York, NY 10176–0799; tel. (212) 986 2200

United States

London Tourist Board (LTB) produces a number of useful free publications. These are available by post from:

**London
Tourist Board**

London Tourist Board, 26 Grosvenor Gardens, Victoria,
London SW1W 0DU; tel. (0171) 932 2000, fax 932 0222
Internet http://www.londontown.com

The LTB also operates the following Tourist Information Centres (TICs) where their very helpful staff can provide you with all kinds of information about where to go and how to get there, including public transport maps, etc., as well as arranging concert and theatre tickets, and booking guided tours and accommodation. London has a further 19 official TICs run mainly by local authorities and providing similar services.

Lost Property

LTB Tourist Information Centres

Victoria Station Forecourt SW1; Underground: Victoria
Open: Easter–Oct. daily 8am–7pm; Nov.–Easter Mon. Sat. 8am–7pm,
Sun. 8am–4pm; tel. (0171) 730 3488

Liverpool Street Station EC2; Underground: Liverpool Street
Open: Mon. 8.15am–7pm, Tue.–Sat. 8.15–6pm, Sun. 8.30am–4.45pm

Waterloo International SE1, Arrivals Hall; Underground: Waterloo
Open: daily 8.30am–7pm

Heathrow Terminals 1, 2, 3 Underground Station
Open: daily 8.30am–6pm

Selfridges, Oxford Street W1 (basement);
Underground: Bond Street. Open during store opening hours

British Travel Centre

12 Regent Street SW1; U\nderground: Piccadilly Circus
Open: Mon.–Fri. 9am–6.30pm, Sat. and Sun. 10am–4pm. Tel. (0171) 730 3400
The British Travel Centre is the joint information centre for the British
Tourist Authority and British Rail, American Express, Export Hotel
Reservations and Edwards and Edwards. It is the first point of call for
information about travel elsewhere in Great Britain.

City of London Information Centre

St Paul's Churchyard EC4, opposite St Paul's Cathedral
Underground: St Paul's. Open: Mon.–Fri. 9am–5pm, Sat. 10am–4pm
This body provides information on the "City" of London i.e. "Inner London".

Visitorcall is a 24-hour phone guide to London operated by the London
Tourist Board and Convention Bureau. Simply dial 0839 123 plus the last
three numbers for the recorded information you are particularly
interested in. Categories include:

Visitorcall

400	What's on this week
403	Current exhibitions
404	Children's what's on
	Sporting events
406	Summer in the parks
407	Sunday in London
411	Changing the Guard
415	Theatre – comedies
416	Popular West End shows
	Tennis at Wimbledon
	Theatre – Shakespeare
422	Rock & Pop concerts
424	Children's places to visit
425	Theatre – Serious plays
428	Street markets
429	Museums
430	Getting around London
431	Guided tours & walks
433	Getting to the airports
438	New productions/booking
480	Popular attractions
481	Palaces
483	Famous Houses & Gardens
484	Day trips from London
485	Pubs, Restaurants and Afternoon Teas
486	Shopping news

Lost Property

Lost property can be reported at any police station. There are also
special lost property offices for articles lost on public transport.

Heathrow: tel. (0181) 745 7727 Gatwick: tel. (01293) 503162	Airports
For items left in black cabs only: Public Carriage Office, 15 Penton Street N1; tel. (0171) 833 0996, Mon.–Fri. 9am–4pm	Taxis
London Transport Lost Property Office, 200 Baker Street NW1 Mon.–Fri. 9.30am–2pm (no telephone enquiries; forms from Underground and bus stations)	Underground and buses

Markets

Every day you will find a street market going on somewhere or other in
London; those listed below are among the most interesting.

Berwick Street, Soho W1; Underground: Piccadilly Circus   General
Mon.–Sat. 9am–6pm
Fruit, foodstuffs, clothing, household wares

Brick Lane E1/2; Underground: Aldgate East, Shoreditch
Sun. 6am–1pm
New and second-hand goods of all kinds

Brixton Market SW9; Underground: Brixton
Mon.–Sat. 8am–6pm, Wed. until 1pm, Fri. until 7pm
Afro-Caribbean: food, clothes, household wares, reggae CDs, etc.

East Street SE17; Underground: Elephant & Castle
Tues.–Thur. and Sun. 8am–3pm, Fri. and Sat. 8am–5pm
Clothes, electrical and household goods, fruit and vegetables

Jubilee Market, Covent Garden WC2; Underground: Covent Garden
Mon. 6am–5pm (antiques); Tues.–Fri. 9am–6pm (all sorts); Sat., Sun.
9am–6pm (arts and crafts)

Leather Lane Market, Leather Lane EC1; Underground: Chancery Lane
Mon.–Fri. 10am–2.30pm; clothes, electrical goods, records, CDs

Petticoat Lane, Middlesex Street E1; Underground: Aldgate
Sun. 9am–2pm
London's most famous street market, noisy, busy and full of real char-
acters, where you can buy almost anything, but specialising in clothes

Shepherd's Bush W12; Underground: Shepherd's Bush
Tues.–Sat. 8.30am–6pm; West Indian, Asian, foodstuffs

See entry   Antiques and
      fleamarkets

Farringdon Road EC1; Underground: Farringdon. Mon.–Fri. 6am–noon   Books

Columbia Road E2; Underground: Old Street. Sun. 8am–12.30pm   Flowers

Leadenhall Market, Whittington Avenue, EC3;   Foods
Underground: Bank, Monument
Mon.–Fri. 7am–3pm
Meat, poultry, fish in Victorian market halls

Portobello Road W11; Underground: Ladbroke Grove, Notting Hill Gate
Mon.–Wed., Fri. and Sat. 8am–1pm (fruit and vegetables); Fri. 8am–3pm
and Sat. 8am–5pm (general); Sat. 8am–5pm (antiques and second-hand)

Smithfield EC1; Underground: Farringdon
Mon.–Fri. 5–10.30am; one of the world's largest meat markets

Motoring

Drive on the left

Drive on the left and overtake on the right, and if you are unfamiliar with driving on the left take special care when starting out. Apart from this, driving on the left is nowhere near as difficult as you might expect.

Do not drive in London

In London it is better not to drive at all, given the congestion and lack of on-street parking, particularly since most tourist places are accessible by public transport.

Right of way

Traffic on the main road generally has the right of way unless a "Stop" or "Give Way" sign indicates otherwise. At roundabouts give way to the traffic coming from the right already on the roundabout. Motorists must stop at road junctions with unbroken double white lines but may edge forward slowly if the white lines are broken.

Speed limits

In Britain the maximum speed limit on motorways and dual carriage-ways is 70mph/112kph (60mph/96kph with a trailer), on other roads out-side built-up areas 60mph/96kph (50mph/80kph with a trailer) and in built-up areas 30mph/48kph. Towing vehicles may not use the outside lane of a three-lane motorway

Alcohol limit

The blood alcohol limit is 0.8 per millilitre.

Petrol

Petrol (gasoline) is sold in litres. Grades obtainable are Four-star leaded (98 octane), Super unleaded (98 octane) and Premium unleaded (95 octane). Diesel and LPG are also usually obtainable in most places.

Tyre pressure

Tyre pressure is measured in pounds per square inch (e.g. 20lb sq.in. = 1.41kg sq.cm).

Insurance

In Britain vehicles only require third-party insurance, so visitors driving their own cars should take out comprehensive insurance to cover their stay.

Motoring organisations

The Automobile Association (AA) and Royal Automobile Club (RAC) pro-vide breakdown services for members of other affiliated motoring organisations, and also operate a joint freephone line for calls for assist-ance from their emergency services.

AA (Automobile Association)

Head Office: Norfolk House, Priestley Road, Basingstoke, Hampshire RG24 9NY; tel. (01256) 320123
Shop: 119 Cannon Street SW1; tel. (0171) 623 5352

AA Breakdown line

Freephone: 0800 887766

RAC (Royal Automobile Club)

RAC House, 1 Forest Road, Middlesex. TW14 7RR 5352
Information: tel. (0181) 917 2500

RAC Breakdown line

Freephone: 0800 828282

Parking
On-street parking

Traffic congestion in London is bad – the average speed is only 11mph/18kmph – and on-street parking is very difficult so it is better not to use your car at all and travel by public transport (see Public Transport). If you do to find a parking space at a meter do not be sur-prised at the high cost for only one hour. Make sure you park only where it is permissible to do so. Parking on double yellow lines; red/pink lines or on the approach to pedestrian crossings is strictly prohibited, although parking on single yellow lines is allowed outside business hours (Mon.–Fri. 8.30am–6.30pm, Sat. 8.30am–1.30pm). Vehicles parked illegally – and that includes parking meters where time has run out – will be clamped and then released only after a long wait and payment of a large fine. The police are also quick to tow away any vehicle illegally parked. If you are unlucky enough to have this happen to you follow the instructions given on the label attached to the vehicle.

Needless to say, London also has its share of official carparks. A free map of these is obtainable from National Car Parks (NCP), PO Box 4NH, 21 Bryanston Street W1A 4NH; tel. (0171) 499 7050.

Off-street parking

Museums and Exhibitions

Admission is free for many of London's museums, but since most museums receive little or no state funding, and have to look elsewhere for support, you may be invited to make a "voluntary contribution" which can either be left up to you or be for a suggested amount. Nor should you be surprised to see museum posters and literature carrying the logos of well-known companies acting as sponsors, or to find museum shops of almost supermarket-like proportions with their own mail-order business as well.

Admission charges

The London White Card, which is issued on a family or individual basis, is valid for three or seven days and for a single price offers the holder unlimited access to thirteen of London's top museums and collections, including the National Maritime Museum, the Natural History Museum, the Science Museum, and the Victoria and Albert Museum. The card can be purchased at any of the participating museums or galleries, Tourist Information Centre, hotels, ticket offices and travel agencies.

London White Card

Last admissions are usually 30–45 minutes before the museum closes. Opening hours are usually 10am–5 or 6pm Mon.-Sat., and from 2 or 2.30pm on Sundays.

Last admissions

List of museums

The relevant entry heading is given for museums which feature in the A–Z section.

Abbey Museum, see Westminster Abbey

Alexander Fleming Laboratory Museum, St Mary's Hospital, Praed Street W2; Underground: Paddington
Mon.–Thur. 10am–1pm, other times by appointment
Laboratory where Fleming discovered penicillin and an exhibition on his life

Apsley House (Wellington Museum), see Hyde Park Corner

Bank of England Museum, see Bank of England

Barbican Art Gallery, see Barbican Centre

BBC Experience, Broadcasting House, Portland Place W1. Daily 9.30am–5.30pm; Underground: Oxford Circus a tour of the BBC studios

HMS "Belfast", see entry

Bethnal Green Museum, see entry

Bramah Tea and Coffee Museum, see Docklands

Museums and Exhibitions

British Museum, see entry

Burgh House, see Hampstead Heath

Cabinet War Rooms, see Whitehall

Carlyle's House, see Chelsea

Chiswick House, Burlington Lane W4; Underground: Turnham Green, then bus
Apr.–Sept.: daily 10am–1pm and 2–6pm, Oct.–Mar. Wed.–Sun. 10am–1pm and 2–4pm;
18th c. stately home

Clink Exhibition, see Southwark Cathedral

Courtauld Gallery, see entry

Crafts Council, 44a Pentonville Road N1
Mon.–Sat. 11am–7pm, Sun. 2–6pm; Underground: Angel
Important exhibitions of contemporary and traditional crafts;
library

Cutty Sark, see Greenwich

Design Museum, see Docklands

Dickens House Museum, 48 Doughty Street WC1
Mon.–Sat. 10am–5pm; Underground: Russell Square, Chancery Lane
The home of writer Charles Dickens from 1837–39, where, among other works. he wrote "Pickwick Papers" and "Oliver Twist".
Letters, furniture and first editions

Dulwich Picture Gallery, see entry

Eltham Palace, Eltham SE9
Thur., Fri. and Sun. 10am–6pm (4pm late Sept.–Mar.), visit by guided tour only at 10 and 11.30am and 1 and 2.30pm; British Rail: Eltham and Mottingham from Charing Cross, then bus 161 from Eltham, buses 161 and 126 from Mottingham.
Beautifully furnished medieval Royal Palace

Fan Museum, see Greenwich

Faraday's Laboratory and Museum, 21 Albemarle Street W1
Mon.–Fri. 10am–6pm; Underground: Green Park
Restored magnetic laboratory of Michael Faraday as it was in 1845 with an exhibition of original apparatus

Fenton House, see Hampstead Heath

Florence Nightingale Museum, St. Thomas's Hospital, 2 Lambeth Palace Road SE1
Tues.–Sun. 10am–4pm; Underground: Waterloo, Westminster
Audio-visuals and memorabilia of Florence Nightingale, founder of modern nursing

Foundling Hospital Art Treasures, see Thomas Coram Foundation for Children

Freud Museum, see Hampstead

Geffrye Museum, Kingsland Road E2
Tues.–Sat., 10am–5pm, Sun. 2–5pm; Underground: Liverpool Street, then buses 22A, 22B, 149
17th–20th c. furniture and household articles in former Ironmonger's Company almshouse with walled herb garden

Gipsy Moth, see Greenwich

Guildhall Art Gallery, see Guildhall

Guildhall Clock Museum, see Guildhall

The Guards Museum, see Buckingham Palace

Ham House, see Richmond

Hayward Gallery, see South Bank

Hogarth's House, Hogarth Lane, Great West Road W4
Apr.–Sept. Mon., Wed.–Sat. 11am–6pm, Sun. 2–6pm; Oct.–Mar. (except for the last three weeks in December) Mon., Wed.–Sat. 11am–4pm, Sun. 2–4pm; Underground: Chiswick Park, Turnham Green
Home of artist William Hogarth

Horniman Museum and Gardens, London Road, Forest Hill SE23
Mon.–Sat. 10.30am–5.30pm, Sun. 2–5.30pm (gardens 8am–dusk); British Rail: Forest Hill from London Bridge
Musical instruments, ethnological and zoological exhibits collected by tea merchant Frederick John Horniman (1835–1906)

House of Detention, Clerkenwell Close EC1
10am–6pm daily; Underground: Farringdon
Victorian underground prison

Hunterian Museum, Lincoln's Inn Fields WC2
Mon.–Fri. 10am–6.30pm; Underground: Holborn, Chancery Lane
Medical collection of Doctor John Hunter (1729–93)

Imperial War Museum, see entry

Institute of Contemporary Arts (ICA), see The Mall

Jewel Tower, see Houses of Parliament

Jewish Museum, Raymond Burton House, 129–131 Albert Street NW1
Sun.–Thur., 10am–4pm (closed Jewish Festivals); Underground: Camden Town
Jewish life and history

Dr Johnson's House, see Fleet Street

Keats' House, see Hampstead

Kensington State Apartments, see Hyde Park · Kensington Gardens · Kensington Palace

Kenwood House (Iveagh Bequest), see Hampstead

Kew Bridge Steam Museum, see Kew Gardens

Kew Palace, see Kew Gardens

Museums and Exhibitions

Leighton House, 12 Holland Park Road W14
Mon.–Sat. 11am–5.30pm; Underground: High Street Kensington
Victorian stately home with art works and romantic garden

Linley Sambourne House, 18 Stafford Terrace W8
Mar.–Oct. Wed. 10am–4pm, Sun. 2–5pm; Underground: High Street Kensington
Home of artist and "Punch" cartoonist Edward Linley Sambourne with 19th c. furniture and paintings

London Butterfly House, see Syon House

London Canal Museum, see Piccadilly Circus

London Dungeon, see London Bridge

London Toy and Model Museum, 21–23 Craven Hill W2
Mon.–Sat. 10am–5.30pm, Sun. 11am–5.30pm; Underground: Lancaster Gate, Bayswater, Queensway

London Transport Museum, see Covent Garden

Madame Tussaud's "Royalty and Empire", see Windsor Castle

Madame Tussaud's, see entry

Marble Hill House, Richmond Road, Twickenham
Apr.–Sept. daily 10am–6pm; Oct.–Mar. Wed.–Sun. 10am–4pm;
British Rail: St Margaret's from Waterloo; Underground: Richmond then bus
18th c. mansion on the Thames, with chinoiserie collection

Marianne North Gallery, see Kew Gardens

Museum of Childhood at Bethnal Green, see Bethnal Green Museum of Childhood

Museum of Cricket in Lord's Cricket Ground, see Regent's Park

Museum of Garden History, see Lambeth Palace

Museum of London, see entry

Museum of Mankind, see entry

Museum of Methodism, see Wesley's Chapel and House

Museum of the Moving Image, see South Bank

Museum of the Order of St John, see St John's Gate · St John's Church

Museum of the Royal Hospital Chelsea, see Chelsea

Museum of Rugby, Rugby Road, Twickenham/Tue.–Sat. 10.30am–5pm, Sun. 2–5pm
British Rail: Twickenham from Waterloo
Multimedia museum in the home of Rugby Union.

Musical Museum, see Kew Gardens

National Army Museum, see Chelsea

National Gallery, see entry

National Maritime Museum, see Greenwich

National Portrait Gallery, see entry

National Postal Museum, see entry

Natural History Museum, see entry

Old Operating Theatre Museum, see Southwark Cathedral

Old Royal Observatory, see Greenwich

Osterley Park House, Jersey Road, Isleworth, Middlesex
Apr.–Oct. Wed.–Sat. 1pm–5pm, Sun. 11am–5pm; Underground: Osterley
then 20 minutes' walk
House and park of Sir Thomas Gresham, founder of the Royal Exchange

Percival Davis Foundation of Chinese Art, 58 Gordon Square WC1
Mon.–Fri. 10.30am–1pm; Underground: Euston
Collection of Chinese objets d'art

Polish Institute and Sikorski Museum, 11 Leopold Road, Ealing W5
Mon.–Fri. 9am–3pm; Underground: Ealing Common
Museum of the Polish government-in-exile in London 1939–45

Pollock's Toy Museum, 1 Scala Street W1
Mon.–Sat. 10am–5pm; Underground: Goodge Street
Dolls, puppet theatres and teddy bears

Prince Henry's Room, see Fleet Street

Public Records Office Museum, Chancery Lane WC2
Mon.–Fri. 9.30am–5pm; Underground: Chancery Lane
National archive with exhibition

Pumphouse Museum, see Docklands

Queen Charlotte's Cottage, see Kew Gardens

Queen's Gallery, see Buckingham Palace

Ragged School Museum, 46–48 Copperfield Road, Bow E3
Wed., Thur., and 1st Sun. in month 10am–5pm; Underground: Mile End;
DLR: Limehouse
Museum about East End of London life, in canalside warehouses once
housing Dr Barnardo's largest ragged school. Includes a reconstructed
Victorian classroom

Ranger's House, see Greenwich

Rock Circus, London Pavilion, Piccadilly Circus W1
Mon., Wed. Thur. and Sun. 11am–9pm, Tues. noon–9pm, Fri. and Sat.
11am–10pm, at Easter and in summer opens an hour earlier;
Underground: Piccadilly Circus
Branch of Madame Tussaud's with animated figures of rock and pop
stars

Royal Academy of Arts, see Piccadilly Circus

Royal Air Force Museum, see entry

Royal Hospital Chelsea, see Chelsea

Royal London Hospital Museum and Archives Centre, St Augustine and St Philip's Church, Newark Street E1
Mon.–Fri. 10am–4.30pm; Underground: Whitechapel

Royal Mews, see Buckingham Palace

Russian Submarine, see Docklands

Science Museum, see entry

Serpentine Gallery, see Hyde Park · Kensington Gardens · Kensington Palace

Shakespeare's Globe Theatre and Exhibition, see Southwark Cathedral

Sherlock Holmes Museum, see Regent's Park

Sir John Soane's Museum, see entry

Southside House, see Wimbledon

Syon House, see entry

Tate Gallery, see entry

Theatre Museum, see Covent Garden

Thomas Coram Foundation for Children, see entry

Tower, see entry

Tower Bridge Exhibition, see Tower Bridge

Tower Hill Pageant, see Tower

Twinings Tea Museum, see The Strand

Victoria & Albert Museum, see entry

Wallace Collection, see entry

Wellcome Museum, see Science Museum

Wellington Museum (Aspley House), see Hyde Park Corner

Wimbledon Lawn Tennis Museum, see Wimbledon
Whitechapel Art Gallery, Whitechapel High Street E1
Tues.–Sun. 11am–5pm, Wed. to 8pm; Underground: Aldgate East
Modern and contemporary art

William Morris Gallery, Water House, Lloyd Park, Forest Road, Walthamstow E17
Tues.–Sat. 10am–1pm and 2–5pm and 1st Sun. in the month; Underground: Walthamstow Central
Home of social reformer William Morris

Winston Churchill's Britain at War Experience, see London Bridge

Woolwich Railway Museum, see Docklands

Music

World-class status   London enjoys world-class status for its music, whether it be classical or the latest contemporary trend. Besides its two opera houses (The Royal

Opera House and English National Opera) it has five top symphony orchestras (the Philharmonia, London Symphony, London Philharmonic, Royal Philharmonic, BBC Symphony) and a number of excellent chamber orchestras (Academy of St-Martin-in-the-Fields, English Chamber Orchestra, London Bach Orchestra, etc.) and choirs (Philharmonia Chorus, Ambrosian Singers, Royal Choral Society, etc.). And there is almost always the chance during a stay in London of seeing stars in concert from the world of rock, jazz and pop.

Information about what's on is published in the daily press and in weekly ratings magazines such as "Time Out" and "What's on in London".

What's On

Even though there may be tickets available on the night it is wisest to book early, especially for the main venues. Box offices usually open at 10am and there are plenty of ticket agencies.

Tickets

English National Opera
The London Coliseum, St Martin's Lane WC2; tel. (0171) 632 8300
Underground: Leicester Square
The Royal Opera
The Royal Opera House, Covent Garden, Bow Street WC2 (box office in Floral Street);
tel. (0171) 304 4000; Underground: Covent Garden
World-famous opera house also home to The Royal Ballet
Closed for refurbishment until 1999

Opera

Sadler's Wells Theatre, Rosebery Avenue EC1; tel. (0171) 863 8000
Underground: Angel
Opera and ballet and dance

London is home to a number of world-famous ballet companies. The Royal Ballet and English National Ballet specialise in the classics, while the London Contemporary Dance School offers the latest in contemporary dance and experimental groups and workshops. Sadler's Wells stages opera in English as well as ballet and dance and often hosts visiting companies.

Ballet and dance

The Royal Ballet
Venue: The Royal Opera House, Covent Garden, see above

Companies

English National Ballet
Venue: The London Coliseum, see above

London Contemporary Dance School
Venue: The Place Theatre, 17 Duke's Road WC1; tel. (0171) 387 0031
Underground: Euston Square

Riverside Studios, Crisp Road W6; tel. (0181) 741 2255
Underground: Hammersmith
Showcase for the Rambert Dance Company's spring workshops in April, and the rest of the time hosts other modern and international dance companies.

Other venues

Barbican Hall, Barbican Centre EC2; tel. (0171) 638 8891
Underground: Barbican, Moorgate
Home of the London Symphony Orchestra

Concert venues

Royal Albert Hall, Kensington Gore SW7; tel. (0171) 589 8212
Underground: South Kensington
Famous as a concert hall for equally famous orchestras

St John's Smith Square, Smith Square SW1; tel. (0171) 222 1061
Underground: Westminster
A baroque church which makes an appropriate setting for 18th c. music

Music

St Martin-in-the-Fields, Trafalgar Square WC2; tel. (0171) 839 8362
Underground: Charing Cross
Popular, free lunchtime recitals (see entry A-Z)

South Bank Centre SE1; tel. (0171) 921 0600
Underground: Waterloo
The South Bank has three concert halls – the Purcell Room, Queen
Elizabeth Hall and the Royal Festival Hall

Wigmore Hall, 36 Wigmore Street W1; tel. (0171) 935 2141
Underground: Bond Street, Oxford Circus
A favourite location for recitals and chamber music

Outdoor concerts

The grounds of Kenwood House on Hampstead Heath make a particularly lovely setting for outdoor concerts from June to August; the Crystal
Palace Concert Bowl also offers music in the open air.

The Proms

The Proms – the BBC Henry Wood Promenade Concerts to give them
their full title – are staged from mid-July to mid-September every year in
the Royal Albert Hall (see Concert Venues) and occupy a very special
place in London's musical life. Programmes range from early music to
specially commissioned modern works. Tickets are not expensive and
the audiences are very mixed. The highlight for many is the Last Night
of the Proms when everyone is in party mood and the conductor has to
keep both Promenaders and performers under control.

Musicals

London can count itself the world's top city when it comes to musicals,
particularly since this is where Andrew Lloyd Webber first stages his
shows. The most popular musicals such as "The Phantom of the Opera"
are usually sold out for six months or more in advance. Favourite musicals include:

**"Beauty and
the Beast"**

Dominion Theatre, Tottenham Court Road, W1; tel. (0171) 656 1888;
Underground: Tottenham Court Road

"Buddy"

Strand, Aldwych WC2; tel. (0171) 930 8800
Underground: Charing Cross

"Cats"

New London, Drury Lane WC2; tel. (0171) 405 0072
Underground: Holborn

**"Jesus Christ
Superstar"**

Lyceum Theatre, Wellington Street, WC2 Tel. (0171) 420 8112:
Underground: Charing Cross, Covent Garden.

"Les Misérables"

Palace, Shaftesbury Avenue W1; tel. (0171) 434 0909
Underground: Leicester Square

"Miss Saigon"

Drury Lane Theatre Royal, Catherine Street WC2; tel. (0171) 494 5000
Underground: Covent Garden

"Oliver!"

London Palladium, Argyll Street W1; tel. (0171) 494 5020
Underground: Oxford Circus

**"Phantom of
the Opera"**

Her Majesty's, Haymarket SW1; tel. (0171) 494 5400
Underground: Piccadilly Circus

**"Starlight
Express"**

Apollo Victoria, 17 Wilton Road SW1; tel. (0171) 416 6054
Underground: Victoria

"Chicago"

Adelphi, Strand WC2; tel. (0171) 344 0055
Underground: Charing Cross

All Hallows-by-the-Tower, see A-Z

Brompton Oratory, see A-Z

St Lawrence Jewry, Guildhall EC2
Underground: Bank, St Paul's

St Mary-le-Bow, see A-Z

St Sepulchre-without-Newgate, Holborn Viaduct EC1
Underground: St Paul's

Labatt's Apollo Hammersmith, Queen Caroline Street W6; tel. (0171) 416 6066
Underground: Hammersmith

Large rock concerts

Royal Albert Hall, see above

Wembley Arena, Empire Way, Wembley; tel. (0181) 902 1234
Underground: Wembley Park

See Nightlife

Jazz clubs and pub music

Newspapers and Periodicals

London is at the heart of Britain's national press, making it one of the world's greatest media centres. Fleet Street had its first news-sheet as early as 1501, but new technology has lately seen many of the national Sunday and daily papers move their production further afield to Docklands. The major dailies have a total circulation of up to 14 million, and as many as 16 million copies of the Sunday papers come off the presses. The British are great newspaper readers, and Londoners are no exception, each with their favourite paper according to their political inclination, opting for "The Times", "Daily Mail", "Daily Express", "Daily Telegraph", "Daily Star" and "Sun" if Conservative, or "The Guardian", "Independent", or "Daily Mirror" if they are more of a Liberal or left-wing persuasion. The "Financial Times" caters for those interested in the Stock Exchange but also has excellent cultural coverage. Londoners' evening paper is "The Standard". Sports fans take "Sporting Life" or "Racing Post".

Newspapers

The Sunday papers are "The Mail on Sunday", "The Independent on Sunday", "The Observer", "Sunday Express", "Sunday Mirror", "Sunday Telegraph", "Sunday People", "Sunday Times" and "News of the World".

Sunday papers

The many periodicals include satirical magazines "Punch" and "Private Eye", while the latest trends in popular music are covered in "Smash Hits", "New Musical Express", and the long-established "Melody Maker". For what's on in London there is "Time Out", the listing magazine which comes out every Wednesday (internet: http://www.time out.co.uk).

Periodicals

Nightlife

London has much to offer for evening entertainment with all its theatres, cinemas and musical shows (see Theatre, Music), not to mention a night out in a pub (see Pubs), but you need to make at least one visit to Soho, too, if only to take in the atmosphere of London's traditional redlight district. Other centres of nightlife are around Covent Garden and in parts of Chelsea such as Sloane Square and King's Road. Since the "in" places change so frequently only those that have stood the test of time are listed

Nightlife

below. It is also worth buying "Time Out" or "What's On In London" to get the full picture of what is on where each evening.

Night clubs and revue bars

Crazy Horse, Swallow Street W1; tel. (0171) 734 6666
Underground: Piccadilly Circus

Legends, 29 Old Burlington Street W1; tel. (0171) 437 9933
Underground: Oxford Circus, Green Park (society meeting place)

Vogue's, 201 Wardour Street W1; tel. (0171) 434 4285
Underground: Oxford Circus, Tottenham Court Road

Madame Jojo's, 8 Brewer Street W1; tel. (0171) 734 2473
Underground: Piccadilly Circus (drag shows)

Raymond Revuebar Theatre, Walker's Court, Brewer Street W1;
tel. (0171) 734 1593
Underground: Piccadilly Circus.

Stork Club, 99 Regent Street W1; tel. (0171) 734 3686
Underground: Piccadilly Circus

Dine and Dance

Restaurants where you can dine and then dance are very popular in London, and are to be found in most of the large hotels. The following venues have also stood the test of time.

Barbarella, 428 Fulham Road SW6; tel. (0171) 385 9434
Underground: Fulham Broadway

Discos and scene clubs

Babushka, 173 Blackfriars Road SE1; Underground: Waterloo a mixture of pub and music club very popular with the younger set

Bar Rumba, 36 Shaftesbury Ave. W1; Underground: Picadilly Circus (jazz, fusion and funk over the long weekend).

Bar Tempo, 96 Pentonville Road N1; Underground: King's Cross (London's most popular Latino club)

The Camden Palace, 1a High Street, Camden NW1; tel. (0171) 387 0428
Underground: Camden Town

The Fridge, Town Hall Parade, Brixton Hill SW2; tel. (0171) 326 5100
Underground: Brixton (always has the newest Brixton sound)

Heaven, Under the Arches, Craven Street WC2; tel. (0171) 930 2020
Underground: Charing Cross (London's number one "house" club and most famous gay venue)

Hippodrome, Charing Cross Road WC2; tel. (0171) 437 4311
Underground: Leicester Square (among the world's biggest discos)

Ny-lon, 84–86 Sloane Ave. SW3; Underground: South Kensington (back to the 1950s, with cocktail bar)

Stringfellows, 16–19 Upper St Martin's Lane WC2; tel. (0171) 240 5534
Underground: Leicester Square (top-class, glitzy disco)

The Wag Club, 35 Wardour Street W1; tel. (0171) 437 5534
Underground: Piccadilly Circus, Tottenham Court Road (where trend-setters meet)

Rock, Folk, Latin

Dingwalls (Camden Jongleurs), Camden Lock, Camden High Street NW1; tel. (0171) 267 1999
Underground: Camden Town

Half Moon Putney, 93 Lower Richmond Road, Putney SW15; tel. (0181) 780 9383
Underground: Putney Bridge

Marquee, 105 Charing Cross Road WC2; tel. (0171) 437 6601
Underground: Leicester Square, Tottenham Court Road (mainly rock and indie)

Rock Garden, The Piazza, Covent Garden WC2; tel. (0171) 836 4052
Underground: Covent Garden (young up and coming pop/rock artists)

Bass Clef, 35 Coronet Street W1: tel. (0171) 729 2476 Underground: Old Street (with good restaurant).

Jazz Clubs

100 Club, 100 Oxford Street W1; tel. (0171) 636 0933
Underground: Tottenham Court Road (tried and tested)

China Jazz, 29–31 Parkway NW1; tel. (0171) 482 3940
Underground: Camden Town (jazz and execellent Chinese food)

Ronnie Scott's, 47 Frith Street W1; tel. (0171) 439 0747
Underground: Leicester Square (London's most legendary jazz club, and still the best)

Comedy Store, 28a Leicester Square WC2; tel. (0171) 426 9144, tickets 344 4444 Underground: Leicester Square

Comedy Club

Opening Times

Mon.-Sat. 9 or 10am–5.30 or 6.30pm, often with late-night opening:
in Knightsbridge and Chelsea, Wed. until 7 or 8pm
in Kensington and the West End, Thur. until 7 or 8pm
in many other areas shops will also stay open later on one of these nights.
Many shops now also open on Sundays.

Shops and department stores

Mon.–Fri. 9.30am–3.30pm but some also stay open later and open on Saturday mornings (see Currency)

Banks

Mon.–Fri. 9am–5.30pm, Sat. 9am–12.30pm (see also Post)

Post offices

See Museums and Exhibitions

Museums

Post

London post offices are open 9am to 5.30pm Monday to Friday and until 12.30pm Saturday, but the post office at Trafalgar Square (24–28 William IV Street) is open for longer (Mon.–Thurs. and Sat. 8am–8pm, Fri. 8.30am–8pm). The head post office is in King Edward Street EC1.

Post offices

Postage stamps are sold in newsagents, shops and other outlets displaying the red sign "we sell postage stamps" as well as from post office counters. Letters under 20g to other EU countries require a 1st Class stamp, but for letters and postcards to non-EU destinations the stamps must show the actual postage rate, not just 1st or 2nd (class). British pillarboxes are red, and some of the old ones carrying the initials of the monarch of the time are still around.

Postage

Abroad and inland: tel. 0800 190 190
Telemessages

Telegrams

Public Holidays

Most public holidays in Britain are also known as "bank holidays" but on some of these, although the banks close, many shops stay open.

New Year's Day (January 1st)
Good Friday
Easter Monday
May Day (first Monday in May)
Spring Bank Holiday (last Monday in May)
Summer Bank Holiday (last Monday in August)
Christmas Day (December 25th)
Boxing Day (December 26th)

Public Transport

Integrated ticketing system

London and its suburbs are served by four main means of public transport – London Transport buses and Underground, the Docklands Light Railway and British Rail trains – and these are covered by an integrated ticketing system. It is also possible to get a Travelcard (see below) which is valid for all four and avoids the necessity of buying separate tickets. London Transport runs a 24-hour information line for enquiries about times, fares and general planning on bus and Underground services, including the Docklands Light Railway.

Information

London Transport, 55 Broadway SW1: tel. (0171) 222 1234 (24-hours)

London Transport's Travel Information Centres, located at Euston, Victoria, King's Cross and Liverpool Street train stations; Oxford Circus,

Docklands Light Railway Station: Canary Wharf

Piccadilly Circus, St James's Park and Hammersmith Underground stations; and Heathrow Terminals 1, 2 and 4, can all supply travel advice and a range of free maps and leaflets, especially "Travelling in London", which is full of useful maps and information to help you get around.

The famous London Underground (or Tube) is still the quickest way of getting around (see *Baedeker Special* p.244/46). Trains run very frequently from 5.30am to midnight from Mon.–Sat. and from 7.30am to 11.30pm on Sundays, usually only taking a few minutes between stations, some of which are closed on Sundays or throughout the weekend. Try to avoid the rush hours during the week between 8 and 9.30am and 5 and 6.30pm. Smoking is not allowed anywhere on the Underground.

Each line has a name and a different colour so you can follow your route. Once you have worked out which lines to take look for the colour coded signs and, since there are trains travelling in both directions, make sure you are on the right platform for the direction in which you want to go. This is made easier by the signs for each platform showing whether trains are north, south, east or west bound. Each train also has its final destination on the front.

Finding your way

The fully automated trains of the Docklands Light Railway (or DLR) connect Docklands (see A–Z) with the rest of the Underground network, and are also a good way of getting to Greenwich via Island Gardens station and the foot tunnel under the Thames. Trains run from 5.40am to around midnight.

Docklands Light Railway

London's famous double-decker buses give you a grandstand view of the streets of the city. They run from early morning to midnight and show front and back what their route number is and where they are going. There are two kinds of bus stop: compulsory, indicated by a red London Transport symbol on a white background, and request, where the colours are reversed. At the latter you have to hold up your hand to stop the bus. To find out about buses which can take disabled passengers contact London Transport's information line.

Buses

The three bus lines which are of most use to visitors since they cover the main attractions are:
No. 9: Kensington–Hyde Park–Hyde Park Corner–Piccadilly Circus–Trafalgar Square–Strand–Aldwych
No. 11: Chelsea–Victoria Station–Westminster–Whitehall–Trafalgar Square–Fleet Street–St Paul's Cathedral–Bank of England
No. 15: Marble Arch–Oxford Street–Regent Street–Trafalgar Square–Strand–Fleet Street–St Paul's Cathedral–Tower

Important bus lines

After midnight special "N" numbered Night Buses run every hour from central to outer London. All except N31 pass through Trafalgar Square and serve theatres, cinemas and entertainment areas – note that all bus stops become Request stops at night.

Night Buses

Red Arrow single-deckers run between important points in the West End and some of the train stations. Payment of fares is by slot machine on board.

Red Arrow Bus

Green Line buses run between central London (starting from Victoria Station) and the outlying suburbs and further afield to tourist destinations such as Bath, Oxford and Stonehenge.

Green Line

For ticketing purposes London is divided into six fare zones. There is just one price for tickets to travel within the central zone and you pay more for each additional zone. Be sure to get a ticket which covers all the zones through which you wish to travel. You can buy your ticket from the bus driver or, on the Underground, from a machine or the ticket office at any station – just say where you want to go. For longer journeys it is

Tickets

Public Transport

High Barnet
Totteridge & Whetstone
Woodside Park
West Finchley
Finchley Central
East Finchley
Highgate
Archway
Tufnell Park

Cockfosters
Oakwood
Southgate
Arnos Grove
Bounds Green
Wood Green
Turnpike Lane
Manor House

Epping
Theydon Bois
Debden
Loughton
Roding Valley † Chigwell †
Buckhurst Hill
Woodford
Grange Hill †
Hainault
Fairlop
Barkingside
Newbury Park

Woodford – Hainault until 1000 hours only

Tottenham Hale ⇌
Walthamstow Central ⇌
South Woodford
Redbridge
Snaresbrook
Wanstead
Gants Hill
Leytonstone
Upminster
Upminster Bridge
Hornchurch
Elm Park
Dagenham East
Dagenham Heathway
Becontree
Upney

Seven Sisters
Blackhorse Road ⇌

sh Town
Kentish Town
Caledonian Road
Camden Road
⇌ North London

Arsenal
Holloway Road
Caledonian Road
Drayton Park
Finsbury Park ⇌

King's Cross
St. Pancras
Angel
Farringdon
Barbican †
Russell Square
Moorgate
Chancery Lane ★
ent Garden
† City
r Thameslink
Blackfriars
★ Temple
kment

Caledonian Road & Barnsbury
Highbury & Islington
Canonbury
Essex Road †
Old Street
Liverpool Street
St. Paul's
Bank
Cannon Street ⇌ †
Monument
Tower Hill
⇌ Fenchurch Street
Mansion House
Tower Gateway

Hackney Central
Hackney Wick
Homerton
Dalston Kingsland
Stratford ⇌
Leyton

Bethnal Green
Mile End
Shoreditch †
Stepney Green
Whitechapel
Aldgate East
Aldgate
Shadwell
Limehouse
Wapping

Bow Road
Bow Church
Devons Road
All Saints
Poplar
Westferry
West India Quay
Canary Wharf
Heron Quays
South Quay
Crossharbour
Mudchute
Island Gardens

Bromley-by-Bow
Upton Park
Plaistow
West Ham
East India
Blackwall
Canning Town
Royal Victoria
Custom House
Prince Regent
Royal Albert
Beckton Park
Cyprus
Gallions Reach
Beckton

Barking ⇌
East Ham

North Greenwich
Silvertown & London City Airport ✈
North Woolwich

River Thames

Rotherhithe
Bermondsey
Canada Water
London Bridge ⇌
Under construction
Surrey Quays

Borough
Elephant & Castle ⇌

New Cross Gate ⇌
New Cross ⇌
Greenwich via Foot Tunnel

Key to Lines

Line		
Bakerloo		
Central		Peak hours only
Circle		
District		Restricted service
East London		
Hammersmith & City		Peak hours and Sunday mornings
Jubilee		Peak hours only
Metropolitan		Under construction
Northern		Peak hours only
Piccadilly		
Victoria		Peak hours only
Waterloo & City †		
Docklands Light Railway †		Under construction
⇌ British Rail		Restricted service

O Interchange stations
⇌ Connections with British Rail
⇌ Connections with British Rail within walking distance
✈ Airport interchange
★ Closed Sundays
★★ Closed Saturdays and Sundays
◊ Mornington Crescent closed for rebuilding

† For opening times see poster journey planners
Certain stations are closed during public holidays

Diary 1A 4.95

251

Mind the gap!

The train thunders into the station, the doors open with a loud hissing noise and the tinny loudspeakers bellow "Mind the gap!", the passengers push their way inside, the doors close and the train moves off – and how! Amid rumbles, screeches and hisses the train travels sometimes at full speed, sometimes crawling or stopping completely for minutes at a time, when you can clearly see that there is a space of only a few inches between the train and the wall of the tunnel and you start to wonder how you would get out if there were a fire or an accident. London's Underground is not for anyone prone to claustrophobia and certainly not for those with a horror of mass transport, for this is the oldest and largest underground network in the world, and yet one of the most efficient.

It comes as no surprise to learn that the idea of constructing a railway under the ground was conceived in London as long ago as the middle of the last century, when traffic problems were already getting out of hand in what was then the largest city in the world. Those travelling into London by rail were obliged to continue their journey into the city by horse-drawn cab or on foot, which could take longer than the original journey. Therefore, in 1854, Parliament authorised the Metropolitan Railway Company to build an underground railway line from Paddington via King's Cross to Farringdon Street. The construction was done by the "cut and cover" method; to avoid the high cost of acquiring land ditches were simply dug along Marylebone Road and Euston Road, supporting walls raised, roofs built over the ditches and the roads re-laid. This line, the world's first underground railway, was opened on January 10th 1863. It bore little similarity to the present-day Underground, being really nothing more than the transfer below ground of a train with several first, second and third class coaches, drawn by a steam locomotive fitted with a special device to prevent the excessive build-up of steam and smoke.

In spite of all the pessimists and prophets of doom – who on earth would want to travel underground anyway? – Londoners were so enthusiastic about this new means of transport that by 1864 no fewer than 259 plans for further underground lines were being discussed. For the time being, however, only one more line, that between South Kensington and Westminster, was opened by the Metropolitan District Railway in 1868. The breakthrough came when a new tunnel-boring technique was developed to replace the rather laborious "cut and cover" method. As long ago as 1848 Marc Isambard Brunel had constructed the first tunnel under the Thames between Wapping and Rotherhithe by using square tunnelling shields to protect the workers. Peter William Barlow converted the square shields to circular ones and thereby in 1870 constructed the Tower Subway between Tower Hill and Bermondsey, through which ran a cable-drawn train – the first underground railway to operate in a "tube" tunnel, even though it remained in service only a few months. Barlow's method was finally improved upon by James Henry Greathead, and with the aid of his Greathead shield the City and South London Railway was built in 1886 and opened in 1890. Today it forms part of the Northern Line and is actually the first modern "tube", for not only was the method of tunnel construction new, the trains were quite different too – specially designed tubular trains without windows, commonly known as "padded cells", drawn by a small electric locomotive powered by conductor rails running parallel to the lines. After that things happened in quick succession: in 1898 the Waterloo and City Line was opened, followed by the Central (1900), Great Northern and City (1904), Bakerloo (1906), Piccadilly (1906) and Hampstead (1907) lines. The disadvantage of the electric locomotive, however, lay in the fact that at each terminus it had to be pulled round to the other end of the train. In 1903, however, the system developed in Chicago by Frank Sprague was introduced; his multiple-unit system transferred the drive units to each end of the train, so that at the terminus only the driver needed to change over. As a result, since 1907 (the year in which it was officially so named), the "Underground" has become London's main means of transport. Since then the network – under the control of the

Rush hour on the tube

London Passenger Transport Board since 1933 – has been rapidly expanded and now carries millions of passengers every day. In the Second World War "the tube" served a completely different purpose; during the German bombing raids in 1940 and 1941 and the V-bomb attacks in 1944 and 1945 tens of thousands of Londoners sought shelter in the stations, some of which also served as underground storage places and workshops.

Wherever you are in London you can see the red circle with the blue bar across it, marking an underground station. That, too, is a part of the success story: in the early stages London Underground developed the idea of

"corporate identity", thanks to Frank Pick who became responsible for the design of underground stations in 1908. He saw to it that the stations, trains both inside and out, timetables and everything else possessed uniform characteristics and a corporate identity. He engaged the calligrapher Edward Johnson, who designed the Underground logo which was introduced in 1916 and is still used today. Pick employed well-known artists to design advertisements some of which have become classic examples of the signwriter's art. In the Second World War "Billy Brown of London Town" appeared on the hoardings; he was specially devised by the cartoonist David Langdon for London Transport in an attempt to educate

Wartime Advert "Billy Brown of London Town"

Londoners in sensible everyday behaviour in war-time London. However, it was a minor employee named Harry Beck whose artistic efforts were to become the best-known of all – he designed the revolutionary map of the London Underground network, model-ling it on an electrical circuit diagram and transposing the lines thereon into a net-work of routes in which only 90° or 45° angles are used. Presenting maps of transport systems in this form became the accepted method throughout the world, and the London Transport Underground Map has since become something of an icon in modern London.

THE NEXT MOVE

AND TAKE A SEASON TICKET

UNDERGROUND

Londoners love their "tube" – what else can they do, for there is little alternative. So they have come to terms with it, read their newspaper or book in the midst of the rush-hour crush and are glad to arrive each morning at their destination. For the London tourist the Underground is an experience every time, as he or she wanders through the underground corridors accompanied by the melancholy sound of a saxophone which must come from behind the next pillar – or the next but one? And anyone who has not yet had to reconcile himself to the trains being full or late will sooner or later see one of the notices which London Transport uses to excuse itself on these occasions: "We apologise for any inconvenience this may cause" – British understatement at its very best.

For those who wish to learn more about the whole London transport system than can be included here a visit to the London Transport Museum in Covent Garden (see entry under Covent Garden) is strongly recommended.

worth buying a return ticket or, after 9.30am (10am on British Rail) but anytime at weekends or on public holidays, a cheap day return.

For tourists the best course is to buy a Travelcard. This allows unlimited travel within the selected zones during the duration of the validity of the Travelcard and covers travel by train, Underground, Docklands Light Railway and buses within central and outer London apart from the Airbus service and some Green Line routes which extend beyond those two districts. Travelcards can be for a day (see below), a week or a month, and are obtainable from London Transport, British Rail stations, Underground stations, and from tobacconists, confectioners and newsagents throughout London displaying the "pass agent" sign. Under-16s pay a reduced rate. To buy your first weekly or monthly Travelcard you will need a Photocard carrying your photograph. Keep your Photocard afterwards since you can use it again if you revisit London.

Travelcard

If you only have a day in London you can buy the One Day Travelcard which entitles you to use all the forms of public transport from 9.30am (10am on British Rail) until midnight; there is no time restriction at weekends or on public holidays. For this only 14 and 15 year olds need a Photocard.

One Day Travelcard

The LT Card is a one day card which can be used at any time on buses, Underground and Docklands Light Railway but not on Night Buses or other special services. Here again only 14 and 15 year olds need a Photocard.

LT Card

The Visitor Travelcard can only be purchased from travel agents at home and abroad. It is valid for the same means of transport as the Travelcard with the advantage that it is available for 1, 2, 3, 4 or 7 days. No Photocard is required and a booklet of discount vouchers for tourist attractions and restaurants is included.

Visitor Travelcard

Make sure you have your ticket before you begin your journey or you may be stopped and have to pay a £10 penalty fare. Many Underground stations have automatic ticket gates in which you have to insert your ticket and take it back as you walk through. You also have to do the same at the end of your journey to get the gates to open to let you through, although this time they will retain the ticket if it has expired.

Keep your ticket

Pubs

No-one can really say they have been to London, or England for that matter, unless they have paid a visit to at least one pub – and this is not simply for the food and drink as much as for the friendly, easygoing atmosphere. If you find a good traditional pub you will soon know why so many of the English look upon their pub as a home from home. They increasingly serve typical bar food such as sandwiches, ploughmans, and pies such as cottage pie, steak and kidney pie and shepherd's pie; some have menus as long as any restaurant. To get served go to the bar, order your drink and pay for it straightaway. There is no need to tip unless the food is brought to the table.

Although compulsory afternoon closing was abolished in 1988, many landlords still keep to the old opening hours, ie:
weekdays 11am–3pm, and 5.30–11pm; Sundays 12–2pm and 7–10.30pm.
   Pubs near tourist attractions and shopping centres are normally open all day; on Sundays, however, many close during the afternoon. The call for "last orders, please" usually means that you have five or ten minutes to order and drink up before closing time.

Licensing hours

From the battery of taps along the bar you will soon realise that pubs serve a variety of beers (see Food and Drink), often from different breweries. These can include mild, bitter, lager and porter, and more

Beer

unusually, mild and bitter, or even a stout such as Guinness. Draught beer is not pressur- ised but pumped by hand. Whether you order a pint (0.57 litre) or half a pint the glass should be brimful with a head. Besides beers from the major breweries such as Worthington, Bass and Whitbread, "free" as opposed to "tied" houses sell "real ales" – reckoned by many to be better – from smaller, independent breweries. Some landlords also stock a number of bottled beers, foreign imports included.

Information about pubs

Pubs range from the traditional and famous to the minimalist and modern and it can be difficult for visitors to find just the right one for them. The following selection should help, and further addresses are available from: Pubs Information Centre, 93 Buckingham Palace Road SW1.

Pub Walks

If you do not want to go alone, you can join one of the convivial guided tours organised by "London Pub Walks" which start out from Temple underground station every Friday at 7.30pm (no advance booking required); information from: Peter Westbrook, Springfield Avenue N10; tel. (0181) 883 2656.

Pub Selection

Anchor Bankside, Bankside, 34 Park Street SE1; Underground: London Bridge. There has been a pub on this site since the 17th c.; the present one dates from the 18th c. Dr Johnson was a regular, and you can still enjoy the same view of the Thames from the terrace.

Bunch of Grapes, 2 St Thomas Street SE1; Underground: London Bridge. This pub has "snob screens" which hid the gentry from the view of the common folk, but nowadays equality rules on its lovely terrace.

Cittie of Yorke, 22 High Holborn WC1; Underground: Holborn. This pub, founded in the 17th c., has one of the longest bars in London.

The Trafalgar Tavern, Greenwich, magnificently situated on the Thames

Dickens Inn by the Tower, St Katharine's Way E1; Underground: Tower Hill. Large pub on several floors, at St Katharine's Dock

The Fox & Anchor, 115 Charterhouse Street EC1; Underground: Farringdon. The "local" for Smithfield Market's butchers offers good square meals early in the morning – no place for vegetarians!

The George Inn, 77 Borough High Street SE1; Underground: London Bridge. Last remaining coaching inn in London with galleried courtyard; very cosy taproom with highly polished wooden tables.

Holly Bush, 22 Holly Mount, Hampstead NW3; Underground: Hampstead. An 18th c. "village" pub tucked away in a cobbled courtyard.

King's Head & 8 Bells, 50 Cheyne Walk SW3; Underground: Sloane Square. Chelsea pub, over 400 years old.

Lamb & Flag, 33 Rose Street WC2; Underground: Covent Garden. A pub has stood on this site since the 15th c. One previous establishment was called "The Bucket of Blood".

Lamb Tavern, 10–12 Leadenhall Market EC3; Underground: Liverpool Street. Restored Victorian pub in Leadenhall Market.

Museum Tavern, 49 Great Russell Street WC1; Underground: Tottenham Court Road. Popular Victorian pub once frequented by Karl Marx and Virginia Woolf.

Prospect of Whitby, 57 Wapping Wall E1; Underground: Wapping. Founded in 1502 and the oldest pub on the Thames, this was for a long time the haunt of smugglers and used to be popular for its grandstand view of public executions.

Salisbury, 89 St Martins Lane WC2; Underground: Leicester Square, Covent Garden. Wonderful Victorian mirrors.

The Sherlock Holmes, 10 Northumberland Street WC2; Underground: Charing Cross. Definitely not the great detective's "local" but full of his memorabilia.

Spaniards Inn, Spaniards Road NW3; Underground: Hampstead. This 18th c. pub, homebase of highwayman Dick Turpin, still has some of its original furnishings.

Trafalgar Tavern, Park Row SE10, Docklands Light Railway: Island Gardens. Magnificent Victorian pub directly on the Thames in Greenwich, already recommended by Charles Dickens.

Williamsons Tavern, Groveland Court EC4; Underground: St Paul's. Reputedly the City's oldest pub.

Ye Olde Cheshire Cheese, 15 Fleet Street EC4; Underground: St Paul's. A Fleet Street institution, founded in the 17th c., which used to be famous as a meeting place for journalists.

Ye Olde Mitre, 1 Ely Court, Ely Place EC1; Underground: Chancery Lane. Dates back to 1514; atmospheric, tucked away down an alley.

See Nightlife   Pubs with music

Railway stations

London has thirteen main railway stations from which trains depart for all parts of the country. Those with connections to the Continent are

Railway stations

Waterloo Station: Norman Fosters glass gallery is the departure point of Eurostar trains

Victoria, Liverpool Street, Charing Cross and Waterloo, the latter being the terminal for Eurostar services through the Channel Tunnel.

To the south
Blackfriars; Queen Victoria Street EC4
Cannon Street; Cannon Street EC4
Charing Cross; Strand WC2
London Bridge; Borough High Street SE1
Victoria; Terminus Place SW1
Waterloo; York Road SE1

To the west
Paddington; Praed Street WC2

To the north
Marylebone; Boston Place NW1
Euston; Euston Road NW1
King's Cross; Euston Road N1
St. Pancras; Euston Road NW1

To the east
Fenchurch Street; Fenchurch Street EC3
Liverpool Street; Liverpool Street EC2

Rail information
SE England, and East Anglia:
 tel. 0345 484950
SW and W England, and S Wales:
 tel. 0345 484950
The Midlands, NW England, N Wales, and W Scotland:
 tel. 0345 484950
E England (except East Anglia), and E Scotland:
 tel.0345 484950
To the Continent:
 tel. 0990 848848

Tickets and information are available from the British Travel Centre (see Information), all stations and British Rail Travel Centres at Heathrow International Airport and Gatwick Airport.

Restaurants

It is easy enough to find a restaurant in London – there is sure to be one round the next corner – but it can actually be quite difficult to choose since there are so many of them, from the most exclusive and expensive to the very cheapest. If English fare is not to your taste there are restaurants from all over the world offering a variety of food unparalleled anywhere else in Europe. London's Chinese and Indian restaurants in particular are extremely authentic and of very high quality. Just remember that good London restaurants can be expensive.

International food at its best

If you find it impossible to cope with being so spoilt for choice, help is on hand from the Restaurant Services: tel. (0181) 888 8080 Monday to Friday, 9am to 7pm.

Restaurant switchboard

Since London has such an enormous number of restaurants the following list can only cover a small proportion. All of them have been inspected by the Automobile Association and have the prestigious AA rosette award for high quality cuisine. The prices given are the average cost of an evening three-course meal (starter, main course, dessert) from the à la carte menu plus VAT.

British Restaurants

Alfred, 245 Shaftesbury Avenue WC2; tel. (0171) 240 2566, £20; Underground: Leicester Square. Informal, café-style restaurant serving simple British dishes.

Traditional

Rules, 35 Maiden Lane WC2; tel. (0171) 836 5314, £25; Underground: Charing Cross, Covent Garden. A stronghold of tradition since 1798, especially salmon from the Scottish rivers and game straight from the shoot.

Savoy Grill, Savoy Hotel, Strand WC2; tel. (0171) 836 4343, £45; Underground: Charing Cross. Top English fare in a top setting, outstanding wine list.

Shepherds, Marsham Court, Marsham Street SW1; tel. (0171) 834 9552, £39; Underground: Pimlico, Westminster (see *Baedeker Special*)

Simpsons in the Strand, 100 Strand WC2; tel. (0171) 836 9112, £30; Underground: Charing Cross, Covent Garden (see *Baedeker Special*)

Wiltons, 55 Jermyn Street SW1; tel. (0171) 629 9955, £50; Underground: Piccadilly Circus, Green Park. Expensive, exclusive and very British; best for fish, oysters and game.

Alastair Little, 49 Frith Street W1; tel. (0171) 734 5183, £22; Underground: Leicester Square, Tottenham Court Road (see *Baedeker Special*)

Modern British

Bibendum, Michelin House, 81 Fulham Road SW3; tel. (0171) 581 5817, £55; Underground: South Kensington (see *Baedeker Special*)

The Brackenbury, 129 Brackenbury Road W6; tel. (0181) 748 0107, £25; Underground: Goldhawk Road, Hammersmith. Wide-ranging, from burgers to excellent Mediterranean fish.

From the cooking-pots
of the Empire!

Let us start with what many other Europeans regard as a virtual contra-
diction in terms – good English cooking. Since 1821 the impregnable bastion
of roast beef – the best in the city – and other classic English lamb and turkey
dishes is **Simpsons in the Strand** ((tel. 0171-835 9112), which of course also
serves an outstanding "English breakfast" including kidneys, smoked fish
and liver, all enjoyed in the atmosphere of a "gentleman's club". Quite new,
less formal, good value for money and yet still offering traditional cuisine is
Shepherds (tel. 0171-834 9552), managed by master chef Richard Shepherd
together with film star Michael Caine. Many of the clientele are equally well
known.

That the English can cook in a modern fashion and be inspired by other
cuisines is proved by a whole range of restaurants. Praised unstintingly by
all the critics is **Qualigno's** (tel. 0171-930 6767), the 1994 Newcomer of the
Year, owned by Sir Terence Conran, which has made itself known not only
through its cooking but also because it has reintroduced cigarette girls.
Lola's (tel. 0171-359 1932), the 1997 Newcomer of the Year, which offers
Mediterranean cuisine at very sensible prices. Superstar Marco Pierre
White's **MPW** (tel. 0171-513 0513) moves in cosmic spheres with prices to
match. Mention must also be made of the old-established **Alistair Little** (tel.
0171-734 5183) in Soho, offering a menu which changes twice daily, and
Bibendum (tel. 0171-581 5817), which has been at the forefront of London
restaurants for a number of years and whose food, equally anchored in both
modern and traditional, is as irresistible as the marvellous Michelin House
atmosphere. Is there a department store restaurant that can be recommended? No problem – Harvey Nichol's restaurant **Fifth Floor** (tel. 0171-
235 5250) is as truly British as the store itself and is capable of producing
magnificent meals in traditional English style. It is also open in the evenings.

One thing we have failed to mention so far – fish and chips, that justly
famous national dish of cod or rock salmon with pieces of potato, fried in
deep fat, sprinkled with salt and vinegar and tradtionally wrapped in a piece
of newspaper, although actually newspaper is now no longer used because
printer's ink is injurious to health. Good quality fish and chips with a wide
choice of fish can be obtained in the **North Sea Fish Restaurant** (tel. 0171-387
5892) and the **Seafresh Fish Restaurant** (tel. 0171-828 0747).

Anyone who finds all this somewhat uninspiring need not worry. In London
there are countless restaurants offering dishes originating from all over the
world. However, two forms of ethnic cuisine in particular of exceptional quality are available – Chinese food, mostly prepared by chefs from Hong Kong,
and Indian in all its regional varieties.

The food offered by Chinese restaurants in, for example, Germany is but a
poor imitation of that served up by London's chefs, both as regards unusual-
ness and authenticity. For anyone wishing to sample a variety of Chinese
food, perhaps for the first time, the answer is a *dim sum*. This will provide
all kinds of refined delicacies – meat, fish and other seafood, vegetables, etc.
– either displayed on a counter or pushed through the restaurant on a trolley
so that the customer can choose what he or she fancies. If in Chinatown the
place to go for *dim sum* is **Chuen Cheng Ku's** (tel. 0171-435 9533). The **Aroma**

is also recommended (tel. 0171-439 2720), but prior reservation is essential as this charming restaurant has only thirteen tables. Anyone who is not afraid of venturing into the outskirts of London will enjoy a fantastic choice of *dim sum* at the *Royal China* (tel. 0181-788 0907) where the interior décor is quite different from the usual portrayal of Chinese folklore. *Eat Well* (tel. 0181-748 6887), *Young's Rendezvous* (tel. 0181-840 3060) and *Local Friends* (tel. 0181-455 9258) also offer *dim sum* which, for the most part, is available only at lunch-time. Classic Hong Kong/Cantonese cuisine is available in the **Imperial City** (tel. 0171-626 3437), in the basement of the Royal Exchange. Those who like their food well spiced should try Szechuan cuisine, the best places for which include *Inn of Happiness* (tel. 0171-321 1931) in St James' Court Hotel, **Hunan** (tel. 0171-730 5712) and *Cheng Dul* (tel. 0171-485 8058). Peking chefs like to fry their food, especially lamb, and use thick noodles – try *Gallery Rendezvous* (tel. 0171-485 4446) in Chinatown. The prince of Chinese restaurants, at least as far as prices and atmosphere is concerned, is undoubtedly the *Oriental* (tel. 0171-629 888) in the Dorchester – genuine Chinese, but only for those with a well-filled wallet. It is much cheaper and quite different in the *Vegetarian Cottage* (tel. 0171-586 1257), which serves the best Chinese vegetarian food.

In London there are over 1500 Indian restaurants, more than in Delhi and Bombay combined. The cuisine ranges from that of north and south India, Pakistan and Nepal to that of Bangladesh.

The splendours of the former British Empire are remembered in *Chutney Mary* (tel. 0171-351 3113), where Indian and English cuisine mingle quite happily.

La Porte des Indes (tel. 0171-224 0055) has received high praise from the critics for its Tamil/Indian/French cuisine. The *Lahore Kebab House* (tel. 0171-481 9738) is one of the best *balti* houses. In this cuisine, which comes from Pakistan and is related to that of northern India, most of the dishes are prepared in an iron pan or wok known as a *karahi* or *balti*. Similar dishes are served in the *Karahi King* (tel. 0181-904 2760), but this restaurant lies a little way out in Wembley. North Indian dishes are also on the menu of the *Malabar* (tel. 0171-727 8800) and *Salloos* (tel. 0171-235 444), where the lamb is most excellently prepared. In southern India vegetarian dishes predominate; the best place for such food in London is the **Ragam** (tel. 0171-636 9098). Very popular for its reasonably priced lunchtime buffets is the *Mandeer* (tel. 0171-224 0660). Somewhat out of town in Finchley, is the *Rani* (tel. 0181-349 4386), one of the best south Indian restaurants which guarantees that no animal products are used in any of its dishes. A number of people from the east of the Indian sub-continent have settled in East London, and many of them patronise the **Shampan** (tel. 0171-375 0475) for dishes from Bangledesh or the *Aladin* (tel. 0171-247 8210).

Now a brief look at the rest of the former British Empire. London's best East African restaurant is the *Mandola* (tel. 0171-229 4734) – how about a *falafel* or lamb stew with a glass of *karkadel* (hibiscus juice)? Dishes from almost the whole of Africa can be enjoyed in the *Calabasth* (tel. 0171-838 1976).

If Caribbean cuisine takes your fancy, try *Smokey Joe's Diner* (tel. 0181-871 1785); the latter is rather a long way out in Wandsworth, but the chef's culinary skills will make the journey worthwhile. Mixed Afro-Caribbean cooking is on offer in *Roots Afric-Carib* (tel. 0171-498 2622).

Fifth Floor at Harvey Nichols, Knightsbridge SW1; tel. (0171) 235 5250, £26; Underground: Knightsbridge (see *Baedeker Special*)

Lola's, The Mall Building, 359 Upper Street, N1; tel. (0171) 359 1932, £30. Underground: Angel (see *Baedeker Special*).

MPW, Cabot Place East, Canary Wharf E14; tel. (0171) 513 0513, £26. DLR Station: Canary Wharf (see *Baedeker Special*)

Leith's, 92 Kensington Road W11; tel. (0171) 229 4481, £34–45; Underground: Notting Hill Gate. Expensive, but first class and stylish.

Quaglino's, 16 Bury Street, SW1; tel. (0171) 930 6767, £35; Underground: Piccadilly Circus, Green Park. The oldest but still the best of Terence Conran's restaurants.

The Restaurant, Hyde Park Hotel, 66 Knightsbridge SW1; tel. (0171) 352 2000, £43: Underground: Knightsbridge. In spite of the poor service and strange furnishings, the critic Siebeck considers it the best cuisine in London.

Fish   Bentley's, 11–15 Swallow Street W1; tel. (0171) 734 4756, £35; Underground: Piccadilly Circus. One of London's most famous fish restaurants. Has been serving fish since 1916 in opulent surroundings.

Café Fish, 39 Panton Street SW1; tel. (0171) 930 3999, £25; Underground: Piccadilly Circus. Busy, bustling fish restaurant.

Foreign Restaurants

American   Christopher's, 18 Wellington Street WC2; tel. (0171) 240 4222, £25; Underground: Covent Garden. American-style burgers, steaks, fish and fries in grand English surroundings.

Belgian   Belgo Noord, 72 Chalk Farm Road NW1; tel. (0171) 267 0718, £20; Underground: Chalk Farm. Mussels, frites and beer (more than 50 brews) and waiters dressed as trappist monks.

Chinese   Fung Shing, 15 Lisle Street WC2; tel. (0171) 437 1539, £15; Underground: Leicester Square (see *Baedeker Special*)

Harbour City, 46 Gerrard Street W1; tel. (0171) 439 7859, £10; Underground: Leicester Square, Piccadilly Circus (see *Baedeker Special*)

Imperial City, Royal Exchange, Cornhill EC3; tel. (0171) 626 3437, £15; Underground: Bank (see *Baedeker Special*)

Kai Mayfair, 65 South Audley Street W1; tel. (0171) 493 8988, £40; Underground: Hyde Park Corner (see *Baedeker Special*)

Ken Lo's Memories of China, 67 Edbury Street SW1; tel. (0171) 730 7734, £28; Underground: Sloane Square, Victoria (see *Baedeker Special*)

Ken Lo's Memories of China, Chelsea Harbour Yard, SW10; tel. (0171) 352 4953, £28; Underground: Fulham Broadway (1 mile).

Ming, 35–36 Greek Street W1; tel (0171) 734 2721, £12–£20; Underground: Leicester Square (see *Baedeker Special*)

The Oriental, The Dorchester, 55 Park Lane W1; tel. (0171) 317 6328, £50; Underground: Hyde Park Corner (see *Baedeker Special*)

Oriental House, 251 Old Brompton Road SW5; tel. (0171) 370 2323, £18; Underground: Earl's Court (see *Baedeker Special*)

Poons, 4 Leicester Square WC2; tel. (0171) 437 1528, £14; Underground: Leicester Square (see *Baedeker Special*)

Royal China, 3 Chelverton Road SW15; tel. (0181) 788 0907, £22; Underground: East Putney (see *Baedeker Special*)

Royal China, 13 Queensway W2; tel. (0171) 221 2535, £15–25; Underground: Queensway, Bayswater (see *Baedeker Special*)

Zen Central, 20–22 Queen Street W1; tel. (0171) 629 8103, £28; Underground: Green Park (see *Baedeker Special*)

Zen Garden, 15–16 Berkeley Street W1; tel. (0171) 493 1381, from £25; Underground: Green Park (see *Baedeker Special*)

ZenW3, 83 Hampstead High Street NW3; tel. 0171 794 7863, £25; Underground: Hampstead.

Le Gavroche, 43 Upper Brook Street W1; tel. (0171) 408 0881, £80; French Underground: Marble Arch. In the top price range with classical haute cuisine from Michel Roux.

La Tante Claire, 68 Royal Hospital Road, Chelsea SW3; tel. (0171) 352 6045, £61; Underground: Sloane Square. Somewhat out of the way, but all the better for that; prizewinning Pierre Koffmann, famous for his innovative cuisine, continues on top form.

Nico at Ninety, Grosvenor House Hotel, 90 Park Lane W1; tel. (0171) 409 1290, £54; Underground: Hyde Park Corner, Marble Arch. One of the best and most innovative French restaurants.

Nico Central, 35 Great Portland Street W1; tel. (0171) 436 8846, two-course meal £27; Underground: Oxford Circus. A modern French style is offered to a good standard.

Al San Vincenzo, 30 Connaught Street W2; tel. (0171) 262 9623, £35; Italian Underground: Marble Arch. Imaginative native Italian food from a talented, self-taught cook.

Orso, 27 Wellington Street WC2; tel. (0171) 240 5269, £24; Underground: Covent Garden. Somewhat more expensive but also such Tuscan-inspired dishes as rabbit with spinach.

River Café, Rainville Road, Hammersmith W6; tel. (0171) 381 8824, £32; Underground: Hammersmith. Tuscan-inspired food with modernist décor in a Thames-side setting.

Greek Valley, 130 Boundary Road NW8; tel. (0171) 624 3217, £8; Greek Underground: St John's Wood (see *Baedeker Special*)

Kalamara's, 76–78 Inverness Mews W2; tel. (0171) 727 9122, £16; Underground: Bayswater (see *Baedeker Special*)

Lemonia, 89 Regent's Park Road NW1; tel. (0171) 586 7454, £17; Underground: Chalk Farm (see *Baedeker Special*)

The White Tower, 1 Percy Street W1; tel. (0171) 636 8141, £35–40; Underground: Tottenham Court Road, Goodge Street (see *Baedeker Special*)

The Bengal Clipper, Butler's Wharf SE1; tel. (0171) 357 9001, £28; Indian Underground: Tower Hill (see *Baedeker Special*)

Bombay Brasserie, Courtfield Close, Courtfield Road SW7; tel. (0171) 370 4040, £25; Underground: Gloucester Road (see *Baedeker Special*)

Chutney Mary, 535 King's Road, Chelsea SW10; tel. (0171) 351 3113, £32; Underground: Fulham Broadway (see *Baedeker Special*)

Gopal's, 12 Bateman Street W1; tel. (0171) 434 0840, £15; Underground: Tottenham Court Road (see *Baedeker Special*)

Indian Connoisseurs, 8 Norfolk Place W2; tel. (0171) 402 3299, £13; Underground: Paddington, Edgeware Road (see *Baedeker Special*)

La Porte des Indes, 32 Bryanston Street W1; tel. (0171) 351 3113. £25; Underground: Fulham Broadway (see *Baedeker Special*)

The Old Delhi, 48 Kendal Street W2; tel. (0171) 724 9580, £20; Underground: Marble Arch (see *Baedeker Special*)

Rani, 7 Long Lane N3; tel. (0181) 349 4386, £13; Underground: Finchley Central (see *Baedeker Special*)

Red Fort, 77 Dean Street W1; tel. (0171) 437 2115, £25; Underground: Piccadilly Circus, Tottenham Court Road (see *Baedeker Special*)

Salloos, 62–64 Kinnerton Street SW1; tel. (0171) 235 4444, £28; Underground: Knightsbridge (see Baedeker Special)

The Star of India, 154 Old Brompton Road SW5; tel. (0171) 373 2901, £20; Underground: Gloucester Road (see Baedeker Special)

Tamarind, 20 Queen Street, Mayfair W1; tel. (0171) 629 3561, £35; Underground: Green Park (see Baedeker Special)

The Veeraswamy, 99–101 Regent Street W1; tel. (0171) 734 1401, £25; Underground: Piccadilly Circus (see *Baedeker Special*)

Japanese

Miyama, 38 Clarges Street W1; tel. (0171) 499 2443, £17; Underground: Green Park. A first-class Japanese restaurant frequented by Japanese Embassy staff.

Suntory, 72 St James's Street SW1; tel. (0171) 409 0201, £50; Underground: Green Park. Very expensive, but sushi at its best if you can afford it.

Wagama, 4 Streatham Street WC1; tel. (0171) 23 9223 and 10a Lexington Street W1; tel. (0171) 292 0990, £12 Underground: Tottenham Court Road and Oxford Circus. In contrast to Suntory, this restaurant offers excellent noodle dishes on long wooden platters at unbeatable prices.

Malaysian-Indonesian

Singapore Garden, 83 Fairfax Road NW6; tel. (0171) 328 5314, £20; Underground: Swiss Cottage. Singaporean/Malay/Chinese inspired diishes in one of London's more animated restaurants.

Thai

Bahn Thai, 21A Frith Street W1; tel. (0171) 437 8504, £25; Underground: Leicester Square, Tottenham Court Road. Among the most interesting Thai food in the capital.

Tui, 19 Exhibition Road SW7; tel. (0171) 584 8359, £22; Underground: South Kensington. Simple black and white surroundings disguise some delicious Thai food.

Hungarian

Gay Hussar, 2 Greek Street W1; tel. (0171) 437 0973, £25; Underground: Tottenham Court Road. London's Hungarian restaurant and an institution in itself.

Shopping

Only Paris can compete with London when it comes to world-class shopping in Europe. In London you can find anything you could possibly want in its vast range of shops, from the most conventional to the highly unusual, but its trumpcards are its antiques and classical English tweeds, cashmere, shirts and the like.

Shopping districts

The greatest variety and selection is to be found in the West End: from Oxford Street, Regent Street and Bond Street – particularly art and antiques – then down to Piccadilly and Jermyn Street, and around Covent Garden and Soho; the other major shopping district takes in Knightsbridge, South Kensington and Kensington with the Brompton Road and High Street Kensington. Chelsea, with the King's Road, is not quite in the same class, but worth looking round nevertheless.

In London you will be spoilt for choice if you want to take home some- **Souvenirs** thing which is typically English – tea or marmalade, perhaps, from, say, Harrods or Fortnum & Mason, a pipe and tobacco, or sweets. When it comes to clothes you could opt for knitwear or even a Burberry trench-coat. Museum shops in for example the British Museum, the V & A, National Gallery and Natural History Museum are also full of good sou-venirs such as art replicas, books and all kinds of knick-knacks.

Most goods (and services) sold in Britain are subject to 17.5% Value Added **VAT refunds** Tax (VAT), which is included in the selling price. Non-EU visitors can get their VAT refunded when leaving Europe by using the Europe Tax-Free Shopping (ETS) scheme. Shops in the ETS scheme (look for the ETS logo) can supply a Tax-Free Shopping Cheque showing the amount of the VAT refund. This is then stamped by Customs as you leave so that it can be cashed at the ETS outlets at airports and other departure points throughout Europe.

Dickins & Jones, 224–244 Regent Street W1   **Department**
★Fortnum & Mason, 181 Piccadilly W1   **Stores**
  (See A–Z, Piccadilly Circus)
★Harrods, 87–135 Brompton Road SW1
  (See A–Z, Harrods)
Harvey Nichols, 109–125 Knightsbridge SW1
John Lewis, Oxford Street SW1
★Liberty's, 210–220 Regent Street W1
  (See A–Z, Liberty's)
Marks & Spencer, 458 Oxford Street W1
Peter Jones, Sloane Square SW1
★Selfridges, 400 Oxford Street W1
  (Enormous, but outshone by Harrods)

See entry   **Antiques**

Bell, Book and Radmall, 4 Cecil Court WC2 (antiquarian)   **Books**
Books for Cooks, 4 Blenheim Crescent W11 (cookbooks)
Cinema Bookshop, 14 Great Russell Street, WC1 (movie books)
Compendium, 234 Camden High Street NW1 (leftist alternative)
Comic Showcase, 76 Neal Street WC2 (comics)
Dillons, 82 Gower Street WC1 (London University bookshop with second-
  hand section)
Forbidden Planet, 71 New Oxford Street WC1 (comics, film, sci-fi)
Foyles, 113/119 Charing Cross Road WC2 (vast)
Hatchard's, 187 Piccadilly W1 (large and traditional)
Map House, 54 Beauchamp Place SW3 (old maps and prints)
R.I.B.A. Bookshop, 66 Portland Place W1 (architecture)
The Travel Bookshop , 13 Blenheim Crescent W11 (travel)

The Cashmere House, 13/14 Golden Square W1   **Cashmere**
Berk, Burlington Arcade W1
Westaway & Westaway, 65 and 92 Great Russell Street WC1

Bendicks of Mayfair, 7 Aldwych WC2   **Delicatessen**
  (Speciality: dark mint chocolate)   **grocery**
Charbonnel et Walker, 1 The Royal Arcade, 28 Old Bond Street W1
  (handmade chocolates)
Paxton & Whitfield, 93 Jermyn Street SW1 (cheese supplier to the Queen)
Grocery departments at Harrods and Fortnum & Mason

The craziest catwalk
in the world

No other city in the world has influenced fashion as much as London. Time and again fashion designers have obtained and do obtain inspiration from the highways and byways of the metropolis. The streets of London – the longest and craziest catwalk in the world. Street-style is the keyword for those in the know in the fashion world. Those who cannot afford exclusive designer clothes create their own individual style, mixing and combining without restraint, cheeky and witty, often odd but never boring. To have style, imagination and courage and knowing where to buy are more important than money, and London has all these things. As well as the traditional hunting-grounds of Camden and Portobello, the young designer boutique of Hyper-Hyper and the Kensington Market seventies revival, there are numerous surprises to be found in Soho and Covent Garden too.

Back in the 1960s "swinging London" was a centre of young fashion. That was when *Mary Quant* seized much of the fashion iniative with her revolutionary "look" and created a new and exciting type of woman. The focal point of her fashion philosophy was the "mini". Like pop music, her ideas were aimed at everybody – make it short, simple and uncompromising was her watchword. Clothes became a way of expressing youth and vitality. In 1955 Mary Quant opened her Bazaar, London's first boutique, in the King's Road. She sold only her own designs, allowing the customers to browse and try on clothes to their heart's content. In 1962 "Vogue" magazine showed her creations, and three years later the "mini-skirt" became the world's top fashion hit. The short haircut or "bob", a style which pointed the way in the sixties, was first experimented with by Vidal Sassoon on Mary Quant, "cutting her hair like she cuts material. No fuss. No ornamentation. Just a swinging line". The cool fashions of Mary Quant can be found today in the tiny shop at 3 Ives Street, Chelsea, SW3.

Made-to-measure tailoring has a long tradition in London. Paul Smith and Ozwald Boateng took the suit, made it modern and thereby injected fresh life into the apparently dead trade of bespoke male tailoring. *Paul Smith* opened his first shop in 1979 in Covent Garden at 41/44 Floral Street WC2. After considerable teething troubles it developed into an oasis for the in-crowd, where one could buy clothes not available anywhere else. Today his creations are sold in thirty countries. Sometimes Smith simply turned the old rules of dress on their heads. He provided classical grey suits with orange linings or combined them with flowered shirts and extravagant ties. More recently he has added ladies' fashions to his repertoire.

Ozwald Boateng knows what it means when one of his customers enthuses about how well his "501" sits on him. He was born in London in 1967, his parents having come over from Ghana. His workshop is at 247 Portobello Road, SW10. As seen by Boateng, the well-dressed, modern man should wear a suit which "sits on him perfectly, emphasises his body in an attractive yet minimalistic and subtle way. The minimalistic approach means that all the jacket buttons must be fastened. That is what I call strength of character – something which will still be regarded as classical in the year 2000". Cost, including one or two fittings, about £1000.

"I like it best when my things make even me laugh". The queen of the London scene is *Vivienne Westwood*, inventor of punk couture and purveyor of provocative forms of dress. The ideas put forward by this eccentric lady are almost all in advance of her time. In her stormy life with Malcolm McLaren, manager of the Sex Pistols, the former primary school teacher discovered her taste for anarchistic costumery in the 1970s and shocked the public with her sado-masochistic gear, the ragged look and sexy wordings on black T-shirts. In 1977 Vivienne and Malcom established London's first authentic punk shop at 430 King's Road: "seditionaries" (agitators) had quickly attained cult status. Since 1980 the shop has been called "World's End". A giant clock shows thirteen hours and goes backwards. The wooden floorboards in the shop are so uneven that it is like walking on the sea, and the furniture is nailed down. Vivienne Westwood's aim is to get rid of petty bourgeois styles of dress. In 1986 her "mini-crini" collection helped crinoline-style fashions to make a come-back. The bodices of her latest collection are tightly laced and "revealing". "Everything I design has an intellectual basis. I am a student of history". She transports herself in a time machine, analyses the fall of the folds in Greek costume and Renaissance textile forms, examines with ironic gestures the possibilities inherent in a classic British material – Harris tweed. She has fashioned costumes for the "Royals" and has adventurously re-created high platform shoes from the spirit of Greek tragedies.

From 1990 to 1992 she succeeded Jean-Charles de Castelbajac as guest tutor at the College of Applied Art in Vienna. In December 1992 the Queen presented her with the Order of the British Empire. Vivienne arrived with her two sons to take tea at Buckingham Palace while wearing no underwear. She allowed her dress to fly up Marilyn Monroe fashion – apart from flesh-coloured tights she was wearing nothing underneath. "I never have the time to find any underwear I like" was her only comment.

Then there are the creations of the Irishman *Philip Treacy* – comical objects made of wire, felt, wickerwork and feathers. They decorate female heads – and not just at Ascot. "Women of the world" are eager to be seen wearing Treacy's extravagant and featherweight creations. That which in the fifties was considered socially essential is now old-fashioned – if you do not wish to attract attention, do not wear a hat. "Today a hat is a symbol of individuality, of style, of indifference to uninvited criticism". The craziest thing about Treacy's hats is that they are wearable, even if they are only a wisp of material or made of long, black feathers. Only a few examples of his work are to be seen in his studio. He himself will create a design to suit the customer and is stimulated in his ideas by all he sees around him. There is this hat of grey beaver fur with eyelashes stuck on it or one made of pink felt in the shape of a steel helmet, another of pink shark-fins, a gaudy red hussar's hat with a black feather – all individually modelled "one-offs" from his studio at 69 Elizabeth Street, SW1.

Shopping

Fashionwear for women	Laura Ashley, 9 Harriet Street SW1 (classic)
	Brown's, 23–27 South Moulton Street W1 (top names in British haute couture)
	Jasper Conran, 6 Burnsall Street SW3 (British haute couture)
	Fenwick, 63 New Bond Street, W1 (latest fashion at reasonable prices)
	Katherine Hamnett, 20 Sloane Street SW1 (British haute couture)
	Pam Hogg, 5 Newburgh Street, Oxford Circus W1 (British haute couture) (wearable designer clothes at affordable prices)
	Hyper, 26–40 Kensington High Street W8 (fashion and designer hypermarket)
	Mary Quant (see *Baedeker Special*)
	Philip Treacy (see *Baedeker Special*)
	Vivienne Westwood (see *Baedeker Special*)
Fashionwear for men	Oswald Boateng (see *Baedeker Special*)
	Burberry's 18/22 Haymarket SW1 (classic trenchcoats)
	Duffer of St George, 27 D'Arblay Street W1 (good value designer fashion)
	Gieves & Hawkes, 1 Savile Row W1 (thoroughly British)
	Harvie & Hudson, 77 & 97 Jermyn Street SW1 (ties)
	Herbert Johnson, 30 Old Bond Street W1 (hats)
	Lock & Co., 6 St James's Street W1 (bowler hats, the original inventor)
	Paul Smith (see *Baedeker Special*)
	Turnbull & Asser, 71/72 Jermyn Street SW1 (famous for shirts)
Fashion wear in general	Agnes B, 111 Fulham Road SW3
	Aquascutum, 100 Regent Street W1 (tweed and raincoats)
	Designer Sale Studio, 241 King's Road SW3 (designer remainders)
	French Connection, 11 James Street and 56 Long Acre W2
	Kensington Market, 49–53 Kensington High Street W8 (70s fashions)
	Next, 160 Regent Street W1
	The Scotch House, 2 Brompton Road SW1
Jewellery	Butler & Wilson, 189 Fulham Road, SW3 (fashion jewellery classics)
	Detail, 49 Endell Street WC2
	Erickson Beamon, 38 Elizabeth Street SW1 (garish)
	Next, 160 Regent Street W1
	Richard Ogden, 28/29 Burlington Arcade W1
	Tom Binns, 30/31 Great Sutton Street EC1
Knitwear	The Irish Shop, 11 Duke Street SW1
	Jaeger, 204 Regent Street W1
	Jane and Dada, 20/21 Christopher's Place, W1 (designer knitwear)
	N. Peal, Burlington Arcade W1 (classic English knitwear)
Leather	Charles Clements, Burlington Arcade W1
	Natural Leather, 33 Monmouth Street WC2
Perfumes	Crabtree & Evelyn, 6 Kensington Church Street W8
	Floris, 89 Jermyn Street SW1
	Penhaligon's, 41 Wellington Street WC2; 66 Moorgate EC2 and 110a New Bond Street W1
Records and CDs	Caruso & Company, 35 New Oxford Street W1 (classical)
	Daddy Kool, 9 Berwick Street W1 (reggae)
	Groove Records, 52 Greek Street W1 (soul)
	HMV, 150 Oxford Street W1 (enormous)
	Ray's Jazz Shop, 180 Shaftesbury Avenue WC2 (jazz)
	Reckless Records, 30 Berwick Street W1 (oldies)
	Rock On, 3 Kentish Town Road NW2 (oldies)
	Rough Trade, 130 Talbot Road W2 (oldies)
	Stern's African Record Centre, 116 Whitfield Street W1 (African music)
	Tower Records, 1 Piccadilly Circus W1 (enormous)

Vinyl Experience, 18 Hanway Street W1 (records, memorabilia, curios)
Virgin Megastore, 14–30 Oxford Street W1 (enormous)

John Lobb, 9 St James's Street SW1   Shoes
Mamolo Blahnik, 49–51 Old Church Street, SW3 (high-class shoe shop).
McAffee, 46 Curzon Street W1 (men's shoes)
Red or Dead, 33 Neal Street WC2 (very hippy footwear).
Robot, 37 Floral Street WC2
The Small and Tall Shoe Shop, 71 York Street W1 (special sizes)
Stephane Kelian, 49 Sloane Street SW1

London Silver Vaults, Chancery House, 53/64 Chancery Lane WC2.   Silver
  See Antiques

Astley's 109 Jermyn Street SW1 (pipes only)   Smokers'
Davidoff of London, 35 St James's Street SW1   requisites
Dunhill's, 18 Jermyn Street SW1
Fribourg & Tryer, 214 Piccadilly SW1
Rothman's, 64 Pall Mall SW1
Smith's Snuff Shop, 74 Charing Cross Road WC2

Asprey, 165/169 New Bond Street W1 (top people's jeweller)   Souvenirs,
Best of British, 27 Shorts Gardens WC2 (just what it says)   gifts, etc.
The Button Queen, 29 Marylebone Lane W1
The Camden Lock Balloon Company, Camden Lock NW1
The Conran Shop, 81 Fulham Road SW3 (everything designed for the
  house and garden is obtainable here).
Cutler & Gross, 16 Knightsbridge Green SW1 (eyeglasses)
L. Davenports & Co., 51 Great Russell Street WC1 (magic)
David Gill, Fulham Road SW7 (design)
Flashbacks, 6 Silver Place W1 (movie magazines, posters, etc.)
The General Trading Company, 144 Sloane Street W1 (the unusual and
  unique: kitchenware, Oriental imports ...)
Italian Paper Shop, 11 Brompton Arcade SW3 (paper)
Knutz, 1 Russell Street WC2 (jokes)
Muji, 39 Shelton Street WC2 and 26 Great Marlborough Street W1 (min-
  imalistic designs from Japan).
Neal Street East, 5 Neal Street WC2 (Oriental imports)
Preposterous Presents, 262 Upper Street N1
James Smith, 53 New Oxford Street W1 (umbrellas and walking sticks)
Space, 214 Westbourne Grove W11 (kitchenware, bathware etc).
Tradition, 5a Shepherd Street W1 (tin soldiers)
Waterford–Wedgwood, 173 Piccadilly W1 (china classics)

Lillywhite's, 24–36 Lower Regent Street SW1   Sportswear
Harrods sports department

Cameo Stamp Centre, 75 Strand WC2   Stamps
London International Stamp Centre, 27 King Street WC2
Stanley Gibbons, 339 Strand WC2

The Tea House, 7 Neal Street WC2   Tea
Twinings, 216 Strand WC2

Hamley's, 188–196 Regent Street W1   Toys

Sightseeing

Sightseeing by Bus

There are two options for sightseeing in London by bus. You can either
take a trip on a double-decker bus on one of the scheduled routes or go on
one of the many sightseeing tours organised by a number of companies.

Sightseeing Tour of London in an open top double decker

Scheduled
bus routes

The best way to gain a first impression of London is to travel on the top deck of one of London Transport's red doubledecker buses, ideally using a Travelcard (see Public Transport), which will enable you to make as many journeys as you want within the time allowed. The routes best suited for seeing something of Central London are:

No. 9: Kensington–Hyde Park–Hyde Park Corner–Piccadilly Circus–Trafalgar Square–Strand–Aldwych
No. 11: Chelsea–Victoria Station–Westminster–Whitehall–Trafalgar Square–Strand–Fleet Street–St Paul's Cathedral–Bank of England
No. 15: Marble Arch–Oxford Street–Regent Street–Trafalgar Square–Strand–Fleet Street–St Paul's Cathedral–Tower

London Transport
Original London
Sightseeing Tours

These 1½ hour guided tours on double-deckers (open-topped in summer), with a live commentary in English by a London Tourist Board guide, are a reasonably-priced way of getting to know your way round the sights of London before setting out to explore on your own. They run every day (except Christmas Day) at 15-minute intervals from 9am to 8pm from March to October, and at 30-minute intervals from 10am to 5pm for the rest of the year.

A recorded commentary in a choice of 8 languages is available as well. Tickets can be bought on the bus or from London Transport Travel Information Centres, London Tourist Board, British Travel Centre or the Tourist Information Centre at Victoria Station (see Information).

Departure points

29 Haymarket (Piccadilly Circus) SW1, Underground: Piccadilly Circus
Marble Arch (Speaker's Corner) W1, Underground: Marble Arch
Victoria Street SW1, Underground: Victoria
Baker Street Underground Station W1, Underground: Baker Street

London Pride

The open-top double-decker bus tours operated by London Pride start every 20 minutes from outside the Trocadero Centre, Piccadilly Circus to

18 destinations, and take 1½ hours. You can hop on and off at any stop on the route. In addition, there is a tour of Docklands. For further information: tel. (01708) 631122.

Many other bus companies also run sightseeing tours in and around London. These can be particularly suitable for larger groups, and include:

Other bus companies

Evan Evans, 26–28 Paradise Road, Richmond; tel. (0181) 332 2222
Frames Rickards, 11 Herbrand Street WC1; tel. (0171) 837 6311
Golden Tours, 4 Fountain Square, 123–151 Buckingham Palace Road SW1; tel. (0171) 233 7030

Sightseeing on foot

One of the best ways of discovering London is to explore its streets on foot by joining one of the many guided walking tours. These usually have a particular theme such as Roman, Medieval or Victorian London, Jack the Ripper, London's Ghosts, historic pubs, the Jewish East End, etc. Themes, times and meeting places (usually at a tube station) are to be found in the listings magazines, or by contacting the tour operator.

Walking tours

City Walks, 147 Offord Road N1; tel. (0171) 700 6931
Footsteps; tel. (01622) 75 4451 (tours in many foreign languages)
Historical Tours, 3 Florence Road, South Croydon; tel. (0181) 668 4019 (walks on historical and cultural themes)
London Pub Walks; tel. (0181) 883 2656
Original Guided Walks, 41 Spelman Street E1; tel. (0171) 247 5604 (East End and Jack the Ripper Walks)
Original London Walks, PO Box 1708, NW6 4LW; tel. (0171) 624 3978 (the most highly recommended). Also offer Explorer Days Out. Fax 0171 625 1932

This trail, which takes in all the historic sights of Central London, was laid out using plaques set in the pavement to commemorate the celebration of the Queen's Silver Jubilee in 1977; London Tourist Board also publishes a trail leaflet.

Signed walks
Silver Jubilee Walkway

From the Museum of London to the Tower of London a signed walk of 1½ miles/2.5km takes you past 21 points on the old London wall, with illustrated panels to inform you along the way.

London Wall Walk

There are some lovely walks – extending for some 37 miles – along the partly restored towpaths of London's Victorian canals. The stretches alongside the Regent's Canal (Regent's Park, London Zoo – see entry Piccadilly Circus in A-Z) and in Paddington's Little Venice are particularly pleasant.

London Canal Walks

For independent tours see Facts and Figures, Sightseeing Tours.

Sightseeing tours

Sport

Spectator sport

Sportsline: tel. (0171) 222 8000 (information about all sporting events)

Information

One of Britain's great national sports and played throughout the Commonwealth, cricket is the ultimate bat and ball game and it can last for days. The mecca for all cricket lovers is Lord's Cricket Ground, with its museum (see A-Z, Regent's Park). London's other great cricket ground is the Oval (Kennington SE11, Underground: Oval).

Cricket

Every pub has its dartboard since darts is the kind of popular game

Darts

anyone can play, but it has been made even more popular by television coverage of the professional championships. The winner is the first to score 301 or 501, but the skill lies in throwing the darts into the right sections of the board, combining doubles, trebles and bullseyes, to get to the target score first.

Football

Britain is the birthplace of football – or soccer as it is also called. London has a number of home teams, namely, Arsenal, Brentford, Charlton Athletic, Chelsea, Crystal Palace, Fulham, Leyton Orient, Millwall, Queen's Park Rangers, Tottenham Hotspur, West Ham and Wimbledon. The top league games usually kick off on Saturdays at 3pm or Tuesday or Wednesday at 7.30 or 7.45pm, although increasingly these dates and times are being changed to suit the needs of television. The highlight of the football year, marking the end of the season, is the FA Cup Final played in May at Wembley Stadium.

Greyhound racing

Greyhound racing, said to be "horse racing for the common man", is very popular. Its London venues are Catford Stadium (Adenmore Road SE6; British Rail: Catford Bridge), London Stadium Hackney (Waterden Road E15; British Rail: Hackney Wick), Walthamstow Stadium (Chingford Road E4; Underground: Walthamstow Central), Wembley Stadium (Stadium Way, Wembley; Underground: Wembley), Wimbledon Stadium (Plough Lane, Wimbledon SW19; Underground: Wimbledon Park).

Horse racing

Ascot and Epsom (see Events, Excursions) are synonymous throughout the world for being where horse racing is truly the sport of kings; the race meetings at the following tend to be more down to earth: Kempton Park (Staines Road East, Sunbury-on-Thames; British Rail: Kempton Park), Sandown Park (Esher Station Road, Esher, Surrey; British Rail: Esher), Windsor Racecourse (Maidenhead Road, Windsor, Berkshire; British Rail: Windsor and Eton Riverside).

Polo

Polo is another royal sport. There are matches every Saturday and Sunday at 3pm at The Guards Polo Club, Smiths Lawn, Windsor Great Park, Englefield Green, Egham, Berkshire; British Rail: Windsor and Eton Central).

Rugby

Rugby, another team ball game invented in England, is much more popular here than elsewhere in Europe apart from France. During the season from September to May the international games, especially England/Scotland, can attract more spectators than football. London rugby grounds include Twickenham (Whittton Road, Twickenham; British Rail: Twickenham), the headquarters of Rugby Union.

Snooker

Snooker is a more complicated version of billiards which, like darts, is very much a pub game but also enjoys television coverage of the professionals.

Tennis

What Lord's is to cricket Wimbledon (see A–Z) is to tennis, since this is where, at the All England Lawn Tennis and Croquet Club (Underground: Southfields), the world's most famous tennis tournament takes place during the last week in June and first week in July every year. There are two ways of getting tickets for Wimbledon: you can either join the queue every morning (the earlier the better!) and hope to get one of the limited number of Centre and Number One Court seats sold each day (though there is a good chance of getting a ground admission ticket), or you can write (after September 1st) to:

All England Lawn Tennis and Croquet Club,
PO Box 98, Church Road,
Wimbledon SW19 5AE
for details about how to enter the ticket ballot (closing date December 31st). There is also the practice of those people who have to leave early

putting their Centre and Number One Court tickets in collection boxes to be resold to those queuing inside the ground.

Participator sports

The Sports Council, 16 Upper Woburn Place WC1; tel. (0171) 273 1500
Information

There are a number of sports centres with swimming pools and other indoor sports facilities. These include:
Sports centres

National Sports Centre, Ledrington Road, Crystal Palace SE19;
tel. (0181) 778 0131
British Rail: Crystal Palace

Chelsea Sports Centre, Chelsea Manor Street SW3; tel. (0171) 352 6985
Underground: South Kensington, Sloane Square

Kensington Sports Centre, Walmer Road W11; tel. (0171) 727 9923
Underground: Latimer Road

Golf is quite popular among the wider public in Britain, where you can play on public courses such as:
Golf

Beckenham Place, Beckenham Hill Road, Beckenham SE6;
  tel. (0181) 650 2292
Brent Valley, Church Road, Cuckoo Lane W5; tel. (0181) 567 1287
Chingford, Bury Road, Chingford E4; tel. (0181) 529 5708
Picketts Lock, Picketts Lock Lane N9; tel. (0181) 803 3611
Richmond Park, Roehampton Gate, Richmond Park SW15;
  tel. (0181) 876 3205

Mounts for horseback riding in Hyde Park can be hired from:
Riding

Ross Nye, 8 Bathhurst Mews W2; tel. (0171) 262 3791
Underground: Lancaster Gate

Hyde Park Stables, 63 Bathhurst Mews W2; tel. (0171) 723 2813
Underground: Lancaster Gate

Ealing Squash Courts, 41 Haven Green W5; tel. (0181) 997 3449.
Underground: Ealing Broadway
Squash

Holland Park Squash Courts, Holland Park, Kensington W8;
tel. (0171) 602 2226; Underground: Holland Park

The Sports Council can supply a list of indoor and outdoor pools in addition to those in the sports centres.
Swimming

There are public tennis courts in many London parks such as Regent's Park which operate a booking system.
Tennis

Taxis

Although nowadays not all necessarily black, London's official taxis, the distinctive black cabs, are almost as famous as its red doubledecker buses and reckoned by many to be the safest and best in the world. They can be booked by telephone or hailed in the street when the yellow FOR HIRE or TAXI sign on the roof is lit up.
Black Cabs

Telephone bookings can be taken round the clock by Dial A Cab on (0171) 253 5000 and Radio Taxicabs on (0171) 272 0272.
Telephone bookings

Telephones

Fares

The fare is shown on the meter which the driver must set going at the start of the journey, and extra charges for evenings and weekends are displayed inside the cab. Journeys in excess of 6 miles/10km can cost more and should be negotiated in advance.

Cab-share

It is possible to share some cabs for the journey from Heathrow to Central London. These cabs have their own rank at Terminal 1 and the fare depends on the destination and the number of passengers.

Complaints

Complaints will be taken up by the police and should be addressed to: Public Carriage Office, 15 Penton Street N1 9PU; tel. (0171) 230 1631, Mon.–Fri. 9am–4pm.

Minicabs

Minicabs are ordinary cars operating a form of taxi service and can only be hired by telephone. They can prove cheaper than black cabs late at night but journeys are not metered so you should agree the fare in advance. The police tend to warn passengers against using minicabs since they are not as closely regulated and there can be the odd unlicensed and unscrupulous driver. If necessary, though, most hotels and pubs can supply you with the number of a minicab firm which they use on a regular basis and which has normally proved reliable.

Women's taxis

Lady Cabs, 12 Archway Close, Archway N19; tel. (0171) 241 4780

Telephones

Public telephones

The old London telephone box

British Telecom (BT), Britain's privatised national telephone company, is in the process of replacing the famous red telephone boxes with more modern high-tech booths but some of the old familiar ones are still about and are being retained in the historic districts of London.

Pay phones accept 10, 20 and 50 pence and £1 coins. To make a call, pick up the receiver, insert the money and dial. A bleeping tone means more money is needed. A growing number of the modern callboxes are green and phonecard only. These phonecards are obtainable to a value of 20, 40, 100 and 200 10p units from post offices, newsagents and other places showing the green phonecard sign.

London dialling codes

Unlike the rest of the country London has two national dialling codes, 0171 for inner London and 0181 for outer London, but you need only use these if you are calling from outside London or from inner to outer London and vice versa.

Long-distance calls are cheaper from Monday to Friday between 6pm and 8am, and cheaper still at weekends from midnight Friday to midnight Sunday. International calls are cheaper from Monday to Friday between 6pm and 8am. The minimum amount for an international call from a public payphone varies depending on the country but on average is £1, so for these it is usually better to use a phonecard. Long-distance calls from your hotel room can be very expensive.

The international dialling code for Great Britain is 44.

From Britain to:

Australia: 00 61
New Zealand: 00 64
Republic of Ireland: 00 353
South Africa: 00 27
United States and Canada: 00 1

Operator (for general enquiries): 100
International operator: 155
Timecheck: 123

Directory enquiries
  London: 142
  Outside London: 192
  International: 153

Television and Radio

Britain has five terrestrial television channels – two public service channels, BBC1 and BBC2, and three commercial channels, ITV and Channel Four and Five, plus a number of stations broadcasting by satellite and cable.

The BBC has five national and numerous local radio stations. The national stations are Radio 1 (rock and pop on FM 97.6–99.8MHz), Radio 2 (light entertainment on FM 88.0–91.2MHz), Radio 3 (arts and classical music on FM 90.2–92.4MHz), Radio 4 (news and general interest on FM 92.4–94.6MHz, MW 720kHz and LW 198kHz), and Radio 5 Live (news and sport on MW 693, 909kHz). London's local BBC station is Radio London (FM 94.9MHz), and there are numerous local and national commercial stations such as Virgin Radio (rock and pop on FM 105.8MHz, MW 1197/1215kHz), Talk Radio UK (news and opinion on MW 1053/1089kHz) and Classic FM (classical music on FM 100–102MHz).

Theatres

London's hundred or so theatres offer the most varied of programmes, ranging from the classics to the avant-garde. Alongside the West End shows and the world-famous Old Vic, Royal Court, Royal National Theatre and Royal Shakespeare Company, there is a whole host of smaller and fringe venues putting on experimental and political drama, workshops and amateur shows. Some theatres specialise in plays by modern authors, while others boast record-breaking runs such as Agatha Christie's "The Mousetrap" which has been playing at the St Martin's Theatre for over forty years. Those listed below are among the most important and most interesting.

Tickets are on sale at theatre box offices and ticket agencies. They are usually in great demand so try and book as early as possible. Prices are reduced for previews, matinées and restricted view seats. The Half Price Ticket Booth in Leicester Square WC2 (Underground: Leicester Square, Piccadilly Circus), sells half price tickets for same-day performances for some West End plays/shows (open: Monday to Saturday from noon for matinées, and 1–6pm for evening performances).

Performance times

Evening performances usually start between 7.30 and 8pm, matinées between 2 and 3pm. Some theatres also put on two evening performances, usually on Saturdays. Most theatres close on Sundays.

Listings

Programme listings appear in the What's On sections of the press and various listing magazines ("Time Out" and "What's On In London"). The London Theatre Guide featuring the programmes of many of London's best-known theatre and arts venues is available from the London Tourist Board and Tourist Information Centres (see Information).

Classic & modern repertoire

Aldwych, Aldwych WC2; tel. (0171) 416 6003
Underground: Holborn, Covent Garden

The Globe, New Globe Walk, Bankside SE1; tel. (0171) 928 6406
Underground: Cannon Street, Mansion House, then on foot over Southwark bridge (theatre is as it was in Shakespeare's time – no technical assistance, spectators stand in the open close to the stage and can boo and cheer – summer season only)

Haymarket Theatre Royal, Haymarket SW1; tel. (0171) 930 8800
Underground: Piccadilly Circus

Old Vic, Waterloo Road SE1; tel. (0171) 494 5460
Underground: Waterloo

Royal National Theatre, South Bank SE1; tel. (0171) 452 3000
Underground: Waterloo
Three theatres: Olivier (1140 seats), Lyttleton (900 seats), Cottesloe (400 seats, experimental theatre)
Some seats are always sold on the day from 10am (all theatres)

Royal Shakespeare Company, Barbican Centre EC2; tel. (0171) 638 8891
Underground: Barbican, Moorgate
Two theatres: Barbican Theatre and The Pit (studio theatre)

Comedies, plays, thrillers

Apollo, Shaftesbury Avenue W1; tel. (0171) 494 5070
Underground: Piccadilly Circus

Comedy, Panton Street SW1; tel. (0171) 369 1731
Underground: Piccadilly Circus

Duchess, Catherine Street WC2; tel. (0171) 494 5075
Underground: Covent Garden

Duke of York's, St Martin's Lane WC2; tel. (0171) 836 5122
Underground: Leicester Square

Fortune, Russell Street WC2; tel. (0171) 836 2238/(0171) 312 1990
Underground: Covent Garden

Gielgud, Shaftesbury Avenue W1; tel. (0171) 494 5519
Underground: Piccadilly Circus

Lyric, Shaftesbury Avenue W1; tel. (0171) 494 5045
Underground: Piccadilly Circus

The Playhouse, Northumberland Avenue WC2; tel. (0171) 839 4401
Underground: Embankment

St Martins, West Street, Cambridge Circus WC2; tel. (0171) 836 1443
Underground: Leicester Square
"The Mousetrap" since 1952

Savoy, Strand WC2; tel. (0171) 836 8888
Underground: Charing Cross

Vaudeville, Strand WC2; tel. (0171) 836 9987
Underground: Charing Cross

Wyndham's, Charing Cross Road WC2; tel. (0171) 369 1736
Underground: Leicester Square

Almeida, Almeida Street, Islington N1; tel. (0171) 359 4404
Underground: Angel, Highbury and Islington

Experimental
and fringe

Lyric Hammersmith, King Street, Hammersmith W6; tel. (0181) 741 2311
Underground: Hammersmith

Riverside Studios, Crisp Road, Hammersmith W6; tel. (0181) 237 1111
Underground: Hammersmith

Royal Court, Sloane Square SW1; tel. (0171) 565 5050
Underground: Sloane Square

Young Vic, 66 The Cut, Waterloo SE1; tel. (0171) 928 6363
Underground: Waterloo

Bush, Shepherd's Bush Green W12; tel. (0171) 743 3388
Underground: Shepherds Bush, Goldhawk Road

Pub theatre

Drill Hall, 16 Chenies Street WC1; tel. (0171) 637 8270
Underground: Goodge Street

Gate, 11 Pembridge Road W11; tel. (0171) 229 0706
Underground: Notting Hill Gate

King's Head, 115 Upper Street, Islington N1; tel. (0171) 226 1916
Underground: Angel, Highbury and Islington

Old Red Lion, St John's Street, Islington EC1; tel. (0171) 837 7816
Underground: Angel

Little Angel, 14 Dagmar Passage, Cross Street N1; tel. (0171) 226 1787
Underground: Angel, Highbury and Islington

Puppet theatre

See Children

Children's theatre

see Music

Musicals

Time

From late October to late March Britain observes Greenwich Mean Time
(5 hours ahead of New York). For the rest of the year the clocks are put
forward one hour to British Summer Time.

Tipping

It is customary to leave a small amount in coins.

Cloakroom

Travel Documents

Hotels	Porters and chambermaids expect a small amount (£1 porters, more for chambermaids)
Pubs	10–15% of the bill for table service but no tipping at the bar
Restaurants	10–15% of the bill if not included as service charge
Taxis	10–15% of the fare

Travel Documents

Passports	All visitors to Britain must have a valid passport unless they are citizens of the Republic of Ireland with which there are no passport controls. In the case of nationals from some Commonwealth countries a visa is required as well, so it is advisable to check before departure with the British Consulate or the British Tourist Authority (see Information).
Vehicle papers	Motorists driving their own car should bring their driving licence, vehicle registration document and Green Card (international insurance certificate). Cars registered abroad must carry the approved oval country distinguishing sticker for their country of origin.

Weights and Measures

Linear	1 inch (in.) = 2.54cm	1cm = 0.39in.
	1 foot (ft) = 30.48cm	10cm = 3.94in.
	1 yard (yd) = 91.44cm	1m = 1.09yd
	1 mile = 1.61km	1km = 0.62 miles
Surface area	1 square inch = 6.45 sq.cm	1 sq.cm = 0.155 sq.in.
	1 square foot = 9.28 sq.dm	1 sq.dm = 1.196 sq.yd
	1 square yard = 0.836 sq.m	1 sq.m = 1.196 sq.yd
	1 square mile = 2.589 sq.km	1 sq.km = 0.386 sq. mile
	1 acre = 0.405ha	1ha = 2.471 acres
Liquids	1 pint (pt) = 0.568 litre (l)	1 litre = 1.76pt
	1 Gallon (gal) = 4.546 litres	10 litres = 2.20gal
	The US pint and gallon are equivalent to 0.83 Imperial pint or gallon.	
Weight	1 ounce (oz) = 38.35 grams (g)	100g = 3.527oz
	1 pound (lb) = 453.59g	1 kilogram (kg) = 2.205lb
	1 stone = 6.35kg	10kg = 1.57 stone

Clothing sizes	**Women**					**Men**				
	UK	32 34 36 38 40				UK	36 38 40 42 44 46			
	EUR	36 38 40 42 44				EUR	46 48 50 52 54 56			
Shoe sizes	UK	3 4 5 6 7 8 9 10 11								
	EUR	36 37 38 39 40/41 42 43 44 45								

When to Go

Although London is worth visiting the whole year round, the weather can be wet or very hot in summer so the best seasons for a visit are spring or early autumn.

Youth Hostels

Reservations for Youth Hostels Association (YHA) member hostels in London can be made through their Central Bookings Office, Rotherhithe Youth Hostel, Salter Road, Rotherhithe, London SE16 1PP; tel. (0171) 248 6547, fax (0171) 236 7681

Reservations

City of London, 36 Carter Lane EC4; tel. (0171) 236 4965, fax 236 7681

Youth hostels in London

Earls Court, 38 Bolton Gardens SW5; tel. (0171) 373 7083, fax 835 2034

Hampstead Heath, 4 Wellgarth Road, Golders Green NW11; tel. (0181) 458 9054, fax 209 0546

Highgate Village, 84 Highgate West Hill N6; tel. (0181) 340 1831, fax 341 0376

Holland House, Holland Walk, Kensington W8; tel. (0171) 937 0748, fax 376 0667

Oxford Street, 14 Noel Street W1; tel. (0171) 734 1618, fax 734 1657

Rotherhithe, Salter Road SE16; tel. (0171) 232 2114, fax 237 2919

London has other hostel-type accommodation for young people, and the term "young" is often stretched to cover a wider age-range. London Tourist Board (see Information) can supply a free booklet "London Accommodation for Budget Travellers". The following addresses fall into this category:

Other hostels

Central Club (YWCA), 16–22 Great Russell Street WC1; tel. (0171) 636 7512, fax 636 5278

London City YMCA, 8 Errol Street EC1; tel. (0171) 628 8832

The London Hostels Association, 54 Eccleston Square, Victoria SW1V 1PG; tel. (0171) 828 3263
This association has at least ten London hostels with around 1100 beds in all.

Index

Index

Principal Sights of Tourist Interest

Note: The places listed above are merely a selection of the principal places of interest in themselves or for attractions in the surrounding area. There are of course innumerable other places worth visiting in London, to which attention is drawn by one or more stars.

Imprint

130 illustrations, 18 maps and plans, 1 large map at end of book

Text: Rainer Eisenschmid, Dr Irene Antoni-Komar, Eva-Maria Blattner

General direction: Baedeker-Redaktion (Rainer Eisenschmid)

Cartography: Christoph Gallus, Hohberg; Franz Huber, Munich; Hallweg AG, Bern (large map of London); London Transport Underground Map

English translation: Margaret Court, Wendy Bell, David Cocking, Brenda Ferris,

Source of illustrations: Archiv für Kunst und Geschichte (1), Baedeker-Archiv (12), British Museum (2), British Tourist Authority (1), dpa (2), Rainer Eisenschmid (61), Frankfurter Allgemeine Zeitung/Lamèr (1), HB-Verlag (15), Bildagentur Lade (2), London Transport (3), Bildagentur Mauritius (1), Kai-Ulrich Müller (15), Museum of the Moving Image (1), Natural History Museum (1), Retinski (1), Dr. Madeleine Reincke (2), Science Museum (1), Wolfgang Stetter (6), Ullstein (8), Victoria & Albert Museum (2), Ulrich Wirth (2), Woodmansterne (1), ZEFA (4)

Front cover: Pictor International, London. Back cover: AA Photo Library (S. Bates)

7th English edition 1999
Reprinted 2000 (×2), 2001

© Baedeker Ostfildern
Original German edition 1998

© Automobile Association Developments Limited 2001
English language edition worldwide

Published by AA Publishing (a trading name of Automobile Association Developments Limited, whose registered office is Norfolk House, Priestley Road, Basingstoke, Hampshire RG24 9NY; registered number 1878835).

Distributed in the United States and Canada by:
Fodor's Travel Publications, Inc.
201 East 50th Street
New York, NY 10022

A CIP catalogue record for this book is available from the British Library.

Licensed user: Mairs Geographischer Verlag GmbH & Co., Ostfildern

Printed in Italy by G. Canale & C. S.p.A., Turin

ISBN 0 7495 1987 8